Follies of the Wise

Follies of the Wise

DISSENTING ESSAYS

Frederick Crews

Shoemaker Hoard

Library of Congress Cataloging-in-Publication Data
Crews, Frederick C.
Folllies of the Wise: dissenting essays/Frederick Crews.—1st Shoemaker & Hoard ed.
p. cm.
Includes bibliographical references (p.   ) and index.
ISBN-10: 1-59376-101-5
ISBN-13: 978-1-59376-101-1
1. Psychoanalysis—History. 2. Freud, Sigmund, 1856–1939. I. Title.
BF173.C796 2006
814'.54—dc22
2005037677

Jacket and text design by David Bullen
Printed in the United States of America by Worzalla

Shoemaker ▓ Hoard
An Imprint of Avalon Publishing Group, Inc.
1400 65th Street, Suite 250
Emeryville, CA 94608
Distributed by Publishers Group West

10 9 8 7 6 5 4 3 2 1

For Isabel Maria Detre and Aaron Frederick Detre

CONTENTS

Acknowledgments   ix

Introduction   3

I. THE ANTISCIENCE

1. The Unknown Freud   15
2. Freudian Suspicion versus Suspicion of Freud   43
3. A Handful of Dust   62
4. Unconscious Deeps and Empirical Shallows   71

II. MODERN DEVILTRY

5. The Revenge of the Repressed, Part I   91
6. The Revenge of the Repressed, Part II   112
7. Demonology for an Age of Science   134
8. The Trauma Trap   153

III. MORE DIAGNOSTIC FOLLIES

9. Keeping Us in Hysterics   173
10. Out, Damned Blot!   187
11. The Mind Snatchers   200

CONTENTS

IV. THE WILL TO BELIEVE

12. The Consolation of Theosophy   219
13. The Esoteric Unconscious   233
14. The New Creationists and Their Friends   254
15. Darwin Goes to Sunday School   270
16. Zen and the Art of Success   282

V. A DISCIPLINE IN CRISIS

17. The End of the Poststructuralist Era   297
18. Kafka in the Clouds   315
19. Call Me Liberal   328

Appendix A: Compromises with Creationism   343
Appendix B: Freud, Lacan, and the Pseudoscientific Academy   351
Notes   365
Works Cited   379
Index   397

ACKNOWLEDGMENTS

Not everyone will like this book, but only Elizabeth Crews, the most astute of editors, knows just how inferior it would have been without her tireless and uncompromising review of drafts. Lacking the initiative and support of Robert Silvers, however, some of my chapters wouldn't have come into existence at all. And I am indebted to my publisher, Jack Shoemaker, for his faith in the book and for shrewd advice about its content.

For their encouragement, assistance, and/or constructive criticism, I want to thank Joan Acocella, Robert Alter, Mikkel Borch-Jacobsen, Glenn Branch, Thomas Chase, Shadia Drury, Dwight Eddins, Edward Erwin, Allen Esterson, John Farrell, Roxanna Font, Pamela Freyd, Peter Freyd, Jacob Fuchs, Adolf Grünbaum, Han Israëls, Stewart Justman, Robert Lescher, Richard Levin, Norman Levitt, Elizabeth Loftus, Malcolm Macmillan, Richard McNally, Gary Saul Morson, Nicholas Murray, Richard Ofshe, Samuel Otter, Kevin Padian, Mark Pendergrast, Richard Pollak, Tom Quirk, Norman Rabkin, Ralph Rader, Alan Rinzler, Ron Roizen, Wallace Sampson, Eugenie Scott, Erik Storlie, Frank Sulloway, Peter Swales, Carol Tavris, Robert Wilcocks, and James M. Wood.

For permission to reprint work that originally appeared in their pages, I wish to thank *The New York Review of Books, The New Republic, Skeptic, The Scientific Review of Alternative Medicine, The Wascana Review,* and *Reports of the National Center for Science Education.* In addition, I am grateful for permission to reuse the following essays: "Freudian Suspicion versus Suspicion of Freud," in *The Flight from Science and Reason,* ed. Paul R. Gross, Norman Levitt, and Martin W. Lewis (New York Academy of Sciences, Vol. 775, ©1996), pp. 470–482; "Unconscious Deeps and Empirical Shallows," in *Whose Freud? The Place of Psychoanalysis in Contemporary Culture,* ed. Peter Brooks and Alex Woloch (Yale University Press, 2000), pp. 19–32; and "The End of the Poststructuralist Era," in *The Emperor Redressed: Critiquing Critical Theory,* ed. Dwight Eddins (University of Alabama Press, 1995), pp. 45–61.

Follies of the Wise

DISSENTING ESSAYS

INTRODUCTION

On the day after Christmas, 2004, as everyone knows, a major earthquake and tsunami devastated coastal regions around the Indian Ocean, killing as many as 300,000 people outright and dooming countless others to misery, heartbreak, and early death. Thanks to video cameras and the satellite transmission of images, that event penetrated the world's consciousness with an immediate force that amounted, psychologically, to a tsunami in its own right. The charitable contributions that then poured forth on an unprecedented scale expressed something more than empathy and generosity. They also bore an aspect of self-therapy—of an attempt, however symbolic, to mitigate the calamity's impersonal randomness and thus to draw a curtain of decorum over a scene that appeared to proclaim too baldly, "This world wasn't made for us." No greater challenge to theodicy—the body of doctrine that attempts to reconcile cruelty, horror, and injustice with the idea of a benevolent God—had been felt by Western pundits since the great Lisbon earthquake and tsunami of November 1, 1755.

On that earlier occasion, mainstream Catholic and Protestant faith received a lesser blow than did Enlightenment "natural theology," which, presuming the Creator to have had our best interests at heart when he instituted nature's laws and then retired, made no allowance for either Satanic influence or divine payback for wickedness. God's indifference, it then suddenly appeared to Voltaire and others, was more complete than any deist had dared to conceive. As for the clerics of the era, they welcomed the disaster with unseemly *Schadenfreude* as a useful topic for sermons. "Learn, O Lisbon," one Jesuit intoned, "that the destroyers of our houses, palaces, churches, and convents, the cause of the death of so many people and of the flames that devoured such vast treasures, are your abominable sins, and not comets, stars, vapors and exhalations, and similar natural phenomena" (Wieseltier 2005, p. 34).

The same opportunity was seized in early 2005 by Hindu, Muslim, Christian, and even Buddhist fear-mongers, and they were joined by, among others, Israel's Sephardic chief rabbi, who proclaimed, "this is an expression of God's great ire with the world" (Wieseltier 2005). But two and a half centuries of increasing scientific awareness had made for a significant difference in lay attitudes. Now the rabbi's callous words—Leon Wieseltier rightly called them "a justification of the murder of children"—met with widespread revulsion. By 2005 only an unschooled person or a blinkered zealot could fail to understand that a thoroughly natural conjunction of forces had wiped out populations whose only "sin" was to have pursued their livelihood or recreation in lowlands adjacent to the ocean.

Theodicy, in this altered climate of opinion, would have to take a subtler tack. Just such an adjustment was made with considerable suavity by the Archbishop of Canterbury, Rowan Williams, in a *Sunday Telegraph* article of January 2, 2005:

> The question: "How can you believe in a God who permits suffering on this scale?" is . . . very much around at the moment, and it would be surprising if it weren't—indeed, it would be wrong if it weren't. The traditional answers will get us only so far. God, we are told, is not a puppet-master in regard either to human actions or to the processes of the world. If we are to exist in an environment where we can live lives of productive work and consistent understanding—human lives as we know them—the world has to have a regular order and pattern of its own. Effects follow causes in a way that we can chart, and so can make some attempt at coping with. So there is something odd about expecting that God will constantly step in if things are getting dangerous. (Williams 2005, p. 22)

Thanks to the *Sunday Telegraph's* provocative headline, "Of Course This Makes Us Doubt God's Existence," Williams's opinion piece raised many an eyebrow, enhancing the archbishop's well-cultivated reputation for theological brinkmanship. On a careful reading, however, his essay appears in a truer light as a traditional exercise in Christian damage control. "Doubt God's existence"? Hardly. It sufficed for Williams that "we are told" about the Lord's plan to allow the world "a pattern of its own"—one that, if it occasionally puts us in harm's way, does so only because the fashioning of a law-abiding cosmos struck the Almighty as the best means for us humans to achieve "productive work and consistent understanding." A more complacent expression of anthropocentric vanity would be hard to imagine.

Having made a conciliatory feint toward heretical thoughts, the prelate went on to slam the door on unbelievers by suggesting that only "religious people" can care about the loss of individual lives within a mass die-off. Through their prayers, Williams related, pious folk "ask for God's action" to assuage the suffering of the maimed and the bereaved. But wait: hadn't the writer just conceded that it's useless to plea for any intervention against nature's laws? That point, we now realize, was only a rhetorical stratagem for exempting the recent tsunami from inclusion among motivated supernatural deeds. The God who had been paring his fingernails when the hundred-foot waves came ashore was now presumably back at his post and ready to be swayed by spoken and silent prayers that would waft toward heaven, even though they lacked any known physical means of doing so.

The point of Williams's essay was not to question theology but to reassert it in the face of other people's misgivings. Viewed from the archbishop's interested angle, the upheaval of earth and ocean served as a trial of faith whose outcome was assured: "The extraordinary fact is that belief has survived such tests again and again—not because it comforts or explains but because believers cannot deny what has been shown or given to them." Although many harsh experiences "seem to point to a completely arbitrary world," convictions about divine mercy will remain in place, because those convictions "have imposed themselves on the shape of a life and the habits of a heart" (Williams 2005, p. 22).

My aim in telling this story is not to scoff at apologetics for otherworldly belief, though I do regard them as uniformly feeble, but to call attention to a clash between two intellectual currents. One is scientific empiricism, which, for better or worse, has yielded all of the mechanical novelties that continue to reshape our world and consciousness. We know, of course, that science can be twisted to greedy and warlike ends. At any given moment, moreover, it may be pursuing a phantom, such as phlogiston or the ether or, conceivably, an eleven-dimensional superstring, that is every bit as fugitive as the Holy Ghost. But science possesses a key advantage. It is, at its core, not a body of correct or incorrect ideas but a collective means of generating and testing hypotheses, and its trials eventually weed out error with unmatched success.

When the Archbishop of Canterbury mentions "effects [that] follow causes in a way that we can chart," he writes as an heir, however grudging, of the scientific revolution. But when he reads the Creator's mind at a remove of more than fourteen billion years, and when he implies that some prayers stand a good chance of being answered, empiricism has given way to lore supported only by traditional authority. That is the kind of soothing potion that people quaff when they either haven't learned how to check the evidential merits of propositions or would rather not risk the loss of treasured beliefs.

If you were to ask the archbishop whether he subscribes to Darwinian scientific principles, I am sure the answer would be yes. So, too, in 1995 Pope John Paul II famously granted that evolution is now "more than a theory." But since the late pope proceeded at once to airbrush humankind from the evolutionary picture and to reassert *for our species alone* the church's perennial creationist legend (see p. 277), it is clear that he was no Darwinian in any meaningful sense. And the same must be said of Rowan Williams. In calling the recent tsunami an entirely natural event he was invoking plate tectonics, a branch of geology whose range of application extends backward by several billion years; but if he were at all sincere about adjusting his perspective to that time frame, he could hardly have gone on to assert that nature's laws were fashioned for the benefit of *Homo sapiens*, a great ape whose entire period of existence has occupied not even a nanosecond of the cosmic hour.

Such inconsistencies, when they are pointed out so baldly, look craven and inexcusable. But that judgment isn't shared outside intellectual circles, and even within them one hears influential voices protesting the encroachment of science on intuitively held truths. Conservatives who aren't already observant believers tend to feel protective toward religion because, in their judgment, it is the only guarantor of precious values that are jeopardized by rampant libertinism. And although theory-minded leftists and radical feminists have no investment in theism, many of them associate science with a masculinist, capitalist, imperialist rapacity that has brutalized Mother Earth; and on these and other grounds some progressives feel entitled to discount any scientific results that contradict the felt verities of ideology.

In addition, some scientists and philosophers who are privately indifferent or hostile to transcendent claims nevertheless seek an accommodation with them. They do so from the best of motives, in order to stem the infiltration of bumpkin "creation science" or its slick city cousin, "intelligent design," into biology curricula. Their hope is to show that scientific research and education have no bearing on issues of ultimate meaning and hence needn't be feared by the pious. To that end, they emphasize that science exemplifies only *methodological naturalism*, whereby technical reasons alone are cited for excluding nonmaterial factors from reasoning about causes and effects. Hence, they insist, the practice of science doesn't entail *metaphysical naturalism*, or the atheist's claim that spiritual causation is not only inadmissible but altogether unreal.

In one sense this is an impregnable argument. Even when science is conducted by ardent believers, it has to disregard theological claims, because those claims typically entail no unambiguous real-world implications, much less quantitative ones, that might be tested for their supportive or falsifying weight. The allegation that God was responsible for a given natural fact can't be either established or refuted by any finding; it is simply devoid of scientific interest. And thus it is true enough that scientists stand under no logical compulsion to profess metaphysical naturalism.

Quite obviously, however, trust in the supernatural does get shaken by the overall advance of science. This is an effect not of strict logic but of an irreversible shrinkage in mystery's terrain. Ever since Darwin forged an exit from the previously airtight argument from design, the accumulation of corroborated materialist explanations has left the theologian's "God of the gaps" with less and less to do. And an acquaintance with scientific laws and their uniform application is hardly compatible with faith-based tales about walking on water, a casting-out of devils, and resurrection of the dead.

Metaphysical naturalism may be undiplomatic, then, but it is favored by the totality of evidence at hand. Only a secular Darwinian perspective, I believe, can make general sense of humankind and its works. Our species appears to have constituted an adaptive experiment in the partial and imperfect substitution of culture for instinct, with all the liability to self-deception and fanaticism that such an experiment involves. We chronically strain against our animality by inhabiting self-fashioned webs of significance—myths, theologies, theories—that are more likely than not to generate illusory and often murderous "wisdom." That is the price we pay for the same faculty of abstraction and pattern drawing that enables us to be not mere occupiers of an ecological niche but planners, explorers, and, yes, scientists who can piece together facts about our world and our own emergence and makeup.

Here it may be objected that myths, theologies, and theories themselves, as nonmaterial things that can nevertheless set in motion great social movements and collisions of armies, confound a materialist or metaphysically naturalist perspective. Not at all. We materialists don't deny the force of ideas; we merely say that the minds precipitating them are wholly situated within brains and that the brain, like everything else about which we possess some fairly dependable information, seems to have emerged without any need for miracles. Although this is not a provable point, it is a necessary aid to clear thought, because, now that scientific rationality has conclusively shown its formidable explanatory power, recourse to the miraculous is always a regressive, obfuscating move.

The present book, however, isn't meant as a sustained attack on religion or as a brief for everything that bears the name of science. Rather, it brings together my recent encounters with various irrational manifestations, some of which in fact are nominally scientific. I have begun with metaphysical issues here because the human penchant for disastrously confusing fantasy with fact is most plainly seen in the impulse to ascribe one's own concerns to divine powers and then to harden one's heart against unbelievers. Although the follies discussed in my chapters are mild when judged against the total historical record of homicidal zeal in the service of misapprehensions, they display most of the features that characterize religious fanaticism, such as undue deference to authority, hostility toward dissenters, and, most basically, an assumption that intuitively held certitude is somehow more precious and profound than the hard-won gains of trial and error.

Like the Archbishop of Canterbury, who allows "habits of the heart" to overrule canons of evidence, many spokesmen for entrenched interests subscribe to a two-tiered conception of truth. They make a token bow to empirically grounded knowledge, but they deem it too pedestrian for mapping the labyrinth of the soul or for doing justice to the emotional currents coursing between interacting persons. Instead of merely avowing that the subjective realm is elusive, however, they then advance their own preferred theory, which is typically sweeping, absolute, and bristling with partisanship.

This book means to suggest, through sample instances in a number of subject areas, that there is no such thing as deep knowledge, in the sense of insight so compelling that it needs no validation. There is only knowledge, period. It is recognizable not by its air of holiness or its emotional appeal but by its capacity to pass the most demanding scrutiny of well-informed people who have no prior investment in confirming it. And a politics of sorts, neither leftist nor rightist, follows from this understanding. If knowledge can be certified only by a social process of peer review, we ought to do what we can to foster communities of uncompromised experts. That means actively resisting guru-ism, intellectual cliquishness, guilt-assuaging double standards, and, needless to say, disdain for the very concept of objectivity.

My mention of experts, however, can't fail to turn a spotlight on my own qualifications, if any, for passing judgment on such diverse and contested matters as natural selection, human motivation and its development, psychological tests, hypnosis, UFO reports, and recovered memory, to say nothing of theosophy and Zen Buddhism. I do lack the requisite background for adding substantive contributions to any of those topics. But *Follies of the Wise* makes no pretense of doing so. I regularly defer to specialists who are conversant with the state of their own discipline and who have already laid out powerful critiques of ill-conceived theories and unworthy dodges. And where the specialists disagree among themselves while honoring the same stringent rules for exposing mistakes, I never venture an opinion.

The question, of course, is how an outsider can be sure that one school of thought is less entitled to our trust than a rival one. In many instances such confidence would be unwarranted. Certain indicators of bad faith, however, are unmistakable: persistence in claims that have already been exploded; reliance on ill-designed studies, idolized law-givers, and self-serving anecdotes; evasion of objections and negative instances; indifference to rival theories and to the need for independent replication; and "movement" belligerence. Where several of these traits are found together, even a lay observer can be sure that no sound case could be made for the shielded theory; its uncompetitiveness is precisely what has necessitated these indulgences.

But then another doubt looms: if bad practices are so conspicuous, why should I or anyone else need to harp on them? At least two reasons come to mind. First, strong factions within such practical endeavors as psychotherapy, projective testing, and social work remain wedded to dubious and harmful notions that are tolerated or even advanced by mainstream guilds. The outrage that some of my essays encountered when first published attests to the challenge they posed to rooted assumptions. And second, charismatic trendsetters in the academic humanities have shown themselves to be credulous about scientifically disreputable notions. Although I can't hope to inhibit such high fliers, perhaps I can encourage some of their potential followers to see that real interdisciplinarity requires vigilance against junk science.

Beyond any social utility these chapters may possess, it suits my temperament to study indefensible pretensions and to note how they cause intelligent people to shut off their critical faculties and resort to

cultlike behavior. Sometimes amusing, sometimes appalling, such devi-
ousness strikes me as quintessentially human behavior. But I don't mean
to set myself apart as a paragon of reasonableness. Having made a large
intellectual misstep in younger days, I am aware that rationality isn't an
endowment but an achievement that can come undone at any moment.
And that is just why it is prudent, in my opinion, to distrust sacrosanct
authorities, whether academic or psychiatric or ecclesiastic, and to put
one's faith instead in objective procedures that can place a check on our
never-sated appetite for self-deception.

Several decades of untranquil experience in the public arena, however, have led me to anticipate only limited success in getting this point
across. To put it mildly, the public in an age of born-again Rapture,
"intelligent design," miscellaneous guru worship, and do-it-yourself
"spirituality" isn't exactly hungering for an across-the-board application
of rational principles. And the culturally slumming, trend-conscious
postmodern academy, far from constituting a stay against popular credulity, affords a parodic mirror image of it. That is the condition I illustrate in Chapter 11, on tales of UFO kidnapping: for opposite reasons,
guileless "abductees" and supercilious Theory-mongers show the same
imperviousness to considerations of mundane plausibility.

A student who signs up for a literature major today, having never
been encouraged to think independently and skeptically, may graduate two years later without having made any headway in that direction.
That is regrettable enough. But if the student then goes on to earn a
Ph.D. in the same field, he or she will probably have acquired a store-
house of arcane terms and concepts allowing that disability to appear
both intellectually and politically advanced. Here is tomorrow's tenured
professor, more impervious than any freshman to the "naive" heresy
that theories can be overturned by facts.

The inclusion in this book of my best-known essays, "The Unknown
Freud" and "The Revenge of the Repressed," brings to mind an especially ironic consequence of my attempts to promote impersonal
standards of judgment. As I will have several occasions to mention
below, advocates of psychoanalysis from Freud to the present day have

responded to the movement's critics by largely ignoring scientific, medical, and logical challenges and focusing instead on the critics' own alleged defects of personality. The result in my case is that I owe such name recognition as I possess mostly to Freudians and their cousins, the recovered memory therapists, who have wanted me to personify the mechanisms of repression and denial and the mood of oedipal rage that must surely lie behind my malicious attacks.

Thus I awoke one day in 1993 to find myself notorious. The difference was made not by what I had recently written (I had been making essentially the same case from 1980 onward) but by where it had appeared: in *The New York Review of Books*, which, rightly or wrongly, the analysts had regarded as their haven. Though my intention all along had been to alert the public to thirty years' worth of important revisionary scholarship by others, I now began to see myself characterized as "the foremost critic of psychoanalysis." It was the Freudians themselves who gladly awarded me that role, the more handily to dismiss all reservations about their craft as the symptoms of one man's neurosis.

My life has rarely been dull over the past dozen years, and for that I must thank my Freudian adversaries. As this book attests, however, psychodynamic theory has by no means constituted my sole concern. If the topic nevertheless keeps surfacing at unexpected moments in this book, that is because psychoanalysis, as the queen of modern pseudosciences, has pioneered the methods and directly supplied some of the ideas informing other shortcuts to "depth."

Intellectually and culturally, the West in the twentieth century did dwell largely in Freud's shadow, but no portion of his legacy is secure today. At such a juncture, I believe, it is important to think carefully about how and why the opinion-setting classes were led astray. What we need is not a new secular god to replace Freud but a clear realization that we already possess, in our tradition of unsparing empirical review, the tools we need to forestall another such outbreak of mass irrationality.

I.

The Antiscience

Chapter 1

THE UNKNOWN FREUD

This review essay, which appeared in *The New York Review of Books*, November 18, 1993, prompted more controversy than any article published in that magazine before or since. The exchanges of letters following that event and, a year later, publication of the essay that constitutes Chapters 5 and 6 are interesting in their own right; they were reprinted in *The Memory Wars: Freud's Legacy in Dispute* (Crews et al. 1995).

Some readers, noting this article's biographical emphasis, interpreted it as an attempt to demean psychoanalysis on illegitimate ad hominem grounds. My objections to the theory as such, however, are stated not only in "The Unknown Freud" itself but at greater length in earlier and subsequent publications (Crews 1986, 1998).

Here and later some redundancies with other chapters have been eliminated, and a few references have been updated to indicate revised or more accessible sources than were originally cited.

I.

That psychoanalysis, as a mode of treatment, has been experiencing a long institutional decline is no longer in serious dispute. Nor is the reason: though some patients claim to have acquired profound self-insight and even alterations of personality, in the aggregate psychoanalysis has proved to be an indifferently successful and vastly inefficient method of removing neurotic symptoms. It is also the method that is least likely to be "over when it's over." The experience of undergoing an intensive analysis may have genuine value as a form of extended meditation, but it seems to produce a good many more converts than cures. Indeed, among the dwindling number of practicing analysts, many have now backed away from any medical claims for a treatment that was once touted as the only lasting remedy for the entire spectrum of disorders this side of psychosis.

Freud's doctrine has been faring no better, in scientifically serious quarters, as a cluster of propositions about the mind. Without significant experimental or epidemiological support for any of its notions, psychoanalysis has simply been left behind by mainstream psychological research. No one has been able to mount a successful defense against the charge, most fully developed in Adolf Grünbaum's meticulous *Foundations of Psychoanalysis* (1984), that "clinical validation" of Freudian hypotheses is an epistemic sieve; as a means of gaining knowledge, psychoanalysis is fatally contaminated by the inclusion, among its working assumptions and in its dialogue with patients, of the very ideas that supposedly get corroborated by clinical experience. And Grünbaum further showed that even if Freud's means of gathering evidence had been sound, that evidence couldn't have reliably yielded the usual constructions that he placed on it. We cannot be surprised, then, by Malcolm Macmillan's exhaustive demonstration (1997) that Freud's theories of personality and neurosis—derived as they were from misleading precedents, vacuous pseudophysical metaphors, and a long concatenation of mistaken inferences that couldn't be subjected to empirical review—amount to castles in the air.

Nevertheless, Freudian concepts retain some currency in popular lore, the arts, and the academic humanities, three arenas in which flawed but once modish ideas, secure from the menace of rigorous testing, can be kept indefinitely in play. There psychoanalysis continues to be accepted largely on faith—namely, a faith in Freud's self-description as a fearless explorer, a solver of deep mysteries, a rigorously objective thinker, and an ethically scrupulous reporter of both clinical data and therapeutic outcomes. That is the image that his own suave texts, aided by the work of loyalist biographers from Ernest Jones (1953–1957) through Peter Gay (1988), have managed to keep before our eyes for many decades now. Surely, the average reader of such works infers, a man who has widened our horizons so decisively must have bequeathed us some irreversible gains in our understanding of the mind.

Not surprisingly, however, the tradition of hero worship is now being challenged as vigorously as are the claims of Freudian therapy and theory. Since the 1970s, a rapidly growing number of independent scholars—including among others Henri Ellenberger, Paul Roazen, Frank Cioffi, Frank J. Sulloway, Peter J. Swales, E. M. Thornton, Morton Schatzman, Hans Israëls, and Phyllis Grosskurth—have been showing us a different Freud, darker but far more interesting than the canonical one. According to their revisionist view, our would-be Prometheus was highly cultivated, sophisticated, and endowed with extraordinary literary power, sardonic wit, and charm, but he was also quite lacking in the empirical and ethical scruples that we would hope to find in any responsible scientist, to say nothing of a major one.

Now we are beginning to discern a notably willful and opportunistic Freud who appears to have thrown together his magisterial-looking claims from various unacknowledged sources—some of them more folkloric than scientific—while passing them off as sober inferences from the data of his clinical practice. Once having arrived at those claims, we see, he adhered to them with a blind, combative stubbornness—though not without willingness to expand the system on an ad hoc basis to encompass newly perceived difficulties. And he promoted that conceptually overstuffed system by means of devious rhetorical maneuvers that disarmed criticism without obliging Freud himself to take the criticism into material account. Through all his conduct, at least from the 1890s onward, runs a note of existential daring and high disdain that could hardly be more remote from ordinary scientific prudence. Fiercely believing in his general vision yet stooping to low tricks in defense of it, this Freud is a saturnine self-dramatizer who defies us to see through his bravado and provides us with tantalizing autobiographical clues for doing so.

Such a figure differs so radically from the Freud we thought we knew that readers may understandably wonder which version comes closer to the truth. But it is really no contest. Until recently, most people who wrote about Freud in any detail were open partisans of psychoanalysis who needed to safeguard the legend of the scientist-genius-humanitarian, and many of the sources they used had already passed through the censorship of a jealously secretive psychoanalytic establishment, whose leaders have been so fearful of open historical judgment that they have locked away large numbers of Freud's papers and letters in the Library of Congress for periods extending as far ahead as the twenty-second century. But as some sensitive documents, having already served their Sleeping Beauty sentences, make their way into the light, and as serendipity turns up others from outside sources, the more improvisational and fallible Freud will necessarily come into ever sharper focus.

Two examples may help to show this link between emergent primary materials and the revisionist portrait of Freud. When the orthodox analysts Marie Bonaparte, Anna Freud, and Ernst Kris first edited Freud's correspondence with his onetime friend Wilhelm Fliess in 1950, they omitted everything that, in their announced judgment, lacked "scientific" interest (Freud 1954). Republication, under different editorship, of the unbowdlerized letters in 1985 showed that the dismissible "unscientific" category had included everything from Freud's cavalier approach to clinical sessions—his writing to Fliess while an early patient was under hypnosis, for example, and his habit of napping while his later psychoanalytic ones were free-associating on the couch—to his naive acceptance of Fliess's dubious theories of periodicity and nasal-genital correspondence. The full letters also put on view the now notorious case of Emma Eckstein, whom Freud had grotesquely diagnosed as "bleeding for love" of himself, whereas she was actually suffering from a half-meter of gauze that Fliess had accidentally left within the remains of her nose after a mad-scientist operation that Freud, too, underwent for his own "nasal reflex neurosis." We will see that the Eckstein story, which Freud's heirs were so anxious to hide from posterity, is no aberration in the wider record; it constitutes an entirely typical instance of Freud's rashness in always preferring the arcane explanation to the obvious one.

As for the second example, the following scarcely believable events may illustrate how previously unexamined (not suppressed) documents can transform our image of Freud. Thanks to a long-neglected and rediscovered cache of letters that avoided becoming time capsules in the Library of Congress, we can now reconstruct the history of Freud's relations with one Horace Frink, a married American patient and protégé who, like many another psychoanalyst of the 1920s, was having an affair with a patient of his own, the bank heiress Angelika Bijur (Edmunds 1988). Despite this redundant testimony to his sexual orientation, Frink was told by Freud that he was a latent homosexual who stood in great peril of becoming an overt one. To avoid that fate, Freud prescribed, Frink would have to divorce his wife and marry Bijur, whom he also urged to divorce her husband, even though Freud had never met either of the allegedly unsuitable spouses.

Freud's transparent aim was to get his own hands on some of the heiress Bijur's money. As he brazenly if perhaps semifacetiously wrote to Frink in steering him toward divorce and remarriage to Bijur, "Your complaint that you cannot grasp your homosexuality implies that you are not yet aware of your phantasy of making me a rich man. If matters turn out all right let us change this imaginary gift into a real contribution to the Psychoanalytic Funds" (Edmunds 1988, p. 45). The divorce and remarriage did occur—soon followed by the deaths of both of the abandoned, devastated spouses, an early suit for divorce by Frink's new wife, and the decline of the guilt-ridden Frink himself into a psychotic depression and repeated attempts at suicide.

It is not recorded whether Freud ever expressed regret for having destroyed these four lives, but we know that it would have been out of character for him to do so. Advancing the fortunes of his movement was for him an imperative that overrode all others. As many casual remarks in his correspondence reveal, he was indifferent to his patients' suffering and quite dismissive of their real-world dilemmas, which struck him as a set of pretexts for not getting down to the repressed fantasies that really mattered. Nor did he care very much, except from a public relations angle, whether those patients improved as a result of his treatment. As he sarcastically wrote to Carl Jung in 1912 about a woman who had been in and out of his care since 1908, "she is beyond any possibility of therapy, but it is still her duty to sacrifice herself to science" (McGuire 1974, pp. 473–474). Frink, it seems, also had to be sacrificed—in this instance to Freud's working capital rather than to his intellectual passions.

What the Eckstein and Frink episodes have most in common is a perfect match between Freud's diagnoses and his immediate self-interest. That fit is obvious in Frink's case. As for Eckstein, by designating her bleeding as psychosomatic Freud was exculpating both his surgeon friend Fliess and himself for having recommended the gruesome and pointless operation. Such stories can only lead us to wonder whether Freud's powers of observation and analysis ever functioned with sufficient independence from his wishes. That, in brief, is the paramount issue confronting Freud studies today.

This is not to say that every Freud scholar is obliged to tackle that issue head on. Of the four books I will examine here, only Allen Esterson's *Seductive Mirage* takes Freud's scientific incompetence as its central theme. In varying degrees, the other three works all convey mixed feelings about Freud's stature and the legitimacy of psychoanalytic claims. But for that very reason, it is instructive to see how convergent their accounts of Freud's imperious style of reasoning prove to be.

Take, to begin with, James L. Rice's informative and subtle study, *Freud's Russia: National Identity in the Evolution of Psychoanalysis* (1993). For Rice, Freud is anything but the objective scientific investigator who insulates himself from cultural impulses and discovers only later, as he maintained, that imaginative writers had anticipated his findings. Instead, he is fully a man of his own time, one whose sensibility, intellect, and specific ideas about the mind were crucially shaped by his reading. And he is also, as Rice puts it, "one of the great egos of our age."

Rice has no trouble perceiving that behind Freud's physicianly manner and his solemnity about the libidinal sacrifices exacted by civilized mores, there lay the nihilism of a disillusioned revolutionary who had deemed the species not worth saving after all. Insofar as it has been noticed, this quality has understandably called to mind the figure of Nietzsche, whose writings Freud disingenuously claimed to have encountered after the psychoanalytic system had been fully shaped. Rice understands, however, that nihilism and spiritual extremism in general had another strong correlate in Freud's imagination: Russia. Freud's family roots lay in Lithuania, where he retained many kin, and where his imagination turned when he thought, as he continually did, about the persecution of Jews and about their efforts to strike back. Up to the early years of Stalin's rule, Rice shows, Freud thrilled to revolutionism and looked to Russia for a political equivalent to his own assault on the tyranny of the despotic superego. Indeed, the Stalinist debacle had much to do with bringing on the futilitarian mood that dominates that most bathetic of "classics," *Civilization and Its Discontents* (1930).

Long before the accession of Stalin, however, Freud feared Russian extremism as strongly as he was drawn to it. As Rice convincingly argues, Freud's notion of ambivalence owed much to his idea of the Russian national character, featuring a supposed savage repressiveness that always gets reimposed after sadistic and erotic uprisings. This creaky formula became his master key to understanding Dostoevsky, about whom he published a celebrated monograph in 1928, "Dostoevsky and Parricide." That essay in turn, as Rice coolly anatomizes it, deserves our attention here as an especially clear instance of the apriorism that vitiates all of Freud's psychoanalytic work, both clinical and belletristic. The fact that we know so much about Dostoevsky from other sources affords us a rare opportunity to compare the record to what Freud self-indulgently made of it.

As Rice explains, in most respects "Dostoevsky and Parricide" is a derivative effort, indebted to views of the novelist that had been popular ever since his enormous Germanic vogue began in 1906. In one key respect, however, Freud's essay was original: its rejection of the idea that Dostoevsky suffered from epilepsy and its substitution of hysteria originating from a primal scene, or a child's discovery of "female castration" through witnessing an act of parental intercourse. Although other analysts within Freud's circle had already made the diagnosis of hysteria on Dostoevsky's part, it is obvious that they were doing so with the blessing of Freud, who had decreed in 1908 that "all those illnesses called hysteroepilepsies are simply hysterias."

Today, thanks to Rice's own work in *Dostoevsky and the Healing Art*

(1985), there is no room for doubt that Dostoevsky, who endured seizures approximately once a month, waking and sleeping, for the last thirty-four years of his life, was a genuine epileptic. As Rice concedes, however, the state of medical knowledge in the 1920s allowed for some uncertainty on that point. In "Dostoevsky and Parricide" Freud advances his erroneous view with a typically guileful show of tentativeness; but then, just as typically, he goes on to treat it as firmly settled. Only with the hindsight granted by the general decline of psychoanalytic authority can we perceive, as Rice does, the perfect circularity of Freud's argumentative procedure. Dostoevsky's epilepsy is brushed aside in order to leave an opening for acts of non-neurological oedipal decoding, acts whose consilience with one another then "proves" that Dostoevsky was never epileptic.

This was by no means the only point of obtuseness in Freud's assessment of Dostoevsky, against whom he bore a gratuitous ill-will. As he wrote to Theodor Reik in 1929, he disliked Dostoevsky because he had already seen too many "pathological natures" in his clinical practice. "In art and life," he reported, "I am intolerant of them." In "Dostoevsky and Parricide" this intolerance takes the form of saddling the novelist with the political cynicism of the Grand Inquisitor and, more remarkably still, with the criminal temperament of Stavrogin. As Rice makes clear, Freud's whole indictment of Dostoevsky as humanity's jailer is built on prosecutorial animus and is buttressed by elementary misunderstanding of the difference between an author and his created characters. We need only add that such misunderstanding is facilitated by psychoanalytic theory, which teaches us to peel away defensive sublimations and to regard as primary whatever psychic materials appear most base.

Dostoevsky was an unlucky man in several ways, but he did have the good fortune to have died without presenting his troubles in person to Sigmund Freud and his epigones. Not so the other notable Russian featured in Rice's study, Sergei Pankeev, or the "Wolf Man," who, beginning in 1910, received some five years' worth of Freud's professional attention. Thanks to the suspenseful case history of 1918 in which

Freud claimed to have removed all of his symptoms and inhibitions, the Wolf Man became the most celebrated of all Freud's alleged cures (see Freud 1953–1974, 17:3–22). Freud knew perfectly well, however, that psychoanalysis had not helped the depressed and obsessive Pankeev at all. By reminding us of this discrepancy and by going into the specifics of Freud's bungling of the case, Rice brings us to the verge of a more general critique of Freudian logic.

Just as he was later to do for Dostoevsky, Freud perceived Pankeev through the distorting lens of "Russian national character." The concept of *Russische Innerlichkeit,* or Russian spiritual inwardness, was especially comforting in Pankeev's case because it served Freud as a private excuse for the Wolf Man's recalcitrance to treatment. But Dostoevsky was already very much on Freud's mind when he first began treating Pankeev in 1910. Indeed, one of the main contributions of *Freud's Russia* is its demonstration that Pankeev and Dostoevsky were curiously interchangeable in Freud's mind. If, for example, a reader of "Dostoevsky and Parricide" wonders why Freud perversely insists on the murderousness of the haunted and harmless novelist, who had been permanently traumatized by a tsarist firing squad, Rice suggests that the answer can probably be found in the severely relapsed Pankeev's announced intention of shooting Freud at the time when the Dostoevsky paper was being composed. For the phylogenetically minded Freud, what one Russian was acting out in 1926–1927 must be what another Russian had secretly harbored in his unconscious fifty years earlier.

The full career of Sergei Pankeev, who was in and out of psychoanalytic treatment for almost seventy years, makes up one of the strangest chapters in the history of Freud's movement. Having lost a millionaire's fortune when (on Freud's advice) he neglected to return to Russia and rescue his estate from the ascendant Bolsheviks, Pankeev adopted the vocation of celebrity charity patient. As the protagonist of Freud's triumphant case history, he allowed himself to be passed from one awestruck analyst to another and even took to signing his letters "Wolfsmann." Later, however, his conspicuous debilitation caused him to be regarded as a bomb that could blow up in the face of psychoanalysis, and he was strongly encouraged, by "pension" payments as well as exhortations, not to tell his story to outsiders. But he eventually did so anyway, spilling his grievances to the Austrian journalist Karin Obholzer in the 1970s and lamenting that, in the final stage of his long Freudian odyssey, "the whole thing looks like a catastrophe. I am in the same state as when I first came to Freud, and Freud is no more" (Obholzer 1982, p. 172).

Yet Pankeev's thralldom to Freud was no greater than that of the analytic community at large, which left the contradictions and implausibilities in Freud's published account of the Wolf Man case entirely unchallenged from 1918 until the 1970s. Even with the aging Pankeev on hand as living evidence that his announced cure was bogus, no Freudian dared to ask whether Freud had tampered with the record to make himself appear a master detective and healer. Rice understands, however, that that is exactly what Freud did.

Involved as he was in a fierce battle against the schismatics Carl Jung and Alfred Adler, each of whom had denied the importance of infantile sexuality in the etiology of neurosis, Freud was determined to find a primal scene to serve as the fountainhead of Pankeev's symptoms. He made it materialize through a transparently arbitrary interpretation of a remembered dream of Pankeev's, from the suspiciously early age of four, about six or seven white wolves (actually dogs, as Freud was later compelled to admit) sitting in a tree outside his window. The wolves, Freud explained, were the parents; their whiteness meant bedclothes; their stillness meant the opposite, coital motion; their big tails signified, by the same indulgent logic, castration; daylight meant night; and all this could be traced most assuredly to a memory from age one of Pankeev's mother and father copulating, doggy style, no fewer than three times in succession while he watched from the crib and soiled himself in horrified protest.

Because he has absorbed the revisionist spirit in Freud scholarship, Rice stands in no danger of being taken in by Freud's posited primal scene. With acknowledgment, he builds upon a trenchant study by the singularly critical psychoanalyst Patrick Mahony (1984), who, though he remains a loyal Freudian, has exposed much of Freud's inventiveness in this instance. For Mahony and Rice alike, the Wolf Man's primal scene lacks all verisimilitude. Freud elsewhere reports that Pankeev's mother disliked sex, for example, yet here he has the wedded pair going at it repeatedly like teenagers on speed, with a one-year-old kibitzer precociously keeping score while observing, from across the room, both his mother's "castrated" genitals and her rapt but suitably passive facial expression—a feat of observation, as Mahony has remarked, that "would exceed the ingenious staging of any pornographic film producer" (Mahony 1984, p. 52).

More tellingly, and more portentously for a final judgment of psychoanalytic claims in general, Freud was never able to convince Pankeev himself that this "terribly farfetched" episode, as Pankeev later called it, had ever occurred. "These scenes from infancy," Freud admits, "are not reproduced during the treatment as recollections, they are the products of construction" (Freud 1953–1974, 17:50–51). That is to say, all such "memories," including the Wolf Man's, were proposed by Freud himself without necessarily involving the patient's cooperation or assent.

Yet having admitted that Pankeev had no recollection of a primal scene, Freud twice reports specific memories on the Wolf Man's part that "confirm" that scene with volunteered details. How strange this is, in view of Pankeev's assurance to Karin Obholzer that, given the customs of his social class, he could hardly have found himself in the parental bedroom where Freud insistently placed him! And to make matters more bizarre, in the course of revising his paper Freud himself came to deny the reality of the primal scene and then to reassert its genuineness, leaving all three propositions to jostle one another in the text. The illogic of Freud's presentation is matched, for absurdity, only by the inherent ridiculousness of the fabricated tale itself.

If the Wolf Man never presented Freud with the required primal scene, from which depths was it hauled up? Rice argues that it was the child Freud, not Pankeev, who slept in his parents' bedroom and who later fancied that he recalled a traumatically enlightening act of intercourse. And it was Freud who was demonstrably obsessed with copulation from the rear and with yet another pivotal feature of the Wolf Man analysis, sexual initiation at the hands of servant girls. One might add the suggestive fact that little Sigismund, according to *The Interpretation of Dreams*, was permanently scarred by a paternal rebuke after he had relieved himself in his parents' bedroom (4:16), thus anticipating, and perhaps determining, what would later be ascribed to the Wolf Man's infancy.

2.

What necessarily falls beyond Rice's purview is the relation of the Wolf Man case, with its fanatical misconstructions and its pathetic outcome, to Freud's normal practice. For a concise sense of that relation, readers can consult an important 1991 article by Frank J. Sulloway (1991) that reviews all of the major case histories and infers that they compose a uniform picture of forced interpretation, indifferent or negative therapeutic results, and an opportunistic approach to truth. We can go further and ask whether, strictly speaking, Freud can be said to have ever practiced psychoanalysis in the sense that he commended to others. Freud generally lacked the equanimity to act on his key methodological principle, that the patient's free associations would lead of their own accord to the crucially repressed material. Some of his own accounts and those of his ex-patients reveal that, when he was not filling the hour with opinionated chitchat, he sought to "nail" the client with hastily conceived interpretations that he then drove home unabatingly. As a distinguished American psychiatrist, Joseph Wortis, recalled from his own training analysis, Freud "would wait until he found an association which would fit into his scheme of interpretation and pick it up like a detective at a line-up who waits until he sees his man" (Wortis 1940, p. 844).

Revisionist students of psychoanalysis agree that one case history in particular illustrates that tendentiousness with especial clarity. This is the 1905 "Fragment of an Analysis of a Case of Hysteria" (7:3–122), a work that forms the topic of Robin Tolmach Lakoff and James C. Coyne's study, *Father Knows Best: The Use and Abuse of Power in Freud's Case of Dora*. Even though "Dora" (Ida Bauer) severed relations with Freud after just three months of tempestuous sessions, Freud's portrait of her has been used as a model in psychoanalytic training—as, in Erik H. Erikson's words, "the classical analysis of the structure and genesis of hysteria" (Erikson 1962, p. 455). But today the Dora case is more often regarded as one long indiscretion on Freud's part. As the first of his fully psychoanalytic cases to be written up, it is relatively candid and vivid in its portrayal of his behavior—so much so that it filled his nonpsychoanalytic contemporaries with alarm. The immediate scandal aroused by the Dora report taught Freud to be more circumspect in subsequent writings, but there is no sign that it altered his peremptory clinical style.

Father Knows Best resembles many another recent study of Dora in approaching the case from a manifestly feminist perspective. It distinguishes itself from most other accounts, however, by showing concern for Dora the actual person, whose escape from Freud's orbit may not have been as free of consequence as other observers have assumed. Though the eighteen-year-old Bauer went to Freud unwillingly, he did represent her last hope of establishing a relationship of trust and mutual respect with an authoritative adult. By betraying that hope in a singularly bullying way, Lakoff and Coyne maintain, Freud helped to ensure Bauer's later unhappiness.

Whether or not this is so, there can be no doubt that, even by the standards of 1901, Freud's treatment of Bauer constituted psychiatric malpractice. Granted, Freud could not have realized what now seems obvious, the sexual aggressiveness of his own behavior in attempting to force prurient suggestions upon his virginal teenage patient. But as Lakoff and Coyne understand, what matters most is the larger picture, namely, that Freud withheld all sympathy from Bauer and assailed her self-esteem at every turn. Abetted by the bias of psychoanalytic theory away from real-life factors and toward sexual fantasy, he tried to convince Bauer that she herself, by virtue of having repressed her latent homosexuality, her fantasies of pregnancy and oral sex, and her memories of childhood masturbation and of the obligatory primal scene, was to blame for a distress that clearly had much to do with the current ugly situation into which she had been plunged by others. But that was not the worst of it, for he also tacitly sought her acquiescence in a scheme that can only be characterized as monstrous.

Lakoff and Coyne offer an exceptionally clear account of Bauer's situation when she consulted Freud. The key facts are these:

1. Her syphilitic father was having an affair with the wife of a close family friend, "Herr K".
2. Herr K himself had taken a sexual interest in Bauer since she was fourteen years old and was now pressing his attentions on her once again.
3. Bauer's father evidently found those attentions convenient, since Herr K's proposed misconduct seemed no worse than his own and might distract Herr K from his role as cuckolded husband, thus leaving the father a free hand with Frau K.
4. When Bauer complained to her father about this, he rebuffed her and sent her off to Freud to be cured not just of her numerous tics and suicidal thoughts but also of her insubordination.

Freud was only too happy to oblige. In Lakoff and Coyne's summary, he demanded that Bauer "become aware of her responsibility for her predicament and on the basis of that awareness, modify her reactions, bringing them into conformity with the wishes of her milieu." Prominent among those wishes was a desire that Bauer give up her antagonism to the pedophilic Herr K, whose intentions toward her had been made plain by a forced kiss when she was fourteen and a direct verbal invitation to sexual activity when she was sixteen, as well as by daily gifts and flowers. Accordingly, Freud labored to show Bauer not only that it had been hysterical on her part to spurn Herr K's original kiss but also that she had been in love with him all along.[1]

It is a pity, Freud tells us, that Dora spitefully cut off the treatment before he could bring her to this useful realization. If Herr K had learned "that the slap Dora gave him by no means signified a final 'No' on her part," and if he had resolved "to press his suit with a passion which left room for no doubts, the result might very well have been a triumph of the girl's affection for him over all her internal difficulties" (7:109–110). In short, a sexually and morally uninhibited Bauer, rounded into psychic trim by Freud, would have been of service to both her father and Herr K, the two predatory males who, unlike any of the women in the story, basked in the glow of Freud's unwavering respect.

It is this last aspect of gender bias that especially catches the interest of Lakoff and Coyne. Using the tools of their academic specialties—Lakoff's is "linguistic pragmatics," and Coyne's is "interpersonal systems theory"—the coauthors take turns exploring the nonreciprocity between Freud and Dora. Freud, they show, overmastered and dehumanized his teenage patient with his badgering. In doing so, Lakoff and Coyne maintain, Freud was redoubling the age-old subjection of women to masculine will by exploiting a power imbalance already inherent in the clinical setting.

Lakoff and Coyne suggest that all psychotherapy relies to some extent on such an imbalance, and they consider it indispensable to therapeutic progress. But psychoanalysis, they feel, tips the scales egregiously, and doubly so when the analyst is male and the analysand female. Freud's personal quirks aside, Lakoff and Coyne argue, psychoanalysis as an institution—with its deliberate coldness, its cultivation of emotional regression, its depreciation of the patient's self-perceptions as inauthentic, its reckless dispensation of guilt, its historic view of women's moral inferiority and destined passivity, and its elastic interpretative license, allowing the analyst to be "right every time"—seems ideally geared to assaulting the very selfhood of insecure female patients.

The point is worth pondering, but the Dora case, precisely because it is one of the worst instances on record of sexist hectoring by a reputed healer, is not representative enough to convey it. If Lakoff and Coyne's primary target was really psychoanalysis rather than Freud personally, they would have done better to show how the standard analytic "power imbalance" warps the conduct of cases in which the therapist behaves more rationally and humanely than Freud did with Bauer.

Contemporary analysts, faced with Lakoff and Coyne's critique, will have no trouble disowning "Dora" and maintaining that *Father Knows Best* overlooks the improved modern state of their craft.

Odd as it may seem, this book must also be judged insufficiently skeptical toward Freud himself. Because their interest stops at Freud's tyrannizing over Bauer and his dismissal of her real-life predicament in favor of "an inspection of [her] internal, pre-existing conflicts," Lakoff and Coyne rashly concede the accuracy of what he asserted about those conflicts. There is, they declare, "no clear reason to dispute any of Freud's interpretations of the material"; he is "precisely on target with every interpretation that reflects poorly on Dora's motives"; and in general, he "often displays a remarkably subtle analytic ear for language as his patients use it," presumably in this case as well as in others (pp. 74, 41, 128, 44). But these compliments defy the by now well-established fact that Freud's hypersensitive ear was chiefly attuned to his own fanciful associations, not to Bauer's. And his reconstructions of Bauer's infantile habits, traumas, and repressions are, transparently, a tissue of flimsy preconceived ideas. As he aptly said in a letter to Fliess when he had known Bauer for scarcely a week, the case "has smoothly opened to the existing collection of picklocks" (Freud 1985, p. 427).

There is, finally, the neglected but overarching issue of whether Bauer was ever a hysteric in the first place. Lakoff and Coyne casually assume that she was, but her immediate family featured a rich array of disorders, from asthma to tuberculosis to syphilis, that would have set off alarms in the mind of a responsible physician. We will probably never know whether Bauer suffered from an organic disease, because Freud made no attempt to find out. Instead, he followed his customary diagnostic procedure, which we have already seen at work with the Wolf Man and in the armchair case of Dostoevsky. That is, he leapt immediately to a conclusion that would permit him to put his trademark suppositions into play and then held to them like a pit bull—later, however, portraying himself as having gradually solved the case with all the prudent objectivity and uncanny astuteness of his favorite literary character, Sherlock Holmes.

3.

Lakoff and Coyne's hesitation about taking too adversarial a position toward Freud and psychoanalysis illustrates the continuing resilience of the Freud legend, which tends to snap back into shape at every point that is not under immediate pressure. To a lesser extent, even James Rice's steadily lucid book on Freud and Russia exhibits the same phenomenon. And so, as we shall see, does John Kerr's otherwise superb *A Most Dangerous Method*. All four authors could have profited from scanning the other revisionist book to be considered here, Allen Esterson's *Seductive Mirage: An Exploration of the Work of Sigmund Freud* (1993). By concisely surveying the whole Freudian enterprise with a skeptical eye, Esterson dispels any impression that some parts of that enterprise have passed beyond controversy.

Except for an incisive discussion of the Wolf Man case establishing that Freud must have invented one of its key figures, the servant girl Grusha, *Seductive Mirage* does not add to our factual knowledge about Freud. Rather, it combines a close scrutiny of his ethics and rhetoric with criticism of his original "seduction theory" and its putative correction; of his major case histories, of his theories of neurosis and dream formation, of his several reformulations of metapsychology, and of his clinical technique and its results. Esterson's book, I should emphasize, is not a polemic written by a longtime foe of psychoanalysis. It is a piece of careful and sustained reasoning by a mathematician who happens to be offended by specious means of argumentation. And its eventual verdict—that every notion and practice peculiar to psychoanalysis is open to fundamental objection—rests on evidence that any reader can check by following up Esterson's cited sources.

Because people do have such a hard time perceiving the nakedness of Emperor Freud, *Seductive Mirage* will prove especially illuminating for the attention it gives to Freud's seduction theory and its sequel, the founding of psychoanalysis per se. After all, to take note of Freud's unsuccess with individual patients like Dora and the Wolf Man leaves the working assumptions of psychoanalysis largely uncompromised. There is always the possibility that Freud simply had little aptitude for therapeutically applying his perfectly sound principles. But if, with Esterson, we uncover grave flaws of reasoning or even outright fraudulence behind the cases that supposedly compelled Freud to adopt those principles, the stakes of the game are considerably raised.

As Esterson relates, up until a certain day in 1897 there was no such thing as psychoanalysis. The method of investigation was in place, but it was producing "findings" of an opposite purport—namely, that hysteria and obsessional neurosis were caused by the repression of actual sexual abuse in childhood. Psychoanalysis came into existence when Freud reinterpreted the very same clinical data to indicate that it must have been his patients themselves, when scarcely out of the cradle, who had predisposed themselves to neurosis by harboring and then repressing incestuous designs of their own. Every later development of psychoanalytic theory would crucially rely upon this root hypothesis, which spared Freud the embarrassment of having to discard his most cherished concept, that of repression. But had he actually discovered anything, and if so, where was his evidence for it?

The controversy over Freud's seduction theory, Esterson reminds us, has concentrated on whether the accusatory tales recounted by his patients were believable. Some feminists and defenders of children follow Jeffrey Masson (1984) in holding that those stories were true and that Freud showed a failure of nerve in renouncing them. Freudians, by contrast, take it for granted that the stories were false. In Peter Gay's words, "for a time [Freud] continued to accept as true his patients' lurid recitals," until he reluctantly concluded that he had been told "a collection of fairy tales" (Gay 1988, pp. 94, 96). But Esterson, drawing on pioneering studies by Frank Cioffi (1972, 1974, 1988) and Jean G. Schimek (1987) among others, demonstrates that both parties have been drastically misled.[2] The question they should have posed to themselves is not *Were those stories true?* but rather *What stories?*

It was Freud himself who taught both his followers and his adversaries to take the seduction narratives seriously as productions of his patients' minds. Beginning in 1914, some twenty years after his work on the pivotal cases, he repeatedly asserted that "almost all my women

patients told me that they had been seduced by their father" and that he
had innocently believed those narratives until their cumulative unlikelihood became too apparent (22:120; see also 14:17 and 20:33–34). But
as Esterson makes unavoidably clear, Freud's papers from the nineties
expose this claim as a cover-up for a very different state of affairs.

"Before they come for analysis," Freud declared in 1896, "the patients
know nothing about these scenes. . . . Only the strongest compulsion of
the treatment can induce them to embark on a reproduction of them"
(3:204). "The principal point," he revealed, "is that I should guess the
secret and tell it to the patient straight out" (2:281). And he confessed
that even after his patients had been "induced" to join in the story making, "they have no feeling of remembering the scenes" thus concocted
(3:204). Here is the heart of the matter. As in the case of the Wolf Man's
and Dora's primal scenes, Freud himself laid down the outlines of the
seduction plots, which were then fleshed out from "clues" supplied by
his bewildered and frightened patients, whose signs of distress he took
to be proof that his constructions were correct.[3]

Freud's motive, in later years, for trying to hide his principal authorship of his patients' "scenes" is easy to discern. The myth of the birth
of psychoanalysis required that some sexual material have been presented to Freud for explanation. Otherwise, even a simpleton would
be able to detect the fallacious means by which Freud segued from the
seduction theory to psychoanalysis proper. In Esterson's words, "having decided that his own constructions [about childhood sexual abuse]
are untrue he concludes that they are not genuine occurrences, but are
phantasies of his patients!" That was exactly the indefensible leap Freud
had taken, but it disappeared from view as soon as he convinced his
critics, and perhaps himself as well, that his patients had come to him
with "lurid recitals."

Given Freud's severe problem with reality testing, it may seem won-
derful that he was able to let go of his seduction theory at all. But here
again, dishonesty and cowardice played a larger role than rationality.
In the spring of 1896 he had already delivered a talk announcing the
seduction theory to Viennese neurologists and psychiatrists, claiming

that his views had been borne out by "some eighteen cases of hysteria," treated on the whole with "therapeutic success" (3:199). We now know from the uncensored Freud-Fliess letters that, at the time, Freud had not resolved a single one of his thirteen cases; nor, despite increasingly frantic efforts, did he ever do so. As the months dragged on and his patients wandered away, disillusioned, each of them became a potential refuter of his seduction claims. Somehow he had to minimize his exposure to the revelation that those people had been neither sexually abused nor cured of their symptoms. His means of doing so was to slap together a new theory whereby it no longer mattered what had happened to patients in their infancy, since in their fantasy life they and every other child who ever breathed had been the would-be seducers— namely, of their opposite-sex parents.

Freud had a plain medical and scientific obligation to retract his seduction theory as soon as he realized its implausibility in 1897. Instead, he publicly reaffirmed it in the following year (3:263). By 1905, in the Dora case history, he was taking the desperate tack of pretending that his published conclusions of 1895 and 1896 had already been fully psychoanalytic; the Dora case, he maintained, would "substantiate" those findings (7:7). And even when he felt secure enough to admit his seduction mistake and turn it to rhetorical advantage, he continued to adulterate the facts. In 1896 the alleged seducers of infants were said to have been governesses, teachers, servants, strangers, and siblings, but in later descriptions Freud retroactively changed most of them to fathers so that a properly oedipal spin could be placed on the recycled material. At every stage, earlier acts of fakery and equivocation were compounded by fresh ones. And this pattern, as Esterson shows in devastating detail, holds for the entirety of Freud's psychoanalytic career.

Dissembling aside, it was no coincidence that the key amendment enabling psychoanalysis to begin its colorful history was one that placed Freud altogether beyond the reach of empirically based objections. Thenceforth, he and his successors could claim to be dealing with evidence that was undetectable by any means other than his own clinical technique—the same technique, as Esterson emphasizes, that had generated the false tales of seduction. Instead of spelling out that technique for the sake of the medically solicitous or the scientifically curious, Freud chose to keep it a mystery that he would unveil only to disciples whom he trusted to accept his word without cavil.

In a word, then, Freud had launched a pseudoscience—that is, a nominally scientific enterprise that is so faulty at the core that it cannot afford to submit its hypotheses for unsparing peer review by the wider community, but must instead resort to provisos that forestall any possibility of refutation. And despite some well-intentioned efforts at reform, a pseudoscience is what psychoanalysis has remained.

4.

It is precisely the institutional emergence of psychoanalysis—its metamorphosis from Freud's personal hobbyhorse to a contentious and internally riven movement—that occupies the final book under consideration here, John Kerr's *A Most Dangerous Method: The Story of Jung, Freud, and Sabina Spielrein* (1993). As its subtitle indicates, this impressive work is essentially a narrative, one that spans the crucial years (1904–1914) of Freud's volatile collaboration and eventual falling-out with Jung. But the narrative is informed at all points by Kerr's discriminating awareness of methodological issues. The story he tells is not just a dramatic tale of professional empire building, ethnic mistrust, erotic complications, and vendettas; it is also an account of the haphazard way in which psychoanalytic doctrine acquired some of its major lineaments. For Kerr, the deeply antiscientific character of Freudianism—with its unformalized procedures, its gratuitous causal assertions, and its appeal to evidence consisting of unobservable buried wishes—left a rational void that could only be filled by exercises of personal power.

Thus readers of *A Most Dangerous Method* who grasp the complex interactions among Jung, Freud, and Sabina Spielrein, the hitherto underappreciated woman who inadvertently sharpened the co-leaders' differences and precipitated their split, will find that they have also acquired insight into the surprisingly negotiable content of psychoanalysis itself. Because Freud was reluctant to say just what he meant by psychoanalysis, and because he was principally concerned to launch an international movement that would leave behind his hapless circle of misfits and drudges in Vienna, it appeared for a while that Jung, his chosen heir, could bend the emerging "science" to spiritualizing purposes of his own. Eventually, of course, Freud proved adamant on large and small points of dogma—but not before he and Jung had freely traded speculations and turned psychoanalytic theory building into a tense dialogue of coded thrusts and parries.

In several respects, *A Most Dangerous Method* serves as an invaluable corrective to received views about the Jung-Freud relationship. Kerr establishes, for example, that in prestige Jung was by no means the supplicant "son" to the authoritative "father," Freud. Because the Zurich contingent commanded a psychiatric clinic and had already published well-regarded research, "it was Jung and [Eugen] Bleuler who put Freud on the scientific map, not the other way around" (p. 9). Similarly, the common assumption that Jung was the less empirically minded of the two thinkers cannot survive Kerr's penetrating discussion. Freud was more suspicious of idealizations than Jung, but the latter, for all his woolly emphasis on a guiding subliminal self, adhered to hypotheses about conflict and regression that required fewer leaps of faith than Freud's.

Whereas Jung believed, plausibly, that the failure of patients to cope with present dilemmas caused them to act regressively, Freud saddled himself with a counterintuitive structure of inextinguishable, polymorphously perverse wishes and repressions that were supposed to become suddenly virulent many years after their formation, dwarfing the patients' contemporary sources of trouble and requiring a mode of analysis that demeaned those sources as trivial. Thus, while Freud treated the patients' unconscious as an obscure and devious text to be deciphered through the cracking of resistances, Jung saw the unconscious as a potential ally that deserved to be courted and activated. Jung may have been naive in his optimism and reckless (as Freud was) about the transmission of ancestral impulses, but his supportive and enabling attitude forestalled the kind of injury that Freud wrought on Dora, the

Wolf Man, and others as he prodded them for "memories" that would shore up his dubious premises.

We are often admonished that Freud's work should not be held accountable to stricter standards than those prevailing in his own day. As Kerr shows, however, Freud's peers understood both the man and his errors more clearly than have the generations that came of age after psychoanalysis had acquired its transatlantic vogue. Freud, observed William James in 1909, is "obsessed with fixed ideas"; in the words of Poul Bjerre, he possessed "an infelicitous tendency to drive one-sidedness to absurdity." His refusal to provide extensive case data to support his notions aroused generally unfavorable comment. As for his therapeutic regimen, James Jackson Putnam remarked in 1906 that it established a "dependence of the patient upon the physician which it may, in the end, be difficult to get rid of." And Putnam added that such unhealthy closeness allows the therapist to impose his sexual pre-occupations through suggestion. As Albert Moll astutely observed,

> Much in the alleged histories has been introduced by the suggestive questioning of the examiner. . . . The impression produced in my mind is that the theory of Freud and his followers suffices to account for the clinical histories, not that the clinical histories suffice to prove the truth of the theory. (p. 245)

Above all, *A Most Dangerous Method* is useful for the light it throws on the ossification of psychoanalysis, during the period of the Freud-Jung struggle, into what Kerr calls "a totalizing worldview." Kerr is at his best when showing how inevitable it was that psychoanalysis be plagued by sectarianism and, in its reconstituted core, patched together by enforced ideological conformity. Running through this book, subtly but insistently, is a parallel between psychoanalysis and a modern totalitarian regime in which propaganda campaigns and heresy trials come to preempt free debate. That analogy becomes inescapable when Kerr recounts the activity of Freud's top-secret "Committee," convened in 1912 by none other than Freud's official biographer-to-be, Ernest Jones, and taking as its mission the shielding of Freud from criticism by promulgating whatever his latest line might be and by heaping ridicule on his opponents. This Orwellian project, which continued until 1926 and remained undisclosed until 1944, guaranteed that the sounding board for Freud's newest fancies, like those of any insecure dictator, would be an echo chamber.[4]

Unsettling though it is, Kerr's discussion of the inquisitorial "Committee" will not be considered either his most original or his most shocking contribution to revisionist Freud scholarship. That distinction belongs to two "love stories," one solidly documented and the other quite speculative, that Kerr regards as having crucially affected Freud's and Jung's perception and treatment of each other. The less certain of those stories shouldn't affect our picture of Freud unless it is borne out by further research. But in the better-established case of Sabina Spielrein's affair with Jung, at least, we gain some valuable insight into the sexual ethics of the earliest psychoanalysts and the sexual politics that affected the shaping of both Freudian and Jungian theory.

Briefly, Sabina Spielrein began as Jung's patient in Zurich, became his soul friend and mistress, drifted into Freud's orbit when the already married Jung deemed her a liability, and gained equivocal acceptance as a Freudian analyst in Vienna, thereafter returning to her native Russia to introduce and champion psychoanalysis until Stalin closed it down as counterrevolutionary.[5] In the course of that career—brought to a barbaric end when Spielrein and the other Jews of Rostov-on-Don were herded into a synagogue and shot by Nazi troops in 1941—Spielrein worked not just with Freud and Jung but also with such other luminaries as Jean Piaget, A. R. Luria, and Alexander Vygotsky, the latter two being for a while her protégés in Moscow.

As Kerr is at some pains to argue, the one point on which Spielrein has hitherto received general credit, that of having anticipated Freud's concept of a death instinct, is largely a misapprehension. On the other hand, Kerr shows, Spielrein has not been properly acknowledged as the prototype of Jung's "anima," the female presence that supposedly occupies a command post within a man's unconscious. But that attenuated form of immortality looks like small recompense for Spielrein's suffering because of Jung's sexual hypocrisy and the icy misogyny with which she was greeted by Freud's small-minded cadre in Vienna.

Freud had heard directly from Spielrein about her involvement with her psychiatrist Jung, and he knew that the aspirations of the pater-familias and hospital officer Jung in Protestant Zurich could have been considerably thwarted by word of that affair.[6] As he incurred more and more of Freud's intellectual displeasure, Jung trembled before the prospect of exposure by Freud, who had a well-known record of deal-ing unscrupulously with former friends.[7] But if Kerr is right, Jung held a higher card that could be played if necessary: Freud himself was the potential subject of an even more damaging story, one about a sexual involvement with his own sister-in-law.

It was Peter J. Swales—by all odds the canniest and most dogged, as well as the most irrepressible, of Freud researchers—who first sys-tematically argued that Freud, during the decades spanning the turn of the century, may have consoled himself for his then sexless, intel-lectually sterile marriage by sleeping with his usual traveling compan-ion and confidante, Minna Bernays (Swales 1982a). The idea has been summarily dismissed by Freudians, who find it incompatible with the high-mindedness they associate with the discoverer of ubiquitous incest wishes. But Swales's essay on the topic abounds in arresting circum-stantial evidence. And we do know for certain that Jung confidentially told a number of people that the morally distressed Bernays herself had revealed the secret to him in person. It is equally clear that something induced Freud and Jung alike to step back from mudslinging and to end their collaboration on relatively civil terms. To put it mildly, the jury is still out on the Freud-Bernays question.

Meanwhile, of course, there remains the less sensational but more important issue of whether anything is salvageable from a once respected body of theory whose evidential grounds have proved so flimsy. On this point, I must say, John Kerr is not always helpful or consistent. At moments he forgets his own powerful account of the psychoana-lytic movement's early and decisive break with the scientific ethos—as, for example, when he refers to Freud as "a systematic thinker of the highest rank," or when he characterizes the typically self-flattering Rat Man case as "a stunning demonstration of the method and a matchless psychological study in its own right." Kerr is also inclined to lay all the subsequent troubles of the psychoanalytic movement at the door of the Jung-Freud clash. Freudians who are willing to come to grips with the shameful side of their history, he tells us, may yet be able to "renovate [psychoanalysis] or build extensions" upon it (pp. 102, 184, 40).

It may be pertinent to note here that *A Most Dangerous Method* began as a dissertation directed by a psychoanalyst, though a relatively critical one, Robert Holt. In a concluding bibliographical essay, Kerr tells us that Holt's (distinctly waffling) book of 1989, *Freud Reappraised*, has served as one of his essential guides to the scientific standing of psychoanalysis. Has Kerr, like the Frank Sulloway of the unrevised 1979 *Freud, Biologist of the Mind*, written a major study of psychoanalysis that is still residually under the spell of the Freud legend? If so, I would like to think that his further development will also follow Sulloway's. For now, I am left wondering which wing of the ramshackle Freudian edifice could be deemed solid enough to "build extensions" on.

A Most Dangerous Method does make a case for psychoanalysis as having been a progressive force at the turn of the century, when psychiatry was burdened with sinister theories of hereditary degeneration and racial inferiority. We should be grateful to the early Freudians, Kerr tells us, for their candor about sex, their cultivation of a developmental perspective, their addressing of the problems and opportunities posed by transference, and their belief in deep and intricate continuities among a patient's disparate productions of symptom and language. Though one could retort that the Freudian craze postponed investigative approaches that have proved more fruitful than psychoanalysis, this perspective has some merit. To be deemed progressive, after all, a psychological movement needn't put forward accurate hypotheses about the mind; it need only raise useful new questions and attract followers who are eager to put aside the older dispensation.

Let us not remain in doubt, however, about whether psychoanalysis remains a vanguard influence today. Incorrect but widely dispersed ideas about the mind inevitably end by causing social damage. Thanks to the once imposing prestige of psychoanalysis, people harboring diseases or genetic conditions have deferred effective treatment while scouring their infantile past for the sources of their trouble. Parents have agonized about having caused their children's homosexuality. Women have accepted a view of themselves as inherently envious, passive, and amoral. And, most recently, even our criminal justice system has suffered episodes of delusion. As I write, a number of parents and child-care providers are serving long prison terms, and others are awaiting trial, on the basis of therapeutically induced "memories" of child sexual abuse that never in fact occurred. Although the therapists in question are hardly Park Avenue psychoanalysts, the tradition of Freudian theory and practice unmistakably lies behind their tragic deception of both patients and jurors.

This claim will, I know, strike most readers as a slur on Freud and his movement. Didn't psychoanalysis arise precisely from a denial that certain alleged molestations were veridical? But we have seen earlier that it was Freud's technique of breaking down resistance that brought those charges into being in the first place, and we have further seen that the same technique, unaltered in any way, saddled Dora and the Wolf Man with initially unremembered primal scenes. By virtue of his prodding, both before and after he devised psychoanalytic theory, to get his patients to "recall" nonexistent sexual events, Freud is the true historical sponsor of "false memory syndrome." Indeed, the modern cases hinge absolutely on Freud's still unsubstantiated notion that children routinely repress anxiety-producing memories—for how else could their initial denial of having been molested be so blithely set aside? Moreover, our incest Pied Pipers are following the most basic, if also the least noted, of all Freudian precedents, a discounting of the suggestibility of patients under emotional stress.

Freud's net legacy, then, may not be quite so positive as the conventional wisdom assumes. While we are assessing it, we can only applaud the efforts of revisionist scholars to restore to us the historical Freud, who, before his own promotional efforts and those of his clandestine "Committee" rendered him sacrosanct, used to be regarded with healthy skepticism. The new Freud studies are having the salutary effect of putting the deviser of psychoanalysis back where he stood at the turn of the century, possessed of a hobbyhorse about the infantile-sexual roots of neurosis and having to win over a sophisticated audience of doubters. The first time around, Freud prevailed by snubbing his most acute critics and posturing before lay readers who knew only that he stood in the forefront of the anti-Victorian camp. This time, it seems, he will not be so lucky.

Chapter 2

FREUDIAN SUSPICION VERSUS
SUSPICION OF FREUD

A BRIEFER VERSION OF THIS CHAPTER WAS DELIVERED AS A LECTURE AT A NEW YORK ACADEMY OF SCIENCES CONFERENCE, "THE FLIGHT FROM SCIENCE AND REASON," HELD IN NEW YORK CITY ON MAY 31–JUNE 2, 1995, AND LATER PUBLISHED IN THE CONFERENCE PROCEEDINGS (GROSS, LEVITT & LEWIS 1996).

I.

Perceptions of Sigmund Freud and of the movement that he founded are so various that I cannot expect, in brief compass, to do more than sketch a position that will appear self-evident to some readers but impossibly strange to others. Some may be offended that I could stigmatize a revered discoverer of fundamental psychological truths as Exhibit A in "The Flight from Science and Reason." Others, however, will have lost any trust in psychoanalysis so long ago that they consider its very mention an anachronism. And many will want to know why they should worry about Freud and his brainchild when the major current threat to our rational and empirical ethos stems from an overt politicizing of intellectual discourse—a phenomenon that looks quite remote from the objective claims, however debatable, of a psychological system.

The only easy portion of my task is to show that Freud's work does remain alive and capable of exerting considerable influence. To be sure, psychoanalysis has suffered a continual and precipitous delegitimation within psychiatry and academic psychology. Yet this development has scarcely begun to dislodge Freudian lore from its pedestal in the popular mind—including the minds of myriad therapists, counselors, and social workers, many of whom do not even realize that they are Freud's legatees.

Since about 1985, in fact, an appalling number of them have been facilitating "recovered memories" of early sexual abuse in precisely the way that Freud himself claimed to be doing with his patients in the mid-1890s, just before launching psychoanalysis as we now know it (see Ofshe & Watters 1994; McNally 2003). While modern recovered memory therapy is often decried as antithetical to the true psychoanalytic spirit, it depends crucially on some of the deepest assumptions of classical analysis—for example, that rendering an anxious patient more dependent and needy within an unequal and volatile relationship is a necessary stage on the path to maturity and freedom; that we must dredge up and abreact allegedly repressed memories of early events if we are to break neurotic patterns; and that etiologically determinative memories can be accurately reconstructed in therapy without fear of contamination by the therapist's biases and hunches. Absent the prior diffusion of those Freudian notions, the grotesque and sometimes deadly fad of modern recovered memory therapy could not have taken root as it did.

Unfortunately, that is not the only connection between psychoanalysis and our epidemic of "repressed abuse." Incredible as it may sound, recent books and articles leave no doubt that some contemporary analysts have abandoned their former emphasis on infantile sexuality and the Oedipus complex and are now, themselves, reverting to Freud's prepsychoanalytic practice of cajoling their patients into believing that they were molested as children (Brenneis 1996; Gartner 1997, 2005). Such a development leaves one disposed both to marvel at the elasticity of Freud's tradition and to put on hold any assumption that its days of producing massive social harm are over.

Since I will be discussing the recovered memory movement at length in Chapters 5–8, however, let me give the rest of my attention here to the survival of Freudianism within American universities. This, too, is no trivial phenomenon. Biographical studies by Frank Cioffi (1974, 1985), Malcolm Macmillan (1991), Max Scharnberg (1993), and others, showing that Freud's "discoveries" rested on misconstrued or nonexistent data, have as yet had curiously little effect on the eagerness of many humanists and some social scientists to adhere to the Freudian outlook or to regard Freud personally as our deepest modern thinker.

When Stanford University, for example, famously expanded its "Western Civilization" requirement, at the outset of the 1990s, to eight alternative tracks of "Culture, Ideas, and Values," Freud was awarded a place in all eight tracks—thus putting him into a tie for top cultural authority with Shakespeare and the Bible and ranking him ahead of Homer, Plato, Aristotle, Sophocles, Virgil, and Voltaire. Again, the *Chronicle of Higher Education* reported in 1992 that 38 percent of all literature professors in America were teaching psychoanalytic theory to undergraduates—a proportion greatly surpassing those for poststructuralism, Marxism, and what the *Chronicle* called "minority approaches." What has been true on the undergraduate level is surely truer for methodologically oriented graduate courses. And merely by opening an academic journal, one can be assured that psychoanalysis prospers among us, not in a few tasteful allusions to the unconscious but in full theoretical strength, with reliance on Freud's most ambitious propositions about the determining power of the repressed.

What is especially striking is that this obeisance to Freud is found on both sides of the barrier between politically engaged poststructuralists and upholders of traditional "humanistic values." Taking an instrumental or situational view of truth, the activists endorse any aspects of psychoanalytic dogma that strike them as conducive to a radical analysis of the bourgeois dispensation. One might expect such opportunism to be sharply rebuked by academics who cling to the master texts and verities of Western culture. But there is a complicating factor: Freud himself, as the Stanford curriculum suggests, is revered as a canonical icon within that culture. Consequently, "soft" academics consider it poor taste to question the shortcuts to psychological profundity taken by adversaries with whom they have nothing in common except contested turf and deference to Freud.

2.

I will concentrate here on the soulful or humanistic variety of Freudianism as it is instanced by two esteemed thinkers: a much-quoted professor of philosophy who is also a lay analyst, and a literary critic known for his defense of humanistic culture and for his dim view of poststructuralism. The philosopher is Jonathan Lear; the critic, Eugene Goodheart. Both Goodheart and Lear freely acknowledge that Freud was no paragon of careful method—but then, neither are they.

In *Open Minded: Working Out the Logic of the Soul*, Lear grants that the first psychoanalyst "botched some of his most important cases" and that "a number of his hypotheses are false, his analytic technique can seem flat-footed and intrusive, and in his speculations he was a bit of a cowboy" (Lear 1998, p. 18). "Looking back," Lear adds, "I regularly find Freud's clinical interventions too didactic and suggestive" (p. 22). Interestingly, however, these embarrassments don't cause Lear to wonder how the Austrian cowboy arrived at other psychoanalytic tenets that are permanently valuable, or how the chronically intrusive clinician could have spared himself from speciously "confirming" them, or how we ourselves can now be satisfied as to their cogency.

Lear does allude to the widely accepted argument that the therapist-patient dyad is too suggestion-prone to serve as a skeptical testing ground for psychoanalytic propositions, but instead of weighing that argument, he dismisses it out of hand. Unexpectedly, and amazingly for a trained philosopher, he takes Freud's *attempt* at objectivity to be sufficient grounds for laying the whole matter to rest:

> It was Freud who first set the avoidance of suggestion as a therapeutic ideal—and it is Freud who devised the first therapeutic technique aimed at achieving it. Psychoanalysis distinguishes itself from other forms of talking cure by its rigorous attempt to work out a procedure which genuinely avoids suggestion. (p. 22)

And that, apparently, is all that need be said.

Lear's porous reasoning here could be shored up only if he were to establish that later analysts have adopted adequate safeguards against the self-deception routinely practiced by Freud. But no such demonstration is forthcoming; and indeed, the chaotic record of psychoanalytic squabbling clearly indicates that Freud's legacy of willful, undisciplined dogmatizing remains fully alive today. We are left to conclude, then, that Lear's enthusiasm for his preferred items of Freudian doctrine lies beyond the reach of any logical considerations at all.

The same inference is made unavoidable by Lear's discussion of the extraclinical probative standards that ought to be applied to psychoanalytic propositions—namely, no standards whatsoever. Like physics, says Lear, psychoanalysis makes causal claims, but those claims, dealing as they do with subjective experience, aren't amenable to experimental testing. Nor does Lear countenance any other impersonal kind of trial. On the contrary, "it is a sign of psychoanalysis's *success* as an interpretive science that its causal claims cannot be validated in the same way as those of the physical sciences" (p. 25; italics as found). Would any other scientific notion be treated so indulgently? If the merits of psychoanalytic thought can be vouchsafed entirely within the subjectivity of people who already subscribe to it, then Freudianism will indeed have clear epistemic sailing—as will the similarly validated theory of the Virgin's bodily ascension to heaven.[1]

For Lear, Freudian theory and the general domain to which it belongs—namely, the psychological understanding of human quirks—are exactly the same thing. No other theory need apply. Thus Lear holds that if Freud is discarded, the price to be paid will be utter brain-dead superficiality. Only one condition, he asserts in *Open Minded*, "would count as a global refutation of psychoanalysis: if people always and everywhere acted in rational and transparently explicable ways" (p. 25). "Are we to see humans as having depth," he asks in mock alarm, "—as complex psychological organisms who generate layers of meaning which lie beneath the surface of their own understanding? Or are we to take ourselves as transparent to ourselves?" (p. 27).

The debate over Freud, Lear assures us, isn't really about the merits of certain hypotheses concerning the mind's development and structure. It's about nothing less than "our culture's image of the human soul" (p. 27). Freud's critics—the present writer is named—are out to deny "the very idea that humans have unconscious motivation"; they want to blot out the entire "complexity, depth, and darkness of human life" (p. 27). Conversely, all honor is due Lear's own guild, the psychoanalysts, who at their best display "profound humility in the face of the infinite complexity of another human being" (p. 26). And as if this weren't enough blarney, he adds that psychoanalysis "begins in wonder that the unintelligibility of the events which surround one do not cause more wonder" (p. 28).

Faced with such a display of tender sensibility, not many readers would be crude enough to break the reverent mood and point out that all of the core tenets of Freudianism have been found by independent researchers to be either false or so ambiguous and confused as to be devoid of scientific meaning (see Erwin 1996; Macmillan 1997). Few of Lear's reviewers in the late nineties, certainly, were so inclined. Not just *Open Minded* but its grateful reception as well instanced a still powerful yearning to set Freud and his movement in a realm apart, where the probing questions that await every other theory of mind are simply disallowed.

As a lay analyst, of course, Jonathan Lear has a vocational *parti pris*. Not so the Brandeis professor of English Eugene Goodheart, who stands outside the therapeutic guild and probably wouldn't even comprehend, much less endorse, Lear's claim that "psychoanalysis is crucial for a truly democratic culture to survive" (Lear 1998, p. 19). It is all the more striking, then, that Goodheart shows the same impulse as Lear to remove Freud from the level playing field of scientific evaluation. The reasons he supplies for salvaging certain articles of the psychoanalytic faith reflect, I believe, something approaching a consensus among those academic humanists who feel that, while Freudianism isn't central to their own worldview, thoroughgoing critiques of psychoanalysis are to be discouraged and deplored.

In a 1995 essay called "Freud on Trial," Goodheart joins Lear in acknowledging that scientific objections have been raised against psychoanalysis. He deflects them, however, in a way that has long been routine within literature departments. "Philosophers of science," he writes,

> do not hold that scientific theories necessarily rise or fall when statements within the theories are falsified. Theoretical survival depends upon the character and degree of falsification. The issue is further complicated if one takes seriously Thomas Kuhn's theory of paradigms in which the demarcation between science and nonscience loses its sharpness. (Goodheart 1995, pp. 236–237)

Although in actuality Kuhn's *Structure of Scientific Revolutions* scarcely touches on the demarcation problem, Goodheart has a point here. Typically, Kuhn holds, a scientific paradigm may remain dominant throughout a protracted crisis during which bothersome anomalies continue to accumulate. But another way of making the same point would be to say that paradigms do crumble when their unfruitfulness has become overwhelmingly evident. Therefore we might reasonably expect Goodheart to assess whether, in the case of psychoanalysis, "the character and degree of falsification" have by now proved worrisome or perhaps even terminal.

Instead, however—and all too characteristically for an academic Freudian apologist—Goodheart shifts ground and introduces a quite different framework of evaluation. Now he sympathetically appeals to Michel Foucault's distinction between mere scientists and "founders of discursivity," of whom Freud is a leading exemplar. In Foucault's reckoning as summarized by Goodheart, founders of discursivity "provide the master texts that determine truth claims" (p. 237). Such thinkers "are not required to conform to the canons of science. Their own discourse constitutes the canon that determines its truth value" (p. 237). If so, Foucault has supplied Freudians with a safe-conduct pass that they can produce whenever their epistemic credentials are challenged.

Goodheart appears at first to welcome this advantage, but he does not feel altogether comfortable with Foucault's blatant stacking of the epistemic deck. Founders of discursivity, he admonishes, always provoke both idolatry and iconoclasm, impulses that are equally worthy of our mistrust. Thus, in Goodheart's view, my own "ferocity" (p. 236) against Freud can be discounted as a typical overreaction to Freud's privileged cultural status. According to Goodheart, a wiser middle course would be to demote the idol Freud to a mere "body of knowledge or knowledge claims, which we may both consult and criticize" (p. 237).

Freud, then, remains enough of a paragon to Goodheart for his propositions to be exempted from scientific canons of validity, but at the same time, the literary critic feels himself at liberty to decide intuitively which Freudian notions to adopt and which to spurn. He remains untroubled by the thought that each psychoanalytic proposition falls squarely within the domain of psychology and should thus, as Freud himself at least formally maintained, be subjected to the same empirical criteria as are brought to bear on every other psychological claim. Like many fellow humanists, Goodheart prefers instead to sample the Freudian smorgasbord on a frankly heuristic basis, appropriating only those ideas that strike him as possessing what he calls "suggestiveness" (p. 237). If there are epistemic pitfalls lurking within that subjective criterion, Goodheart in 1995 had not yet begun to worry about them.

The sheer number of reasons that Goodheart offers for removing Freud from scientific accountability makes one wonder how confident he feels about any one of them. To the halfhearted appeal to Kuhn and Foucault and the more general appeal to heuristics he appends three others: a claim that Freud's sheer "power of narration" (p. 238) provides a kind of emotional truth that we could ill afford to forgo; an assertion that "Freud's achievement occurs in the company of the great masters of modern literature," who "seemed to have arrived at Freud's insights independently" (p. 239); and a final claim that "[t]he evidence for psychoanalytic discovery is to be found . . . in case histories of particular persons . . ." (p. 242), and specifically in "the confirming response of the analysand" (p. 241) to the analyst's interpretations.

It is clear from this last line of argument that Goodheart has drastically misconstrued one of the philosophers of science whom he cites as a properly appreciative and balanced commentator on Freud, Adolf Grünbaum. The burden of Grünbaum's classic critique *The Foundations of Psychoanalysis* (Grünbaum 1984) is that, thanks to the pervasive threat of suggestion and the sheer improbability of gleaning temporally remote etiological inferences from a patient's free associations, Freudian tenets and interpretations cannot be reliably corroborated on the couch. By invoking Grünbaum, Goodheart has stumbled back into the scientific killing fields from which he had hoped to rescue Freud.

Like many another "soft" humanist, Goodheart displays what one might call Freudian Whiggishness, or a special gratitude to Freud for having made us the sage moderns that we now perceive ourselves to be. "In exploring the unconscious and its relation to conscious life," Goodheart avers, Freud "thought he was defining the nature of man, and, to the extent that he succeeded—which is to say, to the extent that we recognize ourselves in the account that he provides, Freud must be the commanding figure of our culture in a way that Weber and Durkheim are not" (p. 243). Goodheart is not saying here that anyone at all can look in his heart and determine just how commanding a figure Freud should be taken to be. It is we literati, we who have honed our sophistication not only on the difficult insights of modernist fiction and poetry but also on Freud's own writings, who constitute the jury and, in part, the very evidence for Freud's majestic stature.

Many other humanists resemble Goodheart in observing no firm distinction between the cause of psychoanalysis and that of high artistic endeavor. Freudianism has graced our cultural landscape for so many decades that the prospect of its removal is perceived as a kind of ecological crime, akin to paving a rain forest to make way for theme parks and drive-in theaters. Yet the humanists' treasuring of Freudian texts *as* culture does not prevent those texts from being further treasured as *explanatory of* culture. For Goodheart in particular, the very act of exalting early modernist literature entails an endorsement of the Freudian ideas that appear to be dramatized, willy-nilly, within those classics. As Goodheart puts it, "[t]he whole panoply of Freudian concepts—the

Oedipal drama in the family romance, the degraded split sexuality that results in impotence, the return of the repressed, and so on—are confirmed in the imaginative literature of the modern period" (p. 239).

Goodheart acknowledges that such confirmation is not scientific proof that Freud was right. But is it any proof at all? The critic's inference suffers from two crucial errors that I myself committed thirty years ago, when I first concluded that the correspondence I found between Freud's writings and those of the author I was then studying, Nathaniel Hawthorne, constituted a validation of psychoanalytic laws (Crews 1966).[2] Those errors cost me a good deal of wasted intellectual effort and eventual mortification, but I see that my public penitence has had a negligible dissuasive effect on other literary academics who are bent upon embracing the very same fallacies.

My first mistake was to overlook the difference between psychological description and psychological explanation. Hawthorne's writings indeed dwell on the themes of incest, patricide, and hidden sexual guilt that Freud explains by reference to the universal and perennial Oedipus complex, but this means only that Freud and Hawthorne shared a preoccupation with the same domain of obsessive-compulsive psychological phenomena. A number of historically and biographically delimited explanations, falling well short of the Promethean claims of psychoanalysis, could be consonant with what Hawthorne, the brooding Romantic artist and ironic student of his Puritan forebears' attempts to stifle sin, fictively represented. A comparable stricture applies to Goodheart's observation of the symmetry between Freudian notions and the rendered worlds of Conrad, Lawrence, Proust, and Mann—doubly so for Lawrence and Mann, whose lively interest in Freud subtracts much of the uncanniness from their exemplification of his ideas.

My mistake number two was a failure to think skeptically about Freud as a late-Romantic literary intellectual in his own right. Freud's sly rhetoric, along with the hagiography that he posthumously channeled through Ernest Jones (Jones 1953–1957), promoted a misperception of him as a mere physician and scientist-drudge who had no time for literature and who was amazed to learn, long after the fact, that his reluctant discoveries about the devious and sex-bespattered human mind had all been anticipated in fiction and drama. That is the bait that Goodheart still finds irresistible in 1995. But the truth is that Freud was a voracious and deeply cultivated reader and that his ideas owed more to Shakespeare, Cervantes, Milton, Goethe, Heine, Schiller, Feuerbach, Schopenhauer, Dostoevsky, and Nietzsche than they did to the turn-of-the-century sexologists whose formulations he also liberally raided.

Great imaginative writers did indeed anticipate Freud, but there was nothing mysterious or confirmatory in the tallying of his ideas with theirs. Quite simply, he plucked their darker intimations about egoism, guilt, and inward drivenness and set them out to dry on the gears and pulleys of an arbitrary explanatory contraption that doesn't work and never did. The "confirmatory" parallelism between literary and psychoanalytic insight has proved to be the most successful of Freud's many hoaxes—made more delicious, in this instance, by a further punishment of the writers for having gotten there first. Although he professed a humble awe before artistic genius, Freud took satisfaction in reducing it to the demeaning banality of infantile determinism. The literary giants, he taught us after he admitted to having read some of them, were only adult babies after all, spinning out symptomatic fantasies that replayed the same oedipal riddle in every instance—the riddle that he alone had solved in a single flash of titanic self-exploration.

3.

Can we—can I—ever have believed this megalomaniacal claim? Yes, the record cannot be willed away. Yet before long, I predict, it is Goodheart's and Lear's current position that will look irrational to most academics. The change is being brought about not by "iconoclasts" and "resentful renegade[s]" (p. 236) like me but by sober historical researchers who keep discovering that none of the great thinker's claims can be taken at face value. A would-be scientist who turns out to have drawn putative psychological laws from samples of a few cases, or one, or even none will not forever be treated as a sacrosanct founder of discursivity.

Indeed, as I hinted earlier, in order to arrive at a radically altered conception of our indebtedness to Freud we need only attend to already extant studies of his borrowings from other writers. Humanists have not been mistaken in looking to Freud for a sense that the human mind is vastly egoistic and cunning. Their mistake has simply been to accede to his subtle but persistent urging that he be considered apart from all other philosophers of the same stripe. The source studies indicate that his real originality is much narrower than has been assumed and that it is confined on the whole to points that are either gratuitous or plainly erroneous.

Consider, for example, what is now known about Freud's relation to Nietzsche, the writer toward whom he most strenuously protested a complete lack of indebtedness. As Ernest Gellner (1985) and Didier Anzieu (1986) indicated a decade ago, and as Ronald Lehrer (1995) has now extensively documented in a book entitled *Nietzsche's Presence in Freud's Life and Thought*, most of what could be termed "insight" in Freud is already there in Nietzsche. In Anzieu's words, Nietzsche

> had some understanding of the economic point of view, which comprises discharge, and transfer of energy from one drive to another. . . . On several occasions he used the word sublimation (applying it to both the aggressive and the sexual instincts). He described repression, but called it inhibition; he talked of the super-ego and of guilt feelings, but called them resentment, bad conscience and false morality. Nietzsche also described . . . the turning of drives against oneself, the paternal image, the maternal image, and the renunciation imposed by civilization on the gratification of our instincts. (Anzieu 1986, pp. 88–89)

But this is just the beginning. As Lehrer shows, Nietzsche's preemption of Freud includes the idea that all actions and intellectual choices are egoistic; that we remain unconscious of the conflicts in our motives; that "[g]ood actions are sublimated evil ones" (Lehrer 1995, p. 36); that "[t]he content of our conscience is everything that was during the years of our childhood regularly *demanded* of us without reason by people we honoured and feared" (p. 37); that forgetting is an active step taken to preserve psychic order (p. 58); that dreams employ symbols to express our primeval selves and our disapproved desires (p. 83); that comedy results from a sudden release of anxiety; and that laughter entails "being malicious but with a good conscience" (p. 40). (All quoted words in this sentence are Nietzsche's.) Lehrer's book also places beyond reasonable doubt Freud's acquaintance with Nietzsche's ideas at various stages of his own development. Paul Ricoeur and others have taught us to think of Nietzsche and Freud together (along with Marx) as partaking of a common "school of suspicion," but it has now come to light that one of those parties attended classes in the other's school.

Freud's exalted reputation will surely dwindle as subscribers to the conventional wisdom begin to absorb findings such as Lehrer's. Deprived of the misconception that Freud unearthed the mind's affinity for self-deceit, they will be obliged to realize that his contribution was that of a systematizer, not a discoverer. And then they will find themselves facing the question that I myself couldn't shake off during my own little paradigm crisis around 1970. What if the Freudian system—the portion of it that was actually new—consists almost entirely of unwarranted reifications and crackpot dogmas?

4.

Observe, for instance, what Freud did with the already familiar insight that our minds operate largely beneath the threshold of consciousness and that our thoughts are shaped in part by bodily needs, self-regard, and ill-will toward rivals. Who would want to deny it? But in Freud's system these dispositions have congealed, unnecessarily, into an inner personage called "the unconscious." And this personage in its

turn allegedly contains homunculi—the ego, the id, the superego—
who employ various stratagems in vying with one another for control
over our actions.

Neither in Freud's case histories nor anywhere else do we find evidence of behavioral manifestations that point unambiguously to the
need for such mythic entities. Their usefulness is not empirical but
rhetorical. Each posited subset of "the unconscious" permits another
strand of contrary motivation to be added to the already tangled explanatory skein, leaving us, if we are sufficiently gullible, so impressed by
the psychoanalytic interpreter's diagnostic acumen that we think we are
witnessing elegant and validated feats of deduction instead of being told
a self-serving detective story in which the very mystery itself—which of
the elves checkmated which others to generate the symptom or dream
or error?—is an artifact of question-begging maneuvers. As Freud's
amused critic Ludwig Wittgenstein brightly put it, to dispense with
the Freudian unconscious would be like having to say, truthfully, "We
do not know who did that" instead of the more impressive but specious
"Mr. Donotknow did that" (Bouveresse 1995, pp. 33–34).

Every distinctive feature of Freudian thought is vulnerable to this
same objection. In Freud's discourse, facts are never more than a warm-
up act for the featured performance of Mr. Donotknow. A freewheel-
ing inventiveness pervades his assertions about the causes and cure of
neuroses, the interpretability of symptoms as somatic compromise formations, the central importance of incestuous and murderous urges and
castration fears in the socialization of children, the necessarily envious
and amoral character of women, the wish-fulfillment theory of dreaming, the origin of medical compassion in childhood sadism, the emergence of sexual identity from a primary base of bisexuality, the insidious
operation of the death instinct, and the indestructibility of all memories,
to say nothing of our enervating Lamarckian inheritance of traumatic
memory traces from the earliest days of the human race.

This last item belongs, of course, not to the supposedly indispensable
core of psychoanalytic theory but to what Freudians somewhat sheepishly designate as Freud's speculative or, in Lear's characterization, his

cowboy side. Gnostic divination, however, was his entire métier. The Oedipus complex was disclosed to him through the same kind of hermetic insight that left him convinced that Shakespeare hadn't written Shakespeare's plays, that Moses was an Egyptian, and that weaving originated when one of our early ancestors twisted together her pubic hairs in chagrin over her nonpossession of the only sexual organ worthy of the name.

In drawing inferences about the exact infantile causes of symptoms exhibited by free-associating patients in his consulting room, Freud the psychoanalyst was engaging in the same cavalier dismissal of other possible determinants that characterized Freud the anthropologist of prehistory. In both exercises of guesswork his corroborative method was to focus on a single hunch, to allow it to exfoliate into further hunches that were equally remote from observation, and then to take the thematic consilience of all those constructions as strong evidence of their basis in reality. By thus mistaking convergences within his own fantasy life for deeply lawful regularities in the world outside it, Freud marked himself not just as error-prone but as chronically delusional.

5.

Such a diagnostic label, however, leaves the most fundamental question about Freud's career farther than ever from a plausible solution. If he was delusional, or even if he was simply wrong in ways that now appear easy to discern, how did he succeed in imposing his reveries on much of the literate West? This is one of the central puzzles of modern cultural history, and it calls for a far more complex analysis than I can offer here. But a strong beginning has been made in Ernest Gellner's admirable but little-read book of 1985, *The Psychoanalytic Movement*, now reprinted by Northwestern University Press (Gellner 1996). Meanwhile, and very much in Gellner's spirit, I would like to propose that Freud has had his way with us chiefly by personifying a uniquely seductive style of hermeneutic license. It is, I believe, his peculiarly Janus-faced relation to the scientific ethos that has made many of us—and academic humanists in particular—willing to overlook his habitual preference for far-fetched explanations.

Of course there are many incentives for being a Freudian, the most common and compelling of which is simply that one has been indoctrinated within the lengthy dependency of a therapeutic "transference." With or without therapy, however, many educated nonscientists have in common an uneasy attitude toward mainstream science, leaving them with a susceptibility—exploited by Freud with formidable brilliance— to irrational persuasion. On the one hand, few secular skeptics are willing to embrace doctrines that appear flagrantly antiscientific. On the other hand, it is common for them to feel at once discouraged and diminished by science, with its grinding laboriousness, its opaqueness to lay comprehension, its strong purchase on technology, its power to command respect and money, and above all, its relentless chipping away at the felt scope of free will and the soul. For such a sense of envy and exclusion the treatment of choice may be Freud's intellectual nostrum, a dose of prescientific and even animistic belief that is made palatable by gestures of scientific prudence.

Now, this hypothesis—that psychoanalysis serves as a kind of metaphysical morale booster for the science-impaired—may meet with an immediate objection from readers who remember Freud's none too bashful grouping of himself with Copernicus and Darwin as the greatest of all deflators of human pride. His own contribution, he explained, was to show that the ego of the frail evolved creature man is not even master in its own house. But do we really find ourselves humbler when we have acceded to Freud's balkanization of the psyche?

True, Freud's system makes the determiner of volition look less like an executive than like a wrangling troika of petulant schemers. But the troika's charge, we recall, has been broadened to cover the generation of symbolically—that is, humanistically—readable symptoms as well as thoughts and deeds. And we, Freud's recruits, are tacitly exempted, just as he exempted himself, from his fatalism about the necessarily beclouded human mind. We are promised a chance to help our leader track meanings in the virgin terrain of the symptomatic, and in doing so, not incidentally, to set ourselves decisively apart from the uniniti-ated as exercisers of godless objectivity and stoicism.

Once we have grasped the evangelistic character of Freud's discourse, much that appears anomalous and confused within it begins to make rhetorical sense. Most commentators who have noted his mythmaking penchant, for example, have tended to characterize him as torn between poetical and positivistic ways of addressing the dynamics of motivation. On one side stands the witches' cauldron of the unconscious; on the other, a rigorous materialist determinism focused on cathexes, quanti-ties of excitation, and thresholds of discharge. But rigor is completely absent from Freud's psychological writings, which contain no data that have not already been tailored to the argumentative point they were enlisted to support.

As for determinism, we ought to distinguish between the assump-tion that all phenomena bear causes and the pretense that through sheer cogitation one can trace each human deed to its precise motivational origin. The latter idea is a marker not of science but of magical think-ing. Where Freud most sternly excludes chance from the realm of the mental, he may sound like he is submitting himself to a taxing discipline; but what he actually asserts is his limitless freedom to assign real-world causal significance to his byzantine and arbitrary interpretations. And that is just the giddy freedom that he dangles before us, his readers and potential disciples.

In this light it is telling that Freud's attraction to science had been aroused in the first place by Goethe's visionary *Naturphilosophie* and that Goethe's Faust, the archetypal trader of his soul for illicit knowl-edge and power, was the foremost of his several key heroes.[3] Indeed, his chief complaint against his early mentor Josef Breuer was that there was "nothing Faustian in his nature" (E. Freud 1978, p. 139). Psycho-analysis as Freud conceived it was a truly Faustian program for removing obstacles to the omnipotence of his own thoughts. His professed ratio-nalism was little more than a fig leaf for his sympathy with folk super-stitions, or what he called "the obscure but indestructible surmises of the common people" as opposed to "the obscurantism of educated opinion" (S. Freud 1953–1974, 18:178). And privately, he was devoted to numerology and telepathy—other arts that leapfrogged purported laws of nature to ratify immemorial beliefs in the uncanny control of matter by mind. In Freud's lurid dreamworld, initially fueled by cocaine as Faust's had been fueled by a narcotic witches' brew (Swales 1983), even tuberculosis and cancer could be brushed aside as mere "somatic compliance" with a psychic leverage that fell barely short of levitation.

All in all, Freud was not an empiricist but a Neo-Platonist—that is, a believer that the tangible world is merely a deceptive screen for innumerable interlinked meanings that can be accessed by anointed persons through direct intuition. His rhetorical guile, however, prompted him to cloak his hermetic urge in materialist atomism, enabling him to wage his stirring war against science while wearing the enemy's own uniform. Likewise, his lofty emphasis on ascetic renunciation and tragic fatalism made a perfect foil for the gossipy prurience that lends his case histories much of their literary allure. Any charlatan can offer us interpretive wildness and voyeuristic titillation, but Freud alone knew how to package them as a courageous adherence to the reality principle.

How does all this relate to the survival of Freud and psychoanalysis in our universities? Obviously, one need not be a Neo-Platonist to be mesmerized by the siren song of Freudianism. An academic can still embrace Freud in the misty way that, for example, Lionel Trilling and his circle did a half-century ago, merely out of a sense that it is the highbrow thing to do. That is roughly where Eugene Goodheart appears to stand today.[4] We can now perceive, however, that Goodheart's and Jonathan Lear's curious two-step with respect to validation—removing Freud's propositions from the scientific arena while ratifying some of them as actual psychological laws—bears a distant kinship to Freud's hollow boast of clinical proof as he indulged an unfettered willfulness of assertion. The strategies are opposite but the intended result is the same, a free ride for controversial ideas about the mind.

But the most fundamental affinity between psychoanalysis and our contemporary humanities lies deeper than any such ideas. Both professions place a value on the sheer production of discourse without end. Thanks to its lax and overlapping rules for drawing inferences, its hospitality to several layers of possible exegesis, its readiness to generalize without regard for counterexamples, and its tolerance of self-contradiction, the Freudian hermeneutic leaves an academic interpreter without even a mathematical chance of having nothing to say. All that is required for self-assurance is the "suggestiveness" that Goodheart commends. Not just the single interpretation at hand but also the whole theory behind it can be considered justified if it allows the interpreter to feel that corroboration is popping up wherever he looks—and of course it always does.

It can be seen, then, that academic disputes over Freud take much of their meaning and importance from a broader struggle over the ethics of intellectual assertion. Insofar as psychoanalysis remains a live issue, I believe that the real choice facing us is not between one point of theory and another but between the rational-empirical ethos and a Faustian pseudoscience that defies it at every turn. The flourishing of academic Freudianism could serve as a kind of fever chart for the sickness of empiricism, which has been weakened not only by explicit theoretical assault over this past quarter-century but also by the failure of "soulful" humanists to hold themselves accountable to empirical canons. If psychoanalysis fails to survive, it will be because empiricism itself is on the mend at last.

Chapter 3

A HANDFUL OF DUST

THIS CRITIQUE OF THE LITERARY CRITIC NORMAN N. HOLLAND'S PAPER
"PSYCHOANALYSIS AS SCIENCE," ALONG WITH A SUMMARY OF THAT PAPER, A
REJOINDER FROM HOLLAND, AND COMMENTARY BY THE PSYCHIATRIST PETER
BARGLOW, WAS PUBLISHED IN THE WINTER 2005 ISSUE OF *The Scientific Review
of Alternative Medicine* (VOL. 9, NO. 2). HOLLAND'S FULL PAPER WAS POSTED
AT HTTP://WWW.CLAS.UFL.EDU/IPSA/JOURNAL/2004_HOLLAND08.SHTML. AS
MY DISCUSSION BELOW MAKES CLEAR, THAT PAPER ARTICULATES A DEFENSE OF
FREUDIAN THEORY ON TWO COUNTS: THAT CERTAIN PSYCHOANALYTIC NOTIONS
HAVE RECEIVED EXPERIMENTAL CONFIRMATION AND THAT PSYCHOANALYSIS
BELONGS TO A DIFFERENT ORDER OF INVESTIGATION FROM OTHER SCIENCES
AND MUST BE JUDGED ACCORDINGLY. THE CONTINUING POPULARITY OF THOSE
TWO THESES IN HUMANISTIC CIRCLES LENDS GENERAL SIGNIFICANCE TO THE
FOLLOWING REBUTTAL.

Norman N. Holland maintains that important parts of psychoanalytic
theory have been experimentally confirmed and that analysts in their
daily practice employ a methodologically sound means of gathering
knowledge. As he recognizes, this judgment stands at odds with the
tacit, all but unanimous verdict of North American psychology faculties. Where psychoanalysis appears at all in the catalogs of well-regarded
university departments of psychology, it usually figures as a prescientific
historical curiosity, not as a viable body of theory. And a study of cita-
tions in the flagship psychology journals concludes that "psychoanalytic
research has been virtually ignored by mainstream scientific psychology
over the past several decades" (Robins et al. 1999, p. 117).

Holland asserts that this snub bespeaks not a considered scientific
assessment but rather "a deep-seated prejudice against psychoanalysis" on the part of psychology professors and textbook authors. The
academic establishment, he holds, has turned its back on a mountain
of studies validating key portions of psychoanalytic doctrine while

disallowing some others. Indeed, according to Holland even the most adamant critics of psychoanalysis are unaware of that literature. The main task that he sets for himself in "Psychoanalysis as Science" is therefore an easy one: he will correct an unfair negative impression by calling attention to the somewhat positive results of *hitherto overlooked* experimental trials.

But how can Holland be sure that those results have been overlooked? One could not tell from his paper that he has read a single page of the revisionist scholarship and reasoning that have revolutionized our perception of the psychoanalytic movement and its claims of scientific validation. His 64 references include no dissenters' texts, and only one dissenter's name, my own, is briefly mentioned. Moreover, Holland's characterization of my position, that I find all of psychoanalytic theory untestable and therefore merely "literary" in nature, is off the mark. I regard psychoanalytic doctrine not as literature but as partly unfalsifiable, partly falsified pseudoscience that, when it was widely believed, caused harm to people whom it demeaned, stigmatized, and misdiagnosed (Crews 1986, 1995, 1998; see also Dolnick 1998).

I do hold that psychoanalytic notions, being so vaguely formulated that they are compatible with any outcomes, tend to be recalcitrant to experimentation. But some psychoanalytic claims inadvertently entail real-world consequences, and those consequences have not been fulfilled. As critics have noted, for example, Freud's hypothesis that paranoia results from repressed homosexuality requires that we not encounter overtly homosexual paranoiacs and that the incidence of paranoia in sexually tolerant communities be lower than in harsh ones. Observation has falsified both predictions, and therefore Freud's hypothesis can be said to have failed on epidemiological grounds.

Unfortunately, the facts and arguments that Holland ignores bear crucially on the question he proposes to answer: whether psychoanalysis deserves to be called a science. He could have learned much, for example, from the work of two major Freud scholars, Frank Cioffi (1998) and Malcolm Macmillan (1997), who have extensively traced Freud's initial confusions and misrepresentations, the many unclarities and cross-purposes that have continued to plague psychoanalytic

doctrine, and the chronic flight from exposure to potential disconfirmation that has typified the entire record from Freud's day through our
own. Science is as science does. If neither Freud nor his successors have
shown a due regard for objections to their pet ideas, psychoanalysis is
ipso facto not a science.

Condensing the findings of Cioffi, Macmillan, and other knowledgeable philosophers of science and historians such as Adolf Grünbaum
(1984, 1993), Edward Erwin (1996), and Allen Esterson (1993), I have
elsewhere put into one long sentence the anti-empirical features of the
psychoanalytic movement (Crews 1995, pp. 61n–62n):

> They include its cult of the founder's personality; its casually anec-
> dotal approach to corroboration; its cavalier dismissal of its most
> besetting epistemic problem, that of suggestion; its habitual con-
> fusion of speculation with fact; its penchant for generalizing from
> a small number of imperfectly examined instances; its proliferation
> of theoretical entities bearing no testable referents; its lack of vigi-
> lance against self-contradiction; its selective reporting of raw data to
> fit the latest theoretical enthusiasm; its ambiguities and exit clauses,
> allowing negative results to be counted as positive ones; its indiffer-
> ence to rival explanations and to mainstream science; its absence of
> any specified means for preferring one interpretation to another; its
> insistence that only the initiated are entitled to criticize; its stigmatiz-
> ing of disagreement as "resistance," along with the corollary that, as
> Freud put it, all such resistance constitutes "actual evidence in favour
> of the correctness" of the theory (Freud 1953–1974, 13:180); and its
> narcissistic faith that, again in Freud's words, "applications of analy-
> sis are always confirmations of it as well." (22:146)

This indictment is sometimes dismissed by Freudians as the rav-
ing of an unhinged mind. The justice of every item, however, has
been conceded piecemeal by a number of psychoanalysts who are still
unready to take in the total picture. And other previously sanguine pro-
psychoanalytic commentators now grant that the Freudian community
has shown none of the traits we associate with serious investigators.

Robert F. Bornstein, for example, whom Holland repeatedly cites as a compiler of positive experimental evidence, recently published an article, significantly entitled "The Impending Death of Psychoanalysis," in which he charged analysts with "the seven deadly sins" of "insularity, inaccuracy, indifference, irrelevance, inefficiency, indeterminacy [that is, conceptual vagueness], and insolence" (Bornstein 2001, pp. 7–11). Bornstein portrays a self-isolated sect that is not just out of step with the march of knowledge but incapable of understanding where it went wrong. In order for Bornstein to bring his revised view into full alignment with that of the revisionist critics (whom Holland is pleased to malign en masse as "the bashers"), he need only grasp that the dysfunctional attitudes he has listed are traceable to Freud's own arbitrary system building, to his dismissal of the need to reconcile psychoanalytic theory with mainstream science, to his heaping of scorn on all who questioned his authority, and to his declarations that backsliders from his movement had fallen into psychosis.

In the estimation of Bornstein and some other would-be reformers, psychoanalysis must now rapidly embrace commonly held scientific standards or vanish altogether from the scene. But what would become of the remaining shards of Freudian theory if their proponents took Bornstein's ultimatum to heart? More than a century has passed since analysts, on no examinable grounds, began launching fanciful propositions about the deep structure of the mind, the stages of psychosexual development, and the unconscious symbolic thought processes in early childhood that supposedly issue in adult mental illness. Medical science has moved decisively away from that approach to explanation, which, as Freud privately observed in acknowledgment of kindred thinkers, harkened back to the "spirit possession" lore drawn upon by the judges in witchcraft trials. (See Chapter 7.)

It would be surprising if such an undisciplined and retrograde movement had received support from well-designed experiments, and it would be no less surprising if the critics of psychoanalysis had failed to address the experimental literature. In fact, Holland's claims on both counts are false. An extensive body of penetrating and disillusioning commentary about pro-Freudian experimentation can be found, beginning with Eysenck and Wilson's small masterpiece of 1973 and running through Edward Erwin's meticulous study of 1996. It is apparent that Holland, who innocently equates the terms "experimental" and "empirical," hasn't pondered these widely discussed and important works. Yet if he had attended to no other writings than my own, he would have found me engaged in pertinent debate with several of the psychodynamically committed experimental authorities on whom he relies: Seymour Fisher, Roger P. Greenberg, Lester Luborsky, and Matthew H. Erdelyi (Crews 1986, 1995, 1998).

As its scientific critics have shown, most of the research admired by Holland suffers from grave and obvious flaws. These studies, having been conducted by people holding a prior affinity for psychoanalysis, are riddled with confirmation bias and demand characteristics:

1. Instead of testing psychoanalytic hypotheses against rival ones that might have fared better under Ockham's razor, the experimenters have used Freudian theory as their starting point and have looked for confirming instances, which have been located with the same facility with which Holland once found oral and anal images suffusing the world's literature.

2. Terms have been construed with suspect broadness; strong causal claims have been reinterpreted as weak descriptive ones; and generous psychoanalytic rules of interpretation have helped to shape positive results.

3. Freudian propositions have been assessed through the application of such questionable instruments as the psychoanalytically tendentious Blacky pictures and the Rorschach test, which already lacked validity before believers in Freudian projection twisted it to their own purposes (Wood et al., 2003). (Holland himself twice appeals to psychoanalytic Rorschach findings as sound evidence.)

4. Signs of unconscious *cognitive* operations have been misidentified as evidence of the very different Freudian unconscious at work (Kihlstrom 1987). (Holland's paper indulges in the same confusion.)

5. Replication of tentative outcomes by independent investigators—
an essential requirement of experimentation in any field—has not
been achieved or even sought.

It is Holland's countenancing of these lax and biased practices that
allows him to proclaim that research "supports an oedipal stage," that
"the penis=baby equation" has been vindicated, that "links between
depression and oral fixation" have been found, and that "Freud's account
of paranoia gets confirmation." Such "confirmation" is a strictly parochial affair, and that is why it has been left out of account by scientifically responsible textbook authors.

Critics of psychoanalysis hold that no *distinctively psychoanalytic*
hypotheses, such as those just mentioned, have earned significant evidential backing. Freudians, however, typically credit psychoanalysis
with having introduced broader notions that were, in fact, already
commonplace in the middle of the nineteenth century. As the great
historian of psychiatry Henri F. Ellenberger observed in 1970, "The
current legend attributes to Freud much of what belongs, notably, to
Herbart, Fechner, Nietzsche, Meynert, Benedikt, and Janet, and overlooks the work of previous explorers of the unconscious, dreams, and
sexual pathology. Much of what is credited to Freud was diffuse current
lore, and his role was to crystallize these ideas and give them an original shape" (Ellenberger 1970, p. 548).

It is only Freud's novelties and unique adaptations, along with those
of his most emulated revisers, that ought to concern us here. Self-
evidently, support for ideas that originated elsewhere, much less those
that express the traditional wisdom of the ages, cannot be counted as
favoring psychoanalysis. Apparently, however, Holland does not consider himself bound by this axiom.

Holland reports, for example, that research has validated such assert-
edly psychoanalytic propositions as "much mental life . . . is unconscious," "stable personality patterns form in childhood and shape
later relationships," "mental representations of the self, others, and
relationships guide interactions with others . . . ," and "personality
development is . . . moving from immature dependency to mature

interdependency." Insofar as these vapid truisms constitute the ground to which psychoanalysis has now fled in its retreat from Freud's heedless guesswork, they illustrate the bankruptcy, not the scientific vindication, of his movement.

In the second half of his argument, Holland seeks to confer respectability on psychoanalysis by assimilating it to sciences that enjoy unchallenged recognition as such. His reasoning here is notably fallacious. By progressing from single inductions to themes and patterns that are then checked for adequacy, he writes, psychoanalysts employ the same "holistic" method as social scientists and some physical scientists as well; and since neither psychoanalysis nor geology nor astronomy attempts to predict the future, "psychoanalysis is not that far removed from geology or astronomy." (Nor, in that one respect, is phrenology or the channeling of ancestors.) Needless to say, a perceived or imagined resemblance between the data gathering in one field and that in another tells us nothing about whether their eventual hypotheses are comparably parsimonious and well supported.

Holland labors to portray the psychoanalytic clinician as a scientist in his own right who cautiously moves from a *theory-free* study of word associations to hypotheses that make full sense of the resultant inferences. Yet he approvingly quotes a pair of experts who point out that the analyst "listens for noises that signify *in psychoanalytic terms*" (emphasis added); he further admits that "Freudians will see Freudian patterns" everywhere; and he adds that "Freudian patients have Freudian dreams and make Freudian statements and focus on Freudian issues"—thus providing the analyst, we may be sure, with more Freudian evidence for the confirmation of his Freudian hunches. Perversely, however, Holland still clings to his ideal vision of the *tabula rasa* clinician-scientist.

Freud, Holland maintains, arrived at his theory in just this inductive manner, building hypotheses from sheer attentive listening in the consulting room. We now know, however, that this hoary legend, propagated by Freud himself and his inner circle, is utterly untrue. Far from suspending judgment as a clinician, Freud typically demanded that his patients agree with his theory-driven accusations of incestuous desires, homosexual leanings, and early masturbation.

As a theorist Freud was a rashly deductive bioenergetic speculator who routinely invented "clinical evidence" to fit his predetermined ideas and who altered the facts again when a new speculation required adornment. Contemporaries accused him with good reason of having plagiarized some of his most basic notions, including repression, infantile sexuality, and "universal bisexuality." When it proved impossible for him to deny such unacknowledged borrowings, he brazenly ascribed them to psychodynamically induced "amnesia" (Ellenberger 1970; Sulloway 1992; Borch-Jacobsen 1996).

Holland's illustrations of Freud's supposed method show that he has not fathomed the cardinal difference between the first psychoanalyst's actual means of reaching conclusions and his seductive rhetorical reconstructions, which offered the trusting reader sequences of ingeniously solved little puzzles that may or may not have preceded his theorizing. Freud's subtle diagnostic skill as manifested in the Wolf Man case history, for example, earns Holland's praise; no one has told him about the cunning fibs in that story that were uncovered by the psychoanalyst Patrick Mahony twenty years ago (Mahony 1984). And in reading Freud's famous "aliquis slip" narrative in *The Psychopathology of Everyday Life*, Holland takes at face value a (probably fictitious) young man's narrated "associations" of liquefied blood and calendar saints. Alas, it has been ascertained that Freud lifted those and other references from a current newspaper article and worked them into a self-flattering and mendacious yarn about Sherlock Holmes–like psychic detection on his part (Skues 2001).

Of course, the fact that Freud himself didn't faithfully employ "the psychoanalytic method" doesn't impugn that method in other hands. Yet it *is* impugned, as Adolf Grünbaum in particular has shown, by the circular procedures that Holland now dimly perceives to be a problem. Whereas Holland would like to believe that a clinician need only exercise "integrity" to avoid imposing his presuppositions on the patient,

Grünbaum makes it clear that question begging in the therapeutic inter-change is structurally unavoidable (Grünbaum 1993, p. 21).

Grünbaum's demonstration is devastating to the claim, still advanced by Holland, that modern psychoanalysis rests on a secure knowledge base. "Psychoanalytic method"—the analysis of (allegedly) free associa-tions, of dreams and slips, and of the "transference"—is much the same as it was a hundred years ago, and it is helpless against the contaminat-ing effect of suggestion. That is why we see so many warring psycho-analytic schools, each boasting "clinical validation" of its tenets.

Holland's final misstep is to bracket psychoanalysis with plate tec-tonics and natural selection, which met with resistance until they were eventually vindicated by consilient findings. The fate of psychoanalysis has been exactly the reverse; it quickly won popular acclaim through its emphasis on taboo breaking but then gradually lost favor as its overweening claims met with no scientific consilience at all. It is that absence of corroboration, not "deep-seated prejudice" or the efforts of debunkers such as I, that chiefly accounts for the moribund state of psychoanalysis today.

Chapter 4

UNCONSCIOUS DEEPS AND
EMPIRICAL SHALLOWS

THE CENTRAL PART OF THIS CHAPTER WAS ORIGINALLY A PANEL PRESENTATION
AT A SYMPOSIUM, "WHOSE FREUD?", HELD AT YALE UNIVERSITY ON APRIL 3–4,
1998. THE PROLOGUE AND EPILOGUE CONVEY SOME IDEA OF MY UNUSUAL ROLE
ON THAT OCCASION. PETER BROOKS, THE ORGANIZER OF THE OTHERWISE ONE-
SIDED SYMPOSIUM, WAS MAGNANIMOUS ENOUGH TO INCLUDE ALL THREE ELE-
MENTS OF THIS ESSAY IN THE ENSUING BOOK, *Whose Freud? The Place of Psycho-
analysis in Contemporary Culture* (BROOKS & WOLOCH 2000). AS BROOKS'S IRATE
INTRODUCTION TO THAT VOLUME SHOWS, HOWEVER, MY ESSAY WAS TAKEN
TO BE LESS AN INTELLECTUAL CONTRIBUTION THAN AN ACT OF ATTEMPTED
SABOTAGE.

AN INTERESTING LIGHT ON THE SPIRIT OF THE YALE CONFERENCE IS CAST IN
JOHN HORGAN'S BOOK *The Undiscovered Mind*. AS HORGAN RELATES, MY TALK
WAS GREETED NOT ONLY WITH A FEW HISSES AND AT LEAST ONE WHISTLE OF
SCORN BUT ALSO WITH SEVERAL BURSTS OF LAUGHTER WHEN NOTHING DELIB-
ERATELY HUMOROUS WAS BEING SAID. HORGAN, WHO HAD SAT IN THE AUDI-
ENCE, EXPLAINS THAT "ANOTHER PANEL MEMBER, ROBERT MICHELS, A PSYCHO-
ANALYST AND PROFESSOR OF PSYCHIATRY AT THE CORNELL UNIVERSITY SCHOOL
OF MEDICINE, PROVIDED A MIMED COMMENTARY, SMIRKING, RAISING HIS EYE-
BROWS, ROLLING HIS EYES, AND SHAKING HIS HEAD IN RESPONSE TO CREWS'S
COMMENTS" (HORGAN 1999, P. 63). DR. MICHELS WAS NOT MISTAKEN IN ASSUM-
ING THAT THE CONFERENCE-GOERS WOULD SHARE HIS MERRY MOOD.

Prologue

When I was invited to participate in the symposium whose proceedings
are recalled in *Whose Freud?*, I accepted with alacrity. Here, I thought,
lay the makings of a lively and fruitful debate not merely about *what* role
psychoanalysis plays in "contemporary culture" but also about *whether*

it deserves to play such a role. If, as I believe, Freudian ideas tell us nothing that is empirically warrantable about the mind but much about the pitfalls of question-begging discourse, then presumably the application of those same ideas to cultural problems will itself run the risk of overconfidence and even circularity. Some panelists, I told myself, will doubtless explain why they consider that worry misplaced or exaggerated, but if others—myself among them—can show that psychoanalysis has no more standing as knowledge than astrology or palmistry, then the perils of "applied analysis" will be made usefully clear.

So much for expectations. When I eventually retrieved the list of symposium participants from my mailbox, I could not recognize among the twenty-nine presenters and panel chairs the name of any critic of psychoanalysis except my own. Nor, in asking around informally among my fellow skeptics, did I discover that any of them had been asked to join in. Even Yale faculty members whose expertise lay precisely in the area of Freud's cultural significance were condemned to the role of spectators; yet their reservations about psychoanalysis were certainly milder than my own. I guessed, then, that the question "Whose Freud?", though by no means settled in advance, was to be negotiated among several schools of psychoanalytic thought, with my own predictable demurral counting as evidence of hospitality, however scant, to extreme perspectives.

Perhaps this was uncharitable on my part, but it was the view I took at the time. So be it, I said to myself. Even if I was being asked to play the token naysayer, I would go to New Haven and nail my theses to the door of the Whitney Humanities Center. I knew that my dissenting judgment stood no chance of giving pause to my fellow symposiasts, but I felt that it ought to be voiced. Thereby, any independent observers who might be present could weigh my reasoning against the justifications of Freudian hermeneutics that, I assumed, would be offered on all sides.

Again—so much for expectations! Even though psychoanalysis finds itself in dire straits everywhere *but* among humanists and a minority of "soft" social scientists, very little was said in defense of Freudian notions during our two-day conference. Apologetics were apparently deemed unnecessary among the like-minded. To my own discordant mind, however, this imperturbability mirrored the epistemic isolationism of the whole psychoanalytic tradition. Notoriously, Freudians have listened only to other Freudians, and they have been inclined to mistake the mere sharing of a controversial set of premises within their own circle for assurance that those premises have withstood all challenge.

Despite the near solidarity lasting through our weekend, I did succeed in provoking a handful of remarks that were intended as refutation of my errors. Those remarks typified attitudes I had encountered many times before. So, of course, I want to make an example of them here. But I will do so only in an extended afterword, leaving my original text exactly as I read it aloud—failed predictions and all. By this means, readers will possess the full basis for comments about my position made by other participants.

Prepared Text

To the question posed in our conference title, "Whose Freud?", I can offer a simple reply: he's all yours. Take my Freud—please! But do you really want him—the fanatical, self-inflated, ruthless, myopic, yet intricately devious Freud who has been unearthed by the independent scholarship of the past generation? Or would you prefer the Freud of self-created legend, whose name can still conjure the illusion that "psychoanalytic truth" is authenticated by the sheer genius of its discoverer?

Let me put this issue concretely by reminding you of the evocative passage in Freud's *History of the Psycho-Analytic Movement* in which he describes the hostility of his Viennese colleagues when he first lectured them on May 2, 1896, about "the part played by sexuality in the aetiology of the neuroses." Who among us hasn't been moved by the story of Freud's sudden realization on that day that he was "one of those who had 'disturbed the sleep of the world'"? It dawned on him, he recalls, that he would never be able to expect "objectivity and tolerance" from straw authorities who lacked his own "moral courage"; thenceforth he would have to pursue the hard path of scientific discovery in "splendid isolation" (Freud 1953–1974, 14:21–22).

That persecuted but dauntless figure is the Promethean hero commended to us not only by Freud himself but also by the house mythographer of psychoanalysis, Ernest Jones, and by subsequent partisans to this day. And it is just the Freud whose borrowed glory can improve the likelihood that one's own broadly psychoanalytic speculations will be deemed valiant and canny rather than, say, politically and academically conformist. If, however, we approach Freud not as our great forebear and patron but as a historical agent like any other, we cannot avoid noticing that the thesis he proposed to that doubting audience in 1896 was the very "seduction theory" that he would privately repudiate sixteen months later. Privately but not publicly, for in that case he would have had to own up not only to his mistake about the causation of hysteria but also to the nonexistence of his boasted cures and, still more damagingly, to the unreliability of both the investigative method and the psychodynamic premises that he would continue to employ for the remainder of his career.

Mental inertia and a reluctance to admit error may help to explain why academic humanists give no heed to such deflationary facts. But by shielding Freud's "insight" from normal skepticism, they also grant *themselves* the luxury of playing the knowledge game with the net down. The most fundamental rule of that game is that a given theory or hypothesis cannot be validated by invoking "evidence" manufactured by that same supposition. The question-begging traits of psychoanalysis—the treatment of tendentious interpretations as raw data; the reflex negation of appearances in favor of reduction to the selfish, the sexual, and the infantile; the ample menus of symbolic meanings and "defense mechanisms" upon which the interpreter can draw to adorn prearranged conclusions; the ever handy wild cards of "the unconscious" and "overdetermination"—all of these constitute a scandal for anyone who subscribes to community standards of rational and empirical inquiry. Yet the very liberties that mark Freudianism as a pseudoscience render it irresistibly charming to humanists in search of instant "depth." (I ought to know; I used to be one of them!) And if, emulating Freud's tactic of pathologizing his critics, Freudian humanists can brand dissenters as suffering from resistance, repression, and denial—in short, from the obsessive-compulsive disorder of "Freud bashing"—then their hermeneutic freedom would appear to be absolute.

Of course, academic Freudians would prefer not to think of themselves as having resigned from the wider intellectual enterprise. More typically, they invoke psychoanalytic notions to address cultural and historical problems and then infer from the very ingenuity of their handiwork, just as Freud did, that the doctrine has thereby proved its fruitfulness. Or, if they have an activist bent, they recast Freudianism to purge it of its patriarchal and conservative implications and then "discover" psychoanalytically that society needs to be realigned in accordance with their ideology.

A bright high school senior could easily detect the fallaciousness of such maneuvers. Unfortunately, however, a bright graduate student in literature, imbued with what now passes for theoretical sophistication, would find nothing to complain about. Such is the intellectually corrupting effect of a self-validating and parochial system of thought. But it is not the antiquated doctrine per se that deserves reproach; the fault lies with professors who not only refrain from teaching standards of empirical adequacy but actively or implicitly denigrate them.

As the first scheduled panelist in this conference and, I gather, the only one who shares the wholly negative view of psychoanalytic theory that is now all but consensual in American psychology departments, I am poorly situated to rebut the more sanguine judgments that will be voiced by others. But at least I can ask uncommitted members of this audience to keep some questions in mind. I will close by commenting briefly on three lines of argument that cannot fail to be broached before our adjournment.

1. You will be told that evidence-based objections to Freudianism are beside the point, since psychoanalysis isn't a body of

propositions but merely a subtle dialogue that weaves a fictive story, thus honoring the sheer ambiguity of experience while enhancing self-awareness of an ineffable but precious kind. This would have come as a surprise to the author of the Oedipus and castration complexes, the ego, id, and superego, penis envy, the vaginal orgasm, the death instinct, the primal scene and the primal crime, and on and on. Psychoanalysis does traffic in subtly guided and indoctrinating dialogue, but its theory has been, and remains, largely a causal account of mental functioning and development. As such, it cannot dodge the criteria of assessment that apply to every such theory. And, of course, it doesn't begin to satisfy those criteria; hence the retreat of latter-day Freudians into the absurd pretense of nonpropositionality.

2. Subsequent panelists will assure you that while Freud made some mistakes, modern psychoanalysis has long since corrected them. When you hear this, please raise your hand and ask which of the ever-proliferating schools of analysis the speaker has in mind and why those schools cannot agree on a single point of doctrine or interpretation. The answer is that the epistemic circularity of Freud's tradition, guaranteeing abundant "confirmation" of every proposed idea, has not been remedied in any degree. Analysts of every stripe still adhere to Freud's illusion that reliable knowledge of a patient's repressed complexes can be gleaned from studying free associations and the transference—even though such study is well-known to produce only those revelations favored by the therapist's sect or local institute.

3. You will doubtless hear that objections to psychoanalytic theory stem from a shallow and outmoded positivism that insists on impossible standards of proof. Wrong again. No philosophy of science, positivist or antipositivist, is entailed in the elementary demand that a theory refrain from justifying itself by appeal to its own contested postulates. That is just everyday rational sense, intuitively grasped by fair-minded researchers in every field, though not by the pundits of postmodernism.

It is precisely because such rationality continues to be exercised with vigor that Freud's ideas, as Edward Shorter observes in his recent *History of Psychiatry*, "are now vanishing like the last snows of winter" (Shorter 1996, p. vii). How ironic it is that well-traveled academics, like bunkered troops on a remote island who haven't heard that the war is over, should be the last to get the news! And now that the point is finally sinking in, how sad it is—and how symptomatic of all that is feeble and dismissible about the humanities today—that humanists can look upon the collapse of a would-be science within its proper domain as a fine opportunity to turn that same doctrine to their own hermeneutic ends!

Afterword

In the excerpts of discussion that follow our four panelists' texts in *Whose Freud?*, readers of the conference proceedings will see that my epistemologically based reservations about psychoanalysis did prompt some commentary, not all of it sharply negative. Robert Michels, for example, dismayed some members of the audience by announcing that he and I "are in agreement about the big picture"—that is, about the impossibility of *verifying* a given theory by *appealing* to that same theory. I will return to that key point at the end of this afterword, since it was challenged head-on by one of our conference's final speakers.

In other respects, Dr. Michels and I could not find common ground. He thought, for instance, that he had caught me saying that any corroboration of a theory would have to come from outside what he (not I) called "one's own group," to which he replied, "That's patently untrue. In fact, one of the characteristics of modern science is that data often can't be understood by anyone who's not a member of a group that understands the methodology and the kind of data that it produces."

This, however, was a straw-man argument, imputing to me the bizarre view that only nonpsychologists are competent to judge psychological theories. Obviously, no one is better qualified to evaluate Freudian claims than are empirically scrupulous researchers within the field of psychology. Michels, however, in raising his meretricious objection, managed to imply that *psychoanalysts themselves* are best suited for this role—rather a different, and wonderfully convenient, proposition.

On this as on other occasions (he and I have crossed swords before, both in person and in print), Dr. Michels admitted that no credible support for psychoanalytic theory or for the differentially positive efficacy of psychoanalytic treatment has ever been presented. This concession places him in a small vanguard of enlightened Freudians who have perused the relevant literature and accepted its clear import. Well, *sort of* accepted it. For, regrettably, Michels always follows this obeisance to research with some very fast talk about where the *real* scientific issue lies—somewhere far removed from the vast terrain he has just ceded to the doubters. And so he gives an impression of being at once empirically scrupulous and upbeat about psychoanalysis.

Thus, in the panel dialogue reproduced in *Whose Freud?*, you can find Dr. Michels saying that "the scientific question"—as if the general cogency of Freudian theory weren't itself a scientific question!—is this: "[D]o interpretations based upon the model that the oral phase precedes phallic interests have a differential and preferable impact on patients when I make them? That's easily testable." Here Michels appears to have forgotten about the placebo effect, to say nothing of the confirmatory bias that makes all anecdotal reporting of "clinical results" a form of science fiction. We don't even know whether his patients improve at all, much less whether they do so at a better-than-average rate, and still less whether their progress can be credited to the brand of psychological dogma to which he makes them privy. Even if we supposed that all of those questions can be answered affirmatively, Michels's hypothesis would remain trivial, because we already know that *false* ideas, supportively presented, can have *positive* therapeutic effects. Thus Michels's "real scientific issue" is just a diversion from what he acknowledges to be the case: the complete failure of psychoanalysis to make good on its scientific boasts.[1]

I will also say a word about Dr. Michels's statement that he is "not troubled by people who challenge the lack of proof, as long as that challenge is a call for inquiry rather than a disparagement of interesting ideas." As Michels is well aware, many if not most of his fellow analysts point habitually to the "clinical proof" of their belief system.[2] He himself, however, grants that all such proof is chimerical. Indeed, he admits that psychoanalytic dogma has by now failed to impress non-Freudian assessors for a hundred years. How far into the future, then, does he think the patience of outsiders should extend? Indefinitely? That would enable him to finish his distinguished career without undergoing a crisis of faith, but from the standpoint of public welfare, no basis has been shown for treating psychoanalytic notions with any more indulgence than those of Scientology or the Unification Church.

Let me turn now to my fellow panelist and sometime Berkeley colleague Judith Butler. In politely raising some questions about my position, Butler gave us to understand that I might profit from cultivating greater philosophical sophistication on the one hand and less unsavory soulmates on the other. Her doubts focused on my reference to *community standards of empiricism*. Both terms, "community standards" and "empiricism," struck her as containing trapdoors that I had failed to notice. Let us first see what she said about "empiricism" and ask whether she had indeed located a fatal weakness in my stand.

Empiricism, Butler said, needs to be grasped in a spirit that makes allowance for the theory-laden nature of "facts." Hence she drew a careful distinction between two possible complaints against a theory: first, that it tautologically derives its conclusions from its own postulates, and second, that it makes use of a "prior conceptualization" in deciding what is to count as data. Butler thought she was agreeing with my appeal to the first complaint but rebuking my endorsement of the second, unreasonable, one. But she was mistaken on both counts.

First, why *shouldn't* a theory "derive its conclusions from its postulates," if the latter are themselves well founded? As post-positivist philosophers of science often remind us, we aren't entitled to care how a given conclusion was originally reached. Maybe it occurred in a dream or by a casting of the I Ching; that would still be none of our business. To complain that an idea wasn't derived inductively would be to exercise that same naive Lockean version of empiricism with which Butler is attempting to saddle me.

Epistemological concern properly arises only when *justifications* of a theory are put forward. My objection is to the notion that a theory can be *proven correct* by sole reference to features that it shares with no other well-regarded theory. If, for example, the proposition that childhood masturbation underlies adult hysteria is justified by citing Dora's fiddling with her purse, or if the castration complex is said to be supported by the fact that many people fear losing their eyesight, no non-Freudian needs to surrender his or her doubts, since in both cases the "proof" appeals to transformational rules unique to psychoanalysis.

Butler is equally wrong in depicting me as believing that a real fact will be found to be unpolluted by theory of any kind. On the contrary, she and I concur in holding that one never arrives at a pure fact in that sense—a fact, in other words, whose discovery hasn't been facilitated by theoretical expectations of one kind or another. We must ask, however, whether a given theory manages to justify itself in relation to facts *other than the ones it has produced for its own purposes.* If not, the theory is in big trouble, and that is exactly the plight of psychoanalysis.

The other term that raised a warning flag for Judith Butler was "community standards." To her ear, the term smacked of "a very interesting desire for respectability" on my part. This is not, I suspect, what most of the other conference participants might regard as my leading vice, but I could see that a concern of Butler's own—expounded in her conference paper—was paramount here. For her, a wish to be empirically respectable must entail a tendency to fall in line with social "normativity" in general, especially as it applies to the imposing of heterosexist values and rules on people who should be left in peace to pursue their own goals and pleasures. What was *very interesting*, then, about my statement of ordinary rational principles—and the point was not lost on Butler's audible rooting section in our conference hall—was my self-alignment with social oppression. The hint was planted deftly and inconspicuously, but there it was: "community standards" meant homophobia.

I take this imputation very seriously—indeed, more seriously than it was meant, for Butler was surely not implying that I had already joined forces with the Pat Robertsons of the world. Rather, she was admonishing me that if I don't watch out I may be mistaken for one of them. Nonetheless, there is something profoundly disturbing here. In a mild and cordial manner, Butler was indulging in a form of McCarthyism that has become routine in university life. For it is now considered acceptable and even chic to ascribe a backward, repressive sociopolitical attitude to those with whom we in fact disagree only intellectually. *That* trapdoor can be sprung at any time to make dissenters disappear, and not just for a day but for a career.

I won't pause here to protest that Butler would find nothing obnoxious in my social views if I were to submit them for her approval; that would be to play the very game I am deploring. But I will emphatically insist that the intellectual values invoked in my talk are not located anywhere at all on the spectrum of ideologies and lifestyles. They are the very values to which lesbian and gay scientists appeal when presenting and defending their hypotheses—hypotheses that will be accorded the same tough peer scrutiny as those emanating from any other quarter. Science cannot be practiced at all without such a tacit understanding that the playing field will remain level. In principle, moreover, the same concern for fairness—that is, for keeping our criteria of propositional adequacy distinct from our private tastes and affiliations—ought to prevail not just in science but in every academic field.

In making this point, which conveys the only thinkable basis for pursuing knowledge that is not corrupted in advance by partisanship, I am aware of sounding like a dinosaur. That is not a sufficient reason, however, for me to alter my conception of intellectual integrity and start trying to please—that is, not offend—those of my fellow humanists who apply political tests to knowledge. To be sure, my adamancy here is cost-free. If, instead of being comfortably pensioned, I were an untenured colleague of Professor Butler's, I might want to sing a more prudent tune; my very livelihood might hang in the balance. But in that case, ought Butler to be implicitly charging *me* with exacting conformity?

Now, rejoining our common topic, I must ask whether Butler's equivocal stance toward knowledge has anything to do with her kindly feelings toward psychoanalysis. Assuredly it does. In her discussion of my paper, she expresses doubt as to "whether there could ever *be* an empirically adequate account of the unconscious." She and I agree that the answer is no. But what, then, should we conclude—that "the unconscious" is, as I am persuaded, not so much a region of the psyche as a blank check that every Freudian can fill out as he or she sees fit? No, according to Butler the fault must lie with empiricism itself. Because she won't regard such traits as untestability, absence of operational content, and self-contradiction as marks against a psychological notion that she can handily adapt to her own ends, the empirical criteria themselves must be downgraded to the status of prejudices wielded in the service of shady interests. This is just what I meant when referring, in my paper, to "the intellectually corrupting effect of a self-validating and parochial system of thought."

The connection, then, is not fortuitous: scratch any academic Freudian and you will find someone whose commitment to disinterested rational inquiry has been compromised to one degree or another. And, of course, the same was true of Freud, who felt entitled to make up his own biological laws and to regard seeming counter-instances as corroborative. Butler's subtle assault on "community standards" is only one, overtly ideological, instance of an anti-intellectual strain that runs through a century's worth of psychoanalytic special pleading. For, whatever they may say when trying to appear philosophically rigorous, all Freudians behave in practice as if they accepted Freud's outlandish dictum that "applications of analysis are always confirmations of it as well" (Freud 1953–1974, 22:146).

It is also possible, however, for an academic Freudian to take one extra step and abandon the whole pretense of "applying" knowledge about the mind to texts that are presumed to "contain" the sought-after psychological meaning. In this connection, I was fascinated by Leo Bersani's thoughtful and candid paper, which I can only hope I am recalling accurately. Bersani has reached a point in his impressive career at which he feels ethically compelled to disavow any style of literary criticism that purports to honor "fidelity to the text." He now sees such intellectual monogamy as implicitly denigrating gay promiscuity, tolerance of which now serves as his test for any adequately ample vision of the good society. Thus Bersani is not even seeking some psychoanalytically grounded understanding of the text that will be more intimate, supple, and unbiased than that of a critical dogmatist. Rather—and this is my own gloss—the very idea of a nubile "object of knowledge" demurely awaiting Mr. Right, its critic-spouse-for-life, is to be eschewed.

Such epistemic radicalism naturally leaves us wondering where if anywhere, for Bersani, psychoanalysis will enter the picture. Feminist, gay, and lesbian theorists have long considered themselves licensed to rewrite Freud's system of thought so as to discount its bourgeois implications while retaining its heady negativity. Bersani, however, seems to be getting tired of the whole enterprise; now he wonders whether there may not be something inherently normalizing in the Freudian outlook.

Yes, of course, psychoanalysis always normalizes, but not always in the same way. It lends an appearance of deep psychological truth to gay and straight ideologies alike. Its cosmetic services are impartially available to pontificating soothers of the bourgeoisie like Erik H. Erikson and to orgasmic zanies like Wilhelm Reich; to the ultra-orthodox shrinks of Park Avenue and to Left Bank Lacanians in suede and sunglasses. Whatever lesson you want to teach, there will always be a Freudian way of putting it.

Psychoanalysis normalizes because, possessing only fake psychological knowledge that changes wildly from one Freudian pundit to the next, it has nothing better to do than to lend the moral inclination of the moment an air of being supported by "findings." You needn't take my word for it. Just read through the rest of *Whose Freud?*, counting all the references to the psychoanalytic significance of *x* and what psychoanalysis tells us about *y*, and then ask yourself: if psychoanalysis "tells us" all of these contradictory things, does it tell us anything at all?

In discussion, Leo Bersani expressed his growing awe for the way each of Freud's texts "enacts a particular relation of the mind to its own interpretations." Among the assembled company, this observation was received with uneasy puzzlement. Auditors could only hope that it might prove to be a compliment of some kind. I heard it quite differently, though, as a sign of crisis on Bersani's part; and I would like if possible to help the crisis along.

Bersani is just now registering the extent to which Freud's reports of patients' symptoms and of those symptoms' meanings unresistingly flatter his theoretical enthusiasms. His writings achieve a poetical density of texture by abolishing the boundary we might expect to find between the honest investigator's fantasy life and the material he is trying to explain. In order to cease being a Freudian, Bersani now needs only to allow this realization to sink in: Freud's "evidence" was conjured to meet the rhetorical need it was meant to fill. Everything fits "geniusly," as Bersani put it, because Freud is a writer of fiction.

Of course, one thing more is required for skeptical detachment from the discourse that famously "never lets go," and that is a resistance to being taken in. Commenting on Bersani's remark, Paul Robinson announced that he has "bad news for Fred Crews. . . . [Freud] is incredibly seductive." I already knew that, having been seduced by Freud myself around the age of thirty-two. But by thirty-seven I was over it, because by then I had been stymied by unanswerable empirical objections and had decided that a literary scholar ought to inquire how an unreliable narrator is accomplishing his seductive tricks. I invite Bersani and Robinson to do the same. They would soon discover, if they don't already know it, that Freud as literary magician is immeasurably more deft than Freud as mental lawgiver. Indeed, it is only when one has realized the capriciousness of his laws that one can grasp how every sentence in his complete psychological writings amounts to an act of cunning self-dramatization.

Meanwhile, of course, the path of least resistance is to remain inside Freud's scholastic universe of linked correspondences. There one can always count on the "aha!" effect, or the sense of confirmation that comes from meeting up with "psychoanalytic insight" that seems to verify one's hunches. As my paper mentioned, most Freudian academics "invoke psychoanalytic notions to address cultural and historical problems and then infer from the very ingenuity of their handiwork . . . that the doctrine has thereby proved its fruitfulness." It isn't easy to forswear this cheap thrill and its attendant promise of discourse (one's own) that will never run dry.

The feedback loop between exercising Freudian hermeneutic privilege and reinforcing one's faith in psychoanalysis works best if one can remain distracted from its perfect circularity. To this end, even trained and certified psychoanalysts will sometimes deny that they have any particular commitment to Freudian ideas. Thus, in our symposium, Meredith Skura told us that she generally eschews theory in her historical inquiries, preferring instead to conceive of psychoanalysis simply as a way of thinking and an attitude toward life. Theory enters her work, Skura said, only in the form of hypotheses that are to be tested by the "so what?" criterion, among others. If, for example, a particular Freudian tenet has helped her to "pull details together" in an illuminating way, she knows she was on the right track.

Alas, any theory whatsoever—phrenological, ufological, what have you—will confirm itself in just this specious manner. The creative rush that one feels as new data effortlessly adhere to old certainties is no substitute for the sober task of inquiring whether there may be other, less dogmatic, ways of making the facts cohere. And doesn't the global "psychoanalytic attitude toward life" amount to a partiality toward Freudian theory? To disavow explicit theory while implementing such an attitude is simply to disguise one's premises from oneself, a retrogressive step in any field.

No such pussyfooting could be charged, finally, against the late Richard Wollheim, who, as our symposium was drawing to a close, displayed a self-assurance about theory that was meant to teach a lesson to fainter-hearted conferees. Wollheim began by expressing displeasure with the timidity of previous speakers, who had shown too much deference to objections that could, in his estimation, be easily neutralized. He threw down the gauntlet to my own contention that one can't prove psychoanalytic theory by merely exercising it. Oh yes, one can, said

Wollheim, who deemed it quite feasible to demonstrate the cogency of Freudian tenets from directly within a clinical context. The devolution of psychoanalysis from science to hermeneutic to mere occasion for "narrative truth," Wollheim said in effect, stops here.

In Wollheim's main example, the object of inquiry was the subtly uncooperative behavior of an analyst-trainee's patient. Disagreeing with the candidate's first effort at explanation of that recalcitrance, her supervisor and conferring colleagues arrived at a better idea: the problem was traceable to the patient's early relations with her mother. Presumably, then, the doctrine of transference was proving its mettle here. For, according to that doctrine, noncooperation within the analysis is often traceable to a childhood attitude that is being reenacted in the consulting room.

Wollheim was pleased to note that since the patient hadn't been involved in the review session, nobody was influencing her; hence the example is suggestion-proof. And he added that a lot of accumulated clinical experience must have gone into the group's solution. That fact seemed to him to vouch for the explanation's plausibility. Since, in this triumph of carefully reviewed interpretation, "a small piece of psychoanalytic thinking helps us to comprehend the situation," the theory behind that thinking had supposedly received strong support.

But had it? In the first place, Wollheim overlooked the dubious impressiveness of a Freudian consensus reached by a group of psychoanalysts who belonged to the same institute. That is the kind of guarantee of sound thinking that has resulted, over time, in everything from witch burnings through the Edsel to the Gulf of Tonkin Resolution. Moreover, how could Wollheim have assured himself that all of the assembled minds were independently converging on the right answer? Isn't it far more likely, given the Machiavellian group dynamics one finds in every analytic institute, that some members were just allowing the supervisor to strut?

More fundamentally, transferential theory was here being "validated" merely by its application to the case at hand, as if there were no conceivable non-Freudian reasons for the patient's stubborn behavior.

There are many such possible reasons, beginning with irritants supplied by a clumsy or overbearing therapist. The theory of transference regularly acts to immunize the psychoanalyst against criticism, pushing the blame backward into the remote past and laying it on the patient herself and/or her parents. We can't say whether or not such a causal misattribution was involved in Wollheim's specimen case, but we can't exclude it, either.

Most fundamentally of all, the "evidence" Wollheim found so persuasive was itself a Freudian interpretation. Only if we already agree with a broadly psychoanalytic account of mental development and structure can an instance of alleged transference be regarded as support for the theory's cogency. As a trained philosopher, one might think, Wollheim could have perceived what was the matter with this nonprobative question begging. The reason he didn't is that he had chosen to remain under the Freudian bell jar, whose stale and breezeless air comes after a while to feel like the atmosphere of reality itself.

I enjoyed my stay at Yale (my alma mater, '55) and had some agreeable conversation with old friends—one of whom, *incredibile dictu*, is an eminent psychoanalyst. (Name withheld to forestall reprisals.) I am also grateful to Peter Brooks for welcoming and, with even greater tolerance, for publishing my animadversions. But I must say that the fiasco of Richard Wollheim's "proof," after so many speakers had dodged the whole issue of validation, struck me as an ironically fitting coda to our symposium. By my lights, the whole event amounted to a two-day pleasure "cruise to nowhere" on the *Titanic*. Those who remain on board for the longer journey will find, I believe, that the iceberg is out there waiting in the dark, the welding is defective, and the lifeboats are all too few.

II.

Modern Deviltry

Chapter 5

THE REVENGE OF THE REPRESSED, PART I

THIS CHAPTER AND THE NEXT ONE WERE PUBLISHED AS A DIVIDED ESSAY IN *The New York Review of Books*, NOVEMBER 17 AND DECEMBER 1, 1994. THE ABUNDANT PROTESTS FROM ADVOCATES OF RECOVERED MEMORY, ALONG WITH MY REPLIES, CAN BE FOUND IN *The Memory Wars* (CREWS ET AL. 1995).

I.

Throughout the past decade or so, a shock wave has been sweeping across North American psychotherapy, and in the process causing major repercussions within our families, courts, and hospitals. A single diagnosis for miscellaneous complaints—that of unconsciously repressed sexual abuse in childhood—has grown in this brief span from virtual nonexistence to epidemic frequency. As Mark Pendergrast shows in his comprehensive study *Victims of Memory: Incest Accusations and Shattered Lives* (1996), if we put together the number of licensed American psychotherapists (roughly 255,000) with survey results about their beliefs and practices, it appears that well over 50,000 of them are now willing to help their clients realize that they must have endured early molestation. Those professionals have been joined by countless untrained operators who use the yellow pages and flea market ads to solicit "incest work." It is hard to form even a rough idea of the number of persuaded clients, because most of them take no publicly recorded action against the accused, but a conservative guess would be a million persons since 1988 alone. The number affected is of course vastly higher, since, as all parties acknowledge, virtually every case sows dissension and sorrow throughout a family.

When one explanation for mental distress rockets to prominence so quickly, we ought to ask whether we are looking at a medical breakthrough or a fad. However, the choice between those alternatives is not always simple. As its main proponents insist, "recovered memory" is by now not just a diagnosis but a formidable sociopolitical movement. In the words of one of that movement's founders, the Harvard psychiatrist Judith Lewis Herman,

> The study of trauma in sexual and domestic life becomes legitimate only in a context that challenges the subordination of women and children. Advances in the field occur only when they are supported by a political movement powerful enough to legitimate an alliance between investigators and patients and to counteract the ordinary social processes of silencing and denial. (Herman 1992, p. 9)

The larger movement in question is, of course, women's liberation, including what Herman calls "a collective feminist project of reinventing the basic concepts of normal development and abnormal psychology . . ." (Herman 1992, pp. 9, ix).

However uneasy one may feel about an ideologically driven "reinvention" of scientific notions, it is possible that the feminist critique of received psychological lore is substantially right. Feminists were certainly warranted, in the 1970s and 1980s, in declaring that the sexual abuse of children was being scandalously underreported. If they now go on to claim that untold millions of victims, mostly female, have forgotten what was done to them, their claim cannot be discredited by the mere fact that it sprang from an activist commitment. Obviously, it needs to be assessed on independent grounds.

Yet such grounds are hard to come by. How can one count authentic cases of repressed memory when the very concept of repression stands in doubt? And what, for that matter, do the champions of recovered memory mean by repression? It is fruitless to press them very hard on this point, since most of them show an impatience with or outright ignorance of conceptual subtleties. Thus in the movement's most influential document, *The Courage to Heal*, first published in 1988, Ellen Bass and Laura Davis proclaim that "none of what is presented here is based on psychological theories." Instead, Bass and Davis appeal directly to "the experiences of survivors"—who, however, may or may not be survivors of abuse, depending on whether they have actually learned the previously repressed truth or succumbed to therapeutically induced delusion.

Although it is no secret that the idea of repression derives from Sigmund Freud, few of the movement's practitioners have actually studied his texts. Consequently, they are unrestrained by certain ambiguities and outright contradictions implicit in the Freudian theory of repression.[1] Freud's uncertainty, for example, as to whether events or fantasies make up the typical content of the repressed gets resolved in favor of events; as Herman puts it in the opening sentence of *Trauma and Recovery*, "the ordinary response to atrocities is to banish them from consciousness." Again, whereas Freud confusingly treated repression as both a conscious and an unconscious mechanism, his activist successors think of it as strictly unconscious—so much so, indeed, that they can routinely regard a young incest victim as leading two parallel but wholly independent lives, one in the warm daylight of normal family affection and the other in continually repressed horror. And while Freud only occasionally portrayed the lifting of repression as yielding undisguised, accurate information about a patient's early past, contemporary "retrievers" entertain no doubts on the point; with the right coaxing, their patients can allegedly reproduce the exact details of their long-repressed traumas.

By today, recovered memory has enlisted the enthusiasm of many psychotherapists who lack the explicit feminist agenda of Herman, Bass and Davis, and other advocates whose views we will examine later. But all parties do share the core tenet of repression—namely, that the mind can shield itself from ugly experiences, thoughts, or feelings by relegating them to a special "timeless" region where they indefinitely retain a symptom-producing virulence. Clinical experience, the therapists agree, has proven the cogency of this tenet in numberless successfully resolved cases.

But has it, really? When arbitrary assumptions leak into "clinical experience," confirming results can be pumped out as easily as bilgewater.

That is why research psychologists would insist that the concept of repression be required to pass tests in which variables are controlled and rival explanations for the gathered data are ruled out. Yet while psycho-analytic loyalists have repeatedly attempted to conduct just such experiments, their positive results have at best shown a compatibility with repression, not a demonstration of its existence. As David S. Holmes concluded after reviewing a sixty-year history of such efforts, "there is no controlled laboratory evidence supporting the concept of repression" (Holmes 1990, p. 96).

Of course, repression cannot be experimentally disproved, either. Since the concept entails no agreed-upon behavioral markers, we are free to posit its operation whenever we please—just as we are free to invoke orgone energy or chakras or the life force. Indeed, as Elizabeth Loftus and Katherine Ketcham remark in their lively book *The Myth of Repressed Memory: False Memories and Allegations of Sexual Abuse* (1994), belief in repression has the same standing as belief in God. The idea may be true, but it is consistent with too many eventualities to be falsifiable—that is, amenable to scientific assessment.

It is possible, however, to mount experimental challenges to corollary tenets that are crucial to recovered memory therapy. That is just what Loftus, a highly regarded researcher and a professor of psychology at the University of Washington [now at the University of California, Irvine], has done in her own experimental work—and that is also why she has been pilloried by the recovery movement as an enemy to incest survivors. *The Myth of Repressed Memory* recounts some of that vilification and tries to head off more of it by taking a conciliatory tone wherever possible. But there is simply nothing to negotiate over. The burden of Loftus's argument is that memory does not function in anything like the way that the recovery movement presupposes.

Loftus offers no encouragement to the retrievers' notion that "videotaped" records of events are stored in a special part of the brain and then suddenly yielded up to near-perfect recall. Empirical science, she reports, has established that memory is inherently sketchy and reconstructive. Whether pleasant or unpleasant, it decays drastically over time, though less so if the experience in question gets periodically "rehearsed"—just the opposite of what the retrievers' theory would predict. Furthermore, memory is easily corrupted, if not with an experimenter's deliberate intervention or a therapist's unwitting one, then with a normal "retrospective bias" that accommodates one's sense of the past to one's present values. Flashbacks to an early age, then, are highly unreliable sources of information about any event. All in all, Loftus finds no basis for thinking that repression, as opposed to a gradual avoidance and atrophy of painful recollections, has figured in a single molestation case to date.

Once we have recognized that a memory can disappear because of factors other than repression, even the best anecdotal evidence for that mechanism loses its punch. Consider, for example, the closely watched case of Ross Cheit, a Brown University professor who has recently proved beyond question that his suddenly recalled 1968 molestation by a music camp administrator was real. But had that abuse been repressed in the first place? In a phone conversation with me on September 7, 1994, Cheit declared that while he takes no position on the existence of repression, he is inclined to doubt that he abruptly and completely consigned his experience to oblivion. A more likely account is that the adult Cheit refocused his faded but unrepressed experiences after he had read a book about pedophilia (as he did) and became morally exercised about it. While this, too, is guesswork, the fact that it can't be ruled out renders Cheit's case useless as a demonstration.

Useless, that is, from the standpoint of logic. For another purpose, that of inducing popular belief in the theory of repression, anecdotes can be powerfully effective. The very idea of repression and its unraveling is an embryonic romance about a hidden mystery, an arduous journey, and a gratifyingly neat denouement that can ascribe our otherwise drab shortcomings and pains to deep necessity. When that romance is fleshed out by a gifted storyteller who also bears impressive credentials as an expert on the mind, most readers in our culture will be disinclined to put up intellectual resistance.

One such narrator, of course, was Freud, whose shifting views about the content of the repressed will prove pivotal to an understanding of the recovery movement's intellectual ancestry. But Freud's stories purportedly explaining tics, obsessions, and inhibitions among the turn-of-the-century Austrian bourgeoisie are beginning to seem not just remote but eccentric. Not so the case histories recounted by the memory retrievers' most distinguished and fluent ally, Lenore Terr, who is not only a practicing therapist but also a professor of psychiatry at the University of California at San Francisco. Terr's deftly written book, *Unchained Memories: True Stories of Traumatic Memories, Lost and Found* (1994), was welcomed both by the Book-of-the-Month Club and by early reviewers who perceived it as a balanced and learned brief for repression.

The publication of *Unchained Memories* has been especially cheering to recovery advocates because Terr is not afraid to challenge their bête noire, Elizabeth Loftus. "[P]sychological experiments on university students," Terr writes, taking dead aim at Loftus's work,

> do not duplicate in any way the clinician's observations. What comes from the memory lab does not apply well to the perceptions, storage, and retrieval of such things as childhood murders, rapes, or kidnappings. Trauma sets up new rules for memory. (Terr 1994, pp. 51–52)

From Loftus's vantage, of course, such a passage begs the question of how these new rules are to be validated without succumbing to the notorious circularity of "clinical experience." Isn't Terr simply handing herself a conceptual blank check? Nevertheless, she scores a strong rhetorical point with her animadversion against hothouse science. If Terr is right about the special character of real-world trauma, we may have to fall back on sheer stories after all.

2.

Among Terr's own stories, none carries more weight than the George Franklin/Eileen Lipsker case, which occupies the first two chapters of her book. The case, in which Terr herself served as an expert witness "to explain," as she says, "'repression' and 'the return of the repressed,'" came to national attention in 1989 with newspaper and television reports of Eileen Franklin Lipsker's long-buried but amazingly lucid recollection of the way her father, in her terrified presence in 1969, had raped her eight-year-old best friend in the back of his Volkswagen bus and then shattered the girl's skull with a rock and covered the body on a wooded hillside south of San Francisco. In Terr's rendering, this story has about it a ring of unanswerable truth, backed up by the soberest of corroborators, a jury in a murder trial.

But Terr's account is not the only one available. It was preceded by Harry N. MacLean's scrupulous book-length retelling of the murder story, *Once Upon a Time: A True Story of Memory, Murder, and the Law* (1994), and now it has been scrutinized by MacLean himself, by Elizabeth Loftus and Katherine Ketcham in *The Myth of Repressed Memory*, and by Richard Ofshe, professor of sociology at the University of California, Berkeley, and Ethan Watters in an even more trenchant book, *Making Monsters: False Memories, Psychotherapy, and Sexual Hysteria* (1994). In view of their findings, the Franklin matter may come to serve as a very different object lesson from the one that Terr intended. If so, a man's freedom hangs in the balance—not the freedom of a good man, surely, but of a man who may have been wrongly convicted.

During the 1990 murder trial in Redwood City, California, it turned out that no concrete evidence implicated Franklin in Susan Nason's death. On the contrary, Franklin's junked van from 1969, located and microscopically studied by police investigators, bore no trace of the twenty-year-old crime. Until a recollection on the part of Eileen's vindictive sister Janice was conveniently revised under therapy, Franklin had a solid alibi for his whereabouts at the time of the abduction. The jury, however, determined with little difficulty that Eileen Lipsker's recovered memory too closely matched the known facts of the unsolved murder to be considered specious. As a result, Franklin is now serving a life sentence in state prison [his conviction was later overturned], and the theory of recovered memory has acquired an imposing trophy.

Lenore Terr appears to have assumed from the outset that Franklin was guilty as charged, and she was eager to make herself useful to the prosecution. Awkwardly, however, her research interest in actual cases of repressed memory was quite new; it seems to have postdated the writing of her 1990 book, *Too Scared to Cry*, which contains no index entry for "repression" and which reports on cases of continuously remembered rather than forgotten trauma. Terr's expertise on sudden recall, moreover, dated from her first interview with Eileen Lipsker herself— and was then swelled by a flood of highly dubious anecdotes about other women's therapeutically prompted visions of incest. But Terr is a thoroughly trained Freudian, and as such she felt qualified, after all, to offer the Franklin jury what she calls "an education" in the reality of repressed memory and its retrieval. Coordinating strategy with the prosecutor and tailoring her testimony, as she now relates, to the job of rendering Eileen Lipsker a wholly credible witness, Terr exceeded the expectations of her temporary employers.

Terr testified that an expert such as herself can readily verify the authenticity of a recovered memory through careful interpretation of the subject's symptoms. In some cases, she continued, the expert can even reliably infer the nature of an unknown trauma. Indeed, she herself claimed to have recently done exactly that, deducing from Stephen King's novels and films the certain knowledge that in his childhood King had watched a playmate die under the wheels of a railroad train.

As Terr now recounts, she mentioned that feat of detection in order to create a helpful analogy in the jurors' minds.[2] She hoped they would see that, like Stephen King in his violence-ridden fiction, Eileen Franklin, for five years after the murder, had symptomatically acted out the awful scene that she had observed but almost immediately repressed. According to prosecutors, between the ages of nine and fourteen Eileen had continually pulled out all the hair from one segment of her crown, leaving what Terr calls "a big, bleeding bald spot" (p. 35). That spot uncannily matched the part of Susan Nason's head that had allegedly been smashed by George Franklin. Eileen, then, had apparently turned herself into a living hieroglyph of a crime that Terr could have inferred all by herself, simply by translating the language of Eileen's symptomatic behavior into its mnemonic source within her repressed unconscious.

In an ordinary trial, caught up in claims and counterclaims about the purport of submitted evidence, the mesmerizing quality of Terr's self-depiction as a Freudian Sherlock Holmes could scarcely have assumed much importance. But this was no ordinary trial. Factually impoverished, it came down to little more than a twelve-person referendum on the photographic return of the repressed. According to the later word of several jurors, and to Terr's great present satisfaction, her testimony was decisive in obtaining George Franklin's conviction.

What most impressed both Terr and the jury about Eileen Lipsker's recovered memory was its extraordinary vividness and precision. The brands of beer and cigarettes consumed by George Franklin at the murder scene; Susan Nason's raising her right hand to ward off the fatal blow; the glint of the sun in her clear blue eyes as George brought the rock down on her head; "a crushed, stoneless, silver child's ring" (p. 4) on the now lifeless hand—all of these details and more were as fresh to Eileen in 1989, Terr says, as they had allegedly been twenty years before. How, then, could they not be authentic and conclusively damning?

One answer to that question was provided at the trial by Elizabeth Loftus herself, an expert witness on the other side. Tests on thousands of subjects have shown conclusively, Loftus told the court, not only that memory always fades with the passage of time but that it readily incorporates "post-event information" (whether true or false) that becomes indistinguishable from the actual event (Loftus & Ketcham 1994, p. 62). Those two facts together suggest that the sharpness of Eileen Lipsker's "memory" must have been caused by recent images—and, as we will see, there was no shortage of such potential contaminants at hand.[3]

With coaching from Terr, however, the prosecution was ready to remove the sting from Loftus's reported findings. Did any of her experiments, she was asked in cross-examination, deal with memories that were two decades old? Wasn't it the case that her experimentally induced distortions of memory affected only some details and not loss of the brute fact that an event had occurred? And had she ever studied a repressed memory? No, she hadn't, for two excellent reasons: she wasn't sure that such memories exist, and even if they do, she couldn't imagine how one could get at them for controlled study.

Regrettably, however, this answer occurred to Loftus after she had left the stand. What she replied instead was that post-event information would probably corrupt a repressed memory in just the way that it assuredly corrupts a nonrepressed one. The concept of repression was thus left unchallenged, and the befuddled jury had no recourse but to side with the rival expert witness—the one who boasted intimacy with the dark and subtle workings of the unconscious.

But Lenore Terr first needed to tiptoe across a theoretical minefield of her own. Her studies of children who had lived through the notorious Chowchilla bus kidnapping and the Challenger explosion had shown unambiguously that such experiences do not get repressed. Why, then, should the jury believe that Eileen Lipsker had repressed her harrowing ordeal? Just in time for the trial, but too late for prior publication, Terr came up with a face-saving theory (Terr 1991). True, she granted, onetime trauma victims always remember the event; but victims of multiple trauma like Eileen Lipsker, whose father had been a bullying drunk and a sexual abuser of two of his other daughters, turn repression into a daily routine. By the time of the murder, according to Terr, Eileen had become an old hand at stuffing bad memories into the mental freezer.

Terr's brainstorm was remarkable in several respects. For one thing, it overlooked the fact, later acknowledged in *Unchained Memories*, that Eileen had always remembered her father's violence around the house. Second, it contradicted universal human experience of protracted duress. Has anyone past the age of, say, six who has survived racial persecution, a famine, a bombing campaign, or a brutal enemy occupation ever forgotten that it occurred? Terr had evidently confused the normal fading of individual instances of repeated, patterned mistreatment with willed unawareness of that mistreatment. And third, Terr was refusing to grant any distinction in memorability between George Franklin's usual brutality and the witnessed rape and murder of Eileen's best girlhood friend.

Beyond the already mentioned dubieties in Terr's version of the Franklin case lie a good number of others emphasized by MacLean,

Loftus and Ketcham, and Ofshe and Watters, and more briefly by Mark Pendergrast as well. The cardinal point is that Eileen Lipsker's certainty that she had attended the murder of Susan Nason did not overwhelm her in a single unprompted flash on what Terr calls "a quiet winter afternoon in 1989" (p. 3). That was the least plausible of five distinct stories that Lipsker kept changing to forestall objections. As the trial record shows, Lipsker, whom Terr characterizes as having known nothing at all about repression, had already been consulting two therapists who were helping her probe her childhood "memories" and her conscious, long-standing suspicions about the murder. Both practitioners employed the theory of repression and had discussed it with her. Moreover, Eileen was aided in producing increasingly bizarre visions of George Franklin committing another murder—this one not just unsolved but completely unknown to police or anyone else—with herself as a witness and of his raping or otherwise sexually abusing her, sometimes in the presence of oblivious family members, from the ages of three through fourteen. She even came to believe that George had physically assisted her godfather in raping her. Incredibly, though, none of these barbarities had left a glint of long-term memory in her conscious mind.

Indeed, as Terr reports, so unaware was Eileen that her subsequently divorced father had been raping her that she went off to live with him for a while at age fourteen, right after the alleged eleven years of violation had ended. Later, the two of them drove across the country together to Florida, employing the back of the VW van, the supposed site of Susan Nason's rape, as their joint sleeping quarters. For Eileen's nineteenth birthday celebration, she took a similar trip with George to Ensenada in the same vehicle. How strange that "the repressed" produced no symptoms or qualms to warn her against taking those risks with the rapist-murderer!

Terr omits any mention of George's second "murder" committed in Eileen's presence, but she does cite the equally implausible memories of incest scenes. In doing so, however, she offers no clue that all this knowledge emanated from a regimen of therapeutic dowsing and that some of it preceded the original murder flashback. This latter fact is important because Eileen's newly formed belief that she had spent her childhood being molested provided her with an extra motive for wanting to see George imprisoned. Terr as author is no more interested in dwelling on such motives than the prosecution was. She uses Eileen's sexual "memories" only in the partisan and highly effective way that they were used in the trial, to establish that a beast like George was just the sort of person who could have raped Susan Nason and then bludgeoned her to death.

The fact that memory therapy lay at the very heart of the Franklin case was manifested in little-noted testimony from one of Eileen's therapists, Kirk Barrett. According to Barrett, as Ofshe and Watters report,

> Eileen's memories "developed" over the course of the therapy sessions and often during the encounter itself. With the relaxation exercises and the free-association techniques, these memories often became more detailed during their hour-and-a-half meetings. . . .
>
> Barrett remembers that from June [1989], when she initially visualized the first element of what was to become the crime scene, through July, Eileen worked both in and out of the sessions trying to sort out the meaning of her feelings, visualizations, and memories. He assured Eileen at the time that it "wasn't important . . . whether her visualizations were real or not," and that they could "sort that out later." In and out of therapy the details slowly cohered into a narrative. One day she came in and reported to Barrett that she had seen a flash image of someone hitting Susan with a rock—but that she couldn't make out who the person was. According to Barrett it was several sessions later, in a highly emotional moment, that Eileen revealed that she was finally able to see the face of the man who killed [Susan]. It was her father's. (p. 257)

Eileen Lipsker originally told her brother that the murder scene had revealed itself to her in hypnosis during her therapy. Later, she told a sister that she had dreamed the crucial knowledge—an equally suggestive fact, since recovered memory therapy often employs either hypnosis or dream analysis or both. Lenore Terr wants us to regard these statements as forgivable "lies" and to put our trust in the more enchant-ing image of Eileen's single flashback to the murder scene. It makes a good deal more sense, however, to suppose that Eileen only belatedly learned that evidence from hypnosis had recently been deemed inad-missible in California courts.

Kirk Barrett's neglected testimony does exculpate Eileen Lipsker in one respect: she had sincerely come to believe that her father was the murderer. Once committed to having him put away, however, she allowed her "memories" to evolve as expediency required, picking up new details and dropping others as newspaper reports disclosed the con-tent of old police records. As Ofshe and Watters remark, virtually the only correct details in her original report were "that Susan had been killed with a rock and that her ring had been crushed—facts that she had told Barrett she had known all her life" (p. 258).

Intriguingly, one of the tiny errors that survived in Eileen's tes-timony, having to do with a confusion between two rings on Susan Nason's hands, corresponded exactly to a mistake made in a newspa-per story in 1969. That could only mean that Eileen's "memories" were tainted by misinformation that she had either heard or, more probably, read in old clippings or on microfilm. Quixotically, however, the judge ruled all journalism from the murder period inadmissible—as if the only possible question to settle were whether Eileen was revealing the sheer truth or telling lies, instead perhaps of unknowingly recycling secondhand lore. Such bits of truth and error were available to her at all times, thanks to the fact that within her family George Franklin had always been considered a suspect in the Nason murder.

There remains the one striking detail that captivated both the jurors and, I am sure, the early readers of Terr's book: the bleeding bald spot that was said to have marred Eileen Franklin's pate for five straight years after the murder. Quite simply, it turns out to be a figment of Eileen's adult imagination. As Ofshe and Watters discovered, more than forty photo-graphs of her in the relevant period —potential exhibits that the pros-ecution wrongly withheld from the defense—show no trace of missing hair. Eileen's mother, Leah, who has changed her mind about George's guilt after finding the narrative in *Unchained Memories* so erroneous, has told Ofshe and Watters that she couldn't have failed to notice any such disfiguration if it had occurred even once. An older and a younger sister have also refuted this claim. If, as Terr believes, every symptom tells a story, in this instance the story is a fairy tale.

Once understood in its true lineaments, the Franklin/Lipsker matter turns out to be highly typical of other recovered memory cases. There is, in the first place, the eerily dreamlike quality of the "memories" themselves, whose floating perspective, blow-up details, and motivational anomalies point to the contribution of fantasy.[4] There is the therapist's reckless encouragement of the client to indulge her visions and worry "later"—usually never—whether or not they are true, along with his "supportive" absence of concern to check the emerging allegations against available knowledge. There is the interpretation of the "survivor's" moral frailties as further evidence that she is a "trauma victim." There is also, we can infer, the therapist's false promise that excavation of the repressed past will lead to psychic mending instead of to the actual, nearly inevitable, result—disorientation, panic, vengefulness, and the severing of family ties. And there is the flouting or overlooking of what is scientifically known about memory, leaving the field free for dubious theories exfoliating from the original dogma of repression.

One remaining feature of the Lipsker case turns out to be reproduced in nearly every controversy over therapeutically assisted recall. The Franklin jury members, like many people who must weigh the credibility of "survivors," felt that they had to accept Eileen's story because she stood to gain nothing and lose everything by accusing her own father of murder. Of course, that was an oversimplification; Eileen felt that the pedophile George was a threat to her own child, and besides, as many observers perceived, she had a distinct taste for fame.[5] In a deeper sense, however, the jury was right: Eileen had opened a Pandora's box of bitterness and recrimination that will probably trouble her for the rest of her life. Nevertheless, the cardinal point about all this self-destructiveness went completely unnoticed. Eileen Lipsker did not decide to send her mind into a tailspin after making rational calculations about the opposing claims of justice and filial loyalty; she was progressively encouraged to do so by therapists who believed that full psychic health must wait upon a vomiting-up of the repressed past.

Disastrously missed at the trial, this cardinal fact slipped away once again on a subsequent Faith Daniels talk show where, for the first time, Eileen Lipsker and Elizabeth Loftus sat down together. "Why would you want to suffer if you didn't have to?" asked one member of the audience who, like nearly all the others, believed Eileen's story and considered Loftus a heartless crank. "Why would you want to put yourself through it? There's no logic behind it" (p. 71). As Loftus now tells us in her book, she smiled stoically as the audience continued to berate her and rally to Lipsker's cause. And then the program was over.

Reading about this episode, one experiences an extreme frustration. Couldn't Loftus have pointed out that other parties besides Eileen had "put her through it"? That, however, was near the outset of the recovered memory craze, when no one yet had an explanatory handle on the burgeoning plague that still besieges us. Now at last, thanks to the inquiries of Loftus and others, it is starting to make an eerie kind of sense.

3.

The Franklin/Lipsker case, so attractive to Lenore Terr as Exhibit A of validated repression, actually shows how a "memory" originating in conscious hunches and resentments can be crystallized by protracted therapeutic suggestion, or the subliminal contagion of ideas between a dominant and a subordinate party. That is what we regularly find when missing elements of recovered memory stories are filled in; where repression was, there shall suggestion be. Indeed, someone who reviews many such cases will eventually realize that the salient question isn't whether or not a bona fide instance of repression can be found, but rather whether there are any limits at all to the malleability of the human mind. Therapists, it seems, are helpful but not strictly necessary to the production of wildly fantastic memories. Given a facilitating belief structure, the compliant subject can use the merest hints as triggers to delusion.

To illustrate this fact, there is nothing quite like the sequence of events recounted in Lawrence Wright's *Remembering Satan* (1994), a short but gripping and brilliantly constructed book that was serialized in *The New Yorker* in May 1993. Wright tells of Paul Ingram, an Olympia, Washington, sheriff's deputy, a born-again Christian, and the chair of his county Republican committee, who was eventually thought to have raped both of his daughters as well as one of his sons innumerable times, to have passed the daughters around sexually as poker nights at home turned into gang rapes, to have hideously tortured the girls and forced them and his wife to have sex with goats and dogs, and to have murdered and cannibalized many babies at huge gatherings of his Satanic cult—where, be it noted, long gowns, pitchforks, and "Viking hats" were de rigueur. The still greater novelty, however, is that Ingram, though he initially remembered none of those atrocities, succeeded in visualizing most of them through the exercise of prayerful introspection. Indeed, he labored so hard to admit to new crimes that his tale-spinning daughters sometimes fell behind his pace.

All this would be hilarious Thurberesque Americana if it were not also inexpressibly sad. Whereas the Franklin household, when Eileen Lipsker went public with her vision, no longer contained a married couple or any children, in the Ingram case a devout family of seven was shattered for good. Moreover, Ingram, who is now serving a twenty-year term in prison after having confessed to six counts of child molestation [he was paroled after serving fourteen years as a model inmate], came close to being joined there by others who were caught in a widening net of lunacy—and at least two of them, who were in fact jailed briefly and then kept under house arrest for five months each, will never recover their reputations. Even those men had to think long and hard about whether they might have unknowingly lived double lives; and Ingram's wife, Sandy, did conclude that she must have been a secret Satanist. She has moved away now and lives under a different name, as does the only one of her five children who hasn't fled Olympia.

What is most arresting about the Ingram calamity is how little suggestion—indeed, how little autosuggestion—was required to set it in motion and then to keep it hurtling toward its climax. Ericka Ingram had a history of making unsubstantiated sexual charges prior to her "realization" at age twenty-two that her father had been raping her. That insight did not occur during therapy but at a Christian retreat in August 1988 at which a visiting charismatic healer told Ericka the news, relayed to her by the Holy Spirit, that she had been molested as a child. Ericka immediately accepted the diagnosis—and she continued to do so. At the sentencing, she was instrumental in seeing that her father received the stiffest allowable punishment, and afterward, like Eileen Lipsker, she advanced her cause on the tabloid talk shows. Still later she denounced a coven of alleged Satanists within the Olympia police department.

During the second day of his questioning, Paul Ingram easily allowed himself to be led into a trance, resulting in his confession to all of the crimes with which he was eventually charged after prosecutors had deleted the witches' sabbath material, which could have raised awkward questions in jurors' minds if the case had come to trial. Ingram's prolific later admissions were facilitated not only by prayer but by "relaxation techniques," one of which he had picked up from a magazine. And two of his sons also developed a knack of instantly becoming "dissociated" in order to provide inquisitors with the required lurid reminiscences.

This is not to say, however, that the Ingram family generated hallucinations entirely under its own steam. To begin with, Paul Ingram's police colleagues exerted unscrupulous (though hardly unusual) pressure on him, extending the second interrogation over a mind-buckling eight-hour period and using his piety as a wedge to confession. They lied to him about what others had revealed and assured him that if he would only begin by admitting his guilt, the relevant memories would come flooding back. By that second day, furthermore, Paul was being advised by a Tacoma psychologist whose recent practice had included Satanic abuse cases, and who later helped Paul's son Chad to conclude that his remembered childhood dreams were proof of molestation. An assistant pastor in the Church of Living Water also helped both Paul and his wife to sustain the cleansing flow of visions. During five months of interrogation, no fewer than five psychologists and counselors kept the heat on Paul, preventing him from ever stepping back to test whether the grimmer yet more tentative of his two memory systems—his "horror movie," as he called it—was anchored to actual events.

When all this pressure has been duly weighed, however, the fact remains that the Ingram case displays a breathtaking readiness on the part of its major players to form lasting "memories" on very slight provocation. And this is important for grasping the explosive potentiality of recovered memory allegations. There was nothing exceptional about the Ingram family's prelapsarian makeup or the Olympia scene in general. Apparently, a community steeped in biblical literalism on the one hand and Geraldo on the other needs only a triggering mechanism to set off a long chain reaction of paranoia.[6] Yet such a community epitomizes a good portion of North America. The potential for mass havoc from "memory"-based accusations is thus no smaller today than it was in the seventeenth century. In fact, it is incomparably greater, thanks to the power of our sensation-seeking media to spread the illness instantaneously from one town or region to another.

As Lawrence Wright properly stresses, one further ingredient acts as a multiplier of trouble. Not surprisingly, it is a shared belief in the theory of repression. Only a few hours into his first grilling, Paul Ingram was ready to state, "I did violate them and abuse them and probably for a long period of time. I've repressed it" (p. 8). His questioners of course held the same view, which took on firmer contours as more psychologists were called in; before long, the official version was that Paul had repressed each of his myriad offenses just as soon as he had finished committing it. A county undersheriff (himself falsely accused of Satanism, but still an enthusiastic believer in its reality) became so enamored of this notion that he started moonlighting as a counselor to survivor groups and writing theoretical papers about the effects of repression.[7] One can only second Lawrence Wright's conclusion: "[w]hatever the value of repression as a scientific concept or a therapeutic tool, unquestioning belief in it has become as dangerous as the belief in witches" (p. 200).

Some secular-minded readers may feel that the Ingram case, in view of its fundamentalist soil and its resultant exotic blossom of Satanism, is too outlandish to tell us much about the prudent and responsible search for incest memories. Yet the more one learns about the scare over "Satanic ritual abuse," the more porous its boundary with the larger recovered memory movement appears to be. According to surveys taken by the False Memory Syndrome Foundation, at least 15 percent of all memory retrievers come to recall Satanic torture in childhood—this despite a lack of evidence to support the existence of any sadistic devil-worshiping cults in North America or anywhere else.[8] The fact is that "memories" of baby barbecues and the like are usually evoked through the same techniques of psychic exploration commended by prestigious academics such as Judith Herman and Lenore Terr. Indeed, as she testified at the Franklin trial, Terr herself has treated "victims" who thought they recalled having been forced to watch ritual human sacrifices.

Until the recovered memory movement got properly launched in the later 1980s, most Satanism charges were brought against child-care workers who were thought to have molested their little clients for the devil's sake. In such prosecutions, a vengeful or mentally unhinged adult typically launches the accusations, which are immediately believed by police and social workers. These authorities then disconcert the toddlers with rectal and vaginal prodding, with invitations to act out naughtiness on "anatomically correct" dolls with bloated genitals, and, of course, with leading questions that persist until the child reverses an initial denial that anything happened and begins weaving the kind of tale that appears to be demanded. As many studies have shown, small children can be readily induced to believe that they have experienced just about any fictitious occurrence. In this respect, however, they do not stand fundamentally apart from their elders. The only real difference is that the grown-ups, in order to become as gullible as three-year-olds, must first subscribe to a theory such as that of demonic possession or its scientific counterpart, Freudian repression. They then become putty in the hands of their would-be helpers.

As it happens, the most impressive controlled illustration of this fact to date came directly from the Paul Ingram case, after the prosecutors—not the defense!—had invited the social psychologist Richard Ofshe to Olympia as an expert on cults and mind control. Perhaps, they thought, Ofshe could cast some light into the murky Satanic corner of the affair. But Ofshe, immediately struck by the conditional quality of Ingram's confessions and their suggestion that a scene was taking place in the mind's eye ("I would've," "I must have," "I see it," etc.), decided to test Ingram's suggestibility by proposing a false memory for him to accept or reject.

"I was talking to one of your sons and one of your daughters . . . ," Ofshe told Ingram. "It was about a time when you made them have sex with each other while you watched." This was one charge that had not been levied and would never be, but one day later, Paul proudly submitted a new written confession:

> . . . I ask or tell Paul Jr. & Ericka to come upstairs. . . . I tell Ericka to knell [sic] and to caress Paul's genitals. When erect I tell her to put the penis into her mouth and to orally stimulate him. . . . I may have told the children that they needed to learn the sex acts and how to do them right. . . . I may have anal sex with Paul, not real clear. . . . Someone may have told me to do this with the kids. This is a feeling I have. (p. 173)

When Ofshe then informed Ingram that this memory was specious, Ingram refused to believe him. "It's just as real to me as anything else," he protested.

Months later, when Ofshe phoned Ingram in jail and begged him not to plead guilty, Ingram wavered but declined. Apart from consideration for the daughters who had so egregiously betrayed him, he cited the likelihood that he was still repressing material that would make the whole case clear. Protected at last from the ministrations of his "counselors," he did change his mind shortly thereafter, but his guilty plea had already been accepted by the court, and two subsequent appeals and many attempts by psychologists to enlighten his parole board fell on deaf ears.

The criminal cases we have examined suffice to show that the "return of the repressed," however bland its uses within the amorphous aims of Freudian therapy, can turn noxious when it is considered by police, prosecutors, jurors, and even accused malefactors to be a source of unimpeachable truth. In the light of the actual recovery movement, however, the Franklin and Ingram examples can be seen to lack a baleful but typical ingredient. So far as we know, neither Eileen Lipsker nor Ericka Ingram (not to mention Paul Ingram himself) was systematically recruited by self-help "recovery" books to believe that certain despicable deeds must have been committed and then wholly repressed.

Just such solicitation—we can think of it as suggestion-at-a-distance—has been brought to bear on myriad vulnerable people, mostly women, by advocates in search of ideological and/or financial gain. The result has been a widespread tragedy that is still unfolding before our incredulous eyes. To lay bare not just its nature but also its causes, both proximate and remote, is a socially urgent task. With the help of several excellent critical works, I will explore that ground in the concluding portion of this essay.

Chapter 6

THE REVENGE OF THE REPRESSED, PART II

HERE IS THE CONCLUDING PORTION OF THE REVIEW ESSAY THAT APPEARED IN
The New York Review of Books, NOVEMBER 17 AND DECEMBER 1, 1994. PUBLIC
AND JUDICIAL UNDERSTANDING OF THE PITFALLS ATTENDING RECOVERED MEM-
ORY HAS GREATLY IMPROVED SINCE THEN.

I.

Throughout the American 1980s and beyond, the interrogation of small
children for their memories of recent sexual abuse played a role in many
a criminal case against accused molesters who had not, in fact, done
anything wrong. The social and financial costs have been enormous.
To take only the most famous example, staff members of the McMartin
Preschool in Manhattan Beach, California, who were accused of every
imaginable horror associated with devil worship, had to endure the
longest (almost seven years) and most expensive ($15 million) trial in
American history before the case collapsed from the weight of its accumulated absurdities. In other instances, draconian sentences are being
served and plea bargains are still being coerced in the face of transparently clear signs that the charges are bogus. Even today, our criminal
justice system is just beginning to erect safeguards against the error
that makes such outrages possible: the assumption that children are still
reliable witnesses after exposure to their parents' and inquisitors' not-
so-subtle hints that certain kinds of revelations are expected of them.

Not even that much progress, however, is being made with respect
to curbing parallel travesties involving the therapeutically manufactured memories of adults who decide that they must have been molested
in their own childhood. On the contrary: by extending their statutes
of limitations to allow for thirty years and more of non-recollection,

our states have been codifying a pseudoscientific notion of repressed-yet-vividly-retrieved memory that can cause not merely injustice but enormous grief and havoc. Obviously, the impetus for such legislative backwardness is not coming from reputable psychological research—which, as we have seen, offers no support to the concept of repression even in its mildest form. The momentum comes rather from a combination of broad popular belief and a relatively narrow but intense crusading fervor.

Since 1988, the most successful communicators of both the belief and the fervor have been Ellen Bass and Laura Davis, coauthors of the "recovery manual" *The Courage to Heal.* A teacher of creative writing and her student, Bass and Davis were radical feminists who lacked any background in psychology. Their knowledge base consisted of stories they had heard from women who clearly remembered that they had been sexually abused in childhood but who had been rebuffed by uncaring therapists and family members. Noting the high numbers of such cases reported within women's collectives, and further noting that other women in such groups eventually produced incest "memories" of their own, Bass and Davis soon decided that repressed abuse must be even more pervasive than remembered abuse. The more likely explanation of the late-blooming cases—namely, that the dynamics of the group encouraged false memory formation by making victimhood into a test of authentic belonging—has yet to dawn on these collaborators.

Precisely because their minds were unclouded by research findings, Bass and Davis uncannily reflected the ideological spirit of their moment and milieu. As Mark Pendergrast relates in *Victims of Memory* (1996), the mounting, and very legitimate, concern about the underreported incidence of real child molestation formed only one corner of the picture. Bass and Davis also spoke to a public mood of impatient moral absolutism; an obsession with the themes, popularized by John Bradshaw and others, of codependency, the "dysfunctional family," and the "inner child"; a widespread susceptibility to occult beliefs; the rise of "lookism" and other manifestations of hypersensitivity to the violation of personal space; and the angry conviction in some quarters that all men are rapists at heart. While Andrea Dworkin and Susan Brown-miller were hypothesizing that American fathers regularly rape their daughters in order to teach them what it means to be inferior, Bass and Davis set about to succor the tens of millions of victims who must have repressed that ordeal.

No single book, of course, can make a social movement. Although *The Courage to Heal* had already sold over three quarters of a million copies before its recent third edition appeared, and although its spinoff volumes constitute a small industry in their own right, Bass and Davis have been joined by a considerable number of other writers who share their slant. Moreover, the recovered memory business quickly outgrew the motives of its founders. By now, as critical books by Pendergrast and by Richard Ofshe and Ethan Watters show, it has evolved into a highly lucrative enterprise not just of therapy and publishing but also of counseling, workshop hosting, custody litigation, criminal prosecution, forced hospitalization, and insurance and "victim compensation" claims.

The recovered memory movement, it must be plainly understood, is not primarily addressed to people who always knew about their sexual victimization. Its main intended audience is women who aren't at all sure that they were molested, and its purpose is to convince them of that fact and embolden them to act upon it. As for genuine victims, the comfort they are proffered may look attractive at first, but it is of debatable long-term value. *The Courage to Heal* and its fellow manuals are not about surmounting one's tragic girlhood but about keeping the psychic wounds open, refusing forgiveness or reconciliation, and joining the permanently embittered corps of "survivors."

In the eyes of the movement's leaders, as many as half of all American women are veterans of sexual abuse. If so, the logic seems to run, you can hardly fail to unearth a victim wherever you look and by however desultory a means of detection. But a revealing game with definitions is being played here. For writers like Bass and Davis, Renee Fredrickson, and E. Sue Blume, sexual molestation occurs whenever the victim thinks—or later comes to believe that she must have thought—that an inappropriate kind of contact is occurring. Blume, indeed, denies that physical touching need be involved at all. "Incest," she explains, "can occur through words, sounds, or even exposure of the child to sights or acts that are sexual but do not involve her" (Blume 1990, p. 5). And still another movement writer denounces what she calls "emotional incest," which can be committed by parents who "appear loving and devoted," "spend a great deal of time with their children and lavish them with praise and material gifts," but do so merely "as an unconscious ploy to satisfy their own unmet needs" (Love 1990, p. 1).

From the standpoint of public health, what's most disturbing here is a likely growth in the number of "false positives"—women who were never molested but who are enticed into believing that they were. The mavens of recovered memory concern themselves almost entirely with means of reinforcing incest suspicions, not with means of checking them against solid evidence pro or con. Their advice to friends and counselors of a woman who has been led to suspect early molestation is generally the same: never cast doubt on those suspicions. So, too, she herself is urged to stifle all doubts. In Renee Fredrickson's words, "You may be convinced that your disbelief is a rational questioning of the reality versus unreality of your memories, but it is partially a misguided attempt to repress the memories again" (Fredrickson 1992, p. 161).

It is little wonder, then, that Bass and Davis, through the first two editions of *The Courage to Heal,* had yet to encounter a single woman who "suspected she might have been abused, explored it, and determined that she wasn't" (Bass & Davis 1992, p. 347). Now, in a third edition that is beginning to sound nervous about "the backlash" in general and pending damage suits in particular, it is admitted that some therapists "have pushed clients to acknowledge abuse . . . that did not occur." But even those few bad apples, in Bass and Davis's still erroneous judgment, cannot "create new memories in their clients"; and the women who change their minds after leaving therapy "represent only a tiny fraction of the millions of actual survivors. . . ."

The "false positives" problem has been exacerbated by the checklists of telltale symptoms that adorn the movement's self-help manuals and advice columns. Smarting from criticism of their earlier checklists, Bass and Davis adopt a warier posture now; nevertheless, they still leave the implication that if you "feel different from other people," incest is a likely cause. E. Sue Blume tells you that you were probably molested if you speak too softly, or wear too many clothes, or have "no awareness at all" of having been violated (Blume 1990, pp. xviii–xxi). If you have checked the questionnaire item "I neglect my teeth" or "There are certain things I seem to have a strange affection or attraction for," Renee Fredrickson knows why (Fredrickson 1992, p. 49). And according to the ubiquitous John Bradshaw, a victim can be spotted either by her sexual promiscuity or, as the case may be, by her lack of interest in sex (Bradshaw 1992, pp. 43–44). These are all sterling examples of what experimentally minded psychologists dryly call a "confirmatory bias."[1]

Once she is drawn into memory therapy, a client will find her suspicions of abuse verified by one or more techniques of investigation that are, in Fredrickson's words, "as unlimited as human creativity" (Fredrickson 1992, p. 141). With or without the therapist's direct assurance that the patient's symptoms are "consistent with abuse," repression can supposedly be dislodged through "feelings work," "body work," "dream work," "imagistic work," "trance work," and "group work"; through the production of journals and pictures that are sure to yield symbols of violation; through the cultivation of flashbacks, which are always deemed to reveal the truth of a past situation rather than compliance with current expectations; through administration of the tongue-loosening "truth serum" sodium amytal; and, of course, through hypnosis, including its deep-end forms of "age regression" and even "past life regression." The considerable body of technical literature showing that none of these methods reliably leads to uncontaminated memories is simply ignored.

The memory movement's feminist affinity should not lead anyone to suppose that its incitement to militant victimhood serves the best interests of women. It is precisely women who make up most of the movement's casualties. Once a patient is invited to believe that her inner child was suffocated at an early age, she may well put the major blame on her mother; that is just what we see in a significant minority of cases. Estrangement between sisters—one converted to hellishly revised memories of their years together, the other refusing to go along—is also a regular aftermath of therapy. But above all, the chief sufferer usually turns out to be the female patient herself.

Survivor manuals preach the doctrine of "abreaction," whereby a patient must painfully relive each repressed memory if she is to stand a chance of freeing herself from it. The experience is guaranteed to be rough. In Lenore Terr's version of this truth, "Clinicians find that once repression lifts, individuals become far more symptomatic. They become anxious, depressed, sometimes suicidal, and far more fearful of items suggestive of their traumas"[2] (p. 52). Bass and Davis agree. "Don't hurt or try to kill yourself . . . ," they feel compelled to advise. "Sit tight and ride out the storm." For many women, however, the storm doesn't end, or else it ends all too abruptly with suicide. And even in the best of cases, a "survivor" is coached to reject the happiest actual memories of her childhood as being inconsistent with the stark truth of molestation. The result is a lasting sacrifice of resilience, security of identity, humor, capacity to show affection, and connection to the people who have cared most steadily about this woman's happiness.

2.

Although much of this woe is irreparable, there is no need for fatalism about its indefinite extension to new cases. On the contrary: the tide is already being turned. The critical books before us follow upon influential exposés by such courageous journalists as Michael Morris, Stephanie Salter, the late Darrell Sifford, and Bill Taylor, along with trenchant warnings by Carol Tavris, Paul McHugh, and Robyn Dawes, among others. And a number of other book-length critiques are just now arriving on the scene.[3] Above all, steady progress in public enlightenment has been forged, over the past two-and-a-half years, by the False Memory Syndrome Foundation, most of whose members are themselves slandered relatives of "survivors."

All three of the most convincing recent books on false memory—those by Elizabeth Loftus and Katherine Ketcham, Richard Ofshe and Ethan Watters, and Mark Pendergrast—address the full tragedy and folly of the recovered memory movement. All are astute, scientifically informed, and compassionate toward the movement's casualties; all contain wrenching accounts of sudden accusation and insult, alienation, family grief, false imprisonment, and death without reconciliation. Any of these overlapping works would serve a reader well as a survey, analysis, and call to corrective action. But the most unflinching and broadest-ranging studies appear to be Ofshe and Watters's *Making Monsters: False Memories, Psychotherapy, and Sexual Hysteria* (1994) and Pendergrast's *Victims of Memory: Sex Abuse Accusations and Shattered Lives* (1996).

As befits a coauthor (Ofshe) whose research specialty has been the tactics of exerting undue influence, *Making Monsters* is finely attuned to the thralldom that would-be healers impose upon their clients, whose mundane initial complaints are typically supplanted by anxiety, suggestibility, and a desperate dependency. What distinguishes this book is its focus on the resultant psychological transformation of patients. For Ofshe and Watters, the speciousness of the so-called memories is incidental to the real tragedy, a "brutalization and psychological torture" of people who get stripped of their actual early memories, infused with fanatical hatred of their parents, and disabled for normal coping in the world beyond the drifting lifeboat of survivorship. The patients themselves become grotesque in the very act of "making monsters" out of the people who nurtured them.

Ofshe and Watters offer us the clearest account of how the very inefficacy of memory treatment—its indefinite postponing of an expected self-restoration—can lock the patient and therapist in an ever more macabre embrace. Thus:

> Therapists often find themselves forced to explain why, after the first series of recovered memories, the client's symptoms do not disappear as promised. The easiest answer is to presume that the abuse must have been more serious than originally thought, and that more repressed memories are hidden in the patient's unconscious. As the

therapist pushes to find more hidden memories, the client, who is already trained in the process, often comes up with still more accounts of having been abused. . . . [Eventually,] the client's worst fears are forged into memories. What could be more psychologically damaging than being raped by one's father? Having to have his baby. What could be worse than having to give birth to your father's child? Having to kill the child. What could be worse than having to kill a baby? Having to eat the baby after you've killed it. What could be worse than all this? Having to do these things during ritualized worship of the Devil. (p. 177)

At such a juncture, readers may suppose, both parties to the "therapy" must surely awaken and realize that they have been taking a magic carpet ride. But for reasons that Ofshe and Watters supply, it doesn't happen. The therapist feels honor bound to avoid "revictimizing" the patient by expressing doubts, and the patient, precisely by virtue of having renounced the actual memories that used to moor her identity, has lost contact with reality and is desperate to retain the therapist's approval. The outcome is a potentially lethal folie à deux.

Ofshe and Watters rightly perceive the Satanic connection as "the Achilles' heel of the recovered memory movement." Radical feminists who prefer all-female "survivor families" to the nuclear family make strange bedfellows with abortion-hating fundamentalists, but the record speaks for itself. "None of us want to believe such stories," write Bass and Davis of the ridiculous tales about babies being forced to eat feces in Satan's honor, "but for the sake of the survivors we must." As *Making Monsters* shows, Bass and Davis's own carte-blanche approach to the authenticating of incest cases leaves them with no way of drawing a line between sane and crazy allegations made by their Christian counterparts from across the ideological tracks.

Making Monsters is a book about iatrogenesis, or the molding of a patient's illness by the incompetent doctor's own ministrations. The authors carry this theme quite far, not just in explaining individual cases but also in challenging an entire disease entity linked to false memory cases, so-called multiple personality disorder (MPD). They are hardly the first parties to express misgivings about this staple of Hollywood, sensational TV, and the criminal courts, where "one of my other personalities did it" has become the murderer's last alibi. But Ofshe and Watters regard MPD as a pure product of suggestion. They see it as a behavioral pattern learned chiefly from hypnotherapists who tend themselves to be believers in Satanic possession and other forms of conspiratorial mind control, and who characteristically prod their patients not only to remember hideous ordeals but also to manifest the dissociated selves that must have been brought into being by flight from those ordeals. With MPD, Ofshe and Watters argue, we stand at the outer edge of medical derangement, yet well within the methodological boundaries of the recovered memory movement.

In their assault on MPD, Ofshe and Watters are joined, independently, by the investigative journalist Mark Pendergrast, whose *Victims of Memory* constitutes the most ambitious and comprehensive, as well as the most emotionally committed, of all the studies before us. Pendergrast's book stands out from the others in several respects. For one thing, it transcribes his numerous interviews with therapists, "survivors," "retractors," and accused "perpetrators," allowing the cruel unreason of the recovery movement to be voiced with a minimum of editorial mediation. Second, he is the author who delves most deeply into the movement's antecedents in witchcraft lore, mesmerism, early hypnotherapy, and the treatment of so-called hysteria—itself a faddish malady whose distribution was suspiciously well correlated with possession of the means to pay for treatment. Third, Pendergrast offers illuminating material about physiological states (sleep paralysis, panic attacks) that have traditionally been mistaken for "body memories" of one lurid kind or another. And it is Pendergrast who devotes the most effort to analyzing the contemporary Zeitgeist in which the recovery movement thrives.

Like Loftus and Ofshe and Watters, Pendergrast offers case histories that will wring the classic emotions of pity and terror from any unbiased reader. But here, too, there is a difference: the most affecting (though by no means the most drastic) of Pendergrast's stories is his own. He himself has lost his grown daughters to the recovery movement. Within therapy that featured the overcoming of repression, both of them came to believe that he did something awful—they won't say what—to one of them, and both have met his pleas for communication with the icy formalism inculcated by *The Courage to Heal*—a book, ironically, that Pendergrast bought and gave to one daughter when she first mentioned that uncrystallized sexual scenes were beginning to haunt her mind. Now both daughters have taken different last names, and in concluding his book with a poignant letter to them, Pendergrast further protects their identities by assigning them fictitious first names as well. Let us hope that they read not just that letter but the whole of *Victims of Memory*, which, though it is hardly addressed to them alone, rests partly on the desperate premise that a 603-page dose of history, logic, and exhortation may be able to turn well-coached zealots back into the amiable young women Pendergrast once knew.

Finally, and understandably, *Victims of Memory* is distinguished by the urgency and specificity of its call to action. Among other recommendations, Pendergrast wants professional associations and licensing boards to stop waffling about repression and to insist that therapists acquaint themselves with what is actually known about memory. He wants reconsideration of laws that have created standing "abuse bureaucracies" and that have rashly extended statutes of limitations. He favors third-party suits for damages against therapists whose implanting of false accusations has destroyed families and livelihoods.[4]

He wants the adoption of higher standards for expert testimony and for the evaluation of therapists' claims that they were mere bystanders to their patients' mnemonic feats. And most pressingly, he asks for a special judicial review of criminal convictions that have been based solely on the alleged retrieval of long-dormant memories or on the manipulated fantasies of small children.

Some people who have always remembered their own sexual victimization will regard the legal and legislative parts of this agenda as regressive, a signal to real molesters that they can exploit children with impunity. Such fears are understandable; pedophiles will undoubtedly try to portray any accuser as deluded by a trick of memory. But that only makes it more imperative that the air be cleared. Until our courts can learn to apply the same evidential criteria to abuse charges that they require for all others, they will remain enmired in phony cases that persecute the innocent and squander resources that are needed to address the real problem of child abuse. Meanwhile, simple justice demands that prison sentences resting on a combination of delusion and misinformation be overturned.

3.

Once the bizarre and sinister features of the recovered memory movement are widely known, sophisticated readers will not hesitate to distance themselves from it. But that very likelihood holds out another danger: bobbing for repressed memories may be perceived simply as a ludicrous, dismissible aberration from a fundamentally sound psychotherapeutic tradition. If that view prevails, we will have learned little of lasting value from the recovered memory fiasco. It is essential to grasp that memory retrieval emerged from mainstream ideas about the psyche and that it bears a strong kinship with every other style of treatment that ties curative power to restoration of the patient's early past.

Despite their feminist affiliation, the champions of survivorship cheerfully acknowledge Sigmund Freud, the male chauvinist par excellence, as their chief intellectual and clinical forebear. They are quite justified in that opinion. Indeed, the ties between Freud's methods and theirs are more intricate and enveloping—and immeasurably more compromising to both parties—than they imagine. Precisely that kinship explains why other therapeutic descendants of Freudianism ought to be doing some soul-searching just now.

Needless to say, it is not classic psychoanalysis to which writers like Bass and Davis feel indebted. They have in mind the prepsychoanalytic Freud, the one who supposedly took pity on his hysterical patients, found that they were all harboring memories of early abuse, "listened and understood and gave them permission to remember and speak of these terrible events" (Masson 1984, p. 9), and cured them by unknotting their repression. Unfortunately (the story continues), he then suffered a failure of nerve; too many fathers were being identified as perpetrators, and patriarchy itself threatened to teeter on its throne. As a result, Freud withdrew into psychoanalysis, a doctrine that ascribes incestuous designs not to adult molesters but, grotesquely, to children themselves.

As I explained in "The Unknown Freud," this fable contains at least one nugget of truth: Freud had no empirical warrant for shifting to an oedipal perspective. The founding of his signature doctrine was indeed a retreat—one designed, however, not to shield guilty fathers but to keep in play his favorite concept of repression—"the cornerstone," as he would later say, "on which the whole structure of psycho-analysis rests" (Freud 1953–1974, 14:16)—after its already announced therapeutic victories had failed to materialize. Freud finally had to cope with the disagreeable thought that his hysterics' "stories" of very early abuse had been peremptory inventions of his own. He did so, however, through a dumbfoundingly illogical, historically momentous expedient, ascribing to his patients' unconscious minds a repressed desire for the precocious couplings that he had hitherto urged them to remember having helplessly undergone. That is how psychoanalysis as we know it came into being.

Even people who accept this correction of the Freud legend may be slow to realize how high and dry it leaves the dogma of repression. Freud and Josef Breuer had first invoked repression in 1893 to cover miscellaneous symptom-producing "things which the patient wished to forget" (2:10); but Freud quickly became uncomfortable both with the random character of the offending thoughts and with his source of information about the repressed, namely, hypnosis. Then, with the seduction theory, he adapted the idea of repression to cover the failure of patients to remember molestations that he soon conceded to have been imaginary. Still later, the concept was stretched to cover fantasies (and some events) whose existence could be known only by positing the action of repression itself. In none of these phases do we encounter raw behavioral data that an outsider would feel obliged to label "the repressed." Thus we really ought to redefine the repressed as follows: "inaccessible and possibly nonexistent psychic material to which the theorist or therapist is nevertheless determined to assign explanatory power." Exactly the same point applies to the repressed as it operates in the discourse of the recovery movement.

Among the many respects in which the memory retrievers' glorification of Freud's "seduction theory" misfires, the least noticed has to do with his alleged sympathy for incest sufferers. It is certainly true that he showed precious little pity for child sexual victims after he became properly "Freudian" and cast children as the would-be seducers. Like Bass and Davis, however, the early Freud was less interested in comforting certified veterans of molestation than in rounding up converts to his all-purpose diagnosis. And the spirit of his interventions, as revealed in his papers and letters of the period, was not compassionate but monomaniacal. It is little wonder that Ofshe and Watters regard him as having "cut the very figure of a recovered memory therapist." Listen to Freud's own words:

> The work keeps on coming to a stop and they keep on maintaining that this time nothing has occurred to them. We must not believe what they say, we must always assume, and tell them, too, that they have kept something back. . . . We must insist on this, we must repeat the pressure and represent ourselves as infallible, till at last we are really told something. . . . There are cases, too, in which the patient tries to disown [the memory] even after its return. "Something has occurred to me now, but you obviously put it into my head." . . . In all such cases, I remain unshakably firm. I . . . explain to the patient that [these distinctions] are only forms of his resistance and pretexts raised by it against reproducing this particular memory, which we must recognize in spite of all this. (2:279–280)

The patient's typical response to such hectoring was an agitation that Freud, like his counterparts a century later, paraded as validation of his guesswork: "The behaviour of patients while they are reproducing these infantile experiences is in every respect incompatible with the assumption that the scenes are anything else than a reality which is being felt with distress and reproduced with the greatest reluctance" (3:204). Note as well how the psychoanalytic concept of resistance (the memory retrievers prefer to call it "denial") was already pulling its weight in the mid-1890s. When Renee Fredrickson now avers that the "existence of profound disbelief is an indication that memories are real" (Fredrickson 1992, p. 171), she is manifesting loyalty to the sturdiest, as well as the most capricious, of Freudian traditions.

Critics of recovered memory have remarked on the movement's puritanical alarmism, whereby a mere touch or look gets invested with traumatic consequences that supposedly remain virulent for thirty years and more. In this respect, too, Freud anticipated the contemporary trend. So long as he cared at all about molestation as an etiological factor, he completely overlooked its real psychological effects, such as fear, moral confusion, and a diminished sense of selfhood. Instead, he dwelt on mechanical cause-and-effect relations between symptomatology and the premature stimulation of one body zone or another. And he regarded masturbation not only as a cause of indigestion, headaches, and lassitude but also as a sign of prior "seduction." The early Freud's truest contemporary heirs are those adults who see toddlers playing doctor and immediately phone the police.

It was Freud, too, who pioneered the modern memory sleuths' technique of thematically matching a patient's symptom with a sexually symmetrical "memory." Before he decided that it made no difference whether a trauma was real or imaginary, Freud was tireless in his pursuit of such causal linkages. Lesions in the mouth were signs that a penis had been there first; dyspepsia or "worm irritation" must have stemmed from the insertion of a tongue or a finger in the former baby's anus; a paralysis of the lower limbs meant that the sufferer had been "required to stimulate the genitals of a grown-up woman with his foot"; and so forth.[5] Freud apparently arrived at such quack conclusions in the same way that his incest-happy legatees do, by taking the symptom as a puzzle to be jointly addressed with the patient and then solving it through direct probing, dream analysis, and the study of tactically selected verbal associations.[6]

The early Freud must also be awarded precedence for the cluster of ideas about memory that has landed so many of our fellow citizens in litigation and/or prison. I refer not just to repression but to the mind's ability to take snapshots of extremely early scenes and reproduce them in detail several decades later. When Lenore Terr, for example, uncritically accepts a man's "memory" from babyhood of his sadistic mother having totally submerged him in the bathtub as he was noticing "light gray walls all around me, a foul smell in the air," she may be defying what is known about brain development, but she is perfectly in key with Freud. Let one example, a letter from 1897, suffice:

> The early period before the age of one and one half years is becoming ever more significant. I am inclined to distinguish several periods even within it. Thus I was able to trace back, with certainty, a hysteria that developed in the context of a periodic mild depression to a seduction, which occurred for the first time at 11 months[,] and [I could] hear again the words that were exchanged between two adults at that time! It is as though it comes from a phonograph. (Freud 1985, p. 226)

Given that Freud here accepts a "phonographic" memory of an adult conversation recorded when the patient was presumably still struggling to say "mama," this passage must rank among his most credulous ever. Yet the claim being made is scarcely more inane than any number of others from the same epoch.

A Freudian's predictable way of handling all such embarrassments will be to say that they predated the birth of psychoanalysis. Yes, but most of them also persisted far beyond it. Long after 1897, Freud continued to badger his patients with ready-made hypotheses and to dismiss their objections as mere resistance; he still took their distress at his morbid insinuations as a further signal of his correctness; he still regarded symptoms as allegories of repressed mental contents; his

Flintstones Lamarckism became more rather than less extravagant; and he never flagged in his quest to forge precise causal links between vividly reconstructed sexual events from infancy (either witnessed or personally endured) and adult mental disturbance. Without the éclat of psycho-analysis, moreover, our memory gurus would never have been drawn to the molestation-minded Freud whom they now prefer. Nor, lack-ing his imprimatur, could they have bandied about notions of repres-sion, abreaction, and unconscious symbolism without feeling a need to argue for their cogency.

A chasm does yawn, however, between the principles of the recov-ered memory movement and psychoanalysis in Freud's most familiar articulation of it. In contrast to Freud's own habit, the ideal Freudian therapist is supposed to be cool, nonjudgmental, and slow to reach closure about diagnoses and thematic connections. He is also asked to honor a number of methodological niceties that deter simplistic trans-lations between any given sign and the event or wish that supposedly brought it into being. There is, for instance, the concept of "screen memories" that are not to be taken at face value, and there are numerous posited defense mechanisms that supposedly warp dreams, symptoms, and errors into relatively obscure compromise formations. Although these refinements brought about an ominous problem of their own—in the full labyrinth of hermeneutic possibilities, how can we ever know which is the true path back to the supposedly originating scene?—they do militate against Bass and Davis's model of extracting repressed truths from the unconscious like so many bills from an automatic teller. Thus a classically trained psychoanalyst would hesitate to claim, as the mem-ory therapists do, that a dream—supposedly a mosaic of infantile and diurnal residues, of wish and defense, of confession and concealment—could be regarded as a direct source of information about the dreamer's early history or the identity of her suspected molester.

Then, too, there is the saving fact that psychoanalysis, in continual retreat from its founding (but unfounded) therapeutic claims, has long since ceased advertising itself as curative in any straightforward sense of the term. That development minimizes the risk that Freudian patients will be devastated in the ways that once beset Freud's personal practice and that now beset the recovered memory profession. "Hysteria," of course, has vanished along with the doctors who battened on it; the psychic mysteries into which Freudian patients now get initiated are reassuringly universal, banal, and devoid of clear implications for changing behavior; and fastidious criteria of selection tend to weed out nearly all applicants who are suffering from anything more wrenching than a wish to know themselves better. Though many recovered memory clients, too, enter therapy with only vague and mild complaints, the incest stories that are forced upon them guarantee a more brutal jarring of their equanimity and identity than any Freudian patient can now undergo.

When all this is said, however, there remains an important core of shared assumptions between psychoanalysis and its hyperactive young successor. These are:

1. To become mentally healthy, we must vent our negative feelings and relive our most painful psychic experiences. The deeper we delve, and the harsher and more bitter the truths that we drag to the surface, the better off we will be.

2. Through the aid of an objective therapist in whom we invest authority, trust, and love, we can not only arrive at an accurate diagnosis of our mental problems but also retrieve the key elements of our mental history in substantially accurate form, uncontaminated by the therapist's theoretical bias.

3. Our minds don't simply keep functioning when consciousness is absent; they feature an unconscious, a unique agency possessing its own special memories, interests, and rules of operation.

4. Everything that we experience is preserved in either conscious or unconscious (repressed) memory; "even things that seem completely forgotten are present somehow and somewhere . . ." (Freud 1953–1974, 23:260).

5. The content of our repressions is preponderantly sexual in nature. Therefore, sexual experiences can be regarded as bearing a unique

susceptibility to repression and can accordingly be considered the key determinants of psychic life.

6. The difficulty we meet in trying to recall our earliest years is attributable not, as neurologists believe, to the incomplete infantile development of our hippocampus and prefrontal cortex, but rather to extensive repression (see, e.g., 7:174–176), which in some instances can be successfully lifted. Inability to recall any other part of our past may therefore be assigned to that same cause.

7. The repressed unconscious continually tyrannizes over us by intruding its recorded-but-not-recalled fantasies and traumas upon our efforts to live in the present. "A humiliation that was experienced thirty years ago acts exactly like a fresh one throughout the thirty years . . ." (5:578).

8. Symptoms are "residues and mnemic symbols of particular (traumatic) experiences" (11:16), and "dreaming is another kind of remembering" (17:51). Consequently, a therapist's methodologically informed study of symptoms and dreams can lead (through however many detours) to faithful knowledge of an originating trauma.

9. Challenging though it may be, this work of reconstruction is made easier by the existence of a universally distributed store of unconscious equations between certain symbols and their fixed sexual meanings.

10. As a result of all these considerations, the most prudent and efficient way to treat psychological problems is not to address the patient's current situation, beliefs, and incapacities but to identify and remove the repressions that date from much earlier years.

All ten of these principles are erroneous or extremely open to doubt. Yet they are so widely believed as to constitute what Richard Wollheim and Thomas Nagel, among others, regard as the psychological common sense of our era (Wollheim 1993; Nagel 1994). For Nagel, indeed, this popularity serves as actual proof that Freud must have been on the right track; if the Freudian revelation has convinced people as savvy as ourselves, Nagel thinks, there must be something to it.[7] He might entertain second thoughts after realizing how the common sense of the 1990s, not unlike that of the 1690s, has run amok when taken literally by demonologists.

As Freud well appreciated when he chose as his epigraph for *The Interpretation of Dreams* Virgil's line about stirring up hell, psychoanalysis is already demonology. That is, it allegorizes the psychologically unknown as a dark power that must be coaxed forth, scrutinized, and kept in check by professionals who, incorruptible themselves by virtue of their faith and training, sniff out the hidden corruption of others. This sanctioned prurience is the thread that Mark Pendergrast traces from witch persecutions through mesmerism to hypnotherapy to psychoanalysis itself and, full circle, to the detection of Satanic abuse. Exactly that same compatibility between preindustrial and modern forms of superstition, we may recall, proved the undoing of the Freudian Christian Paul Ingram, who wrote in his diary after conferring with his fundamentalist pastor, "John thinks several spirits are in me yet, still in control of my unconscious. . . . [It] may take someone like John to guide me around my defenses" (Ofshe & Watters 1994, p. 172).

According to his confidant Sándor Ferenczi, the early Freud used to hurl himself body and soul against the forces that had invaded his patients' minds. He "worked passionately, devotedly, on the curing of neurotics," wrote Ferenczi in his diary, "(if necessary spending hours lying on the floor next to a person in a hysterical crisis)." Those were the work habits not of a fifty-minute psychoanalyst but of an exorcist. It was only after many therapeutic setbacks, Ferenczi reminded himself, that Freud came to call patients "a rabble," good for nothing but "to provide us with a livelihood and material to learn from" (Ferenczi 1988, p. 93). Eventually, his private pessimism about ever being able to cast out our psychic demons crept over his whole affluent institution, which now, in the 1990s, stands suddenly naked before the only skeptics it can't ignore, the insurers who decide what is and isn't a reimbursable form of treatment. The exorcist's fervor has passed into coarser and more passionate hands such as those of Bass and Davis.

But this is not to say that psychoanalysis is doomed to stand by helplessly while young fanatics strut upon the stage that Freud built. Since every Freudian concept and commitment is revisable in a pinch, we may yet see the emergence of a hybrid psychoanalysis that has borrowed new vitality from the recovered memory movement. Portents of such an eventuality can already be found. The psychoanalyst Lawrence Hedges, for example, has recently proposed that therapeutically retrieved molestation scenes are not exactly false; they may be screen memories for inferrable bad experiences suffered "[i]n utero and in the earliest months of life" (Hedges 1994, p. 15). In a book from the Analytic Press, Lynda Share similarly proposes that the interpretation of adult dreams can give us detailed knowledge of real traumas from early infancy (Share 1994). And in *Feminist Psychoanalytic Psychotherapy*, Charlotte Krause Prozan, who sensed which way the wind was blowing long ago, reports that whereas analysts used to be watchful for penis envy in women patients, today "we are looking for sexual abuse" (Prozan 1992, p. 207).

In a follow-up book Prozan offers a case history that dramatically embodies the blending of elements from standard psychoanalysis and therapy for repressed abuse. Prozan's treatment of "Penelope" was classically Freudian in its ground rules, in its heavy reliance on dream interpretation, and in its length—fourteen years. Although Penelope never did recall any molestation, Prozan wasn't fazed; as she reminds us, "[t]he phenomenon of not remembering . . . is in itself a symptom indicative of a severe traumatic experience" (Prozan 1993, p. 270). As an appointed termination date loomed, the frantic Penelope surrendered at last to Prozan's thirteen-year insistence that her dreams—of setting fires, of a van crashing into a house, of being shot by a man, of sex with Prozan herself—admitted of no other explanation than the enduring of anal rape by a family friend when she was nine years old.

Exiting psychoanalysis at age forty-nine, Penelope was still smoking, drinking, and binge eating—the behaviors she had entered treatment to bring under control. Now, as well, she was estranged from her unbelieving mother and sister. But she was glad, at least, to have puzzled out the identity of her abuser, "[t]hat SON OF A BITCH! It's totally his fault!" And she was eagerly looking forward to full-throttle survivorship in what she called "the days of being powerfully angry" (Prozan 1993, pp. 303, 308).

The disapproval that most psychoanalysts would feel upon reviewing this case is less significant than their substantial sharing of Prozan's axioms about the repressed unconscious, its modus operandi, and its amenability to symbolic decoding. Their confidence about such matters stems from the same source that encourages writers like Bass and Davis to trust their own findings—once again, "clinical experience" and its replication by other members of their sect. As Thomas Nagel innocently puts it, each doubtful hypothesis "has to find its empirical support in countless other applications to other patients in other settings." That is exactly the home-team approach to validation that produces abundant support for "facilitated communication," Satanic mind control, UFO abductions, previous incarnations, and telepathy—this last a favorite pastime of Freud's.

In a refreshingly sane essay, Paul R. McHugh, director of the Department of Psychiatry and Behavioral Science at the Johns Hopkins Medical Institutions, has depicted a long-term struggle, within the mental health disciplines, between what he called empiricists and romanticists—between, that is, those who bind themselves to methodical study of facts and those who "rely upon feelings for evidence, on metaphors for reality, on inspiration and myth for guidance" (McHugh 1994, p. 17). The essay is especially pertinent because it relegates both psychoanalysis and recovered memory therapy to the romanticist camp, where they surely belong. But it also relegates them to history's ashcan. In McHugh's opinion, the empiricists are winning hands down, because their insistence on real-world testing allows them to deliver what they promise, proven remedies for specific complaints.

In the long run this victory does look inevitable. For now, however,

I remain mindful of an earlier observation of McHugh's—that every ten years or so, "psychiatric practice has condoned some bizarre misdirection, proving all too often [that] the discipline has been captive of the culture" (McHugh 1992, p. 498). Out in the rough-and-tumble psychotherapeutic marketplace, to which our mental health associations discreetly turn their backs, Freudian clichés are breeding promiscuously with those of religious zealots, self-help evangelists, sociopolitical ideologues, and outright charlatans who trade in the ever seductive currency of guilt and blame. So long as "Freud's permanent revolution," as Nagel calls it, retains any sway, the voodoo of "the repressed" can be counted upon to return in newly energetic and pernicious forms.

Chapter 7

DEMONOLOGY FOR AN AGE OF SCIENCE

This article, first published in *Skeptic* magazine, May 1997, grew out of a talk I gave in January of the same year for the Justice Committee's "Day of Contrition–Revisited Convocation" in Salem, Massachusetts. The convocation was meant to rally support for alleged sexual male-factors who had been imprisoned as a result of coerced testimony from children or the therapeutically recovered memories of adults.

I.

This tricentennial observance of the Massachusetts Day of Contrition cannot fail to provoke somber and resolute thoughts in everyone who sees a parallel between the judicial horrors of the 1690s and those of the 1980s and 1990s. Although Salem has a further and more positive resonance for some of us who love the classics of American literature, the town inevitably calls to mind the aura of demented legalism that made the execution of so-called witches appear to be the only available course of action in 1692. Salem's own Nathaniel Hawthorne, for one, could not escape that theme, and without doubt it helped to color his imagination and make him a lifelong brooder about irreparable wrongs. One wonders what he would have said about the contemporary manias that have brought us here in protest today.

In his years as a struggling young author, Hawthorne frequently dwelt upon his Puritan ancestors, the authorized persecutors of heretics, and brooded about their less-than-noble motives. Was it simply religious fanaticism, he asked himself, or was it also prurience and sadism that impelled his great-great-great-grandfather, Major William Hathorne (1607–1681), to sentence a possibly psychotic Quaker woman to be stripped to the waist, bound to the tail of a cart, and whipped through the streets of Salem? "Feeling [the] symptoms [of sin] within the breast," Hawthorne wrote with a precocious scorn for manifest pretensions, "men concealed it with fear and shame, and were only the more cruel to those unfortunates whose pestiferous sores were flagrant to the common eye" (Hawthorne 1882–1889, 2:287).

And then there was Hawthorne's great-great-grandfather, Judge John Hathorne (1641–1717), who favored the death penalty not only for witchcraft but also for heresy, and who played a significant role in the judicial killings of 1692. Hawthorne had less to say about that tumultuous episode than we might have expected, but there can be no doubt that it fed both his morbidity and his irony. Men like John Hathorne struck him as being at once half deranged and intimidatingly vigorous and decisive—filled with a misguided conviction that made his own democratic mildness and self-doubt look like the consequence of some long hereditary degeneration. He *wanted* to represent those old Puritans as having hid from sexual self-knowledge and as having struck out obtusely at representatives of their own rejected impulses, but somehow the furtiveness he expected to find in his forefathers always appeared more descriptive of his own uncertain self. The real temper of the hanging, whipping, unhesitant Hathornes lay beyond his envious and belittlingly psychologizing grasp.

I have begun with this apparent digression partly because I happen to have published a book about Hawthorne in the mid-sixties, in my early days as a professor of literature—a book that pursued a Freudian line of argument that I now feel to have been largely mistaken (Crews 1966). But my mistake at least had its roots in what might be called Hawthorne's own proto-Freudianism. Any number of Hawthorne's sentences sound as if they had been plucked directly from the less technical, more Dostoevskian pronouncements of Freud. And the Viennese witch doctor, as Vladimir Nabokov maliciously but acutely called him, could only have applauded the idea that the judicial severity of John and William Hathorne must have taken its impetus from unconscious guilt, reaction formation, and projection. That was just what Hawthorne and Freud had most in common: a penchant for discounting altruistic motives and regarding consequential deeds as stemming from discomfort with the sordid contents of one's own mind. And, of course, we cannot deny that they both may have been right.

But we who have come to Salem are not here to play guessing games about motives. The issue before us is a practical one: how to right a public wrong that keeps recurring in new forms. If we are to take an effective stand not only against the current madness but against future versions of it as well, analytic understanding—but not necessarily *psycho*analytic understanding—of episodes like the 1692 witch hunt is imperative. Indeed, I want to suggest that Freud's and Hawthorne's emphasis on twisted personalities is exactly what we least need, because it obscures factors that we *can* satisfactorily grasp and control. It is not necessary, I will argue, that we peer into the hearts of judges and accusers, ferreting out their stifled lusts and compunctions. All we need is the right set of precautions, so that when a certain style of volatile illogic makes a renewed appearance, we can say, "No; here is the mistake you're making, and we won't allow you to break up families and send people to prison on such a faulty basis."

I can put this matter concretely by reference to a scene that most of us have recently observed. In the recent film adaptation of Arthur Miller's play *The Crucible*, none other than John Hathorne himself makes an appearance at one of those riveting, anguished moments when the whole hoax of demonic possession seems ready to unravel. Young Mary Warren has decided to confess that the bewitched girls have been faking it. Very well, then, says Hathorne, let's see you fall into a fit here and now. Mary tries and tries, but can't manage to swoon—and so Hathorne and the other examiners are reinforced in their belief that demons have taken charge of Salem, and the awful farce continues. Any private fantasies that Hathorne may conceivably be entertaining about Mary Warren at this moment are making no difference to the outcome. What matters is Hathorne's unawareness that fits can be induced in suggestible people by social contagion but are recalcitrant to the kind of tense effort Mary is making here (Spanos 1996). Let us be fair to the Puritan judges: surely they wouldn't have gone forward with their persecution if they had been able to realize that nothing in the events engulfing them was mysterious enough to call for a transcendent explanation.

The question, however, is whether even today we have a sufficient comprehension of popular delusions to reach agreement about the cognitive mistakes that allow them to flourish. Precisely because our culture is now predominantly secular and scientific, our latest witch hunts are couched in professional idioms that tend to lull our skepticism—the idioms, namely, of therapeutic concern, of deterministic depth-psychological forces, of social-scientific objectivity, and even of data-laden laboratory research. In order to become sufficiently alert, it is not enough that we recognize the outlandishness of certain kinds of claims, such as Mom and Dad's ritual barbecuing of babies on the patio's Weber grill. When patently ridiculous charges are made against parents or caregivers accused of sexual crimes, those charges are typically peeled away by shrewd prosecutors so that they can't devalue the "evidence" for other and more plausible-looking crimes by the same defendant. If we can't demonstrate the fallacies riddling *all* testimony that has been contaminated by the illegitimate way in which reputed memories were formed, we will go on allowing innocent people to be railroaded into prison.

Clarity on this point may be impeded by the fact that we are here to consider two kinds of rashness whose kinship is not immediately obvious. Most closely allied to the events of 1692 are the Little Rascals– or Wenatchee-style "sex ring" frenzies, with their uncontrolled propagation of rumor and their ever-widening net of accused parties. Rather different in appearance are the accusations, mostly but not exclusively sexual in nature, made by one adult against another based on "recall" of childhood memories that were supposedly repressed or dissociated until they emerged in therapy. I will be giving most of my attention to this second category of dubious charges, not because they are more destructive—far from it!—but because it is harder to reach consensus about the reforms they call for. We can all agree that coercive and unvideotaped interrogation of children must stop. But when it comes

to memory therapy, does the problem lie with ill-trained and impetu-
ous practitioners, or, as I suspect, is the most "scientific" training in
this art—such as we find, for example, in Kenneth S. Pope and Laura
S. Brown's high-toned *Recovered Memories of Abuse* (1996)—scarcely
better than the worst?

Let us begin by asking what is shared between our two classes of
misplaced zeal. We could say that both kinds of cases batten on the
fallibility of memory, but there is only a distant resemblance between
so-called recovered memory twenty years after the fact and a child's
coerced consent to a social worker's or detective's insinuations about
what happened in the daycare center or church basement a few weeks
or months before. The credentialed authorities require no theory
of psychogenic amnesia in order to assert that the children had
simply been afraid to relate what they had undergone until the helpful
psychologist brought out the anatomically correct dolls and went to
work establishing a schedule of reinforcements for eliciting "the truth."
We must look instead to theoretical understanding of the real common
denominator here—namely, *suggestion*, or the unremarked flow of ideas,
feelings, or "recollections" from a dominant to a subordinate party, so
that the latter has the impression of having arrived at those ideas, feelings, or recollections independently.[1]

Right away, however, I want to head off a likely misapprehension. It is
wrong to think of suggestion as a phenomenon that operates completely
apart from the consent of the influenced person. There is always a proffered benefit for going along with the suggester's notion. As both versions of *The Crucible* indicate through their unresolved ambiguities, we
cannot always establish a clear border between an effect of suggestion
and an outright dissimulation. Even a faked panic attack can become
a real one in the acting, and a falsehood can acquire the strength of a
conviction once the consequences of being found out have escalated.
As in *The Crucible* once again, the whole community, or that part of it
that fixes rewards and penalties, can become an agent of suggestion,
transmitting the message that persistence in an already consequential
pretense is *de rigueur*; and those who get the message can be self-aware

to a degree yet increasingly "sincere" as their options narrow and their expected role is delineated more urgently.

That pattern is as common today as it was in 1692. Thus a child, learning from an interrogator that approbation and freedom from more grilling will be forthcoming only when certain alleged incidents are agreed to, may be conscious of fibbing when he or she first assents to the interrogator's demand; but soon thereafter the stakes will be raised, and the child's reality-testing criteria for recalling what did or didn't happen will be an early casualty (Ceci & Bruck 1995). The same confusion doomed Paul Ingram in Olympia, Washington, when he was assured by his fellow sheriffs that the relevant memories of his crimes against his daughter would come flooding back just as soon as he signed a confession (Wright 1994). And of course there is the far more usual case of the young adult whose therapist has convinced her that surcease from her worsening depression, disorientation, nightmares, and hallucinations will come only after she has recalled the identity of the "perpetrator" who is ultimately responsible for them. That promise of relief is rarely fulfilled, but meanwhile, the patient gets sucked into a vortex of paranoid survivorhood, and further "memories" are sure to follow.

Daycare pupils, when being insistently debriefed, and patients undergoing recovered memory therapy necessarily show signs of stress, just as wrongly accused criminal suspects do under intense and prolonged questioning. It is usual in all three types of inquiry to encourage visualizations and hypothetical role playing that raise the subject's anxiety level and create uncertainty as to what really happened; then it is a small step to turn conditionals into declarations of fact (Ofshe & Leo 1997). Rational reflection tells us that the grilling itself is probably responsible for the victim's mounting vertigo in such situations, but rational reflection is exactly what is often missing from all three contexts. The criminal investigator is looking to extort a confession; the questioner of children wants confirmation of what he thinks he already knows; and the recovered memory therapist has staked a whole practice on obscuring the difference between fantasized images and recall of events. Consequently, all three inquirers are prone to the same error, that of interpreting the subject's agitation as confirmatory evidence of the hypothesized deed, consciousness of which is now supposedly rising to the surface of the subject's mind.

This is the twentieth century's version of Salem's "spectral evidence," whereby a seeming or actual fit was taken as proof that demons were flying across the room from an accused person to the tormented one. Of course, most—not all—detectives and social workers rule out the likelihood of demonic influence, but they honor exactly the same forensic logic as the Puritans did, excluding from consideration the suggestive effect of their own conduct and belief system and assuming instead that an invisible agency must be at work in causing the subject to be miserable. It makes little difference whether that agency is thought to be Satan's or that of a mental homunculus who hoards the toxic secrets of the past. In both cases the key point is that Ockham's razor, or a preference for explanations entailing the fewest number of unproven assumptions, is being laid aside: an explanation relying on mechanisms that may not exist is forestalling a straightforward analysis of influence and reward in the here and now.

Once we have grasped the link between blindness to suggestion and diagnostic "wildness," a clarifying light is shed on some important and otherwise puzzling matters. Why do different schools of psychotherapy encounter such disparate kinds of ailments? Why, for example, do a minority of practitioners unearth almost all the cases of past-life regression, forgotten-then-remembered incest, and multiple personality (or "dissociated identity") disorder? If suggestion weren't being exercised, wouldn't those cases be more evenly distributed? When we look closely, we discover that the "multiples" are rarely identified prior to therapy but more typically during its course. What an eloquent and appalling fact! Moreover, the treatment regimens that regularly unearth dramatic but unreproducible findings about the repressed past tend to rely heavily on hypnosis and/or related techniques of inducing compliant states (Orne 1959). The egregious cases of wrongly implanted belief that end up in court, we must conclude, are just the tip of a vast iceberg. It seems that the profession of "dynamic" (conflict-oriented) psychotherapy, for all its good intentions, is prone to an epistemological naiveté that produces the very same results as outright fraud would do.

2.

One might think that the correction of this deplorable state of affairs would be an uppermost concern of our professional therapeutic guilds. Unfortunately, however, the reality is that too much money, power, and self-regard are already committed to practices that are scientifically and medically indefensible. Witness the much remarked failure of the American Psychological Association's Working Group on Investigation of Memories of Childhood Abuse, composed equally of clinicians and academic psychologists, to agree on the very existence of a serious problem of malpractice, much less on its solution. Their quarrel came down to a stark confrontation between two kinds of expertise, with experimental prudence about the nature of memory going *mano a mano* with "clinical knowledge," alias the memory business as it has been practiced throughout the past decade. Since the healers and the researchers occupied different epistemic universes, they could do little besides fire off bitter critiques of one another.

Interestingly, both parties in the APA working group were able to cite abundant research findings in support of their positions. If one equates science with an arraying of supportive empirical studies, then each side was impressively "scientific." The clinicians, however, did a most unscientific two-step that is characteristic of recovered memory apologetics:[2] they invoked findings about the physiological effects of *known* trauma when, of course, the whole issue is whether a trauma "recovered" in therapy ever occurred in the first place; and they bridged the gap between such technical-looking irrelevancies and that main issue by invoking a special privilege for clinically acquired knowledge. The theory of recovered memory, they claimed, is validated by "one hundred years of case descriptions" going back to early reports by Freud and Pierre Janet (Alpert et al. 1996, p. 138)—reports, they neglected to mention, that utterly failed to demonstrate their imputed link between trauma and repressed or dissociated mental contents.[3] But more shocking than that omission was the therapists' begging the question of faulty premises by appealing to the sheer number of clinical findings that have been derived from those very premises.

The working group's memory researchers acquitted themselves much better, as one would expect from the prominent role that the study of suggestion has played in academic psychology for the past eighty-five years, ever since the secret of the horse Clever Hans's power of computation was unlocked by attention to his master's inadvertent signals. Our whole idea of a well-designed experiment in psychology and other social disciplines is based largely on precautions against the contaminating effects of "demand characteristics" that shape a subject's responses (Orne 1962) and "experimenter effects" that arise when the same person who devised a study is allowed to score its results (Rosenthal 1994). Not surprisingly, then, the APA's researchers couldn't countenance the therapists' claim that clinical experience, a notorious breeding ground of self-validation, ought to be considered a uniquely reliable source of knowledge about the causes and effects of dissociated consciousness (Ornstein et al. 1996).

If being on guard against suggestion is both the theoretical and the practical key to averting future witch hunts, however, I must point out that we are a long way from being adequately forearmed. Even the APA's psychology professors tended to fall in with the clinicians' assumption that suggestion operates only when certain obvious techniques of relaxing self-control are "improperly" used. Such an emphasis scapegoats the marginal practitioners in a field that regularly and "respectably" turns its clients into converts to the therapist's pet notions, often without recourse to "truth serums" or hypnosis. Indeed, an awareness of being hypnotized is sometimes all that a sophisticated patient needs to discount any belief claims that may emerge from the session, whereas suggestion may work most efficiently when neither party realizes it is taking place (Borch-Jacobsen 1996a, 1996b). In particular, the more pains a recovered memory therapist takes to be tentative and modest about the likelihood of a hidden history of sexual abuse, the fewer alarm signals may be triggered and the greater the likelihood that the patient will reach the same conclusion "on his own."

And this brings me to a pivotal observation. Witch hunts and their modern derivatives are facilitated not just by the bare phenomenon of suggestion in the torture chamber, the consulting room, or the police station but by the demonological character of the suggester's background assumptions—that is, by a sanctioned worldview whereby possession of the subject's psyche by alien forces is regarded as a normal possibility. When John Hathorne in *The Crucible* finds that Mary Warren can't self-induce a fit, he doesn't just tell himself that his experiment has reached a negative finding; rather, he falls back on the only alternative available to him, the theory of Satanic infestation of souls. In like manner, our doctors of recovered memory have at the ready a theory of split-off mental contents amounting to a second self within the subject; and that theory is evidently more palpable to them than their own cognitive and emotional dominance within the therapeutic dyad. Moreover, the very fact that the dogma of repression/dissociation recommends itself as "science"—the fruit of unimpeachable discoveries from the laboratory and the clinic—makes it an ideal modern conveyor of illusions.

Whether it was actually Freud or Janet who bequeathed us our psychodynamic version of haunted consciousness is a debated point. Janet himself repeatedly complained that Freud's "repression" was a plagiarized version of his own "dissociation" (e.g., Janet 1914–15), which has come to stand for a more radical kind of forgetfulness and self-division but which originally covered much the same ground as Freud's idea. But it was Freud whose system of thought permeated our medical and intellectual culture, becoming, as it were, the water in which the sharks of memory therapy could swim. And it is the precedent of Freud's "seduction theory," which he abandoned in 1897 without correcting the method of investigation that had generated it, to which the modern advocates of recovered memory have appealed.[4]

Moreover, the distance separating psychoanalysis from recovered memory therapy has recently begun to narrow in an ominous manner. Although some Freudians continue to deny the fact,[5] it is no longer a secret that American psychoanalysis now harbors a thriving branch of recovered memory practice, differing in no essential respect from Freud's quest for "seductions" in the mid-1890s. Nor is this the first such reversion in psychoanalytic history. The same thing happened once before when Sándor Ferenczi decided around 1930 that Freud had been right the first time about his patients' childhood abuse.[6] As both Ferenczi and the new recovered-memory Freudians could attest, to move from "psychoanalysis proper" back to the seduction theory requires only a minor adjustment of perspective—the same adjustment that Freud had made in the opposite direction when he decided that his patients must be repressing their sexual fantasies rather than their memories of violation.

Tellingly, historians now recognize that the Freudian idea of the repressed unconscious arose from a series of missed opportunities to take proper note of suggestion. First there was Jean-Martin Charcot's mistaken inference that his hypnotized "hysterics," when they suffered temporary paralyses of their limbs, were showing their underlying medical conditions rather than the effects of coaching and hypnosis itself. Freud's witnessing of those specious demonstrations in 1885–1886, and especially his agreement with Charcot's inference that unconscious trauma-generated ideas must be triggering the patients' paralyses (Spanos 1996; Borch-Jacobsen 1997), became the unshakeable core of his faith in the mind's capacity to will itself into ignorance of its own traumatic past. Second, Freud extended the applicability of Charcot's faulty insight by adopting Hippolyte Bernheim's use of posthypnotic suggestion in psychotherapy while overriding Bernheim's caution about using hypnosis as a biographical investigative aid.[7] And third, Freud regarded or pretended to regard Breuer's Anna O. (Bertha Pappenheim) as someone whose hysterical symptoms had been banished through memory retrieval. On the contrary, we can now perceive Pappenheim's dubious "cure" to have been yet another case of hypnotic suggestion and autosuggestion—a case in which the disease itself, whatever its underlying reality, was given shape by the proffered treatment and by the patient's own hypochondriacal fertility of imagination.

Before long, of course, Freud dispensed with hypnosis as an overt clinical tool. But the outlines of his theory of mind were largely settled by the time he did so, and his suggestion-based "clinical validations" of his patients' reconstructed childhood vicissitudes continued apace. Those reconstructions depended crucially on an ur-premise that would allow both Freud and his recovered memory successors to be supremely confident of their ability to peer into the past—the principle, namely, that thematic material surfacing in therapy must have radiated forward from the big bang of an originating childhood trauma. Yet no evidence in favor of that proposition has ever been found. It is, quite simply, a throwback to the tribal witch doctor's belief in "like makes like" magic, whereby both diagnostic and curative significance is ascribed to mere imagery contained in dreams and trances (Scharnberg 1993).

As the American psychiatrist John Whitehorn, writing of schizo-phrenia, observed in 1952, the "ready disclosure of . . . psychoanalyti-cally 'symbolic' material may be compared to the disclosure of inti-mate housekeeping details by the collapse of the facade of a bombed apartment house. Many schizophrenic patients happen, by reason of their particular form of reaction, to drop the social facade maintained so meticulously by ordinary mortals" (quoted by Guze 1992, p. 16). In this analogy, the bomb corresponds to the actual, probably biochemical, cause of schizophrenia. But for merely unhappy people being treated both aggressively and psychodynamically, the bomb more typically goes off in the doctor's office, where symptom manufacture is encouraged as progress toward confrontation with the repressed, and where the patient learns to attach a soul-wrenching, often accusatory autobio-graphical significance to the fruits of suggestion.

In Freud's therapeutic work, the path to that illusion was consider-ably smoothed by his doctrine of transference—perhaps the one aspect of his system still endorsed in name by all psychodynamic schools. When patients showed ingratiating or hostile responses to Freud's overbearing manner and wild surmises, reference to transference allowed him to maintain that he was just acting as a neutral screen for the projection of early oedipal conflicts. His assertion that he was not the real object of the patients' feelings served at once to "prove" the hardihood of early neurotic patterns and the need for more therapy, to make the patient doubt her very capacity to say what she meant, and to delegitimize any efforts to criticize Freud himself or to redress the drastic inequality between the two parties—an inequality that itself pushed the deprived and humbled initiate toward eventually becoming a disciple of the Freudian system (Gellner 1996).

By now, of course, "narrativists" and "constructivists" within dynamic therapy have emptied transference and its corollary, the therapist's own "countertransference," of most of their original meaning. But those concepts get reinvigorated in a new and sinister way when analysts decide to part company with the Oedipus complex and go into business as recovered memory practitioners. Appealing more often to Janet's dissociation than to Freud's repression, they now fancy that they can communicate, through sheer empathy, with those fragments of the patient's personality that must have been split off when the putative sexual trauma occurred:

> As I come to occupy my patient's internal world, to reside experientially within it, I surely come to know, in the most intimate of ways, my fellow inhabitant's [sic], her internal objects and their accompanying self-representations. I interact with them, I act like them, ultimately I will become them! (Davies 1996, p. 209)

Even more remarkably, this mediumistic feat on the analyst's part is actually taken to be corroborative of the fateful deed.

Here we witness the complete triumph of suggestion over inferential prudence. Like other recovered memory therapists, this psychoanalyst is unconcerned that she herself may have helped to shape her patient's "internal objects." The patient as a troubled individual has virtually disappeared, replaced by voices that only the therapist/adept can hear and identify. When such pretensions are advanced as cutting-edge theory, the veil of cool empirical rationality momentarily drops away; countertransference is refigured as channeling; and we find ourselves effectively restored to the seventeenth century, the last age in which significant numbers of learned Western doctors believed that they could coax out demons from the afflicted.

I, too, hear voices at this juncture—a chorus of psychoanalysts protesting, "This has nothing to do with us! You are talking about rogue therapists who are flouting the circumspect and open-ended ethos of psychoanalysis as it has developed after Freud. Psychoanalysis is not about victimization but about allowing clients to realize who they are and to set their own goals." To which I reply: psychoanalysis is many things to many people, and right now a fierce battle over its proper character is being waged before our eyes. Let the old-line Freudians worry about establishing what constitutes orthodoxy and heresy; our concern is with preventing harm. And it is quite apparent that the psychoanalytic model of the mind, once it gets rejoined to Freud's original project of intuiting long-past acts of molestation, is a formidable instrument for generating anguish and injustice.

3.

It is, indeed, precisely a *theoretical* kinship, a shared conception of mental self-division, that links our contemporary hunt for "perpetrators" both to Freud's nineteenth-century effort and to the campaign against bewitchment in 1692. On this point I can summon an impressive witness, Sigmund Freud himself.[8] It is a little-known but significant fact that Freud was an avid student of witchcraft and its detection. In 1897 he bought a copy of the infamous *Malleus Maleficarum [The Hammer of Witches]*, the fifteenth-century persecution manual that makes a brief appearance in *The Crucible*; and he was a great admirer of Johann Weier, the sixteenth-century Dutch author of *De Praestigiis Daemonum et Incantationibus ac Veneficiis [On the Deceptions and Incantations of Demons and on*

Poisoners], a book widely credited with having slowly—all too slowly!—taught civil and religious authorities to disbelieve in the very existence of witchcraft.[9]

Freud's regard for Weier would appear to comport well with his famous secular rationalism, but nothing is ever simple when one is dealing with the founder of psychoanalysis. Like Weier, Freud was intrigued by reports that a certain number of accused witches actually came to admit that they *were* witches. In Weier's sensible judgment, torture was causing some victims to hallucinate and others to end their ordeal by agreeing to charges that they knew to be false. The crafty Freud, however, begged to differ. At first, during the period of his "seduction theory," he hypothesized that the "witches" may have been victims of sexual abuse whose repressed unconscious retained a sense of devilish goings-on. Later, once he had decided that his patients hadn't been forced into perverse acts in childhood, he changed his mind about the witches as well. Now their references to demons stood not for molesters but only for "bad and reprehensible wishes, derivatives of instinctual impulses that have been repudiated and repressed" (Freud 1953–1974, 19:72).

These seemingly opposite views on Freud's part are alike in one chilling and critically important respect: they take no account whatsoever of the circumstances in which confessions were extracted from the accused. As Freud told the Vienna Psychoanalytic Society in 1909, speaking about visions of flying through the air and consorting sexually with the Devil, "We find unmistakably infantile elements in those fantasies that were not created under torture but merely squeezed out by it" (Nunberg & Federn 1967, 2:123). Which is to say that in Freud's view, "witches" *were* guilty, not of sorcery but of lewd and twisted thoughts rattling about in their heads. Confessions of witchcraft, then, properly interpreted, were just a matter of getting in touch with the repressed.

Freud evidently felt that he had the very best authority for regarding witches as hysterics. In his 1893 obituary of his idol Charcot, he praised the latter for having "thrown the whole weight of his authority on the side of the genuineness and objectivity of hysterical phenomena" (Freud 1953–1974, 3:19)—phenomena that Charcot, who "drew copiously upon the surviving reports of witch trials and of posses-sion" (3:20), regarded as having been objectively validated in precisely those records. Thus Freud adopted Charcot's own tunnel vision of the Christian West's most gruesome aberration, ascribing "hysteria" to the victims rather than to the perpetrators of a vast atrocity. In doing so, Freud celebrated in Charcot the very flaw that would eventually tarnish both of their scientific reputations: a refusal to make allowance for coer-cion, compliance, collusion, and outright malingering in the production of supposedly objective "symptoms," from the dungeons of the Middle Ages through the demonstration amphitheater in the Salpêtrière.

It was left to Breuer and Janet, Freud's obituary essay went on, to realize that Charcot's work with hypnotically provoked paralyses must entail the idea of a "splitting of consciousness" (3:20), the only assump-tion that might explain why "a hysterical patient is overcome by an affect about whose cause he asserts that he knows nothing" (3:19). That, of course, was exactly the Salem judges' way of accounting for the "symp-toms" displayed by Abigail Williams, Mary Warren, and the others: a second self must have taken up residence within them. Knowing about the girls' dissimulation, we must find the analogy troubling.

Freud, however, was positively exhilarated to reach across the centu-ries and salute his spiritual colleagues, the diagnosticians of possession. "By pronouncing possession by a demon to be the cause of hysterical phenomena," he averred, "the Middle Ages in fact chose this solution [the splitting of consciousness]; it would only have been a matter of exchanging the religious terminology of that dark and superstitious age for the scientific language of today" (3:20). Or, as he would put it with a certain defiance thirty years later, "The demonological theory of those dark times has won in the end against all the somatic views of the period of 'exact' science" (Freud 1953–1974, 19:72).

Because of this perceived theoretical kinship, Freud could not bring himself to condemn the torturing inquisitors of the Middle Ages. Their stern measures were hardly his own, but he had to admit that they had been efficacious in teasing the unconscious into surrendering its shameful contents. As he wrote to Wilhelm Fliess in 1897, he could now understand "the *harsh therapy* of the witches' judges" (Freud 1985, p. 227; emphasis added). And indeed, it was not just theory but also therapeutic practice that bound him to the witchcraft inquisitors.

Freud himself, in the mid-1890s, was prodding his patients into concocting "scenes," not of witchcraft but of forced sexual initiations purporting to have set in motion the workings of neurosis.[10] "Would you believe," he wrote to Fliess in 1896, "that the reluctance to drink beer and to shave was elucidated by a scene in which a nurse sits down *podice nudo* [with bare buttocks] in a shallow shaving bowl filled with beer in order to let herself be licked . . . ?" (Freud 1985, p. 218). Or a few weeks later: "Would you please try to search for a case of childhood convulsions that you can trace back . . . to sexual abuse, specifically to *lictus* [licking] (or finger) in the anus[?] . . . For my newest finding is that I am able to trace back with certainty a patient's attack that merely resembled epilepsy to such treatment by the tongue on the part of his nurse. Age 2 years" (Freud 1985, pp. 223–224). Or consider the following passage from a letter written in the same month, January 1897; the patient in this instance is the posthumously notorious Emma Eckstein, whose nose Fliess had surgically disfigured with Freud's connivance two years earlier. "Imagine," writes Freud, "I obtained a scene about the circumcision of a girl. The cutting off of a piece of the labium minor (which is even shorter today), sucking up the blood, after which the child was given a piece of the skin to eat" (Freud 1985, p. 227).

Here we find ourselves, astonishingly, standing within the horror-movie portals of "Satanic ritual abuse." Thanks to his Lamarckian assumptions about the hereditary transmission of memory traces, Freud suspected that the fantasies he was extracting from Eckstein actually pointed to the existence of dark cults and sordid practices near the dawn of civilization. "I am beginning to grasp an idea," he wrote in the same letter: "it is as though in the perversions, of which hysteria is the negative, we have before us a remnant of a primeval sexual cult, which once was—perhaps still is—a religion in the Semitic East (Moloch, Astarte). . . . I dream, therefore, of a primeval devil religion with rites that are carried on secretly . . ." (Freud 1985, p. 227). And it is at this moment that Freud expresses solidarity with the witch interrogators. They may have been wrong about their victims' connection to dia-bolical cults *just then*, he seems to say, but they were only off by a few thousand years. Here is Freud approximating the role of Hawthorne's zaniest monomaniac, Ethan Brand.

Of course, no social harm can come from attempts to intuit pre-antiquity on the basis of one's patients' imagery; it is just gnostic folly pure and simple, like declaring oneself a reincarnated gladiator or druid priestess. But plenty of harm attached to Freud's taking the "scenes" as proof of childhood sexual abuse. A representative passage from the let-ters to Fliess shows how callously he went about the business of bullying a patient and setting her against her dumbfounded father:

> When I thrust the explanation at her, she was at first won over; then she committed the folly of questioning the old man himself, who at the very first intimation exclaimed indignantly, "Are you implying that I was the one?" and swore a holy oath to his innocence.
>
> She is now in the throes of the most vehement resistance, claims to believe him, but attests to her identification with him by hav-ing become dishonest and swearing false oaths. I have threatened to send her away and in the process convinced myself that she has already gained a good deal of certainty which she is reluctant to acknowledge.
>
> She has never felt as well as on the day when I made the disclo-sure to her. In order to facilitate the work, I am hoping she will feel miserable again. (Freud 1985, pp. 220–221)

If Freud had enjoyed a wider and more sympathetic audience in the 1890s, it seems that he could have ended the decade by writing not *The Interpretation of Dreams* but a macho version of *The Courage to Heal.*

The founding gesture of "psychoanalysis proper" was a step back from wild accusations toward inconsequentiality; no one could be held criminally accountable for the fact that neurotics were suffering from their own fantasies. In its social effects, however, Freud's eventual psychology was far from inconsequential. As the feminists who founded

our recovered memory movement correctly alleged, classical psychoanalysis actually gave child molesters an alibi by ascribing seductive
designs to small children themselves and by dismissing accounts of
always remembered rape as mere "screen memories" defending against
those oedipal wishes (Simon 1992). We are paying dearly today for the
understandable anger generated by such quackery.

Should we at least be grateful that psychoanalytic theory as it is usually apprehended produces more introspection than litigation? Obviously not, since that theory lends itself so readily to new therapeutic fads
purporting to find evidence of past crimes in "the repressed." Three
times thus far, from Freud's "seduction" phase through Ferenczi's own
to our present crisis, we have seen outbreaks of inquisitorial mania based
on the same premises about the hidden unconscious mind and its pre-
eminently sexual concerns; and the last of these eruptions has become
what the others might well have been, a mass delusion.

Ironically, it is when psychoanalysis swerves from philosophical posturing back toward the medical model—that is, toward attempted correlations between specific neurotic manifestations and specific etiolo-
gies (Guze 1992)—that it becomes dangerous again, because at such
moments its old vice of construing themes as causes assumes a lunatic
forensic cast. If we persist in regarding classical analysis and its tamer
offshoots as "science" while condemning seduction theories as perversions of an otherwise well-founded doctrine, then we can count on the
emergence of new recovered memory movements ad infinitum.

Chapter 8

THE TRAUMA TRAP

This chapter appeared in the March 24, 2004, issue of *The New York Review of Books*. In considering two works of very different perspective and merit, it showed that, even after the plague of recovered memory had been brought largely under control in North America, its theoretical champions were continuing to advocate dangerously erroneous notions about traumatic memory and appropriate treatment for its effects.

I.

Every now and then a book appears that can be instantly recognized as essential for its field—a work that must become standard reading if that field is to be purged of needless confusion and fortified against future errors of the same general kind. Such a book is *Remembering Trauma*, by the Harvard psychology professor Richard J. McNally (2003). To be sure, the author's intention is not revolutionary but only consolidating; he wants to show what has already been learned, through well-designed experiments and analyses of records, about the effects that psychological trauma typically exerts on our memory. But what has been learned is not what is widely believed, and McNally is obliged to clear away a heap of junk theory. In doing so, he provides a brilliant object lesson in the exercise of rational standards that are common to every science deserving of the name.

McNally's title, *Remembering Trauma*, neatly encapsulates the opposing views that, for a whole generation now, have made the study of trauma into psychology's most fiercely contested ground. Are scarring experiences well remembered in the usual sense of the term, or can some of them be remembered only much later, after the grip of a self-protective psychological mechanism has been relaxed? This is the pivotal issue that McNally decisively resolves. In the process, he also sheds light on a number of related questions. Does memory of trauma stand apart neurologically from normal memory? Does a certain kind of traumatic experience leave recognizable long-term effects that can vouch for its historical reality? What memory problems typify post-traumatic stress disorder, and does the disorder itself "occur in nature" or is it a cultural construct? And is memory retrieval a well-tested and effective means of helping adults to shed depression, anxiety, and other psychological afflictions?

One extended trauma, a public one, that won't be soon forgotten by the involved parties is central to McNally's argument. I refer to the great sex panic that gripped this continent from about 1985 to 1994. It wasn't just an epidemic of runaway fear, rumor, and persecution but a grimly practical test of the theories whose currency made it possible. And the theories at issue were precisely those that are exhaustively reviewed in *Remembering Trauma*. McNally uses that chapter of our history to show just how much damage can be done when mistaken ideas about the mind get infused with ideological zeal.

In the 1980s, as McNally relates, daycare workers risked prosecution and imprisonment on the coerced testimony of bewildered and intimidated three-year-olds who were prodded to "remember" nonexistent molestations. Meanwhile, poorly trained social workers, reasoning that signs of sexual curiosity in children must be "behavioral memories" of rape, were charging parents with incest and consigning their stunned offspring to foster homes. And most remarkably, whole communities were frantically attempting to expose envisioned covens of Satan worshipers who were said, largely on the basis of hypnotically unlocked "memories," to be raising babies for sexual torture, ritual murder, and cannibal feasts around the patio grill.

In the same period many psychotherapists, employing hypnosis, dream analysis, "guided imagery," "age regression," and other suggestion-amplifying devices, persuaded their mostly female patients to "remember" having been molested by their fathers or stepfathers through much of their childhood, in some cases with the active participation of their mothers. The "perpetrators" thus fingered were devastated, embittered, and often publicly shamed, and only a minority of their accusers eventually recanted. Many, in fact, fell in with their therapists' belief that young victims of sexual trauma, instead of consciously recalling what was done to them, are likely to develop multiple personalities. Disintegrating further, those unfortunates were then sent off to costly "dissociative identity" wards, where their fantasies of containing five, a dozen, or even hundreds of inner selves were humored until their insurance coverage expired and they were abandoned in a crazed condition. At the height of the scare, influential traumatologists were opining that "between twenty and fifty percent of psychiatric patients suffer from dissociative disorders" (van der Kolk & van der Hart 1991, p. 432)—disorders whose reported incidence plummeted toward zero as soon as some of the quacks who had promoted them began to be sued for malpractice.[1]

What we experienced, McNally shows, was a perfect storm, with forces for mischief converging from every side. The fraudulent 1973 best seller *Sybil* had already helped to relaunch the long-dormant fad of multiple personality and to link it to childhood sexual abuse.[2] Beginning in the early 1980s, the maverick Swiss psychoanalyst Alice Miller taught many American readers what Sigmund Freud had once believed, that memories of early abuse are typically repressed and must be therapeutically unlocked if the resultant neuroses are to be cured. Jeffrey Masson's melodramatic book of 1984, *The Assault on Truth*, misrepresenting Freud's "seduction" patients as self-aware incest victims rather than as the doubters that they remained, fanned the feminist anger that Miller had aroused, encouraging women to believe that molestation by fathers must be pervasive.[3] Self-help manuals such as *The Courage to Heal* (Bass & Davis 1988) then equipped scientifically ignorant psychotherapists with open-ended "symptom checklists," ensuring that their patients would be diagnosed as suffering from buried memories of violation. And all the while, Geraldo Rivera and less cynical alarmists were whipping up fear of murderous devil cults.

If the origins of our mass delusion were complex, its dissipation in the mid-1990s is easily explained. Like the Salem witch hunt three centuries earlier, the sex panic had no internal brake that could prevent its accusations from racing beyond all bounds of credibility. The stirring motto "Believe the children" began to sound hollow when preschoolers who finally agreed that they must have been inappropriately touched went on to describe having been dropped into a pool of sharks or turned into a mouse. The medical records of some alleged rape victims showed that they had still been virgins at a later period. In one notorious case, influential at first in promoting recovered memory but later in discrediting it, a woman who got her father sentenced to life in prison for a murder/rape she had remembered in hypnotic trances went on to recall his killing of another person who proved to be wholly imaginary (see pp. 96–105). And many patients, when urged to dig deeper after producing a vague scene or two, reduced the process to self-travesty by conjuring surreal orgies with Daddy's bridge partners, visiting uncles, and the family pets.

One recovered memory case in particular, less absurd than most but nevertheless lacking in prima facie plausibility, set in motion what the movement's loyalists now bitterly characterize as "the backlash." In 1991 the future "betrayal trauma" psychologist Jennifer J. Freyd, after her therapist had pointedly asked her in their second encounter whether she had ever been abused, suddenly "remembered" that her father had continually molested her between the ages of three and sixteen (see Brown et al. 1998, p. 16). It was Freyd's mother, Pamela, convinced that she would surely have noticed some effects of countless domestic sex crimes against her daughter, who then made contact with other recently accused parents and established the False Memory Syndrome Foundation. Under Pamela Freyd's leadership, the foundation (on whose advisory board I serve) gathered and disseminated the most authoritative scientific judgments about trauma, memory, and suggestive influence—judgments that swayed enough jurists, legislators, and journalists to bring a healthy skepticism into play.

What put Jennifer Freyd's "memories" in question wasn't just their dissonance with her mother's close observation. By alleging fourteen years' worth of molestations that had been unknown to her conscious mind prior to a therapist's prompting, Freyd was invoking an outlandish new defense mechanism. Granted, some psychologists still believed in repression, or the sequestering of a disagreeable thought or memory inside "the unconscious"; and others subscribed to dissociation, the more radical knack of "splitting the self" so quickly that no narrative memory of the trauma gets formed at all. But Freyd's story, like many others that surfaced during the sex panic, stretched those principles to cover any number of serial traumatic incidents, as if a person could be subjected to the same outrage hundreds of times without taking cognitive note of it.

This cumulative forgetting of harmful experience is what the social psychologist Richard Ofshe disdainfully named *robust repression*—a startlingly maladaptive behavior that, if actual, ought to have aroused wonder and consternation from the earliest times until now, if indeed it didn't lead to the extinction of our species. Before the American 1980s, however, it had apparently never once been remarked. Could robust repression itself have been robustly repressed throughout the millennia?

Most recovered memory advocates have ducked the conundrum of robust repression, and some have dismissed it as an alien notion devised by their adversaries. But the alleged phenomenon, McNally shows, is nothing other than the "massive repression" posited by such prominent traumatologists as Judith Lewis Herman, Judith L. Alpert, Lenore C. Terr, and Jennifer Freyd herself, each of whom understood that claims of sudden access to a long string of previously unsuspected horrors require a basis in theory. What could that basis be? McNally makes short work of the only systematic attempts, Terr's and Freyd's, to maintain that serial traumas are easier to forget than single ones. Moreover, all such efforts are doomed to be question begging, because the only evidence favoring robust repression consists of the very memories whose authenticity hangs in doubt.

The same stricture applies, however, to repression and dissociation per se. Those notions became current in the 1880s and 1890s when

Freud and Pierre Janet independently attempted to trace the then fashionable complaint of hysteria to pathogenic hidden memories and to
expunge the ailment through hypnotically induced recall. Freud, by far
the more influential figure, clung to repression—though rendering it
progressively more elastic and ambiguous—even while repeatedly distancing himself from the diagnostic and curative claims he had inferred
from its supposed workings.

Before he was finished, Freud had conceived of repression as both a
conscious and an unconscious process acting upon feelings, thoughts,
ideas, and fantasies as well as memories. Such profligacy left repression
without any operational meaning; "the repressed" was simply any material that Freud, who was given to ascribing his own punning associations to his patients' minds, chose to identify as having been dismissed
from awareness. Yet the long vogue of psychoanalysis kept the concept
alive, enabling it to be virulently readapted, a century after its formal
introduction, to the same task of recruiting patients to victimhood that
had preoccupied its champion in 1895–1896.

As McNally explains through deftly analyzed examples, it isn't just
therapists and their patients who fail to ask prudent questions about the
repression or dissociation of trauma. The body of research purporting
to validate those mechanisms is riddled with procedural errors, most of
which stem from naive trust in the retrospection of subjects who have
already been led to believe that they must have undergone a trauma
that was then sequestered from memory. Along with such other inquirers as David Holmes (1990) and Harrison G. Pope, Jr., et al. (1999),
McNally understands that a good test of repression or dissociation has
to be *prospective*. That is, it must track down people who are known with
certainty to have lived through ordeals that would be expected to have
triggered a self-protective loss of memory, and it must then ascertain
how many of those people are unable to recall the event.

Holocaust survivors make up the most famous class of such subjects,
but whatever group or trauma is chosen, the upshot of well-conducted
research is always the same. Like Holmes and Pope, McNally finds
that no unanswerable evidence has been adduced to prove that anyone,

anywhere, has ever repressed or dissociated the memory of any occurrence. Traumatic experiences may not always remain in the forefront
of memory, but, unlike "repressed" ones, they can be readily called
to mind again. Unless a victim received a physical shock to the brain
or was so starved or sleep deprived as to be thoroughly disoriented at
the time, those experiences are typically *better* remembered than ordinary ones. Thus Judith Herman's much quoted maxim, "The ordinary
response to atrocities is to banish them from consciousness" (Herman
1992, p. 1), would appear to be exactly opposite to the truth. And once
that fact is understood, the improvised and precarious edifice of recovered memory theory collapses into rubble.

2.

It would be a serious mistake, however, to assume that reckless trau-
matology has now been permanently laid to rest. The conviction that
fathers are naturally prone to incestuous rape is still current. In some
academic departments, a dogged literalism about the repression/disso-
ciation of trauma has become oddly wedded to postmodernist suspicion
of science.[4] Furthermore, most of the "trauma centers" that sprang up
in the 1990s to study and treat psychogenic amnesia are still operating under the same assumptions as before. As for the theoreticians of
recovered memory, they continue to use their positions of authority in
universities, hospitals, and professional organizations to advance the
views whose hollowness McNally has exposed, and they can still count
on a surprising level of support from their colleagues.

Consider, in this regard, the following example of deafness to the lessons of the sex panic. Each year the American Psychiatric Association,
the body that sets the most basic guidelines for sound practice in our
mental health professions, bestows its Manfred S. Guttmacher Award
on what it deems to be the best recent publication on legal psychiatry.
The prize for 1999 went to a 768-page tome by Daniel Brown, Alan
W. Scheflin, and D. Corydon Hammond, *Memory, Trauma Treatment,
and the Law* (1998). The authors characterize themselves as "voices of

moderation in the middle" opposing "zealots on both sides" (p. 1). Their book, however, consists largely of sophistical pleading for already lost causes: the forensic value of therapeutically retrieved memories, the genuineness of multiple personality disorder, the likelihood that some reports of ritual abuse cults are accurate, and the desirability of allowing evidence obtained through hypnosis to be admissible in court.

Memory, Trauma Treatment, and the Law isn't just a disingenuous book, hiding its partisanship behind a screen of sanctimony; it is also a noxious one. Lightly granting the possibility that therapy may occasionally lead to pseudomemories, it trivializes the problem, deeming it serious only "when the patient takes legal action or publically [*sic*] discloses abuse" (p. 37)—as if the suffering of privately shattered families counted for nothing. And the book's strategy of superficially "reviewing the literature," citing both skeptical and (always more numerous) credulous studies and then tilting the scales toward the latter, merely simulates scientific neutrality.

These authors' activism in the cause of recovered memory was well-known long before they collaborated on their prize-winning volume. Daniel Brown and Alan Scheflin had often served as expert witnesses minimizing the hazards of memory retrieval, claiming to have found overwhelming experimental support for the concept of repression, and denying that a therapist could ever deceive a patient into thinking that she suffered from multiple personality; and their collaborative papers were similarly one-sided.[5] In 1995, moreover, Scheflin had delivered a warmly received address to a Texas conference held by the Society for the Investigation, Treatment and Prevention of Ritual and Cult Abuse, whose other speakers asserted, inter alia, that there were 500 Satanic cults in New York City alone, committing 4,000 human sacrifices per year, that Bill Clinton was serving as the Antichrist in the worldwide Satanic fraternity of the Illuminati, and that the False Memory Syndrome Foundation is "a Central Intelligence Agency action." Expressing solidarity with the assembled psychotherapists whose diagnoses of ritual abuse were exposing them to malpractice suits, Scheflin counseled them on the best means of foiling the supposed legal machinations of "the false memory people," whom he characterized as the "enemy."[6]

But it is the hypnotherapist D. Corydon Hammond, well-known for his low regard for experimental research on memory,[7] whose name on the title page of *Memory, Trauma Treatment, and the Law* ought to have prompted especial wariness among the Guttmacher judges. Like Scheflin, Hammond has affirmed the reality of both Satanic abuse cults and multiple personality disorder. But whereas Scheflin stops short of asserting a proven link between those two phenomena, Hammond is on record as a flamboyant true believer.

In a notorious 1992 lecture at a conference on sexual abuse and MPD, Hammond revealed his conviction that many MPD sufferers have acquired their split personalities through subjection, from early childhood onward, to ritual sexual abuse, sadistic torture, and mind control programming. The aim of the programmers, he disclosed, has been to produce remotely guided "alters" who, unbeknownst to their core selves, will be slaves to a worldwide intergenerational cult that is organized into "Illuminatic councils." The cult, said Hammond, is headed by a shadowy "Dr. Greenbaum," a Hasidic Jewish collaborator with the Nazis who once assisted in death camp experiments and later used the CIA to further his nefarious ends. "My best guess," Hammond confided,

> . . . is that they want an army of Manchurian Candidates, tens of thousands of mental robots who will do prostitution, do child pornography, smuggle drugs, engage in international arms smuggling, do snuff films, . . . and eventually the megalomaniacs at the top believe they'll create a Satanic order that will rule the world. (Hammond 1992)[8]

These colorful fantasies are significant, but not because they point to a failure of reality testing on Hammond's part. Closely related ideas were voiced in the heyday of the recovered memory movement by other prominent MPD specialists such as Bennett Braun and Colin Ross. What matters is that Hammond and the others all claim to have learned about the grand cabal from their hypnotized patients, who, until they were placed in trances, hadn't even known they were molestation victims, much less robotic smugglers, whores, and assassins.[9]

As Brown, Scheflin, and Hammond now put it in arguing in favor of hypnotically obtained evidence in the courtroom, "for some victims, hypnosis may provide the only avenue to the repressed memories" (p. 647). Exactly. Without that means of exchanging and embroidering false beliefs, Hammond himself could never have learned from his patients about the evil Dr. Greenbaum and his thirst for absolute power over us all.

The illogicalities and distortions in *Memory, Trauma Treatment, and the Law* do not go unremarked in McNally's *Remembering Trauma*. Thus, when Brown et al. cite one study as evidence that "amnesia for Nazi Holocaust camp experiences has also been reported," McNally quotes that study's rather different conclusion: "There is no doubt that almost all witnesses remember Camp Erika in great detail, even after 40 years" (McNally 2003, p. 192). And when Brown et al., again straining to make psychologically motivated amnesia look commonplace, cite another study to the effect that "two of the 38 children studied after watching lightning strike and kill a playmate had no memory of the event," McNally informs us that those two children "had themselves been struck by side flashes from the main lightning bolt, knocked unconscious, and nearly killed" (p. 192).

Such corrections, however damning, are peripheral to McNally's fundamental critique of Brown and his colleagues. The heart of the matter is that Brown et al. have miscast the entire debate over recovered memory by marshaling evidence against a straw-man "extreme false memory position." Supposedly, the extremists hold that all refreshed memories of abuse are necessarily wrong. Then one could put the extremists in their place just by citing a few cases of authenticated recall. But as McNally shows, critics of recovered memory fully allow that a period of forgetfulness can precede a genuine recollection. Indeed, that pattern is just what we would expect if the young subject at the time of the act, never having been warned against sexual predators, was unsure how to regard that act. What the critics deny is that "memories" of trauma, surfacing for the first time many years later, are so intrinsically reliable that they can serve as useful evidence that the experience was real.

Brown, Scheflin, and Hammond want *that* extremism to be embraced once again by the legal system that has finally learned to distrust it.

It would be reassuring to think that the American Psychiatric Association's Guttmacher jury merely skimmed *Memory, Trauma Treatment, and the Law* and misconstrued it as a bland eclectic survey. Already in 1991, however, another Guttmacher Award had been bestowed on coauthor Scheflin for a work that made several of the same legal arguments (Scheflin & Shapiro 1989). A more likely explanation for the subsequent prize is that Brown et al., having mounted a brief for the deep knowledge and expert testimony of theory-minded clinicians, were gratefully perceived as siding with mental health providers against their adversaries. If so, a larger question comes into view. What role did our major societies representing psychotherapists—the American Psychoanalytic Association, the American Psychological Association, and the American Psychiatric Association itself—play in condoning or actually facilitating the recovered memory movement, and how much enlightened guidance can we expect from them in the future?

3.

As I have noted on several occasions,[10] and as McNally confirms, in the 1990s recovered memory therapy made significant inroads into the practice of North American psychoanalysis. Even today, feminist clinicians bearing diplomas from analytic institutes are probing for missing memories of abuse and vigorously defending that practice in psychoanalytic books and journals. But the American Psychoanalytic Association, representing over 3,000 members, has turned a blind eye to this trend—and one can understand why. The psychoanalytic movement is already embattled, and too much about the historical ties between Freudianism and recovered memory would prove embarrassing if attention were called to it. The elected custodians of Freud's legacy have no desire to confront his early phase as a self-deceived abuse detecter; or to admit the precedent he set, during that phase and thereafter, in treating dreams, tics, obsessional acts, and agitation in the consulting room as "behavioral memories" of inferrable traumas; or to revisit the grave doubts that have been raised about repression; or to be reminded of the way psychoanalysts, until quite recently, insulted real victims of molestation by telling them that their "screen memories" covered a repressed desire to have sex with their fathers.[11] No longer given to excommunicating dissidents, the tottering Freudian patriarchy has made its peace with "recovered memory psychoanalysis" by pretending that it doesn't exist.

The largest of the three societies riven by the issue of recovered memory, the 150,000-member American Psychological Association (hereafter APA), is nominally responsible for quality control in the administration of therapy by the nation's clinical psychologists. Hence one APA division's commendable effort in the 1990s to identify the most effective treatment methods for specific complaints such as phobias and obsessive-compulsive disorder. That initiative, however, met with disapproval from APA members whose favorite regimens had not been found to give superior results. Some practitioners worried that insurers would use the list of approved treatments as an excuse to cut off reimbursement for all but the preferred therapies, and others complained that the association seemed on the verge of putting soulless experimentation ahead of clinical know-how. For now at least, the organization as a whole is not recommending treatments, to say nothing of disavowing dangerous ones (Glenn 2003). Recovered memory thus gets the same free pass from the APA as "attachment therapy," "therapeutic touch," "eye movement desensitization and reprocessing," and the hypnotic debriefing of reincarnated princesses and UFO abductees.[12]

This reluctance to challenge the judgment of its therapist members is deeply rooted in the APA's philosophy. Ever since 1971, when the association gave its blessing to Ph.D. and Psy.D. programs that omitted any scientific training, the APA has guided its course by reference to studies indicating that the intuitive competence of clinicians, not their adherence to one psychological doctrine or another, is what chiefly determines their effectiveness.[13] Those studies, however, were conducted before recovered memory practitioners, using a mixture of peremptory guesswork and unsubstantiated theory, began wrenching patients away from their families and their remembered past.

In 1995 the APA did publish a brochure, "Questions and Answers about Memories of Childhood Abuse," which can still be found on the "APA Online" website. The document combined some prudent advice to patients with soothing reassurance that "the issue of repressed or suggested memories has been overreported and sensationalized." Further inquiry into the phenomenon, it said, "will profit from collaborative efforts among psychologists who specialize in memory research and those clinicians who specialize in working with trauma and abuse victims."

But the APA directors already knew that such collaboration was impossible. In 1993 they had established a "task force," the Working Group on the Investigation of Memories of Childhood Abuse, self-defeatingly composed of three research psychologists and three clinicians favorably disposed to retrieval, and the task force had immediately degenerated into caucusing and wrangling. After years of stalemate, the group predictably submitted two reports that clashed on every major point, and the abashed APA, presented with this vivid evidence that "clinical experience" can lead to scientific heterodoxy, initially declined to circulate photocopies of the two documents even to its own members except by individual demand.

Meanwhile, the organization repeatedly compromised its formal neutrality. In 1994, for example, the APA's publishing house lent its prestigious imprint to a book that not only recommended recovered memory therapy but recycled the most heedless advice found in pop-psychological manuals. The book, Lenore E. A. Walker's *Abused Women and Survivor Therapy: A Practical Guide for the Psychotherapist*, touted hypnotism as a legitimate means of gaining access to "buried memories of incest" and "different personalities" within the victim (pp. 425–426). Walker provided a list of telltale symptoms, any one of which might indicate a history of forgotten molestation. These included "ambivalent or conflict ridden relationships," "poor body image," "quiet-voiced," "inability to trust or indiscriminate trust," "high risk taking or

inability to take risks," "fear of losing control and need for intense control," "great appreciation of small favors by others," "no sense of humor
or constant wisecracking," and "blocking out early childhood years"
(p. 113)—years that in fact are not remembered by anyone.

Then in 1996 the APA published and conspicuously endorsed another
book, *Recovered Memories of Abuse*, aimed at equipping memory therapists and their expert witnesses with every argument and precaution
that could thwart malpractice suits (Pope & Brown 1996). The book's
coauthors were well-known advocates of recovered memory treatment, and one of them, Laura S. Brown, was actually serving at the
time on the deadlocked task force. She had also supplied a foreword to
Lenore Walker's bumbling *Abused Women and Survivor Therapy*, calling
it "invaluable and long overdue" (p. vii). Unsurprisingly, then, *Recovered
Memories of Abuse* characterized false memory as an overrated problem
and drew uncritically on much of the research whose weaknesses Richard McNally has now exposed. The APA's unabated promotion of that
book, even today, suggests that the organization remains more concerned with shielding its most wayward members than with warning
the public against therapeutic snake oil.

There remains, once again, the American Psychiatric Association—
"the voice and conscience of modern psychiatry," as its website pro-
claims. Putting aside the fiasco of the 1999 Guttmacher Award, we
might expect that a society representing 38,000 physicians, all of whom
have been schooled in the standard of care that requires treatments to be
tested for safety and effectiveness, would be especially vigilant against
the dangers of retrieval therapy. Thus far, however, that expectation
has not been fulfilled.

To be sure, the Psychiatric Association's 1993 "Statement on Memories of Sexual Abuse" did warn clinicians not to "exert pressure on
patients to believe in events that may not have occurred. . . ." Yet the
statement inadvertently encouraged just such tampering by avowing
that the "coping mechanisms" of molested youngsters can "result in a
lack of conscious awareness of the abuse" and by characterizing "dissociative disorders" as a typical outcome of that abuse. Those remarks

constituted a discreet but unmistakable vote of confidence in multiple personality disorder and its imagined sexual etiology. And indeed, a year later the fourth edition of the Psychiatric Association's *Diagnostic and Statistical Manual of Mental Disorders (DSM-IV)* reaffirmed the validity of MPD under the more dignified and marketable name of dissociative identity disorder.

The Psychiatric Association's 1993 declaration on abuse memories performed still another service, a subtle one, for the repression/dissociation lobby. In explaining "implicit" memory—the kind that is exercised in the routine execution of skills or in the coloring of emotions by past impressions that aren't being explicitly called to mind—the statement proffered a curiously strained example. "In the absence of explicit recall," it said, implicit memory can torment "a combat veteran who panics when he hears the sound of a helicopter, but cannot remember that he was in a helicopter crash which killed his best friend." Here was an elision of the crucial gap between merely not thinking about a past event, as in the normal operation of implicit memory, and having total, psychologically motivated amnesia for that event.

Knowledgeable readers would have seen that in taking this unusual step, the statement's drafters were lending their authority to one controversial interpretation of post-traumatic stress disorder (PTSD), which the Psychiatric Association had first stamped as genuine in *DSM-III* of 1980. But why should a primarily martial ailment have figured even indirectly in a position paper on childhood sexual abuse? The mystery vanishes, however, if we know that the recovered memory movement's favorite means of courting respectability has been to fold the symptoms of repressed/dissociated abuse into PTSD.

In 2000 the Psychiatric Association's trustees, eschewing risky flights into theory, approved a lower-profile "Position Statement on Therapies Focused on Memories of Childhood Physical and Sexual Abuse." This declaration, however, was more pussyfooting than its predecessor. The validity of recovered memory treatment, it whispered, "has been challenged" in some quarters. While pointing out that memories can be altered as a result of suggestions from "a trusted person or authority figure," the drafters tactfully refrained from mentioning that the suggesting party is usually a therapist. And clinicians were advised to avoid "prejudging the veracity of the patient's reports" of abuse, as if false reports were typically delivered to therapists out of the blue, without influence from confabulation-enhancing devices employed within the treatment. The absence of any mention of those devices, such as hypnosis and sodium amytal, marked a step backward from the association's 1993 statement.

These equivocations neither helped nor impeded the already withering recovered memory movement. As we will now see, however, the movement's hopes of a comeback have been pinned on the Psychiatric Association's fateful decision to treat post-traumatic stress disorder as an integral and historically invariable malady. And that decision was a medically unwarranted one. As McNally indicates with reference to several recent studies, PTSD, like Victorian hysteria and like recovered memory itself, can now be understood as an artifact of its era—a sociopolitical invention of the post-Vietnam years, meant to replace "shell shock" and "combat fatigue" with an enduring affliction that would tacitly indict war itself as a psychological pathogen.[14] However crippling the symptoms associated with it may be for many individuals, the PTSD diagnosis itself has proved to be a modern contagion.

Once certified by the American Psychiatric Association as natural and beyond the sufferer's control, post-traumatic stress disorder began attracting claimants, both civilian and military, who schooled themselves in its listed symptoms and forged a new identity around remaining uncured. By now, as McNally relates, PTSD compensation is demanded for such complaints as "being fired from a job, one-mile-per-hour fender benders, age discrimination, living within a few miles of an explosion (although unaware that it had happened), and being kissed in public" (p. 281). According to Paula Jones among others, PTSD can even be the outcome of a consensual love affair. In view of such examples, the attempt to subsume forgotten abuse under post-traumatic stress makes more cultural than scientific sense; the same atmosphere of hypersensitivity and victimhood brought both diagnoses to life.[15]

As McNally shows in his concise and undemonstrative style, the national sex panic left its mark on each successive version of the Psychiatric Association's bible, which in turn congealed folklore into dogma. The 1980 *DSM-III* entry on post-traumatic stress disorder, mindful only of wars and other shocking disasters, had defined a PTSD-triggering event as one that falls "generally outside the range of usual human experience" and that "would evoke significant symptoms of distress in almost everyone." In 1994, however, the fourth edition generously expanded the category of precipitating causes to include "developmentally inappropriate sexual experiences without threatened or actual violence or injury." Thus a single-minded therapeutic sleuth could now place a questionably retrieved incident of infantile genital fondling on the same etiological plane as the Bataan death march or an ambush in the Mekong Delta.

It was the diagnostic manual, once again, that removed the largest obstacle of all to the merger of post-traumatic stress and recovered memory. The key sign of PTSD, as first conceived, was that accurate recollections of the trauma keep intruding on the patient's conscious mind; this was just the opposite of repressed or dissociated memory. But between *DSM-III* and its revised edition of 1987, PTSD patients were discovered to have been harboring a convenient new symptom. In 1980 they had shown only some incidental "memory impairment or trouble concentrating" on daily affairs, but the updated edition replaced routine forgetfulness with "inability to recall *an important aspect of the trauma*" (emphasis added).

This retroactive infusion of amnesia into the clinical picture of PTSD explains why the Psychiatric Association's illustrative helicopter pilot could have been troubled by a memory that had left no conscious imprint on his mind. Here, too, was the opening needed to give dissociation an appearance of hard-scientific concreteness. Post-traumatic stress, it was now claimed, short-circuits narrative memory and finds another, precognitive, channel through which it can flood the subject with anxiety. Accordingly, diehard recovered memory theorists took up a last refuge in neurobiology, now maintaining that dissociated sexual abuse generates signature alterations of brain tissue.

With the arrival of McNally's *Remembering Trauma*, there is no longer any excuse for such obfuscation. It makes no sense, McNally shows, to count forgetfulness for some "aspect of the trauma" within the definition of PTSD, because normal people as well as PTSD sufferers get disoriented by shocking incidents and fail to memorize everything about the event, even while knowing for the rest of their lives that it occurred. Likewise, it has never been established, and it seems quite unbelievable, that people can be haunted by memories that were never cognitively registered as such. Nor can specific brain markers vouch for the reality of a long-past sexual trauma, because, among other reasons, those features could have been present from birth. "It is ironic," McNally reflects, "that so much has been written about the biological mechanisms of traumatic psychological amnesia when the very existence of the phenomenon is in doubt. What we have here is a set of theories in search of a phenomenon" (p. 182n.).

Remembering Trauma is neither a polemic nor a sermon, and McNally offers little counsel to psychotherapists beyond warning them against turning moral disapproval of pedophilia into overconfidence that they can infer its existence from behavioral clues observed twenty or thirty years after the fact. But another lesson is implied throughout this important book. Attention to the chimerical task of divining a patient's early traumas is attention subtracted from sensible help in the here and now. The reason why psychotherapists ought to familiarize themselves with actual knowledge about the workings of memory, and why their professional societies should stop waffling and promulgating misinformation about it, is not that good science guarantees good therapy; it is simply that pseudoscience inevitably leads to harm.

III.

More Diagnostic Follies

Chapter 9

KEEPING US IN HYSTERICS

THIS CHAPTER ORIGINATED AS A REVIEW OF ELAINE SHOWALTER'S 1997 BOOK *Hystories: Hysterical Epidemics and Modern Media*. IT APPEARED IN *The New Republic*, MAY 12, 1997.

I.

For over a decade now, the object of keenest interest within American interdisciplinary scholarship has been a disease, and a possibly nonexistent one. As Elaine Showalter, Princeton's Avalon Foundation Professor of the Humanities and past president of the Modern Language Association, puts it near the outset of her own latest contribution to that field, *Hystories*,

> While physicians and psychiatrists have long been writing obituaries for hysteria, scholars in the humanities and social sciences have given it new life. Social historians, philosophers, anthropologists, literary critics, and art historians have taken up the subject of hysteria because it cuts across historical periods and national boundaries, poses fundamental questions about gender and culture, and offers insights into language, narrative, and representation. (Showalter 1997, p. 7)

This statement is certainly right about the disillusionment of the medical authorities. By now it is reasonably clear that hysteria, which was once thought to cause nervous women and some men to experience paralyses, seizures, tics, linguistic impediments, and hallucinations, is not a stable disorder with characteristics that occur independently of social expectations. As a relatively fixed cluster of symptoms, it evaporated after the Victorian heyday of its chief theoreticians, Jean-Martin Charcot, Pierre Janet, Josef Breuer, and the early Sigmund Freud—a likely sign that the malady was coaxed into approved forms largely by the therapeutic interventions that were meant to cure it. Hysteria was probably an umbrella term that covered diverse phenomena, including symptoms of organic disorders, some outright malingering, and psychogenic suffering of a kind that suited the temper of the age.

Strictly speaking, of course, an ailment cannot "pose questions about gender and culture" and "offer insights into language, narrative, and representation." That is the work of the academics, who would have graced us with their thoughts on those matters with or without hysteria as a pretext. But their enthusiasm for hysteria is understandable. In the nineteenth century, it served as a magnet for masculinist and racialist notions that are now often assumed to have occupied the inmost layer of the smug Victorian mind. Indeed, one common way of regarding the disease, amply developed in Showalter's influential study of 1985, *The Female Malady: Women, Madness, and English Culture, 1830–1980*, is to say that its diagnosis and treatment were a medicalization of misogyny itself.

As we learn from Marc Micale's comprehensive recent survey of hysteria studies, *Approaching Hysteria* (1995), that idea of Showalter's has been variously assessed as fertile and regrettably one-dimensional. Showalter herself, however, is sure that she occupies the cutting edge of research in this field. She, Micale, and a few others, she declares in *Hystories*, constitute "the New Hysterians," who understand that hysteria has always been "a body language for people who otherwise might not be able to speak or even to admit what they feel" (p. 7). And her group is in touch with findings in all of the disciplines that matter. The New Hysterians have established themselves, she proudly reports, "at the busy crossroad [*sic*] where psychoanalytic theory, narratology, feminist criticism, and the history of medicine intersect . . ." (p. 81).

In the academy as presently constituted, that methodological lineup appears thoroughly suitable and unproblematic. Showalter sees nothing here requiring further explanation. Yet it may not be immediately obvious to an outsider why two fields of study, medical history and the structure of narrative, are being matched with two vortexes of controversy, psychoanalysis and feminism. Is this intellectual-ideological hybrid really the best available equipment for making sense of hysteria? And don't rival allegiances within the contentious Freudian and feminist traditions dictate very diverse apprehensions of the social past?

This latter question is especially pertinent to "hysterical" women, whom Freud either cured or persecuted, depending on one's perspective. If, like Showalter, one is inclined to settle for "equity feminism" as opposed to the "gender feminism" that feeds on rage against men, one will be sympathetic to misdiagnosed "hysterics" but wary of glamorizing their helplessness and histrionics. And that tendency will be reinforced if, again like Showalter, one feels more comfortable with classical Freudian notions than with the radical view (very common among gender feminists) that psychoanalysis needs to be purged of its oppressive patriarchal features. Showalter's theoretical affinities, never cogently defended, thus press her continually toward a middle-of-the-road outlook that could pass for sheer reasonableness but is, I am afraid, more a matter of dodging trouble and taking refuge in received ideas.

Until now, the clearest instance of this weakness has been Showalter's inability to be consistent about whether she regards hysteria as an authentic malady; she has supported both sides without appearing to notice that she is contradicting herself. As I have already mentioned, her usual view is that hysteria was less an affliction than a somatic idiom for otherwise silenced people—an attractive hypothesis that is, however, somewhat incommoded by the managerial style of such wealthy and manipulative hysterics as Breuer's "Anna O." (Bertha Pappenheim) and Freud's "Frau Cäcilie M." (Anna von Lieben). Yet in *The Female Malady* Showalter also upheld Charcot's opposite, briefly influential, but fiercely contested judgment that hysteria was a true disease whose manifestations were visited upon, not suggested to or invented by, the sufferer. "Through careful observation, physical examination, and the use of hypnosis," she wrote there, "Charcot was able to prove that

hysterical symptoms, while produced by emotions rather than by physical injury, were genuine, and not under the conscious control of the
patient" (Showalter 1985, p. 147).

That last claim was already out of step with informed opinion
when it was published in 1985. To be sure, Charcot did regard hypnosis as crucial to an understanding of hysteria, whose symptoms, he
believed, were produced when a trauma sent the organism into a quasi-
hypnotic state. By "rehypnotizing" his resident hysterics and putting
them through their symptomatic paces, supposedly without their conscious awareness of obeying an instruction, Charcot imagined that he
was demonstrating both the integrity of hysteria and its isolation from
conscious will. But in truth he had proved little more than his own gullibility. His critics and later students were able to show that coaching
and suggestibility, not to mention dissimulation, amply account for all
of Charcot's hypnotic results.

Why does this matter? In fact, the point is momentous. The young
Freud sat reverently at Charcot's feet in 1885–1886, enthralled by what
he would eventually regard as hypnotic evidence of "split consciousness."
It was on that basis that he would begin his fateful quest for unconscious
mental causes of neuroses. In 1888, prefacing his translation of Hippolyte Bernheim's book *Suggestion*, he explicitly rejected the idea that
Charcot could have obtained his findings through suggestion, since otherwise "[w]e should not learn from the study of major hypnotism what
alterations in excitability succeed one another in the nervous system of
hysterical patients . . . ; we should merely learn what intentions Charcot
suggested (in a manner of which he himself was unconscious) to the subjects of his experiments—a thing entirely irrelevant to our understanding alike of hypnosis and of hysteria" (Freud 1953–1974, 1:78). Here is
Freud as Quixote, taking the measure of his first windmill.

The more clearly we realize that Showalter in 1985 was quite justified
in regarding hysteria as jointly "constructed" by doctors and patients,
the more ludicrous it seems that Freud could have dismissed the threat
of suggestion not just in Charcot's case but throughout his own career.

The joke, however, was lost on Showalter, who has always displayed a novitiate's piety toward the founding legend of psychoanalysis. Like Breuer, whose Anna O. case she also badly misinterpreted in *The Female Malady*, Charcot is an indispensable "precursor" in that legend, and Showalter was therefore unable to adopt a sufficiently critical view of his mistakes.

2.

In *Hystories*, Showalter finally takes a harder line toward both Charcot and hysteria. But now she is able to keep the hysterical ball in play by deliberately blurring the line between hysteria as a mental illness of individuals and the popular notion of "mass hysteria," or waves of fear, morbidity, and physical unease that ripple through collectivities in the grip of shared delusions. Her central claim is that hysteria recurs in more or less regular cycles and that we today, like the Victorians, are living through a peak phase of the phenomenon. For Showalter, the chief hysterias of our time are chronic fatigue syndrome, Gulf War syndrome, recovered memory of childhood sexual abuse, multiple personality disorder, Satanic ritual abuse, and alien abduction, all of them resulting from a contagion of erroneous ideas.

Showalter does a creditable journalistic job of marshaling informed opinion about each of her six American "hysterias." Even so, misgivings arise from the outset. For one thing, the author builds no conceptual bridge from individual pathology to the social dynamics of rumor formation. Is it hysterical to pick up a faddish idea about UFOs or about why one is feeling listless? Do we gain anything by labeling as hysterical, for example, the serene self-immolators of Heaven's Gate? The desired linkage of such instances with hysteria à la Charcot, Janet, Breuer, and Freud is little more than semantic. And even within her modern instances, Showalter has yoked together vastly disparate phenomena, from merely mistaken and correctible beliefs on the part of normal people through paranoid phantasms and lasting physical debility. She is even willing to count as hysterical the panic of Japanese subway riders in the wake of a poison gas attack, as if there were no distinction to be drawn between well-founded fear and pure delusion.

Furthermore, there is something peremptory about Showalter's list of recent hysterias. She has conjoined two items on which the medical jury is still out—chronic fatigue syndrome and Gulf War syndrome—with four others whose iatrogenic (doctor-induced) and hallucinatory basis is by now evident to most observers. Malingerers and copycats we have always with us, but it seems especially early, while investigations into possible toxic exposure are still under way, for Showalter to be asserting so categorically that Gulf War syndrome simply "does not exist" (p. 206).

By casting the hysterical net as widely as possible, Showalter is apparently seeking to gain certain tactical advantages. For example, she wants us to believe that our hysteria-plagued society urgently needs the ministrations of literary critics, without whom the "story" of hysteria would supposedly be indecipherable or vulnerable to ingenuous literal interpretation. We must turn to fiction, she maintains, if we are to fortify ourselves against present and future hysterical outbreaks, for novels "can tell us a lot more about the causes and cures of hysteria than most of the self-help books on the market" (p. 99). And again, it is critics, with their keen attunement to genre conventions, who can save us from the fallacy of thinking that similarities among "hystories" (reports of abduction, etc.) are a warrant of their truth.

Showalter is right to emphasize that popular narratives in our time have been transmitters of destructive misapprehensions about the mind. Think of *The Three Faces of Eve* (1957), *Sybil* (1973), and *Michelle Remembers* (1980), which have variously primed Americans to believe in Satanism, multiple personality, and repressed memories of sexual abuse. Understanding the conventions and structure of those books, however, is of negligible utility. What we chiefly need to know about them is that their stories are false; they call not for formal analysis but for research into their suspect origins. A literary critic could conduct such research as well as the next person, but Showalter has not even perceived its value, so bent is she upon commentary of a more usual but irrelevant kind.

On its face, *Hystories* appears to say that we Americans are living through one of the most perilous junctures of our history. Showalter points out that we are approaching the year 2000, a perfect witching hour for mass hysteria. Millennial panic is drawing us inexorably toward an Armageddon in which "traumatists and ufologists, experiencers and abductees, survivors and survivalists" (p. 5) will all join forces against public sanity. This "coming hysterical plague" (p. 207) may yet be averted, but only if we mobilize all our resources of prevention. As a sample of such preparedness, Showalter walks us through the hysterical and paranoid themes of *Batman Forever*, one of many cultural products that are allegedly laying the groundwork for a new Salem on a nationwide scale.

The reader who finds all this hard to swallow needn't feel apologetic; Showalter doesn't really believe it herself. On the penultimate page of her book she admits that

> [t]he hysterical witch-hunts of our own time may be waning. . . . People accused of abuse on the basis of recovered memory are being acquitted. Convictions have been overturned. Retractors are taking back their accusations of satanic ritual or childhood abuse. Journalists in Britain and the United States have taken up the cause of those falsely accused. Books and TV documentaries have helped turn the tide of credibility. . . . (p. 206)

Thus Showalter's own attempt to whip up a little hysteria, if only to lend urgency to her discourse, eventually comes to naught.

3.

Watching Showalter's manifest argument self-destruct, one has to wonder whether she doesn't have some other end in view. There are grounds for inferring that *Hystories* was conceived in mindfulness not of millennial frenzy but of something quite opposite, precisely that turning of the tide against recovered memory, acknowledged as a seeming after-thought. Showalter has perceived that the therapeutic craze of the later eighties and early nineties, whereby patients have been encouraged to concoct images of early sexual violation and then to suppose that those images must be memories, is rapidly becoming both an intellectual and an ethical liability. Sensing the movement's imminent collapse, she wants to assure us that she never meant to endorse it.

I single out recovered memory as the core "hysteria" in Showalter's list for two compelling reasons. First, that theme is actually the com-mon denominator of all four of her syndromes that involve delusions and not just physical symptoms. Belatedly "recalled" childhood sex-ual abuse, multiple personality, Satanic ritual abuse, and interplanetary abduction all tend to blossom on the same branch, namely, suggestive prompting by therapists who use hypnosis and/or related techniques to bring the client's perceived history into alignment with a favorite diagnosis. Indeed, the "memory" of Satanic rites and the emergence of "dissociated alters" are simply later stages of the search for more and more grisly instances of sexual abuse. And it is only in therapy, typically, that the lost souls who suspect that they may have been wafted into hov-ering spaceships succeed in "remembering" for certain that it was so.

Second, Showalter tells us, in a commendable act of self-criticism, that she must now reconsider her declaration at the end of *The Female Malady* that "the best hope for the future is the feminist therapy move-ment," including "women's self-help groups" (p. 59). She recognizes that just such groups, at the very time she was exalting them, were cru-cially responsible for launching the recovered memory movement; and she sees that even today they remain a breeding ground of false sexual accusations. *Hystories* is Showalter's vehicle not just for correcting her mistake but for challenging the whole conception of "women's ways of knowing"—a conception that, for many radical feminists and distraught women under their influence, has turned the suspicion of early sexual violation into a foregone conclusion.

This is a worthwhile purpose on Showalter's part, but it immedi-ately comes up against a delicate point of diplomacy. Just how much recantation can she afford without jeopardizing her stature within the fiercely politicized field of women's studies? Feminists, she asserts, owe a primary obligation to the truth (p. 158), yet she also knows that the very concept of truth has taken a pummeling from some of her sisters as an oppressive phallocentric ideal. Showalter is not about to walk the plank on behalf of truth-for-its-own-sake. Instead, she adopts a politic stance of more feminist than thou. Feminism itself, she points out, possesses its own "strong enlightenment, rationalist tradition" (p. 158); hence she will "ask feminist questions" (p. 11) about the conspiratorial illusions of our time. And with less fanfare, she will backpedal and equivocate whenever her challenge to radical feminism threatens to become a permanent estrangement.

Note, for example, how Showalter professes to be scandalized that Lynne Cheney

> draws a sinister analogy between women's studies discussions and therapeutic coercion: "Indeed, there are many parallels between the recovered memory movement and feminism as it has come to be practiced on campuses. The encouragement—even the requirement—in feminist classrooms to confess personal views and traumas establishes an environment very much like the one that exists in victim recovery groups." Feminist activists are understandably angry about these attacks. . . . (p. 10)

Now, Showalter knows perfectly well that the "recovery group" approach to pedagogy is practiced and openly advocated by some feminist academics,[1] and she also knows that many women students, with little or no assistance from therapists, have disastrously acquired "memories" of sexual abuse when their seminar leaders and classmates effectively demanded that they do so. For Showalter to make that charge, however, would be a virtual declaration of academic civil war. Instead, she rounds up the usual suspect, the impenitently conservative Cheney, and offers her as a hostage to the militants.

Showalter's distaste for factional strife may also account for the emphasis she now places on male hysteria. As she uneasily remarks, hysteria is "a term that particularly enrages some feminists because for centuries it has been used to ridicule and trivialize women's medical and political complaints" (p. 8). But if the recovered memory movement is hysterical—and Showalter insists that it is—then she herself is bestowing the h-word on the feminist mainstays of that movement. Only by stipulating that men, too, fall victim to hysteria—including "our war veterans" (p. 142) who "had to deal with frightening gossip" in the Persian Gulf (p. 141)—can Showalter acquire some insurance against the accusation of having betrayed her sex.

Once that insurance has been purchased, Showalter feels confident enough to dissent not only from recovered memory theory but also from a peculiarly defeatist, victim-minded style of feminist thought that fed into it. This is the 1970s modified-Lacanian doctrine of Hélène Cixous, Julia Kristeva, Catherine Clément, and Luce Irigaray, according to which the whole realm of rational knowledge was ceded to men while "absence" and "lack" were celebrated as innately feminine. Those voluble champions of muteness elevated the nineteenth-century hysterical woman to heroic status and proclaimed that "the discourse of the hysteric" was the true speech of womankind, to be cherished in defiance of such patriarchal straitjackets as grammar and syntax. Not so, objects Showalter, joining what has by now become a chorus of protest against "essentialist" stereotyping about the incoherent female mind.

Again, however, the thinness of Showalter's critique is painfully apparent. In her view, it was only a lapse of prudence for Parisian feminists to chant in 1972, *"Nous sommes toutes des hystériques!"* (p. 57). In doing so, "they came dangerously close to acting like hysterical divas" (p. 57), and those among them who were psychoanalysts accordingly found themselves penalized by their Freudian or Lacanian establishments. For Showalter, playing Dear Abby for the moment, the lesson is clear: "Claiming hysteria is not the wisest strategy for professional success" (p. 57). But what about the Freudian/Lacanian *premises* of French feminism? Shouldn't they be reviewed and weighed for cogency?

If Showalter were to undertake such an inquiry, it could lead to awkward questions about her own unexamined psychoanalytic assumptions.

Discretion is therefore preferable. Thus when she relates that Cixous and company located the origin of hysterical female discourse in "the pre-Oedipal phase of feminine development, when the baby daughter takes the mother as her primary object of desire" (pp. 56–57), Showalter observes only that the idea possessed "tremendous intellectual and emotional appeal" (p. 56). Evidently, her professed allegiance to enlightenment standards does not extend to a concern for the empirical basis of theories about the mind.

4.

Here we return to a source of confusion in Showalter's work that is even more consequential than her bending to every feminist breeze. I mean her unreflective loyalty to the broad outlines of the psychoanalytic revelation. That loyalty appears to be tested at various moments in *Hystories*, partly in response to cited objections that I myself have posed. But the Freudian unconscious remains Showalter's master key not just to psychological sophistication but to the alleviation of mental woe everywhere. As she puts it, "Freud's message never got through to millions of people, who still distrust and fear the unconscious and its power over us. As a result, they suffer needlessly" (p. 9).

I would like to say that Showalter and I disagree about psychoanalysis and leave it at that, but something more symptomatic of "humanistic" complacency is on display here: a bland refusal to think consecutively. Remarkably, Showalter concedes the truth of nearly every negative observation about Freud and psychoanalysis that comes to her notice. Those concessions, however, leave her argument completely unaffected, as if she were just going through the motions of acknowledging a distant, boring debate. Her faith in Freud has about it a dreaminess that can't be penetrated by mundane considerations of evidence and logic.

Showalter grants that Freud was a self-publicizing "showman" (p. 38) who was less interested in curing his patients than in turning them into exhibits of his pet notions. More significantly, he was a "stubborn, bullying interrogator" (p. 42) who "pressured his patients to produce narratives congruent with his theories" (p. 41). And she further admits that when Freud adopted his oedipal explanation of the psycho-neuroses, his system of thought became (in Richard Webster's quoted words) "almost completely freed from the constraints of empirical reality" (p. 42). Does it not follow that we should hesitate to adopt that system as our own lens upon reality? But the issue is never raised.

In this respect Showalter proves to be typical of her fellow New Hysterians, who are uniformly partial to psychoanalysis though often stern toward its creator. Take Sander L. Gilman, an eminent cultural historian and still another recent president of the Modern Language Association, whose dust-jacket blurb for *Hystories* calls it "the standard for all future studies of mental illness and culture." In learned and pro-vocative books such as *Freud, Race, and Gender* (1993) and *The Case of Sigmund Freud* (1993), Gilman goes farther than any accused Freud basher toward reducing psychoanalysis to a manifestation of one mad-cap improviser's eccentricity. For Gilman, Freud's universal castration complex was his attempt to pin on the human race what Germanic anti-Semites were saying about the circumcised Jews, and again, his psychol-ogy of women is presented as yet another deflection of racist slanders. These charges saddle Freud with a craven furtiveness that sits ill with the Promethean legend he took such pains to promote, but Gilman's startling indictment never causes him to reconsider his own Freudian-ism. Some commitments, I suppose, are just too deep for thought.

Showalter herself is far more protective of Freud the man than Gil-man is. Indeed, when she has to decide which movements to approve and which to shun, she applies a simple litmus test: do these people show sufficient respect for the discoverer of the unconscious? The French feminists, for example, despite their "appealing" manipulation of Freud-ian developmental notions, placed themselves beyond the reach of her forgiveness when they depicted Freud as the male oppressor par excel-lence and characterized his female patients as martyrs to a sexist insti-tutional practice.

Preeminent among those rehabilitated hysterical "stars" and

"supermodels," as Showalter scornfully calls them, stands the teenage "Dora" (Ida Bauer), whose brief treatment at Freud's hands ended rancorously when she refused to accede to his view of her as an oedipally fixated bisexual whose symptoms had been prompted not by her gruesome family predicament but by early masturbation and a desire to suck her father's penis. Showalter is uncomfortable with that diagnosis, but her outrage is reserved for those feminists who have called Freud, not Dora, the real hysteric in the case. "They made Freud the fall guy, pinning the blame for Dora's symptoms onto him . . ." (p. 58). And again: "Dramatizing the psychoanalyst's hysteria, reducing his theories to performance or farce, is another way of fending off the specter of the unconscious" (p. 109). It is time, decrees Showalter, to forsake the perverse outlook that prizes "women's stories" over "doctors' studies" (p. 93), the latter presumably being trustworthy because doctors know best—especially if their name is Freud.

The doctor in Dora's case, however, was not just wrong but relentlessly cruel, and his cruelty was fed by the theory of mental conflict that Showalter sentimentally misconstrues. Freud's harrying of Dora rested on his Charcot-inspired conviction that hysteria was as regular in its laws of operation as epilepsy or syphilis and on his utterly mechanical view of its causation. That is why he could write to his friend Wilhelm Fliess, soon after beginning his attempt to break Dora's will, that the case had "smoothly opened to the existing collection of picklocks" (Freud 1985, p. 427). Freud was sure he could force to the surface an admission of a specific early practice, event, or fantasy (masturbation, the primal scene, an incest wish) to match each symptom. The contrast with Showalter's empathetic, socially aware, symptom-as-protest conception of hysteria could hardly be greater—but she draws no insight from that fact.

On the crucial topic of recovered memory, finally, Showalter's psychoanalytic partisanship once again requires her to don blinders and give out useless advice. She is eager to believe that the alleged link between Freudianism and recovered memory is merely a defamation by "one-sided" and "vitriolic" extremists such as me. But as she mentions in passing (p. 17), therapeutic epidemics can only get going if they possess a theoretical superstructure. And though Showalter won't come near to admitting it, nothing could be more obvious than that the theory behind recovered memory was drawn almost entirely from the Freudian picture of the mind.

For Showalter, predictably, the key to halting outbreaks like the recovered memory madness is to "defend Freud's insights and try to restore confidence in serious psychotherapy" (p. 12), mainly psycho-analysis. But psychoanalysis not only evolved from a recovered memory inquisition—Freud's "seduction theory" of the mid-1890s—it contains a built-in potentiality of reversion to that state. When disheartened analysts, sensing public resistance, tire of ascribing murderous and incestuous designs to small children and of telling real victims of early molestation that they are suffering only from illusory "screen memo-ries," the hunt for oedipal fantasies can get swiftly replaced by a hunt for repressed sexual abuse and its "perpetrators." Just such a turn was taken around 1930 when Freud's anguished disciple Sándor Ferenczi, chafing against the master's icy and controlling ways, decided that his women patients deserved sympathy as probable survivors of early molestation. And since the 1980s it has been happening once again.

When Showalter at last awakens to this appalling phenomenon, she will doubtless say that the analysts in question haven't chosen the best style of feminism or Freudianism and are behaving badly—in fact, just like a pack of hysterics. A more effective response might be to call in question the whole unproven idea that colloquy between a therapist and a patient can reliably unlock repressed secrets from the patient's early childhood. And to that end, a truly skeptical history of "dynamic" psychotherapy and its favorite diseases might be an important source of illumination. Unfortunately, it isn't likely to be forthcoming from any of Showalter's New Hysterians.

Chapter 10

OUT, DAMNED BLOT!

THIS REVIEW OF *What's Wrong with the Rorschach? Science Confronts the Controversial Inkblot Test* APPEARED IN THE JULY 15, 2004, ISSUE OF *The New York Review of Books*. IT IS CLOSELY RELATED TO CHAPTER 8, IN THAT BOTH ESSAYS CALL ATTENTION TO OUTSTANDING WORKS OF CRITIQUE AND POINT OUT THE ENCOURAGEMENT OFFERED BY THE AMERICAN PSYCHOLOGICAL ASSOCIATION TO PRACTITIONERS OF DUBIOUS SCIENCE WHO HAPPEN TO BE STRONGLY REPRESENTED WITHIN THE ORGANIZATION.

I.

"It's a Rorschach." That bit of everyday speech, referring to any equivocal stimulus that elicits self-betraying interpretations on all sides, is one sign among many that, in the popular mind at least, the vaunted inkblot challenge has no rival as psychology's master test. In actuality, the Rorschach is now administered for diagnostic purposes somewhat less frequently than the low-maintenance, question-and-answer Minnesota Multiphasic Personality Inventory (MMPI), which asks the subject to agree or disagree with such flatfooted assertions as "I often feel sad." But neither the public nor Rorschachers, as the zealous and clannish guardians of the blot technique are known, take much interest in "superficial" self-report tests such as the MMPI. The mind's hidden layers, it is assumed, can be tapped only through unguided responses to images lacking determinate content; and the Swiss psychiatrist Hermann Rorschach's ten cards with bisymmetrical shapes, introduced to an initially unimpressed world in 1921, are thought to have confirmed their uncanny power in countless applications.

This judgment is shared in large measure by American clinical psychologists and other professionals who have occasion to administer personality tests. As we learn from a provocative and important book by James M. Wood, M. Teresa Nezworski, Scott O. Lilienfeld, and Howard N. Garb, *What's Wrong with the Rorschach?*,[1] some 80 percent of American Ph.D. programs in clinical psychology still emphasize the Rorschach in required courses; 68 percent of specialist programs in educational psychology teach Rorschach technique; and the test is employed by roughly a third of all psychologists evaluating parents in custody cases, criminals facing sentencing or parole, and children who may or may not have been abused. Until very recently, testimony by Rorschach experts has gone largely unchallenged in our courts.

Necessarily, then, *What's Wrong with the Rorschach?* is not just a history of the test's evolution and periodic vicissitudes. It is also, and with increasing social concern as the story approaches the present, a continual assessment of the merits and pitfalls of projective testing. Since the four authors have themselves been participants in recent debate about the Rorschach, there is no pretense of neutrality here. But Wood and his colleagues do aim at objectivity and fairness, and if they err at all it is on the side of mercy. Readers of *What's Wrong* will find no more lucid primer on the requirements of scientific prudence as they relate to the authentication of psychological tests.

An avid reader of both Freud and his Zurich colleague Jung, Rorschach conceived of his test as a nonsectarian aid to psychoanalysis, impersonally determining an individual's "experience type" *(Erlebnistypus)* without presuming to favor one psychodynamic faction or another. The idea was to present all test takers with the ten loose printed cards, half of them in black and white and half including some colors, displaying an identical sequence of images. (It was long thought that Rorschach created his cards simply by folding each wet, multiblotted page in half along its vertical axis. It now appears, however, that he either painted entire shapes or subtly altered his blots with watercolors to produce desired effects.) For each card the test giver would ask in the most neutral tone, "What might this be?"; he would capture the subject's responses fully and exactly in a *protocol*, or written record; and he would subsequently arrive at a singular personality profile by sifting that record for telltale features such as the kinds of forms named, focus on whole shapes or details, emphasis on movement versus color, and rigid literalism versus a comfortably imaginative accommodation to the imperfect resemblance between the blots and any real-life form.

Movement- and color-based responses were of paramount importance in Rorschach's system of weighing personality. He believed that test takers who offer a high number of movement ("M") responses are, paradoxically, turned inward or "introversive"; intelligent and creative, they nonetheless are awkward and socially inept. In contrast, subjects who favor color ("C") responses are "extratensive," or adroit in company but restless and impulsive. Someone who registers a high number of both M and C scores qualifies as "dilated" or "ambiequal"—a healthy blending of introversive and extratensive traits. But low and similar numbers of M and C responses stigmatize the subject as "coarctative," or lacking in both creativity and emotional stability.

These rules were far from modest in scope. The close association between creativity and social clumsiness, were it to be upheld by evidence from other sources, would in itself constitute a major discovery, and so would the posited link between social adeptness and impulsivity. In addition, it would be remarkable if those and other constellations could be inferred with certainty from such utterances as "The bug is bleeding" and "It looks like a skull." And this is to say nothing of Rorschach's most expansive boast, which was that his test would be found capable of ascertaining personality differences between regional populations and even whole races.[2] Did he have grounds for making such sweeping claims, or was he capriciously assigning the equivalent of fortune cookies to his unsuspecting volunteers?

There is much in Rorschach's only book, *Psychodiagnostics*, that might encourage us to regard him as a crank. Bizarrely, for example, he insisted that a movement response be scored if the subject conjured a child sitting at a desk or a vampire sleeping in a coffin, because "muscular tension" was supposedly implied. And although a dog performing in a circus exhibited Rorschach movement, a cat catching a mouse or a fish darting through water did not, because, according to the founder, significant motion had to be "human-like" in function. Meanwhile,

Rorschach tagged as "pedants" or "grumblers" any testees who concentrated on details as opposed to whole images; those who interpreted white spaces were probably troublemakers; and those who hesitated before commenting on the multicolored cards must be exhibiting "color shock," thereby betraying themselves as neurotic repressers of emotion.

Rorschach argued, quite sensibly, that by examining the average test results (later called "norms") for many people whose personality traits had already been determined by other means, administrators could learn whether a given kind of response was actually well correlated with a given trait. Yet before he died from a perforated appendix just nine months after the publication of *Psychodiagnostics*, Rorschach had found time to accumulate test results for only 405 independently categorized subjects, and their types were drastically skewed toward schizophrenia (188 examples) and other pathologies he had encountered in his hospital rounds. Only 117 ordinary people, scattered amid his assorted "morons," "imbeciles," "senile dements," and so forth, had been sampled. Given such a sketchy evidential base, it isn't surprising that *Psychodiagnostics* was slow to find admirers; the wonder is that its complex scoring system was finally adopted with so few reservations.

The Rorschach found its true welcome in the world's headquarters of psychological typecasting and "adjustment," the United States. Wood engagingly tells how the test finally caught on here in the 1930s, flourished in the forties and early fifties, weathered a crisis of doubt in the later fifties and sixties, and then surged again until, a decade ago, skeptics began to nip at its heels once more. Along the way, different groups of American enthusiasts devised their own scoring rules to yield the kinds of results that interested them. Through it all, however, Rorschachers have kept faith with the founder's ten inviolate cards, which have been granted the kind of awe once reserved for texts dictated directly from the sky.

The Rorschach conquered North America and much of the Western world before any part of its rationale had been subjected to stern experimental trial. In seeking to explain this striking fact, Wood notes that inkblot games and tests were current even before Rorschach launched his own version. His key departure—the attempt to gauge a subject's whole personality and not just a faculty of imagination—fit nicely with the growing sway of psychoanalysis, and more particularly with the Freudian ideas of projection and free association. Again, Americans who preferred the more cheerful Jungian conception of the psyche responded favorably to Rorschach's adaptation (with significant differences) of Jung's already celebrated dichotomy between introverts and extraverts. Moreover, in balancing a "romantic" emphasis on deep intuition against an "empiricist" battery of codes and tables for figuring scores, the Rorschach proved at first serviceable, and then virtually indispensable, to the burgeoning American profession of clinical psychology, which was developing its own romantic pretensions but needed an objective-looking diagnostic tool to offset the inherent subjectivism of the one-on-one interview.[3]

2.

Reasons for popularity, of course, are not the same thing as scientific justifications. Wood et al. remind us that if a given instrument of testing in any field is not to cause havoc, it must be both valid and reliable. In brief, it must measure what it purports to measure and it must yield approximately the same results when readministered in new conditions or by other examiners.

Hermann Rorschach had accepted those criteria in principle, and most of his followers have paid due obeisance to them. But at every juncture where the test stood in peril of being decertified by negative findings, Wood shows, its promoters backed off from empirical accountability and expanded the scope of their claims. The story told in *What's Wrong*, by turns appalling and amusing, reads like a parable of the larger struggle between science and pseudoscience, with the latter always managing somehow to issue itself a new reprieve from execution.

When the Rorschach began to attract American followers through

word of mouth in the 1930s, it brought to prominence an initially reluctant but subsequently flamboyant champion, Bruno Klopfer, whose talent for salesmanship and deafness to criticism were responsible in part
for the high morale of American Rorschachers in the forties and fifties.
A refugee from Nazi Berlin, Klopfer had studied with Jung in Zurich
and had learned how to score various psychological tests there, including the Rorschach. He was barely surviving as a research assistant in
Columbia's anthropology department when eager graduate students
learned of his expertise and pressed him into moonlighting as their
Rorschach trainer.

Although Klopfer's real passion had been psychoanalysis, not assessment, he soon contracted a taste for interpreting Rorschach's still
untranslated pronouncements and for devising novel inkblot rules that
hadn't occurred to the master. Before long he possessed a grand career
and an adoring crew of disciples who fed his insatiable ego. As Wood
explains, this elevation of one individual to guruhood added mystification to an already dubious mind-reading program and further postponed a reckoning with the need for evidential support.

In the Rorschach scheme as first conceived, a subject's summed scores
for responses in each category of interest—color, say, or white-space
shapes—corresponded directly to a certain trait of personality. Klopfer
accepted some of those equivalences, but on the whole he found the idea
behind them too rigid for capturing the subtleties of human character.
What was needed, he argued, was "configural" interpretation, whereby
a highly experienced and gifted judge (guess who?) would draw "holistic" inferences from an intuitive contemplation of *all* of the subject's
scores on the test. The Rorschach "artist" could justify this method by
creating anonymous ("blind") profiles on the basis of protocols com-
piled by others and then by checking the profiles against case histories
or against delayed personal acquaintance with the test takers. The artist himself or someone from his circle of admirers would let the rest of
us know, anecdotally, how well he had done.

Klopfer's fans considered him a virtual oracle, and he was inclined
to agree. He even claimed that, through analysis of Rorschach scores

alone, he could discriminate between cancer patients with fast- and slow-growing tumors. But all of his pretensions were proven hollow when neither he nor other famous virtuosos could exhibit any diagnostic acumen in circumstances that were properly secured against cheating. Though many Rorschachers still revere Klopfer's memory, he now appears to have been only a colorful buffoon.

Wood and his fellow research psychologists are only peripherally concerned with Klopfer's foibles. Their target here is the whole idea of "clinical validation," whereby hypotheses are checked not against impersonal trials of their adequacy but against testimonials, case studies, and assessments of success made by parties with a stake in the outcome. That method inevitably risks being undermined by "confirmation bias," or the natural human tendency to misread evidence in one's own favor. And confirmation bias runs wild in subjective evaluations of Rorschach profiles, thanks to such factors as the wide applicability of the test's vague personality descriptors and the contradictions that crop up within a given subject's scores, tempting the evaluator to seize upon apparent hits and ignore the misses. Even blind Rorschach interpretation per se, Wood points out, isn't always what it seems, because the examiner often has advance knowledge about the population of test takers—for example, a ward full of mental patients.

Bruno Klopfer's disdain for controlled studies was shared by American psychoanalysts, whose own absolute trust in clinical validation had come straight from Freud. The Rorschach, they perceived, could serve as a technical adjunct to their relatively unstructured explorations of patients' minds. Predictably, they imbued the test with a symbol-decoding function that Rorschach himself, decades earlier, had pondered and rejected as unproductive. According to the Freudians, subjects gazing at the ten plates were really seeing projections of their unconscious desires and neuroses—conditions that pointed to a need for further months or years on the couch. And needless to say, those inferences, too, were clinically validated without incurring any risk of disconfirmation.

At the height of the Freudian vogue, Rorschach's Cards IV and VII became known to analytically inclined authorities, though not to unsuspecting test takers, as the "Father" and "Mother" images.[4] A woman who pointed out, plausibly, that the "arms" on the Father card are skinny was said to be in the grip of penis envy; and if she likened the Mother to a stuffed animal, she thereby convicted herself of what one expert called "a refusal to grow up and assume heterosexual responsibilities." "So it went with all the cards," Wood observes. "Card V revealed childhood memories of having seen one's parents engaged in intercourse. Card VI reflected unconscious attitudes toward sex and 'phallic worship.' Card IX revealed 'anal' concerns and paranoia. Card X revealed 'oral' fantasies" (p. 112).

In this vein of instant diagnosis no one surpassed the psychoanalyst Robert Lindner, the author of *Rebel Without a Cause*. Lindner identified forty-three Rorschach responses amounting to cries for help. Does the subject perceive "some sort of tool" in Card II? Then he is suffering from "hesitancy in coming to grips with an underlying sexual problem." Does he compare a portion of Card X to an extracted tooth? He is a chronic masturbator. And if, when perusing Card IV, he is rash enough to mention both decay and death, he is probably suicidal, and "there is a fair prospect that [he] will benefit from convulsive therapy" (p. 113).

All of the eminent American Rorschachers from the thirties through the fifties were sympathetic to Freudian dream interpretation, and they felt the tug of the popular psychoanalytic tide. After considerable hesitation, for example, and not without misgivings about diluting his authority, Bruno Klopfer made room in his scoring system for Mother and Father symbolism. Yet the main benefit of the Freudian trend accrued to those tradition-minded Rorschachers who resisted it. In doing so, they identified themselves as the party of scientific restraint—even though their own rules for interpreting color, movement, and form responses as indicators of personality had never been proven cogent, either.

From the outset of the Rorschach's wild American ride, some psychologists who believed in the test's general soundness understood that empirical standards couldn't be indefinitely brushed aside in the lordly Klopfer manner. Two highly regarded Rorschach theorists,

Samuel Beck and Marguerite Hertz, argued vigorously that Klopfer's "configural" blending of scores was perpetuating a deadly subjectivism and placing each individual rule of interpretation beyond the reach of disproof. Beck and Hertz won an appreciative following by associating themselves with "psychometrics," the statistically based controls that are now universally honored in experimental psychology if not in its clinical counterpart. As they emphasized, the psychometric ethos mandates that test procedures be standardized; that reliability be verified, not just promised; and that norms be gathered in enough volume to put the announced meaning of scores beyond dispute.

Beck and Hertz could endorse psychometrics because they were initially sure that research would confirm most Rorschach rules while weeding out a few unsupportable ones. That confidence inspired many loyalists as well as outsiders, from the forties through the sixties, to submit Rorschach hypotheses to objective review. But the results proved devastatingly negative. Correlations between predicted traits and independently observed ones were found to be either nonexistent or too weak to be trusted. Test results varied unacceptably among examiners with differing styles of self-presentation. And meanwhile, crippling statistical blunders were unearthed in the more optimistic reports. As the most sophisticated of the critics, Lee J. Cronbach, wrote in 1956, "It is not demonstrated that the test is precise enough or invariant enough for clinical decisions. The test has repeatedly failed as a predictor of practical criteria. . . . There is nothing in the literature to encourage reliance on Rorschach interpretations" (Wood et al. 2003, p. 178).

Here was one of those moments when Rorschachers faced a clear if painful choice between loyalty to science and loyalty to beliefs in which they had invested much money, time, and self-esteem. As usual, most of them opted to close ranks. Even Samuel Beck ignored the ominous findings and began taking a kinder view of clinical validation after all. And most of those who did refer to the experimental literature, having sifted it for scraps of encouragement, refused to acknowledge what it was plainly saying about the test's fundamental inaccuracy.

When practitioners of a quasi-medical fad exempt themselves from

answerability to empirical trials, one usual consequence is a proliferation of alternative schools. By the late 1950s, Wood reports, no fewer
than five American Rorschach regimens were current, not to mention
other inkblot tests that heretically departed from the original cards.
Credentialed psychologists, rapidly increasing in number but not in
methodological sophistication, felt free to draw upon all five incompatible codes as if they were passing down the line at a salad bar. To
the increasingly restive dissenters, what had been true all along was
now overwhelmingly apparent: the Rorschach was a revealing projective test not of its respondents' quirks but of the preconceptions held
by its advocates.

3.

By the mid-1960s the Rorschach had earned the distrust of most psychologists who were keeping up with the mainstream journals. In 1974,
however, the technique underwent a surprising resuscitation at the
hands of the American clinician John E. Exner, whose often revised
and supplemented book, *The Rorschach: A Comprehensive System*, would
become the most influential of all Rorschach texts.

Seeking consensus among the quarreling Rorschachers, Exner assembled an eclectic quilt of the best elements, as he judged from painstaking
surveys, in all of the competing regimens while adding many categories of his own, including new measures for egocentricity, depression,
obsessive style, and "hypervigilance." In itself, such a combination of
winnowing and amplifying wouldn't have set Exner apart from many
another Rorschach pundit. But he silenced most doubters by conspicuously embracing psychometric standards, including the provision of
abundant, broadly representative norms and barrages of scientific references purporting to document both the validity and the reliability of
his Comprehensive System.

In Exner's hands the test regained a level of respect not enjoyed
since the early fifties, and his domination of the Rorschach scene has
been all but total for three decades now. In 1997 he received an "Award

for Distinguished Professional Contributions to Knowledge" from the Board of Professional Affairs of the American Psychological Association, which credited his Comprehensive System with having revived "perhaps the most powerful psychometric instrument ever envisioned"; and as recently as April 2004 his life's work was honored through a conference jointly sponsored by Harvard Medical School and the Massachusetts Mental Health Center.

As *What's Wrong with the Rorschach?* demonstrates, however, the imposing Comprehensive System is really a production of smoke and mirrors. Exner's claims for the high reliability of his technique, it turns out, have rested on a misconstrual of accepted statistical terminology. Further, his famous compilation of norms was vitiated by a major sampling error that went unremarked for more than a decade. The cited studies underpinning his rules have been mostly unpublished and unshared work by the least trustworthy of judges, a team of enthusiasts employed by his own subsidiary, Rorschach Workshops, Inc. And the inflated reputation of those studies has been sustained by the Rorschach Research Council, yet another Exner satellite.

In Exner's code, "reflection" answers, such as "clouds reflected in a pond," indicate narcissism. Even one reflection response within a protocol, Exner admonishes, can tell a psychologist that "a nuclear element in the subject's self-image is a narcissistic-like feature that includes a marked tendency to overvalue personal worth" (p. 205). This is a grave matter, because Exner, taking a page from Freud, has held that "homosexuals and sociopaths" are highly narcissistic. Detection of those dubiously bracketed personality types thus rests in part on the perception of symmetries in forms that simply *are* symmetrical.

Wood's critique leaves me convinced that Exner's pseudo-precise method for inferring diagnoses from weighted combinations of Rorschach scores is even riskier than Bruno Klopfer's impressionistic holism. Take, for instance, the Comprehensive System's Egocentricity Index, which is figured by tripling the number of a subject's reflection responses, adding the number of "pair" responses, and dividing the sum by the total number of all responses. If any one of the component rules here is invalid, so is the whole index, in which case its automatically applied mathematical formula will cause many more misdiagnoses than Klopfer's case-by-case guesswork.

The Comprehensive System has done less than nothing to remove the most serious flaw in all previous Rorschach schemes, including Hermann Rorschach's own: their tendency to overpathologize, or to err on the side of abnormal characterizations. In one study from the 1980s, in which mental patients and ordinary citizens were blindly intermingled, Comprehensive System judges classified nearly 80 percent of the normal subjects as depressed and as harboring serious problems of character. And in 2000 three skeptical researchers, examining the Rorschach scores of 100 behaviorally normal California schoolchildren, reported that in Comprehensive System terms the children

> may be described as grossly misperceiving and misinterpreting their surroundings and having unconventional ideation and significant cognitive impairment. Their distortion of reality and faulty reasoning approach psychosis. These children would also likely be described as having significant problems establishing and maintaining interpersonal relationships and coping within a social context. They apparently suffer from an affective disorder that includes many of the markers found in clinical depression. (pp. 236–237)

When the Exner system is relied upon to assess individual children or candidates for the priesthood or pilots suspended for drunkenness or convicts seeking parole, a form of roulette is being played with their fate. James Wood offers a chilling example from a custody dispute in which he himself was consulted too late to affect the outcome. Inkblot scores had suggested that the ex-wife, who had repeatedly charged her ex-husband with physically and sexually abusing his children, was seriously disturbed, lacking in empathy, and incapable of forming rational judgments. Those were the conclusions implied by such damning symptoms as her having seen, in two cards, the shape of a paper snowflake (incorrectly scored by the examiner as a "reflection response") and the supposedly depressive image of a Thanksgiving turkey carcass—

corresponding, as it happened, to leftovers that were then sitting in her refrigerator.

Meanwhile, the ex-husband's Comprehensive System protocol assured the authorities that he was more or less normal. As Wood learned from available records, however, the man had beaten at least one of his three previous wives, had married this fourth one under an assumed name, had broken two of her teeth shortly after their wedding, and had both battered and molested his young son. Thanks in large part to the two errant Rorschach profiles, full custody of the endangered son was awarded to his sadistic father.

If a psychological test cannot discriminate reliably between signs of pathology and casual associations such as the remembered turkey carcass, it is a public menace and ought to be dropped forthwith. Oddly, however, Wood et al. are reluctant to say so. Partly out of deference to colleagues who have devoted their careers to the Rorschach and partly because some of the authors themselves still harbor confessed "romantic" sympathies, they take a firm stand only about the urgency of getting the Rorschach out of the courtroom. On other points, such as the possible usefulness of inkblots in "psychodynamic exploration" that could be "analogous to dream interpretation," they express cautious interest and call for further research (pp. 191, 279).

Here Wood et al. appear to have put in abeyance their own decisive critique of clinical validation. Both dreams and Rorschach responses can be "explored" with disastrous effect; think of the role played by dream analysis in recovered memory therapy, and think of Robert Lindner's suggestion that shock treatment may be indicated when Rorschach answers reveal a desperate mental state. The story told with admirable patience and logic in *What's Wrong with the Rorschach?* speaks more clearly than its authors do here at the end. This test is a ludicrous but still dangerous relic of the previous century's histrionic love affair with "depth," and the only useful purpose it can serve now is as a caution against related follies.

Chapter 11

THE MIND SNATCHERS

THIS DISCUSSION OF SEVERAL RECENT BOOKS ON "UFOLOGY" WAS PUBLISHED IN
The New York Review of Books, JUNE 25, 1998. AT FIRST GLANCE, THE TOPIC MAY
APPEAR SIMPLY RIDICULOUS. THE ESSAY TAKES ITS INTEREST, HOWEVER, FROM
CONSIDERING BOTH THE GULLIBILITY OF A CELEBRATED HARVARD PSYCHOLO-
GIST, NOW DECEASED, AND A POSTMODERN ACADEMIC'S REFUSAL, ON POLITICAL/
THEORETICAL GROUNDS, TO DRAW OBVIOUS CONCLUSIONS ABOUT THE BASELESS
NATURE OF UFO REPORTS. FOR AN EXCELLENT RECENT STUDY OF THE ABDUC-
TION PHENOMENON, SEE CLANCY 2005.

I.

According to a *Time*/CNN poll, 64 percent of Americans now believe
that creatures from elsewhere in the universe have recently been in
personal touch with human beings, and among the believers, roughly
half subscribe to the thesis of alien abduction (CNN Interactive 1997).
One such mortal, Whitley Strieber, has "received nearly a quarter of a
million letters claiming contact" (Strieber 1998b, p. 86) in the eleven
years preceding his report. Indeed, many people, most of them mere
students of the topic rather than "experiencers," think that the aliens,
having subjected abductees to breeding experiments in parked spaceships or secret underground laboratories, have already produced a race
of hybrids who will someday rule or even replace us.

The hybrids may in fact be shopping and commuting all around us
as I write. And even if they aren't, their mixed parentage could help to
explain the familiar images found in abduction memories like the following, culled from each of the three books under review here:

> He's got on a, a multistriped t-shirt. . . . And some, like little blue
> shorts. . . . They had sophisticated-looking toys, like maybe they
> got them out of Edmund's Scientific or something. . . . They have a

yo-yo. . . . It looks like an Etch-a-Sketch screen, except it's filled with all sorts of stuff. (Jacobs 1999, pp. 137, 139, 141, 152)

They were dressed like 1920s thugs, and came into the bedroom with old fashioned Tommy Guns, aiming at me and blazing away. (Strieber 1998b, p. 99)

Beth Collings saw a naked man in an enormous white cowboy hat. . . . Karla Turner . . . mentions two people she knows who have seen aliens disguised as hillbillies. Katharina Wilson had an experience with an alien masquerading as Al Gore. (Dean 1998, p. 121)

Once recollections of this kind are taken to be authentic, guesswork as to the aliens' true nature and purpose becomes irresistible. What if, for example, Katharina Wilson's visitor wasn't just masquerading as Al Gore but *was* "Al Gore"—the hybrid or body snatcher who has already replaced the man from Tennessee? And if so, the alien takeover of our executive branch surely wouldn't have stopped at the second in command. Consider this provocative observation by the renowned abduction expert David M. Jacobs:

> Because the late-state hybrids are mainly human, they have strong sexual drives but little conscience. It is as if they have human attributes but lack human controls. Even if they do have a conscience, they know that the human victim will immediately forget what has happened to her. The hybrid might assume that there is no lasting effect upon the human and he therefore can do and say anything he pleases with impunity. (Jacobs 1999, pp. 206–207)

Could the space creature who assumed the form of Bill Clinton have been hideously mocking us when it kept invoking "executive privilege"?

Of course there are difficulties to be ironed out before speculations along these lines can become fully respectable. One of them has to do with distance. In the planets circling our Sun, no creatures besides ourselves are known for their partiality to tourism. What, then, about the next nearest star, Alpha Centauri? Voyaging from that vicinity at the generous estimate of a million miles per hour, our current visitors would have had to wave goodbye to their loved ones around the time of Moses—and then, having briefly played doctor with their favored specimens, some white Americans, they could look forward to devoting another three millennia to the return trip. Would it, to quote Prufrock, have been worth it, after all?[1]

To the unlikelihood of such persistent travel must be added the fact that modern UFO incidents, from the still hotly debated Roswell, New Mexico, Air Force case of 1947 until now, can be accounted for in rationally acceptable mundane terms.[2] Misleading optical effects, half-waking dreams, sleep paralysis, tricks of memory, paranoid delusions, temporal lobe lesions, intoxication, fraud, and faddism are abundantly familiar to us, whereas the UFO thesis, even without the added burden of abduction tales, flouts the known laws of nature at every turn. Lacking even a scrap of credible physical evidence, ufologists have had to fall back on an appeal to numbers. How, they ask, could so many trustworthy witnesses be wrong about having spotted a spacecraft? Well, just replace "spacecraft" with "witch," "ghost," "angel," "Loch Ness monster," "Abominable Snowman," or "face of Mother Teresa on a bun," and you have your answer.

If all parties to the UFO controversy subscribed to the rule of Ockham's razor and to David Hume's reservations about the miraculous, the issue would have been laid to rest a whole generation ago, when Philip J. Klass's *UFO's Explained* (1974) deflated the best brief for visitation then extant, J. Allen Hynek's *The UFO Experience: A Scientific Inquiry* (1972). Empirically speaking, nothing has changed since then; it is still the case that "you can't get here from there." Yet UFO claims, far from abating or becoming more humble, have expanded in number, extravagance, and fervor, and there is no reason to think that any deployment of evidence or logic can now discourage them.

At the time of the Hynek-Klass exchange, the bone of contention was sightings: could any of the supposedly glimpsed celestial objects be spaceships from elsewhere? To be sure, a number of witnesses had also laid claim to very bizarre personal dealings with aliens, but "responsible" ufologists considered such reports fraudulent, and so-called contactees were regarded as a discredit to the cause. The sobriety of that cause depended on the aliens' continued elusiveness. So long as they kept darting about the heavens so coyly, only pausing occasionally to hover over a swamp or chase a car, their technically inclined human monitors could also maintain a low profile, venturing no inanities about the contents of the baffling extraterrestrial mind.

2.

In 1981, however, Budd Hopkins published his wildly popular *Missing Time*, and UFO advocacy underwent a major reversal. The physics of space travel was no longer deemed greatly interesting. Instead, credence was invested in one limited form of human-alien contact—namely, abduction. And that vogue is still going strong today, though certain of the faithful, taking a less dire view of alien actions and motives than Hopkins had, prefer gentler terms such as "visitation" or simply "experience." But the difference is only a matter of coloration, since all parties concur in maintaining that the uninvited guests have been seizing people for hours of "missing time" and tampering with their bodies and minds.

The abduction stories are supposedly warranted not by their verisimilitude but by the sincerity and emotional agitation with which they are narrated. Thus UFO validation, like much else in our nominally scientific era, has taken an inward turn. Although most citizens distrust abduction reports, others cannot withhold their sympathy from patent victims. They are ready to second Harvard's former resident ufologist and prophet of higher consciousness, the late John Mack, who complained that the inclusion of "a hostile debunker" on a radio or television program about abduction "constitutes a human rights violation of an authentic minority."[3]

David Jacobs and Whitley Strieber share with Mack and Hopkins the highest popularity among abduction/visitation believers. Such eminence requires that they keep the dissenters at bay by making a grave show of answering empirically based objections. Strieber in particular is a master of such guile, nominally welcoming experimentation and tantalizing his readers with the prospect of physical proofs that never quite materialize. His and Jacobs's scientific concern is UFO-like: now you see it, now you don't. Jacobs speaks for both authors when he declares that it just doesn't matter how the aliens got here. Maybe they did so, suggests this Temple University history professor, by surfing the "astral plane," or by popping out of "a parallel universe," or by "traveling on thought patterns"—their own or even ours. "The question is not how aliens get here," says Jacobs insouciantly, "but whether they *are* here. The 'how' is ultimately a technological detail" (Jacobs 1999, p. 90).

Once such formalities are out of the way, the encounter expert is free to expand his claims at just those points where they might be considered most vulnerable. You needn't wonder, for example, how astronauts from another planetary system can give comprehensible orders to monolingual Yankee earthlings; the aliens, Jacobs and Strieber assure us, can read our thoughts and communicate with us telepathically. Again, if only one person in a crowd sees the intruders approach and leave, that is not because they are imaginary but because they have a knack of putting anyone they please into a trance. If an alleged abduction has left doors and windows locked, leading to a suspicion that the whole thing was a dream, the theory comes to the rescue by positing an ability on the aliens' part to waft both themselves and us through solid walls. If some of the hypnotically recalled visitors bear a suspiciously human aspect, that's not because people tend to dream about other people but because some UFO denizens must be hybrids. And if women who thought they had been impregnated by aliens turn out not to be pregnant at all, that is because their offspring have already been extracted in a second, but this time amnesiac, violation.

Both Strieber and Jacobs have recourse to the classic sophistry of all ufologists, ascribing a cumulative weight to reports that, when regarded one by one, are lighter than air. ("Individually," says Strieber, "the stories are incredible. But taken together, they are beyond the incredible" [p. 93].) What compels assent, they declare, is the otherwise unaccountable congruence of detail from one narrative to another. In fact, however, there is nothing unaccountable about it. Descriptions of spaceships and aliens have always followed the specifications laid down by Hollywood in films such as *The Day the Earth Stood Still* (1951),

Close Encounters of the Third Kind (1977), and *E.T.: The Extra-Terrestrial* (1982); by scare-mongering TV docudramas such as NBC's sensational and slanted *The UFO Incident* (1975);[4] and by books like Strieber's own runaway best seller of 1987, *Communion.*

Indeed, authors like Strieber, Jacobs, Hopkins, and Mack are best understood not as neutral compilers of abduction experience but as theoretically committed generators and standardizers of it, each of whom attracts the type of report he is known to favor. Their works at once provide templates for future dreams or nightmares, filter out or minimize anomalous material, and establish the author as an inspirational figure holding special insight into the extraterrestrials' plans. If you suspect that ETs are up to no good, Hopkins or Jacobs will help you fit the evidence into a satisfying conspiratorial thesis. If, on the other hand, you prefer the mushy Steven Spielberg approach, Mack or Strieber will soothe you with assurances that the aliens, despite their occasional rudeness, are really our tutors, having come all this way just to raise our ecological awareness and enhance our spirituality.

However earnestly intended, these mind-numbing books can shake loose some very big bucks for their authors and their shamelessly cynical publishers, who surely realize that they are not merely widening their companies' profit margins but fomenting public delusion. Twenty or thirty years ago, for reasons of self-respect, most houses would have thought twice about lending their imprint to such ludicrous stuff. Not today; there's no business like UFO business. The prospect of striking it rich again with another blockbuster like Strieber's *Communion* or Hopkins's *Missing Time* is just too tempting to pass up.

As an entrepreneur, no one in the UFO community quite compares to Whitley Strieber. He was already a successful writer of horror fiction before he decided that he himself was an experiencer with a story to tell. His *Communion*, having prompted a $1 million advance from Beech Tree Books, was rushed into print in 1987 to steal a march on Random House and Hopkins's sequel volume *Intruders*, whose anticipated audience indeed defected to Strieber. (Hopkins was evidently born too soon to benefit from the reign of benevolent cooperation that the Strieber-style aliens are preparing for us.) As for Strieber's latest effort, *Confirmation*, a publicity bulletin from St. Martin's Press pointed to the happy conjunction of its release with the debut of Hollywood's much ballyhooed film *The X-Files*. But Strieber himself would not want to be associated with such crassness. He prefers to call attention to the altruistic-looking Communion Foundation, a tax-exempt, donation-soliciting enterprise that, by gathering "research" and further testimony of the desired kind, can provide the raw material for even more best sellers.[5]

Strieber was a latecomer to the UFO movement and even to its abduction-theory phase. His fellow ufologists, especially those whose interest was sparked by aeronautic phenomena, have always regarded him with cool suspicion. And well they might, for Strieber manages to be all things to all readers who grant him an initial suspension of disbelief. Alternating among autobiographical narrative, other victims' stories, and expert-sounding discussion of tests and gadgets; doling out well-spaced *frissons* in the Stephen King manner; yet also telling the spiritually hungry how much the aliens care about them, Strieber leaves his competitors looking like understudies who are still trying to memorize a master thespian's lines.[6]

One element in Strieber's original success, though it has fallen away as his fame has grown, was his willingness to make personal revelations that a less nimble persuader would have hesitated to disclose. In *Communion*, for example, he acknowledged a propensity for telling sensational tales about his past that he believed at the time of telling but later realized were false. One might think that such a confession would diminish his value as a witness to otherworldly entities floating around his bedroom. On the contrary, Strieber's show of candor was a brilliant stroke, conjuring an image of pained vulnerability that rendered his *outré* narrative more credible and poignant to millions of readers who could empathize with his struggle.

When the aliens paid their first call at Strieber's upstate New York cabin in the backwoods, they had to deactivate a distinctly unrural alarm system and foil his nightly check of all closets and crannies for small intruders. After that incident, his composure hung in the balance until the kindly Budd Hopkins helped him regain control—an intervention that Hopkins may regret by now. But "control" may not be quite the *mot juste*. Strieber has a record of hearing voices and switching his religious sympathy among Christian denominations, medieval mysticism, Zen Buddhism, earth-goddess witchcraft, and Gurdjieffian Theosophy.

In any event, Strieber has reserved his most daring maneuver for his latest volume, *Confirmation*. His earlier books, he now asserts, were never intended to say that the extraterrestrials are already among us; he had just wanted to raise the issue of whether they were or not. Now, however, he is sure not only that the ETs have arrived but also that they have inserted "unknown bright objects" in his brain (Strieber 1998b, p. 221). Using those implants as remote control devices, he implies, the spacepersons forced him, unknowingly, to alter the original neutrality of his drafted books. On now rereading the bound versions, he is amazed to find them unambiguously stating the actual truth: "that spiritually evolved aliens were here trying to influence humankind in a positive way" (p. 221). Anticipating (and also augmenting) Strieber's sales figures, it seems, the aliens made him their chosen vessel for spreading the good word.

That such cosmic gall can pass unchallenged among Strieber's loyal readership may suggest how deeply he and other visitation authorities have tapped into the will to believe. As many observers have noted, the feelings that find expression in UFO doctrine are multiple and deep.[7] They range from religious yearnings and a sense of anomie and threatened autonomy to resentment of dryly materialistic laws of science and a conviction, based on individualistic contrarianism, that the government's belittlement of UFOs is a strong point in their favor. These are dispositions, not arguments, and therefore skepticism has nothing in its arsenal that can touch them.

That fact in itself is of no great consequence. Insofar as the UFO obsession constitutes just another form of supernatural belief, it can be regarded as a comforting hobby. And as hobbies go, a rage for flying saucers would seem preferable to, say, the racing of dune buggies across fragile desert terrain. But there is a catch: the troubled people who come to see themselves as abductees are not hobbyists but genuine victims, though not in the way they think.

As David Jacobs relates, "Most abductees say the phenomenon has had a devastating effect on their personal lives" (Jacobs 1999, p. 225). One can gather what he means by attending to the following fragment of a case that was brought to him:

> Then the hybrids told Beverly that they could take her body whenever they wanted and that she was always vulnerable and never safe. One hybrid raped her, and she was forced to perform fellatio upon another. They pinched her, twisted her skin, and hurt her without leaving marks. They pushed an unlit candle into her vagina. They then told her she had caused her children to be abducted. . . . On another occasion hybrids made her envision her six-year-old daughter walking into a room ringed with naked hybrids who had erections; she was led to believe that her daughter would be raped by all of them. (p. 205)

Even Strieber, whose correspondents generally represent the uplifted-and-enlightened end of the contactee spectrum, admits that "[s]ixty percent specifically mention fear. Twenty percent report negative encounters" (Strieber 1995, p. 96).

3.

The first impulse of most readers, I suspect, once they are made aware of such needless terror, is to pathologize the sufferers: they must be exceptionally disturbed if not outright crazy individuals. No doubt that is true of some of them, but as a generalization it falls flat. One need only peruse *NOVA*'s excellent program of February 27, 1997, "Kidnapped by UFOs?," to become acquainted with self-perceived abductees who are intelligent, articulate, and rational in all respects but one, their memories of close encounters. And that impression is borne out by every study that has attempted, always fruitlessly, to find predictive factors for susceptibility to the UFO illusion.[8]

It is inappropriate, then, to set apart self-perceived abductees as psychotics or, more mildly, as "hysterics" who have failed to contain an internal buildup of pressure, be it repressed "shame, guilt, or helplessness" (Showalter 1997, p. 207) or some vague millennial anxiety. The spotlight should be turned instead on the Pied Pipers who induce false belief, not only through their books and films and talk shows but also, in many instances, through their one-on-one practice of quack therapy with patients who have consulted them about their unnerving nightmares featuring ETs.

Nearly always in such consultations, the fateful source of error turns out to be abuse of hypnosis. The great facilitator of anguish over abduction is not mental illness on the victims' part but hypnosis in the hands of their would-be supporters. Those dabblers, many of whom lack any training beyond a quickie night school course, have failed to learn the most important fact about hypnosis: that the emotions and "recollections" generated in a hypnotic session needn't refer to anything but the suggestive pressure exerted by the hypnotist himself.

It is no coincidence that, of the four leading abduction boosters, three—Mack, Hopkins, and Jacobs—use "time regression" hypnosis as their key means of gaining information about contact with aliens. As for Strieber, he himself submitted to hypnosis so as to resolve doubts about his initial encounter of December 1985, and he credits countless mailed-in stories without investigating what role hypnotic anamnesis may have played in their production. Although all four authors make token gestures of caution against hypnotic confabulation, their actual prudence in that regard is nil. Indeed, Mack can even write, with childlike ingenuousness, that the United States leads the world in abduction reports, with England and Brazil coming next, "chiefly because of the availability of practicing hypnotists and therapists working with abductees in these countries."9

As the *NOVA* video made clear, there is nothing unusual about the way most abduction memories are formed. They begin with sleep paralysis, the same condition of half-awake dreaming that once fed into widespread and catastrophic delusions of possession by witches, incubi, or Satan himself.10 Alarmist books and programs about alien invasion take the place of religious folklore in shaping the preliminary interpretation that scientifically uninformed Americans overlay on such experiences. But, typically, it is only in the office of a true-believer hypnotist or other quasi-Mesmeric practitioner that the hunch congeals into "truth" and becomes a lasting threat to the dreamer's equanimity. When David Jacobs tells us, for example, that many abductees "live in fear that it will happen again and feel guilty that they cannot protect their children," he is largely describing the outcome of his own meddling as a biased hypnotic detective.

Here, inevitably, we arrive at the theme of recovered memory. Not surprisingly, abduction reports began multiplying just when, in the 1980s, false memories of "repressed" or "dissociated" incest trauma became a national epidemic. Abduction memories and memories of "forgotten" childhood sexual abuse are conjured in exactly the same way, by applying an unsubstantiated psychodynamic theory to the images unearthed by hypnotherapy, dream analysis, and assorted techniques for stimulating and guiding fantasy. Although the sex abuse specialists see recollections of alien contact as screen memories for incest while the abductionists take the opposite view, they are all playing the same noxious game.

But this parallelism could also give us cause for optimism about the likely fate of the abduction fad. Thanks to the harm it has caused and the attention it has drawn to pseudoscientific notions about the mind that were shared by judges and juries only a few years ago, the recovered memory movement is now in retreat, and the therapists who swelled its ranks are being sued by some of the awakened "retractors" whom they deceived. There is every reason to expect a similar end to the scare over extraterrestrials. Though general UFO belief will surely go on indefinitely, the folly of abduction "memory" can be halted if, through public education and counseling, "abductees" themselves come to realize what has been done to them.

4.

As someone who spent his employed decades in a congenial university setting, I would like to think that academics will be prime contributors to this effort. And perhaps they will. But another recent book about the UFO phenomenon offers a reminder that the contemporary academy, riven as it is by a chasm that has continued to widen since the 1970s, cannot be counted on as a bastion against irrationalism. In *Aliens in America: Conspiracy Cultures from Outerspace to Cyberspace* (1998), Jodi Dean, a political scientist at Hobart and William Smith Colleges, strikes an attitude that is more disturbing in its way than anything said by Professors Mack and Jacobs.

While those tenured apologists have worked amid well-earned ostracism and ridicule from their colleagues, Dean, who has already composed one book of feminist theory and edited another (Dean 1996, 1997), here wields the current idiom of poststructuralism and postmodernism in a way that must have favorably impressed peer evaluators and the staff of Cornell University Press. Yet if *Aliens in America* is a mainstream work, the mainstream has become a turbid meander. The problem is not the author's hospitality, per se, to the alien abduction hypothesis; indeed, she repeatedly assures us of her perfect indifference to all claims proffered by the UFO movement. But indifference itself—a studied refusal to acknowledge any criteria of judgment except sheer subversiveness toward an imagined establishment—is precisely the scandal here.

As a sociologist of cults and conspiracies, Dean might be expected to show us how the abduction zealots debase the language of scientific prudence, simulating a concern over fraud, error, and hypnotic confabulation while appealing to faith at every turn. She does allude more than once to the UFO literature's abundant but meaningless invocation of the majority culture's "scientific and juridical standards." But those standards figure in her book not as our common rational heritage but merely as technocratic idols to which the powerless are forced to pay homage. She herself takes pride in doing without them altogether.

What counts for Dean is that a UFO report, however discreetly it may be couched, is "a political act" that "contests the status quo" (Dean 1998, p. 6). "Those of us attracted to left-wing causes," she says, "to critical positions against political, governmental, and corporate authorities, or maybe just to underdogs in general may feel at home in ufology" (p. 60). Abductees are especially praiseworthy because "[t]hey hold on to their experiences, resisting the efforts of interpreters to compile them into coherence" (p. 122). Mere persistence in UFO delusion, then, constitutes useful sabotage of the evil empire—"the techno-global information society that is America at the millennium" (p. 6)—which nevertheless, Dean implies, remains in total command of our lives.

But if our oppressors pay no heed to alien abduction, where does the subversion come in? The answer is that it resides entirely in Dean's own head. The politics that animate her are focused not on concrete developments but on conceptual fuzzballs such as "contestation," "thematics," "cultural space," "essentialization," "reinscription," and "the originary moment." In the never-never "site" where she "interrogates the production of knowledge" and deconstructs "the social imaginary," points are awarded to any act or notion that can be counted as "anti-hegemonic."

It scarcely matters to Dean, then, that our popular culture, in which she herself shows every sign of being uncritically immersed, devours the "subversive" abduction tales like so many Big Macs; nor does it matter that the state of Nevada is drawing tourists to an official Extraterrestrial Highway commemorating alien contacts; nor that one can now attend an abduction conference held on the grounds of MIT and then read a sympathetic account of it in the upscale and none too revolutionary *New Yorker*. Nor does Dean care that writers like Strieber, Hopkins, Mack, and Jacobs, in the tradition of religious quietism, "contest the status quo" by encouraging millions of people to point their hopes and fears heavenward instead of acting in their material interest.

This is not to say that Dean leaves real historical circumstances entirely out of account. Both the Cold War and its stepchild, NASA, are continually cited in *Aliens in America* as the backdrop against which ufology acquired its revolutionary cast. But if we had to rely on Dean for our knowledge of the Cold War, we would never realize that it had something to do with thwarting Soviet expansionism. For her, as for other post-Vietnam academic radicals, "Cold War containment culture" was just an instrument for imposing American values on the world, penalizing social nonconformity, and hounding imagined "enemies within."

Then there is NASA, which in Dean's view has served no other function, either military or scientific, than to wage a "theatrics of space," a global skywriting campaign that could "win the Cold War and the ratings war" (p. 11) by upstaging the Russians with flashier stunts than theirs. Ignoring abundant evidence that the Air Force and the Pentagon, not NASA, have been ufology's perennial bugbears, Dean takes it as axiomatic that UFO buffs share her loathing of the space program. In the private mental Nintendo that she mistakes for politics, abduction survivors achieve their highest score by serving as anti-astronauts. Their tales of kidnapping "tell about ways of being human that transform the representations of agency and spectatorship found in space imagery . . ." (p. 7). And imagery is all that finally matters.

Dean does recognize that someone who has become convinced he was kidnapped by ETs may thenceforth be subject to paranoid fears. At that point her reader momentarily entertains the hope that compassion will set in, prompting Dean to back off from ideologizing the abduction theme. But nothing of the sort occurs. Rather, Dean rushes to embrace paranoia itself on political grounds. True or false, paranoid conspiracy theory recommends itself to her as "an appropriate vehicle for political contestation" (p. 8), obliging the rest of us to think about "victimization, colonization, surveillance, and the 'technologizing' of reproduction and the body" (p. 46).

Nevertheless, Dean perceives a flaw in the paranoid mindset: it is too fixated upon truth. The paranoiac, she says, thinks that answers really lie "out there" but are concealed by sinister forces, whereas she herself suffers from no such illusion:

> Faced with gigabytes of indigestible information, computer-generated special effects, competing expert testimonies, and the undeniable presence of power, corruption, racism, and violence

throughout science and law, voters, consumers, viewers, and witnesses have no criteria for choosing among policies and verdicts,
treatments and claims. (p. 7)

By way of illustration, Dean cites the O. J. Simpson trial, in which
"DNA evidence entered by the prosecution was not as compelling as
what, for many, was a personal experience of discrimination and harm"
(p. 8). She comments: "Given the political and politicized position of
science today, funded by corporations and by the military, itself dis-
criminatory and elitist, this attitude toward scientific authority makes
sense" (p. 8).

For Dean, all that's certain is the undecidability of every issue. Yet
even here the discourse of the alien gives her a vanguard feeling: it
"marks a dissolution of the boundaries of the intelligible so complete
that any exclusion seems arbitrary, repressive" (p. 61). Since ufology
instructs us that there are "myriad perspectives on the world, each with
its own legitimate claim to truth" (p. 108), the wisest course would be
to venture no assertions and take no action. "Passivity makes sense,"
Dean observes, "if we lack perspective, if we lack even the possibility of
perspective because all possible points from which to assess our situations have collapsed into one another" (p. 173).

In this light it is significant that the object of greatest scorn in *Aliens
in America* proves to be the late Carl Sagan, a fellow academic who
shared Dean's interest in UFO abduction but publicly challenged its
reality. She has certainly chosen the right adversary to epitomize everything that she is not. Yet because rationality itself is anathema to her,
she cannot begin to come to terms with Sagan's argument against the
likelihood of space intruders. Instead, she lamely attempts to show
that he "confirms the importance" (p. 55) of alien abduction simply
by discussing the topic at length. Since Sagan placed himself "in the
UFO discourse, . . . his very critique reaffirms its claim to scientific
status" (p. 59). Furthermore, "Sagan isn't as skeptical as Hopkins
because he, Sagan, works within a worldview that he doesn't question.
. . . He doesn't even know where we are now, when people are skeptical
to the point of paranoia" (p. 70).

Having thus expressed her contempt for critical reasoning, Dean faces the problem of putting her own propositions into some kind of order without sounding like yet another slave to thought. Her solution is to "link" ideas free-associatively, citing as precedent the analogy of website links that nonhierarchically connect everything with everything else. In Dean's rhetoric, links—between alien abduction and alien immigration, the race issue and the space race, a new breed of men (astronauts) and the breeding of new men—replace logical operations while retaining a vaguely syllogistic air, as if her mere ability to pun between themes amounted to proof of something momentous.

Precisely because Dean's links are too easily "clicked," however, they fall short of meaning anything definite even to her. All of her key terms lead her in circles, and at times she is reduced to a kind of stammering:

> It is an age of aliens, an alien age when alien images and alien copies and copies of aliens appear unpredictably and unannounced in places they shouldn't, in places we can't understand, in multiple, contradictory, alien places. (p. 4)
>
> The interesting phenomena involve more than belief in aliens and UFOs. . . . These phenomena include the interest in aliens on the part of those who don't believe, in aliens as fashion statement or icon of techno-globalism or globo-technocism. The interesting phenomena involve the myriad acknowledgments in networked information cultures of the extraterrestrial gaze. (p. 11)

The editors at Cornell University Press—unless they have already been supplanted by space invaders—are apparently wagering that such babble is the academic lingua franca of the future. If it is, Carl Sagan, himself a distinguished member of the Cornell faculty and a champion of clear prose, won't be missed. I suspect, however, that what *Aliens in America* really announces is a dead end. Here the gestural radicalism of Paris 1968 has reached its futilitarian nadir, where sheer disablement—the inability of traduced people to free their minds from haunting and debilitating images—is hailed as the nearest imaginable thing to freedom.

But the fiasco is intellectual as well as political. For decades now, we have been told that "knowledge" is not a legitimate goal of striving but merely a shibboleth for enforcing the dominance of a class, race, or gender. From that position it follows that the correct way to assess an idea is not to test its congruence with established facts but simply to ask whose interest it serves. And once this anti-empirical habit comes into play, it automatically creates sympathy for whatever notions are rejected by the ruling group. The process of rehabilitating "marginalized" conceptions stops at nothing—not even, we now perceive, at the most comical excesses of the abduction mania.

"The aliens have landed," writes Jodi Dean with slacker sarcasm. "Resistance is futile" (p. 61). On the contrary, *Aliens in America* helps to clarify, through its very stagnancy and incoherence, just where resistance ought to be applied.

IV.

The Will to Believe

Chapter 12

THE CONSOLATION OF THEOSOPHY

A LONGER VERSION OF THIS CHAPTER AND THE NEXT ONE APPEARED AS A TWO-PART ARTICLE IN *The New York Review of Books*, SEPTEMBER 19 AND OCTOBER 3, 1996. THEY ARE MEANT TO BE READ AS A SINGLE UNFOLDING NARRATIVE AND ARGUMENT.

I.

During my several decades of teaching literature at Berkeley, one of my favorite offerings proved to be a large introductory lecture course on modern British and American authors. I always found it a pleasure to lead wary but game lower-division students at least partway into the rarefied, highly wrought worlds of Joyce, Faulkner, Woolf, Stevens, and their contemporaries. Notoriously, however, modernism comes with some awkward ideological baggage. My distaste for Lawrence's preaching against insubordinate women and for Pound's fulminations against "the Jews" made it hard for me personally to cope with such noxious rant, to say nothing of asking California sophomores, steeped in egalitarianism and innocent of history, to put it into some ameliorating perspective.

The juncture in each semester that I approached most warily, though, was the hour when an accounting had to be made of W. B. Yeats's magical beliefs and practices. Here was perhaps the greatest of modern poets, the one who could most fearlessly and eloquently address perennial human concerns about sexual striving, wounded pride, lost love, bodily decay, shattered dreams, and helplessness before blind forces; but here as well was someone who needed—and not just for the sake of his muse—to believe in palmistry, crystal gazing, astral travel, the secret governance of history by phases of the moon, and a spirit world that could be commanded through ritual incantations. How, I wondered, could such a "sentimentalism of the intellect," as Yeats's father justly called it, square with the poet's exultation in his capacity to face cold reality without flinching? Moreover, I knew what to expect at the end of my necessarily equivocal lecture: the blocking of my exit by a small but intent cluster of students who would clamor for further news about those 2,000-year cycles that really, professor, *really* make everything fall into place at last, and where do I sign up for this Golden Dawn?

That Yeats was in earnest about his esotericism cannot be doubted. As his bemused friend Pound observed in a letter of 1919, "Bit queer in the head about 'moon,' whole new metaphysics about 'moon,' very very very bughouse." Neither Pound's sarcasms nor John Butler Yeats's paternal chiding could shake the poet's conviction that, in his own words from 1892, "The mystical life is the centre of all that I do and all that I think and all that I write." Like some of my students a century later, Yeats felt that gnostic beliefs and rituals were less a rearguard protest against the iron rule of science and materialism than the advancing edge of an emergent mass consciousness. As he put it, "I have always considered myself a voice of what I believe to be a greater renaissance—the revolt of the soul against the intellect—now beginning in the world."[1]

But until Yeats became a distinguished personage, that voice was a mere echo of a far more confident one. Like others who pined for lost certainties, Yeats had fallen under the spell of one of the gaudiest characters of the nineteenth century. This was Helena Petrovna Blavatsky, cofounder, with Henry Steel Olcott, of the burgeoning Theosophical Society, and a catalyst of unorthodox neo-religious stirrings in America, England, the European continent, India, and elsewhere.

For sheer chutzpah, there has never been anyone quite like Madame Blavatsky. Born in Russia and descended from Russian-German aristocrats, she fled at age seventeen from an ill-considered marriage and kept on moving for the next quarter-century. During her passage through much of the world, she kept acquiring assorted occult/religious notions, meanwhile liberally inventing other travels and adventures that would enhance her self-portrayal as an initiate into secret brotherhoods.

When Blavatsky settled in New York in 1873 at age 42, she looked to be just another table-rapping spiritualist. Indeed, Blavatsky and Olcott had come together, platonically, over their common interest in the summoning of ghosts—an object of naive awe for him, a workaday meal ticket for her. But she would soon one-up her fellow mediums by copiously plagiarizing and synthesizing esoteric texts and by making claims of paranormal contact with Tibetan "Masters" or "Mahatmas" whom she had allegedly visited in person. Thus she came to be known as an authority on the world's religions and ancient cults, which all proved to have derived from an aboriginal, long-suppressed doctrine that had been revealed to her in telepathic trances and in letters that were "precipitated" by psychic express into her antechambers and train compartments.

Blavatsky moved her society's headquarters from New York to India in 1878 after the American press, which had gotten wind of her vulgar deceptions as well as her zany stories, showed a determination to keep her in the satirical limelight. But the move wasn't just expedient; HPB wanted to tip Theosophy's scales away from too exclusive an emphasis on Western esotericism—the body of thought that yoked together magic, alchemy, Hellenistic and Renaissance Neo-Platonism, the Kabbalah, the Tarot pack, and communication with spirits—and toward the more mystical, higher-toned Eastern tradition that included Vedanta and Mahayana Buddhism.[2] The result was a still more awkward mishmash of dogmas that would have troubled even the chronically credulous if HPB hadn't kept them marveling at her paranormal demonstrations—some of which, however, were once again being publicly exposed as shams. When she moved, one last time, to London in 1887, it was because the skeptics were back on her trail; a commission of the Society for Psychical Research, investigating her stunts at Adyar (near Madras), had pronounced her an accomplished fraud. Yet Blavatsky's apparent persecution by "materialists" only enhanced her glory in the eyes of neophyte admirers like Yeats, who was easily persuaded by a dashing Indian disciple, Mohini Chatterjee, to join the Theosophical Society's magic-minded Esoteric Section in London.

To be sure, when the hypersensitive Yeats actually met Blavatsky, he was taken aback by her coarseness of manner. Nor could he ever quite bring himself to believe in the existence of her Himalayan Masters. In turn, HPB was made so uneasy by Yeats's insistence on performing foolish magical experiments—trying, for example, to raise the ghost of a flower from its ashes—that she soon exacted his resignation. Yet Blavatsky had placed her stamp on his mind indelibly. Without her encouragement to pierce the veil of maya, Yeats would have been deprived of the prophetic strain and several of the odd but passionately held beliefs that helped to lend his verse its uniquely rapt quality.

2.

If Yeats's case were unique, we could dismiss it as a curious foot-note to modern cultural history. But from the 1880s straight through the 1940s an imposing number of prominent figures, from Kandin-sky and Mondrian through Gandhi and Nehru to Huxley and Isher-wood, intersected the Theosophical orbit long enough to have their trajectory significantly altered by it. As some of those names imply, moreover, the movement distinguished itself from most esoteric fads by resonating with consequential forces of sociopolitical change. Blavatsky and Olcott's political message—internationalist, pacifist, socially progressive—appealed not only to the enlightened bourgeoisie of England and America but also to indigenous leaders in colonized lands such as India and Ceylon, where the Theosophical Society estab-lished impressive beachheads. And although its enrolled membership, worldwide, never exceeded 45,000, it spawned a number of related asso-ciations—most notably, perhaps, Rudolf Steiner's "Anthroposophy"—that exert a continuing influence on reformist and utopian thought.

One is tempted to assume that such an effective movement must have been only superficially irrationalist in emphasis. After all, the Theo-sophical Society's charter sounded almost like a university catalog, refer-ring soberly to "the encouragement of studies in comparative religion, philosophy and science" and to "the investigation of unexplained laws of nature." But it wasn't comparative religion that instructed Madame

Blavatsky about "the Lord of the World," who, she reported, had dropped to Earth from Venus with various helpers whose own assistants included her two chief personal Masters. Nor was it science that taught Theosophists to construe pure spirit as a sufficient cause of events ranging from remote communication between individuals to the secret pre-arrangement of whole historical epochs by celestial busybodies.

How could otherwise discerning people have subscribed to such preposterous ideas? To address that question, one turns expectantly to scholarly treatises on esotericism in general and Theosophy in particular. But one quickly finds that most of the historians are themselves occult partisans who, for example, "objectively" weigh the likelihood that enlightened beings paid astral visits to Olcott and others, making flowers appear in midair, causing an indoor rain shower, and so forth.[3] One such expert avers that experimental science is "hardly capable of accounting for" the correspondences that "unite all visible things and likewise unite the latter with invisible realities" (Faivre 1994, p. 34), and another maintains that work such as Blavatsky's "demolishes the pretensions of science by adducing a mass of evidence against the premises of materialism" (Godwin 1994, p. 305). Such writers can't tell us why occult ideas have proved seductive; they merely illustrate the problem.

So, too, the esoteric historians' gratitude toward the propounders of transcendent doctrine leaves them reluctant to be candid or vivid about the shamming, squabbling, and jockeying for power that inevitably characterize the daily conduct of any movement that traffics in unconfirmable ideas. Consider, for example, what becomes of Madame Blavatsky in the hands of K. Paul Johnson (1994, 1995), the best-informed but hardly the most trustworthy commentator on Theosophy. Though he acknowledges HPB's light regard for the truth and reluctantly explodes several features of her legend, Johnson airily maintains that she "devot[ed] all her energies to the enlightenment and liberation of humanity" (K. Johnson 1995, p. 226). Her lies, he declares, were told with the most selfless of motives, to protect the identities of her politically active tutors in Egypt and India, the real-life prototypes

of her fanciful Mahatmas Koot Hoomi and Morya: "Most of her public life was an effort to serve hidden Masters without betraying their
secrets" (K. Johnson 1995, p. 244).

Such piety obscures both the cynical glee Blavatsky must have taken
in perpetrating ruses and the obvious self-interestedness of her concocted "Master letters," which, far from expressing sublime and eternal
truths, mirrored her own opinions and advanced her immediate tactical ends vis-à-vis jealous rivals. At the same time, Johnson's emphasis
on her role as a handmaiden to male sages occludes the very traits of
HPB's that we can still admire: her feisty independence and impetu-
ousness, her spurning of a conventional feminine role, her impatience
with petty hypocrisy, her earthy humor, her well-founded scorn for her
lieutenants, and her shrewdly accurate gauging of other people's eagerness to be gulled.

Happily, though, the story of modern esotericism is not the exclusive
property of esotericists. Now we have Peter Washington's invaluable
*Madame Blavatsky's Baboon: A History of the Mystics, Mediums, and Misfits
Who Brought Spiritualism to America* (1995), a work that makes cogent
sublunar sense of HPB and much of her progeny. Not coincidentally,
it is also a comic triumph, a deliciously deflating narrative about quirky
lawgivers—dreamers, power trippers, pedophilic poseurs—and their
unruly rank and file, "the neurotic, the hysterical, the destructive and
the downright mad."

Yet Washington is by no means merely a naysayer. He shows
empathy with seekers who found themselves orphaned by the loss of
traditional faith. Moreover, he credits some of them with a clear awareness of the difference between what Aldous Huxley would call Theosophy's "bunkum about astral bodies, spiritual hierarchies, reincarna-
tions and so forth" and its standing as "a good enough religion—its
main principles being that all religions contain some truth and that we
ought to be tolerant . . ." (Washington 1995, p. 313).

Washington's portrait of HPB is especially nuanced and convincing. He sees that she was never really in control of her temperament,
her finances, or her courtiers, whom she couldn't resist needling

impishly; but he also detects in her an endearing note of self-mockery—
as when, for example, she describes herself, in a letter of 1883, being
feted in India by discomfited British officials and their wives. Writing
in the third person, the 245-pound Blavatsky depicts her own

> graceful, stately person, clad in half-Tibetan, half-night-dress fash-
> ion, sitting in all the glory of her Calmuck beauty at the Governor's
> and Carmichael's dinner-parties; HPB positively courted by the aide-
> de-camps [sic]! Old "Upasika" [one of her several nicknames] hanging
> like a gigantic nightmare on the gracefully rounded elbows of mem-
> bers of the Council, in pumps and swallow-tailed evening dress and
> silk stockings, smelling brandy and soda enough to kill a Tibetan yak.
> (Washington 1995, pp. 64–65)

Could this be the obedient figure depicted in K. Paul Johnson's defer-
ential studies? It is a stronger person altogether—self-invented, whim-
sical, and enormously amused by the inconvenience she is causing those
who play by the official rules.

This ironic flamboyance on HPB's part comes across vividly in Washington's telling. Of particular note is her almost affectionate quarrel
with Darwinian biology, a body of theory whose emphasis on chance
adaptations and raw necessity was diametrically opposed to her spiritualizing and teleological approach to causality. The theory of evolution through natural selection, she was well aware, had been acquired
through more legitimate labors than her own, and she acknowledged
Darwin's preeminence in a characteristically high-spirited private gesture. Her prize possession, as Washington reports, was "a large bespec-
tacled [stuffed] baboon, standing upright, dressed in wing-collar,
morning-coat and tie, and carrying under its arm the manuscript of a
lecture on *The Origin of Species*" (pp. 44–45). And as Washington shows,
much of HPB's magnum opus, *The Secret Doctrine* (1888), reads like a
hashish-induced satire on *The Descent of Man*, with interplanetary spirits preempting the ancestral role of apes.

But Washington also sees that when it came to established Christianity, Blavatsky's whimsy disappeared; she wanted the whole religion

overthrown. The touchy, divisive "Personal God" of the Judeo-Christian tradition, she felt, had strutted his bloody hour on the historical stage and should now give way to a mellow, nonspecific pantheism. If her means of imparting conviction were meretricious, the conviction itself in this major instance was not.

3.

As Washington's narrative reveals in fine detail, the dilemma that kept HPB continually off balance—how to advance sincerely held principles that had become entangled with improvised nonsense—was bequeathed to her associates when she died in 1891. Most of *Madame Blavatsky's Baboon* is given over to that largely farcical but sometimes poignant aftermath. Washington's masterly telling of the story is not just a chronicle but, implicitly, a parable about the progress of any religion from visionary zeal through the consolidating of a privileged and corruptible priesthood. The fact that HPB was never so innocent as to believe herself a divinely instructed messenger would appear to set Theosophy apart from many another religion, but the more important difference is that it remained a comic-opera affair: no intimidation of the wretched, no collusion with rapacious potentates, no burning of heretics, no genocidal crusades.

After HPB's earthly remains were maneuvered into the grave, the manifest topic of Theosophical debate became how best to honor her legacy; but of course the real question was who should rule. Narrowly partisan letters from the Masters and even from Blavatsky's own shade now began floating like aerial leaflets into the hands of the schemers who stood to gain from them. HPB herself was eventually "occulted" to the status of an Ascended Master sitting between Morya and Koot Hoomi in spirit heaven, and a whole new theology began to crystallize around her. Meanwhile, every tendency she had tried to suppress—Christ worship, ecclesiastical solemnity, apostolic succession, sexual libertinism—blossomed in one cranny or another of the ungovernable international movement.

Insofar as leadership was maintained, furthermore, it was nothing to boast about. Most prominently, there was the ubiquitous and ritual-happy Annie Besant, who remained president from 1907 until her death in 1933. Besant had been a fiery Victorian atheist and socialist, and at the helm of the Theosophical Society she retained her genius for fund-raising and public relations. But esoteric notions, once they had taken hold, appear to have addled her judgment. At once the new president began establishing superfluous suborders—the Preparation League of Healers, the Imperial Services League of Modern Thought, the Prayer League, and so forth—while courting for herself such extra titles as Very Illustrious Most Puissant Grand Commander of the British Jurisdiction of the Co-Masonic Order. Dottiness overtook her long before senility set in for good. In 1925, for example, she and others attempted to locate the Hungarian castle of one of HPB's lesser Masters, the Count of Saint-Germain, by choosing a seemingly random but divinely inspired destination from a railway timetable. The "Dark Forces," she concluded after a week of vexatious train hopping, were responsible for the party's having gotten no farther than Innsbruck.

Besant's choice of trusted associates was a continuing source of imbroglios and recriminations. Above all, she remained steadfastly loyal to Charles Leadbeater, who remained in positions of authority for twenty-five years after the first of many plausible accusations of child molestation were voiced against him in 1906. Leadbeater specialized in cosmological systematizing and in divining the past incarnations of himself and other Theosophists, who had all, it seems, been related to one another not only in earthly ages but on other planets as well. It was Leadbeater, too, who accepted a bishopric in the "Liberal Catholic Church" of James Wedgwood—an even more improbable personage who shared Leadbeater's fondness for invented ranks, beribboned frocks, and pubescent boys, and who once told the police, after having been observed visiting eighteen public lavatories within a two-hour period, that he was seeking a friend who had "gone wrong" in a previous life.

Leadbeater was also instrumental in engineering the Theosophical

Society's greatest and most ironic success, the grooming and selling of Jiddu Krishnamurti, the "World Teacher"—supposedly an incarnation of Maitreya, the messianic Buddha—to a holiness-parched international public. Washington leaves us to surmise whether Leadbeater's quasi-abduction of this fourteen-year-old son of an impoverished Indian Theosophist was motivated more by lust or by ambition to play John the Baptist to a new savior. What we do know is that Krishnamurti, who confessed after twenty years of grooming for guruhood that he had never finished reading a single Theosophical book, remained a virtual prisoner of the society's directorate from 1909 until the day in 1929 when he publicly renounced not only occultism, ceremony, and hierarchy in general but the Theosophical Society in particular.

The irony of Krishnamurti's career, Washington demonstrates, lay in the spectacular aftermath of that renunciation. His Theosophical handlers had so exasperated him with their transparently hollow mumbo jumbo, while nevertheless convincing him that he was a chosen vessel of some kind, that he could turn his manufactured celebrity to a sane end, namely, informing millions of seekers that there were no Masters and no fixed paths—nothing to follow but their inner light. Unfortunately, Krishnamurti lived long enough to see even this mild lesson twisted into "flower power" narcissism. Even more sadly, grave risks of egotism and insulation from needed criticism awaited the increasingly pampered sage who would show people everywhere how to distrust all ideas except his own. Still, by thwarting the plans of Leadbeater and Besant to turn him into a living god and by preaching self-reliance and toleration, Krishnamurti perpetuated the more viable element in HPB's confused original vision.

Was the mature Krishnamurti, then, a great exemplar of the Theosophical outlook or an exasperated rebel against it? Washington doesn't resolve the question, but he frames it for us in a stimulating way by pairing Krishnamurti with an equally extraordinary personage, his manic antagonist G. I. Gurdjieff. These two figures stand out from all others in *Madame Blavatsky's Baboon*, marking the most divergent paths that share a starting point in the teachings of HPB. Whereas Krishnamurti disdained systematic assertion and took a meditative and pacifist approach to every issue, the anarchically charismatic Gurdjieff—"a cross between guru and carpet dealer" (p. 196), as Washington characterizes him—blended gnostic cosmology and numerology with an aggressively impulsive policy of disorienting and humbling his adherents, supposedly so as to cut through their defensive layers of acquired personality and arrive at the core of being within. But Washington seems more inclined to believe that Gurdjieff had founded an eccentric personal cult—one that sadistically exploited his disciples' yearnings for remission from bourgeois respectability.[4]

Washington feels that if Gurdjieff discarded the Theosophical Society's platform of harmony and fraternity, he couldn't have been a Theosophist with a capital "T":

> If Theosophy represents the idealistic tendencies in early-twentieth-century Europe—the currents of feeling which gave birth to the League of Nations, social democracy and youth movements—Gurdjieff is part of the complementary fascination with barbarism and primitivism which colours the politics of Fascism and works of art from Lawrence's novels to Stravinsky's early ballets. Gurdjieff's doctrine was war and his method of teaching was to stir up productive strife with all the means at his disposal. (p. 170)

This contrast is well drawn, yet insofar as it absolves Theosophy of blame for Gurdjieff's excesses, it is open to dispute. Washington's whole book manifests the incapacity of Blavatsky, Olcott, and their heirs to keep the Theosophical urge within prescribed doctrinal bounds. Once HPB had set the precedent of combining a flouting of decorum with fraudulent assertion of contact with divine powers, the emergence of a madcap Pied Piper like Gurdjieff could not be regarded as a complete surprise.

Gurdjieff also appears closer to the Theosophical mainstream if we set his temperament aside and concentrate instead on what people took away from his "Work"—a communal but far from egalitarian blending of menial tasks with dancing, chanting, breath exercises, and metaphysical pep talks. To the jaundiced Washington, the quintessential Gurdjieffian acolyte may have been Katherine Mansfield, whom

Gurdjieff had scrubbing carrots in cold water at midnight just before her final tubercular collapse. But many survivors of the Work, which continues even today in unpublicized communes, never repented of what they took to be an enlightening discipline focused on the core message that they must awaken from the slumber of routine existence. That was just what they were hearing from Krishnamurti as well, without seeing any need to choose between the two otherwise disparate sources of advice.

4.

It scarcely matters, in any event, who should and shouldn't be called an authentic Theosophist. What remains puzzling is the still unresolved "Yeats problem." In some of the most striking instances of Theosophical allegiance and self-transformation, the celestial flummery and mock science provided by Blavatsky and others *did* play a central role. Wild assertions about lost continents, interplanetary visitations, and ranked angelic hosts superintending the universe were either countenanced or actively embraced by well-educated and otherwise discriminating people. Once again, how can we explain it? What benefit could have been great enough to make such a sacrifice of judgment appear worthwhile?

A clue can perhaps be found in another noteworthy career that is overlooked by Washington, that of Henry A. Wallace, Franklin Roosevelt's vice president. Wallace was a leading agronomist who knew as much about hybridizing corn as anyone alive, a crusading secretary of agriculture who pleaded for the wise husbanding of Earth's resources, an astute advocate of free trade and of the concept that led to the Marshall Plan, an early proponent of racial integration, and a voice of restraint in the tense early years of the Cold War, whose eventual end he clearly foresaw. Yet he was also a zealous Theosophist, schooled in Blavatsky's doctrines by none other than Yeats's friend George W. Russell ("AE"), and a firm believer in what he called "an order of reality which can be contacted by people who have certain types of perception" (White &

Maze 1995, p. 25). Indeed, the competent and well-traveled Wallace was no less a moonbeam climber than Yeats himself.[5]

Wallace's excellent biographers Graham White and John Maze make it clear that without his esoteric beliefs, he could not have become the pragmatic activist that he was. They also supply the crucial mediating factor that makes such a paradox understandable: Wallace needed to get out from under a sense of religious paralysis. Freed by Theosophy from a confining Presbyterian obsession with individual sin and damnation, he found that he could allow his equally Christian zest for good works to operate without impediment on a universal scale. Wallace could match or surpass the nonconformist righteousness of his forefathers only by adopting a still more heterodox creed than theirs—one that vested enormous (if illusory) power in supplicants who had acquired a proper awe for nature's hidden correspondences.

Yeats's case was very different, but it was no less involved with the search for a way to detach religious and creative impulses from any entrenched creed. The poet was driven toward magic by the force of his father's rationalistic arguments against organized religion— arguments that he found himself incapable of refuting. With his churchly leanings thus thwarted but with his yearning for certainty and closure more urgent than ever, Yeats was disposed to reach directly for supernatural insight. That was just what Blavatsky was urging all of her lapsed-Christian contemporaries to do, and it wasn't just her opinion, she emphasized, but that of history's all-star team of sages and of the living Masters, too.

We might well ask what was to be gained, intellectually, by scrupling over the resurrection of Jesus but asserting general reincarnation, or by putting one's own psychedelic visions and prophecies in the place of St. John's. But cogency of assertion was less crucial to Yeats than establishing his autonomy, and Theosophy aimed its lessons precisely at self-development. Despite the alleged immemorial antiquity of its doctrines, it was a do-it-yourself religion, allowing the believer to regard his own reveries as authorized from the other side. As the once shy, now bold Yeats put it, "All that we do with intensity has an origin

in the hidden world, and is the symbol, the expression of its powers . . ."
(Ellmann 1948, p. 95).

There can be no escaping the fact that in our nominally empirical,
technology-driven age, the creativity and initiative of many significant
achievers have been bound together with transparently absurd beliefs
and practices. While Theosophy has hardly been the sole locus of such
enabling supernaturalism, it is the most blatantly counterscientific one
to have been taken up by serious thinkers. Mere faith in a Creator, after
all, tends to leave the laws of physics and chemistry (if not always of biology) unchallenged, but the Theosophical mindset specifically trumped
those laws with the assertion of a Prospero-like power that Gurdjieff's
explicator P. D. Ouspensky aptly called "the miraculous." Yet it was
precisely that illusion of omnipotence—the fancy that all things are
possible when the will is attuned to hidden sympathies—that proved
efficacious as a solvent to inhibitions.

Nevertheless, cases like those of Yeats and Wallace may leave us
more indulgent toward Theosophy than the full record warrants. To
judge from them, one would conclude that nothing but psychological
and social benefit can result from surrendering one's critical judgment
to a gnostic way of knowledge. It may be, however, that Theosophical
occultism was benign only because the people who adopted it had been
schooled since childhood in public-spirited ideals.

What happens, we may wonder, when occult assumptions are seized
upon by malcontents who are not disposed to settle for the tolerant
eclecticism that formed the heart of Aldous Huxley's "good enough
religion"? And what if broadly gnostic means of acquiring "knowledge" have infiltrated our mainstream institutions, producing widely
accepted dogmas that are neither true nor harmless? There is more
to be said about these matters than can be found in the dryly satirical
pages of *Madame Blavatsky's Baboon*. By turning in the next chapter to
other books and to a somewhat broader conception of irrationalist loy-
alties, I will reopen the question of modern occultism in a more dis-
quieting key.

Chapter 13

THE ESOTERIC UNCONSCIOUS

Since this chapter and Chapter 12 were originally a two-part article, the following text assumes a reader's acquaintance with the preceding chapter.

I.

With the publication in 1995 of Peter Washington's admirable study *Madame Blavatsky's Baboon* (1995), readers gained access to a judicious as well as an entertaining account of Theosophy, a late-nineteenth- and early-twentieth-century movement that conjoined religious syncretism to esotericism on the one hand and liberal idealism on the other. In England, the United States, and India as well as elsewhere, Washington shows, Theosophy generated much bizarre metaphysics, absurd pomp, and petty factionalism, but it also exerted a surprisingly invigorating effect within the lives of many adherents. And its immediate political influence, too, appears to have been largely benign, for Theosophy allied itself with irenic internationalism and the self-determination of colonized "natives."

Or so the indigenous activists were at first led to believe. But as they sooner or later discovered, Theosophy was never meant to be a catalyst of revolution. Helena Petrovna Blavatsky had no taste for violence or even for social disorder, and her anti-imperialism was so flimsy and opportunistic that at different times she volunteered to serve as both a British and a Russian spy (see Johnson 1994, pp. 213–214, 226–227). And more generally, Theosophy sent the world a mixed message about human equality—a contradiction, we might say, between brotherhood and "the Brotherhood," those distant Mahatmas who allegedly served as deputies of the Rulers of the Universe and who deigned to communicate telepathically only with the top level of Theosophical initiates.

As Washington observes, furthermore, the emergence from Central Asian obscurity of the conflict-thirsty G. I. Gurdjieff during World War I suggested, however faintly, a potential opening of Theosophy toward the militant right. In practice, to be sure, Gurdjieff remained a one-man movement and took little interest in the great powers and their bloodbaths. Indeed, whether he found himself in the turmoil of revolutionary Russia or in Nazi-occupied Paris, he showed a notable talent for placating whichever Caesar happened to be ruling at the moment. But Washington perceptively glimpses an affinity between Gurdjieffian cruelty and the ethos of purgative primitivism that led D. H. Lawrence among others—and the later Yeats could have been mentioned in the same connection—to flirt with proto-fascist authoritarianism as an alternative to bourgeois soul death.

Nor should we ever be surprised when occultism does link arms with reactionary ideologies. Sooner or later, the gnostic habit of thought battens upon vitalism, the belief in a life force that cries out to be unshackled from convention. And fascist doctrine stands ready to give vitalism a nationalistic and nostalgic twist: we must inhale the spirit of our warrior ancestors, who knew no democratic legalism and harbored no pity for the unfit and the foreign.

As it happens, this is something more than a theoretical scenario. If we retrace our steps to the 1880s and follow the vogue of Blavatsky's *Secret Doctrine* (1888) not in England or America but in Germany, we encounter a sinister and portentous counterhistory that rates only a passing footnote in *Madame Blavatsky's Baboon* and no mention at all in books by esoteric devotees. Astonishingly, the most hellish of all totalitarian ideologies, Nazism, bore more than a casual relationship to ideas of Blavatsky's that she had promulgated with a very different politics in mind.

The second volume of *The Secret Doctrine* featured an evolutionary myth about our planet's seven "root-races," five of which had already made their successive debuts. Humanity, Blavatsky revealed, had declined to a spiritual nadir with race number four but was now on the rise again, as our own fifth root-race worked its way toward superior incarnations that would eventually produce the god-men of root-race seven. Our ancestors' greatest disgrace, furthermore, was thought to have occurred when the slimy Lemurians of root-race four had inter-bred with still lower creatures. And although that fateful miscegenation had occurred eons before the Theosophical Society began preaching racial harmony, the chief magi who dispensed wisdom to Blavatsky by thought transference from Asia, Koot Hoomi and Morya, had alleg-edly disclosed to her colleague A. P. Sinnett that one "sub-race" within the fifth root-race—namely, the Aryan—possessed the highest spiri-tual potentiality.

Of course, Theosophical notions about race hadn't been flashed directly from heaven or even from Tibet. They were related, however loosely, to academically fashionable inquiries into the origins of mod-ern languages, myths, and religions by such scholars as Jakob Grimm, August Schleicher, and Max Müller. Comparative linguistics appeared to show that a primordial ethnic group—often designated by that same name, Aryan—spoke the tongue from which every later Indo-European strain derived. And parallel investigations of folktales and belief systems also yielded family trees, suggesting that modern cultural divergence, with all its potential for fatal scapegoating, was less a matter of geog-raphy and tradition than of persistent, indeed ineradicable, hereditary traits. Much Victorian academic discourse thus tended toward racist stereotyping, even before Darwinian theory inadvertently exacerbated matters by supplying a biological dimension to the game of invidi-ous classification. With the advent of Social Darwinism, people who already felt that Africans, Chinese, and Jews were throwback types, and who correspondingly regarded their own Caucasian race as humanity's advancing edge, could couch their prejudices in the idiom of natural selection.

Such was the volatile climate into which Blavatsky's insouciantly improvised theology, history, and anthropology were launched. For a few years, to be sure, her influence looked harmless enough. When, with Olcott's assistance, the first German Theosophical Society was founded in 1884, its initial appeal was felt mainly by members of the left-liberal *Lebensreform* movement, who were typically fond of rural communes, vegetarianism, alternative medicine, nudism, and the like. But as Nicholas Goodrick-Clarke shows in his fine 1985 study, *The Occult Roots of Nazism*, Theosophy was to make its strongest impact on the *völkisch* right, which was nationalistic, hierarchical, authoritarian, racist, and obsessed with modern degeneracy from an ideal past that had supposedly been ruled by Aryans in the narrower Teutonic sense of the term.

The Secret Doctrine needed only minor revision to be accepted as a liberating gospel by radically reactionary "Ariosophists"—Austrian and German followers of Guido von List (1848–1919) and Jörg Lanz von Liebenfels (1874–1954), who in the years before the Great War began prophesying an imminent era of German world hegemony. Like Blavatsky, the Ariosophists despised Christianity, which they regarded as having empowered a sickly underclass and as having hijacked and corrupted a Germanic sun-worshiping cult that deserved to be revived as such. Blavatsky's fancy that humans had descended from gods became serviceable when it was scaled down to include only people of a certain lineage. As for her secret brotherhood, it found an exact counterpart in the German esotericists' posited corps of ancient Aryan man-spirits known as *Armanen*. And her idea of race mixing as the root of decadence struck a responsive chord in thinkers who were unsure of their own social credentials, eager to find an all-purpose explanation for the troubles of modernity, and vexed by the close Central European presence of Slavs and Jews, who impressed them as being ever more numerous, alien, and controlling.

The Occult Roots of Nazism traces the path by which Ariosophists, who were more interested in nostalgic gestures than in day-to-day politics, passed along their myths and symbols to more militant anti-Semitic and nationalist organizations, which in turn lent inspiration to the Nazi Party after the bitter debacle of World War I. Among the symbols thus transmitted, none stirred more emotion than the swastika, which Blavatsky herself had helped to raise to prominence, incorporating it into the very seal of the Theosophical Society. Originally an Eastern

sign of fertility and fortune, that emblem meant for Blavatsky's followers the spinning electro-spiritual force by whose means the Sons of God
and their executive agent, Fohat, set and kept our universe in motion.

By the time that Hitler personally put his finishing touches on the
Nazi emblem, Ariosophists had long since identified the swastika with
a Teutonic rune whose meaning, it was thought, had been rendered
inaccessible for millennia thanks to the supplanting of Aryans by inferior races. Hitler placed the swastika within a red field signifying the
purity of Aryan blood and, within that, a white disk that stood for the
sun. But the swastika itself still meant roughly what it had conveyed to
Blavatsky, the principle of sun-based holy energy. Simply, that principle
had now become the property of a single culture. For a fervent Hitlerite,
to contemplate the Nazi flag was to be mystically transported into the
Ur-German heroic past—and, not incidentally, to harden one's heart
against groups that were disqualified by ancestry from an intuitive rap-
port with Wotan worship and its runes.

Goodrick-Clarke is scrupulously reluctant to conclude that the various lodges and orders of occult German nationalism directly produced
the Nazi phenomenon. It is true that Heinrich Himmler retained his
own private occultist and allowed him to develop much of the symbolic
bric-a-brac of the initiatory, blood-conscious, mystery-minded S.S.
But as Goodrick-Clarke stresses, Hitler was from the outset a modern-
izer and a mass-party man; he ordered the lodges closed as soon as he
took power, while mobilizing for his own ends the *völkisch* and xeno-
phobic sentiment that Ariosophists had cultivated in a more backward-
looking spirit. What Teutonic occultism offered the Third Reich, then,
was chiefly a set of metaphors and legends that blended into a psychologically potent cocktail of resentment, pride, and longing for a
homogeneous martial state. The eclectic, self-amused, live-and-let-
live Blavatsky would have been appalled by what she had accidentally
set in motion.

Even so, we should not overlook the broad epistemic likeness
between Theosophical dreamers and the ideologues who smoothed
the way for the terroristic Nazi state. The common factor was their

shared rejection of rational empiricism. By pretending that reliable knowledge can be obtained through such means as clairvoyant trances and astrological casting, the original Theosophists encouraged their German colleagues to "uncover" in prehistory just what they pleased, and the resultant myth of how Aryan hegemony was broken by quasi-simian races formed a template for the infectious post–World War I story of betrayal by Jewish materialists and the vindictive Allies. The whole visionary apparatus—the vitalistic sun cult, the mystic brother-hood, the pygmy usurpers, the lost ancient continents, the millennial cycles, even the idea of a conspiracy by a cabalistic "Great International Party" of diabolical antitraditionalists—was already there in *The Secret Doctrine*. There needed only a specific historical grudge and a fevered demagogue to set in motion the march toward paranoid eugenics and actual extermination of the "polluting" social elements.

2.

We need to remind ourselves, after such an example, that esoterically acquired convictions are not always and everywhere a menace. In a stable democracy such as our own, manifest occultism tends to produce more amusement than terror. And, in fact, a direct line of descent connects Theosophy to an array of ludicrous and generally harmless New Age practices that now surround us, from astrology, crystal gazing, home-opathy, and pyramid power to Wicca nature worship, prophecy, chan-neling, past life regression, goddess theology, belief in extraterrestrial visitation, and obeisance to self-designated gurus and ascended mas-ters. (Indeed, two of Blavatsky's own Masters have reappeared in per-son, ageless and helpful as ever, in the Great White Brotherhood that is said to guide our American contemporary Elizabeth Clare Prophet, aka Guru Ma.) Although one can agree with the late Carl Sagan's conten-tion that such fads reflect a popular revolt against science and a lamen-table resurgence of superstition (Sagan 1996), it would be perverse to mention them in the same breath with Nazi ideology.

Sagan did, however, single out one occult atavism that can bear deadly consequences: it is the psychotherapeutic practice (discussed at length in Chapters 5–8) of persuading clients that their neurotic symptoms derive from repressed or dissociated memories of child-hood sexual abuse and torture. Just what that practice has to do with occultism may not be immediately evident. But as Sagan remarked, the trancelike state in which patients typically "retrieve memories" of previously unsuspected traumas brands recovered memory ther-apy as a modern variant of spiritualism; and that connection is only strengthened by the not infrequent "remembering" of subjection to devil-worshiping cults.

Sagan's point needs to be placed in a broader historical and con-ceptual frame, however, if the manifestly silly conjuring of Satanic "memories" is not to be mistaken for a rare departure from a ther-apeutic tradition that otherwise stands above reproach. Although many people tend to assume that psychotherapy rests on authenti-cated discoveries about the mind, the talking cure was actually born in a climate of occultism; it retained its gnostic affinities in the *anni mirabili* of its modern flowering; and it has yet to make an altogether clean break from those affinities. Contemporary therapists who are struggling to render their profession more accountable to ethical and empirical norms may not realize it, but they are at war with an irra-tionalist legacy that deserves to be identified as such.

As several scholars have established in increasingly convincing detail, the key thinkers who pointed therapy toward the retrieval of forgot-ten trauma—Charcot, Janet, Breuer, and Freud—were deeply if indi-rectly indebted to a parlor healer, theorist of the paranormal, and proto-Theosophist, Franz Anton Mesmer, who enjoyed an enormous vogue in the late eighteenth and early nineteenth centuries.[1] Not coinci-dentally, this was the same Mesmer who triggered the American and European craze of spiritualism, which in turn provided the young Hel-ena Blavatsky with her livelihood as a medium. Thus Theosophy and psychotherapy share a key forebear—one who had written his medical thesis on planetary influences and who inspired the founding of a quasi-Masonic, symbol-mongering "Society of Harmony" that declared the human race to be capable of registering mystic sympathies with every cranny of the universe.

The theatrical Mesmer, clad in a robe emblazoned with Rosicrucian alchemical signs, had "magnetized" people whose later counterparts would be classified as hysterics, supposedly redirecting their warped fields of electrochemical energy into wholesome channels. Like psychotherapists a century later, he induced hypnotic trances and provoked "crises" that were considered prerequisite to cure; and like them, he placed truth value on the "information" that was thus speciously fed back to him from his own suggestions. And so did his immediate followers, the Marquis de Puységur and the Chevalier de Barberin, who turned Mesmerism directly into the modern therapeutic path by minimizing the importance of imagined magnetic fluid and emphasizing instead both the psychic attunement of the healer to the patient's hidden illness and the providing of advice about everyday problems and relationships.

Jonathan Miller (1995) has traced the steps whereby medical and scientific thinkers gradually stripped Mesmerism of its occult trappings, reducing it to mere hypnosis and thus preparing the way for recognition of nonconscious mental functioning. As Miller emphasizes, the resultant "unconscious," corresponding to "the processes which are integral to memory, perception, and behavior" (J. Miller 1995, pp. 28–29), has little in common with the custodial and repressive Freudian unconscious, whose twentieth-century sway among theoreticians actually retarded the development of cognitive psychology as we now know it. The psychoanalytic unconscious, too, ultimately derived from Mesmerism, but from its subsequently discredited side—that is, from the unsustainable claim that hypnotic states bring to expression reliably veridical memories that must therefore have been stuffed away in some normally forbidden corner of the psyche.

In the practice of Mesmerism, the news that came back from hypnotized subjects tended to be reports of time travel and spirit contacts. Hence Mesmer's vogue among esotericists and his disrepute among the more secular-minded. His nineteenth-century medical avatars aimed

lower, but they fell victim to his key fallacy of mistaking mere suggestibility for telltale evidence of buried trauma. Hypnotized subjects can
produce quite real physical manifestations that arise entirely from compliance with the hypnotist's wishes. Overlooking that key fact, Charcot
and his followers ingenuously accepted the symptomatology of "hysteria" as it was acted out under the influence of hypnotic collusion. As
Mikkel Borch-Jacobsen puts it in his indispensable *Remembering Anna
O.*, the eventual hypothesis of the dynamic, repressing unconscious "was
(and is) simply an end run around the hypothesis of simulation, by way
of arguing that the hysteric's right hand doesn't know (or forgets, or
represses) what the left hand is doing" (Borch-Jacobsen 1996b, p. 71).

Borch-Jacobsen shows that Josef Breuer's "Anna O." case of 1880–1882
—the fountainhead of all modern "cures" through memory retrieval—
involved an especially egregious instance of such misinterpretation.
Like other talented "hysterics" who honed suffering into a full-time
reproach to family members and to a misogynistic social order, Bertha
Pappenheim specialized in histrionics that were probably both inspired
and amplified by hypnotism. Her symptoms largely reproduced the tics
and convulsions that had been featured, just months before she began
consulting Breuer, in sensational and much-discussed Viennese stage
demonstrations of Mesmeric power by one Carl Hansen. And most
of those symptoms, far from being permanently removed by Breuer's
treatment as Breuer and Freud would later deceptively maintain, sprang
up within that treatment, were rewarded with habituating doses of morphine and chloral hydrate that had been meant to alleviate a very real
facial neuralgia, and partook of a doctor-patient *folie à deux* that would
end only when, pressed to do so by his neglected wife, Breuer abandoned the fruitless "cure."

At that point Pappenheim, half in spite and half in self-reproach,
ventured to assert that she had been simulating afflictions from the
outset. If so, Breuer's much-vaunted ability to banish individual symptoms by encouraging her to talk about them becomes all too readily understandable. What we know for certain is that Pappenheim
had stage-managed the course of treatment, which involved the

hypnotic and autohypnotic production of fantasies and hallucinations to which she herself ascribed a purgative effect. The Anna O. case thus resembled, in Henri Ellenberger's words, "the great exemplary cases of magnetic illness in the first half of the nineteenth century . . . in which the patient dictated to the physician the therapeutic devices he had to use, prophesied the course of the illness, and announced its terminal date" (Ellenberger 1970, p. 484). In a word, the founding example of modern psychotherapy was just another instance of Mesmerism in the chatty mode of Puységur and Barberin.

3.

From the mid-1880s through the early nineties, Freud himself was renowned in Vienna as a suggestive healer. His practice then rested squarely on the use of hypnosis—a tool he would later sheepishly characterize as borderline "mystical" (Freud 1953–1974, 11:22)—to allay tumultuous emotional crises and induce supposedly cathartic memories. Some of his medical colleagues suspected that neither the memories nor the cures were authentic—a conclusion that Freud himself eventually embraced, but not before contracting a permanent fondness for the repression etiology of neurosis. Tellingly, when Freud and Breuer broached their theory of hypnotically deciphered hysteria in 1893, its earliest favorable recognition came from a paranormal enthusiast and a founder of the Society for Psychical Research, F. W. H. Myers (see Jones 1953–1957, 1:250). The same society would later welcome Freud as a corresponding member (Jones 1953–1957, 3:397).

As Peter J. Swales recounts, the children of Freud's most important patient in that period, Anna von Lieben (the "Frau Cäcilie M." of *Studies on Hysteria*), detested him as "'*der Zauberer*,' 'the magician,' come to put their mother into a trance yet again and to accompany her through her fits of ravings, screamings, and long declamatory speeches" (Swales 1986, p. 50). Freud kept the immensely wealthy Anna's treatment going, without any discernible benefit on her side, for five years, often with twice-daily sessions. Interestingly, Anna was already a morphine addict, and Freud had no hesitation about feeding her habit. Indeed, that was his regular means of bringing her eruptions to subsidence. As Swales observes, the key insights that this inventive "hysteric," whom Freud repeatedly called his "teacher," gave him into repressed trauma, dream interpretation, sexual fantasy, transference, the conversion of ideas into symptoms, and cathartic "abreaction" were all contaminated not just by hypnotic suggestion but by Anna's chronically doped and dependent state—a factor that is never directly mentioned, much less duly weighed, in Freud's fragments of her case history in *Studies on Hysteria*.

The later abandonment of hypnosis by Freud and others by no means immunized psychotherapy against such epistemic folly; it merely rendered the question-begging effect of clinical suggestion harder for either the practitioner or the patient to recognize. Freud himself likened his "pressure technique"—the next method he used to extract the desired kinds of memories—to both hypnotism and crystal gazing (Freud 1953–1974, 2:271). And he candidly observed that his final and supposedly objective tool of free association also produced a state that "bears some analogy to . . . falling asleep—and no doubt also to hypnosis" (4:102). As Borch-Jacobsen emphasizes in a significant article (1996a), psychoanalysis never did adopt precautions against the visionary generation and misconstrual of pseudomemories.

Moreover, a gnostic tendency lay at the very heart of analytic work as the mature Freud conceived it. In drawing on a privately determined symbology to assign thematic meanings to dreams, associations, errors, and symptoms (productions that can easily be taken to signify anything whatsoever), and then in leaping inferentially from those arbitrary interpretations to putative childhood "scenes" that had to be "recalled" or at least acknowledged if a cure was to occur, classical analysis didn't just resemble divination; it was the very thing itself. And in this light, Freud's lifelong paranormal sympathies—almost always treated as a minor biographical curiosity—deserve to be considered an integral part of the record.

As Ernest Jones's otherwise flattering biography concedes in its startling chapter entitled "Occultism," Freud displayed "an exquisite oscillation between scepticism and credulity" where occult topics were concerned (Jones 1953–1957, 3:375). The expressions of doubt, however, were partly diplomatic and partly aimed at holding in check an embarrassing affinity for "the uncanny" and "the omnipotence of thoughts." Freud engaged in magical propitiatory acts and tested the power of at least one soothsayer; he confided to Jones his belief in "clair-voyant visions of episodes at a distance" and "visitations from departed spirits" (Jones 1953–1957, 3:381); and he even arranged a séance of his own with his family members and three other analysts. He also prac-ticed another hermetic art, numerology, attaching fated meaning to cer-tain room, phone, and ticket numbers and uncritically accepting such bizarre fancies as Wilhelm Fliess's assertion that the day of a woman's death ought to coincide with the onset of her daughter's menstrual period. Nor, though he and Fliess fell out at the turn of the century, did he ever renounce his allegiance to such notions.

Perhaps most significantly, Freud was strongly attracted to mental telepathy, an unconfirmed paranormal phenomenon that, though it needn't be linked to manifestly occult beliefs and practices, neverthe-less entails the very power that Madame Blavatsky and others touted as their pipeline to Theosophical wisdom. Jones himself was barely able to dissuade Freud from publishing a credulous paper of 1921 entitled "Psycho-analysis and Telepathy" (Freud 1953–1974, 18:177–193). But Freud, who plainly told his inner circle of his "conversion to telepathy" (Jones 1953–1957, 3:394), could not be altogether hushed.

In a 1922 paper called "Dreams and Telepathy," Freud tried to assume a neutral pose but let slip an affirmation of "the incontestable fact that sleep creates favourable conditions for telepathy" (18:219). In a 1925 paper on "The Occult Significance of Dreams," he speculated that a telepathic message might make itself known only by being incor-porated into a dream (19:138). And in a chapter of his 1933 *New Intro-ductory Lectures* entitled "Dreams and Occultism," he analyzed one such dream containing news that, he suspected, had traveled telepathically between a father and a distant daughter (22:31–56). He even surmised, as Blavatsky had done before him, that telepathy had been our "original, archaic method of communication between individuals" (22:55).

In his 1921 paper, Freud noted that both telepathy and psychoanalysis meet with disbelief from learned skeptics but appeal to a folk sense of uncanny causality, and he expressed solidarity with what he called "the obscure but indestructible surmises of the common people against the obscurantism of educated opinion" (18:178). He went even further in "Dreams and Occultism," declaring, "It would seem to me that psychoanalysis, by inserting the unconscious between what is physical and what was previously called 'psychical,' has paved the way for the assumption of such processes as telepathy" (22:55). And having decoded to his satisfaction the telepathic dream I have already mentioned, he admitted that "it is only the *interpretation* of the dream that has shown us that it was a telepathic one: psycho-analysis has revealed a telepathic event which we should not otherwise have discovered" (22:38).

Something more than politeness may have been involved when, in turning down the proffered editorship of a journal devoted to ESP, Freud wrote, "if I had my life to live over again I should devote myself to psychical research rather than to psychoanalysis" (Jones 1953–1957, 3:392). One can see why Freud's predilection for telepathy made Jones so uneasy. As the latter told his colleagues in a circular letter, public knowledge of the fact would serve those whose "opinion has always been that psychoanalysis is a branch of occultism" (3:394).

Now, believing in telepathy is by no means the same thing as subscribing to the existence of an astral plane; Freud was no Theosophist. On the contrary, by expanding his sense of what the mind can discern on its own and of what two minds can accomplish at a distance, he hoped to forestall any need to invoke the supernatural within his "science." But that science itself rested largely on conclusions gleaned uncritically from fantasy-producing trance states—and not just from those of drugged and hypnotized patients like Bertha Pappenheim and Anna von Lieben. There was also Freud's own cocaine-aided "self-analysis," a rash of visions supposedly granting him access to memories from the earliest years of his life—memories that, in fact, his undeveloped brain would have been incapable of storing at all, much less of preserving for decades in pristine form. Without such self-telepathy, as it were, we would never have been told about the parricidal and incestuous urges that supposedly tyrannize every human mind.

Freud's sense that unconscious power can annul the strictures of physics and biology remained one of the peculiarities of his thought.[2] In that sense, despite many eloquent protestations to the contrary, he decisively cast his lot with occultism and against science. And likewise, a hermetic strain in Freudian speculation, whereby fanciful instinct theories are extended analogically from the personal psyche to prehistory and thence to the totality of organic nature, has remained prominent from Freud himself and his fervently occultist disciple Sándor Ferenczi—the "Court Astrologist of Psychoanalysts," as he jestingly called himself (Jones 1953–1957, 3:386)—through Geza Róheim and Norman O. Brown.

The most recent exemplar of that tradition is the American philosopher-psychoanalyst Jonathan Lear, who perceives between Freud's lines a vitalistic revelation that "the divine is immanent in nature" and that all forms of life are suffused with a love that seeks to articulate itself (Lear 1990, p. 221). In *Love and Its Place in Nature* Lear voices the familiar irrationalist cry that if Freud's insights cannot be scientifically corroborated, then the "bounds and methods" of science will have to be "redrawn" (p. 220). As he elaborates, "If science is to treat archaic mind as its subject matter, the science should be conceived as growing out of and completing the archaic expressions it is striving to understand" (p. 97). Madame Blavatsky would have heartily concurred.

4.

It is not Freud, however, but his rival and sometime protégé C. G. Jung who affords us the most arresting insight into the linkage between occultism and the therapeutic ethos. Among the formative influences on Jung were writings on ancient mysteries by the Theosophist G. R. S. Mead, who had actually served as Madame Blavatsky's secretary. As Richard Noll reminds us in an important study published in 1994, *The Jung Cult*, Mead

> viewed his impressive scholarly work as a personal path to spiritual renewal and wisdom (gnosis). All of his writings are focused on bring- ing the reader closer to his or her own personal mystical experience of gnosis through the ideas of the ancient adepts. For Mead, as for Jung, scholarship was holy work. Jung's post-Freudian work (after 1912), especially his theories of the collective unconscious and the archetypes, could not have been constructed without the works of Mead on Gnosticism, Hermeticism, and the Mithraic Liturgy. (Noll 1994, p. 69)

Noll leaves us in no doubt that Jung was himself an esotericist—not just a scholarly student of the alchemical and astrological traditions but a believer in a solar-based life force and in the power of hermetic sym- bols to reorganize the psyche and even provide a kind of salvation. His collective unconscious and his archetypes, nominally scientific enti- ties, are in fact occult constructs, since no known physical process can explain how the individual can tap into the memory bank of the entire species and summon powers that reside nowhere in particular. As Jung himself put it, "the main body of the collective unconscious cannot be strictly said to be psychological, but psychical" (Noll 1994, p. 102). Fur- thermore, the therapeutic regimen that Jung began to develop around 1912 constituted a full-fledged *völkisch* mystery cult, featuring a buried pagan layer of the unconscious mind, direct experience of God as what Noll calls "an inner sun or star that was the fiery core of one's being" (p. 141), and communion with one's ancestors in the Land of the Dead.

These were all standard features of Ariosophy and its fellow back-to- Wotan movements in Germany and Austria. Indeed, Jung drew several of his vitalistic and race-conscious notions from leading exponents of those movements, and he taunted the Jewish Freud by making pointed references to them in his letters. Though Anglo-American Jungians continue to deny it, Jung's thought, in Noll's words, "arose from the same Central European cauldron of neopagan, Nietzschean, mystical, hereditarian, völkisch utopianism out of which National Socialism arose." Thus it is surely no coincidence that Jung initially welcomed Hitler's ascension and, at least for a while, cheerfully accepted the challenge of hewing to "Aryan science" in matters of psychology, declaring that Jewish notions were incapable of answering to the creative Germanic soul (Jung 1934).

It should also be clear by now that Jung was a far more committed occultist than Blavatsky herself. We know that Blavatsky slapped together her claims from published sources and faked her mediumistic feats. As Noll relates, however, in 1913 Jung began to cultivate private visionary experiences through a trance technique that he later named "active imagination":

> In these visions he descends and meets autonomous mythological figures with whom he interacts. Over the years . . . a wise old man figure named Philemon emerges who becomes Jung's spiritual guru, much like the ascended "masters" or "brothers" engaged by Blavatsky or the Teutonic Brotherhood of the Armanen met by List. Philemon and other visionary figures insist upon their reality and reveal to Jung the foundation of his life and work. . . . These visionary experiences . . . form the basis of the psychological theory and method he would develop in 1916. (p. 210)

Sometimes, however, Philemon had to be put on hold while other voices, especially an insistent female one, clamored to be heard:

> Jung then wondered if his unconscious was forming an alternate personality. . . . He decided to interact with the voice, . . . [employing] a technique used by the spiritualist mediums: "I thought, well, she has not the speech centers I have, so I told her to use mine, and she did, and came through with a long statement. This is the origin of the technique I developed for dealing directly with the unconscious contents." (p. 203)

Thus was born the notion of the anima, every man's female second self. (A woman's corresponding "animus" appears to have been a chivalrous afterthought.) But before he generalized and psychologized the spirit-woman in that manner, Jung took her to be an ancient matriarchal deity who had literally taken up residence in his mind. It only remained for him to conclude that he himself, in Noll's words, "had undergone a direct initiation into the ancient Hellenistic mysteries and had even experienced deification in doing so" (p. 213). As Jung eventually revealed to his followers, that is exactly what he thought had occurred during one of his many trances in 1913. In fact, he was inclined to believe that he had temporarily occupied the being of Jesus Christ himself.

By comparison with that apotheosis, all of Theosophy's transcendental claims appear fairly modest. After all, Blavatsky, Sinnett, and the others never avowed that they themselves were divinities. But they did assert that pagan mysteries contain the necessary means of restoring psychic integrity to wan victims of modern materialism, and that was exactly Jung's message as well. As he put it forcefully in a letter to the stunned Freud, psychoanalysis ought to

> revivify among intellectuals a feeling for symbol and myth, ever so gently to transform Christ back into the soothsaying god of the vine, which he was, and in this way absorb those ecstatic instinctual forces of Christianity [to make] the cult and the sacred myth what they once were—a drunken feast of joy where man regained the ethos and holiness of an animal. (Noll, p. 188)

Freud's own lesson—that the ego should make peace with its buried demons, the better to control them—was rather more dour and conservative. However, it was no less a product of romantic speculation about ancestral memory, impish inner personages (the ego, id, and superego, each with its own motives, knowledge, and tactics for getting its way), and the grave consequences of trying too hard to deny expression to our instincts. And, of course, one must be a spiritualizing philosopher in the first place to conceive of animality as something to be bargained with rather than as a pervasive fact of our constitution. In this sense Jung, Freud, and Blavatsky were all closer to one another than any of them was to Darwin or Pavlov.

5.

None of this means that psychotherapy is doomed to be a hermetic art or that it serves no useful function, nor even that contemporary Freudians and Jungians, whom I have thus far ignored, retain Freud's and Jung's own predilection for the paranormal. Nor does the genealogical link between Ariosophy and Jungianism condemn the latter as a tool of reactionary indoctrination. All such pronouncements on the basis of origins alone must be resisted as illogical and antihistorical.

At the same time, an awareness of the gnostic strain in Freud and Jung does cast a suggestive light on the central issue that now confronts, and radically polarizes, the therapeutic community throughout the West: whether caregivers should address themselves to helping clients cope with their current dilemmas as they perceive them or, rather, send those clients on a regressive search for a hypothetical early past and initiate them into "knowledge" of repressed traumas and introjected personages. There is all the difference in the world between "taking a history"—investigating the relationships and vicissitudes that have predisposed the patient to act in self-defeating ways—and *producing* a previously unsuspected, artifactual history that is dictated by boilerplate diagnostic expectations. The cabalistic penchant lingers precisely insofar as therapists insist that true healing must entail a confrontation with some predetermined class of memories, powers, insights, buried selves, or former incarnations. And it is no coincidence that the dangers of drastic harm are all clustered at that end of the therapeutic spectrum.

The worst of those dangers is surely the evincing of "multiple personalities" from a patient who came to therapy with a far milder complaint (N. Spanos 1996; Acocella 1999). As Carl Sagan recognized, this is a fairly common though not inevitable outcome of recovered memory treatment, which can pass the disintegrating victim along to the snakepit of a "dissociated identity" ward from which the only exit may be either suicide or the exhaustion of insurance benefits. What Sagan didn't realize, however, is that a growing number of certified psychoanalysts, such as Richard Gartner (1997, 2005) and Adrienne Harris (1996), having found it more ideologically attractive to smoke out long-past sexual abuse than to rehearse the same old oedipal fantasies, had already begun bringing "split-off selves" to cathartic expression in analytic therapy.

As I showed in earlier chapters, this practice reprises the recovered memory quackery that Freud himself was practicing in the mid-1890s, when he brutally overrode his patients' denial of having been molested in early childhood and told them that he detected the nature of their traumas in their current symptoms of constipation, sores in the mouth, and so on. In that period Freud was convinced that merely by attuning his psyche to a patient's speech he could hear what two adults had been saying in her presence when she was eleven months old (Freud 1985, p. 226). Amazing—but scarcely more so than the contemporary analyst's feat of getting to know little girls, grown-up molesters, and skittish adolescents through acts of empathy with the adult patient whose mind harbors all of these dissociated "introjects." When the psychoanalyst Jody Messler Davies writes of her patients' split personalities, "I interact with them, I act like them, ultimately I will become them!" (Davies 1996, p. 209), nothing but a crystal ball need be added to render her spiritualist premises explicit.

Whether practiced by Freud in 1896 or by his memory-scouring heirs a century later, the combination of coaxed belief and induced crisis, with the therapist's conjectures then "verified" by the agitated patient's discomfiture on the couch, amounts to a perfect recipe for creating panic and delusion. Empathetic therapy, it seems, has made no lasting gain in prudence since the eighteenth century. Indeed, Mesmerism looks like a pleasant diversion in comparison with modern treatments that result in the destruction of families and the prosecution of innocent people.

Nevertheless, it should be noted that therapeutic harm does not correlate directly with the degree of outlandishness in a practitioner's diagnosis. Take, for example, the patients who form the research base for the late, sublimely gullible Harvard psychiatrist John Mack, who accepted UFO abduction stories at face value (Mack 1994). Having been hypnotically reinforced in the belief that alien kidnappers once diddled them in hovering spacecraft, those patients must be regarded as classic victims of therapeutic occultism. Yet they tend on the whole to be only mildly dysfunctional. The explanation is simple: these people weren't raised by the creatures who supposedly abused them. In contrast, the relatively plausible allegation that one must have been raped by one's father characteristically shatters the identity of the patient who falls prey to such a staple notion in the professional folklore of our time.

If occult concepts per se were psychologically noxious, we would expect Jungian ministrations in particular to wreak havoc on their clients, many of whom come away from therapy believing in fortune-telling, mystical "synchronicity," communion with pantheistic sources of wisdom, and similar willful notions. But those beliefs seem to render them only more cheerful, self-trusting, and tedious at parties. Once again, then: as we saw in the case of Theosophy versus Ariosophy, it is not a weakness for illusions that renders a doctrine or a therapeutic regimen deadly but a preference for illusions that blame a live human "perpetrator" for whatever discontents are being magnified.

But social harm apart, we might venture to hope that psychotherapy, as an institution that likes to maintain good-neighbor relations with science, will someday make a clean break with its gnostic component. All those therapists who acquire "knowledge" by first applying suggestive pressure and then disregarding its influence on their findings are more akin to mediums than to physicians. Do they really want to continue down the yellow brick road that has led from Mesmer and Puységur through Freud and Jung to the latest promises of cure via channeling, rebirthing, and past life regression? And will their guilds never tire of issuing discreet caveats about "going too far" with diagnostic procedures that actually go in circles?

If I remain pessimistic about a thoroughgoing reform of psycho-therapy, it is because of the unquenchable human thirst for meanings that can ease our doubts, sanction and regulate our urges, and flatter our self-conception. Established religion, Theosophy, and psychotherapy as it is often—by no means always—practiced have all plied the same trade, and with degrees of popular success that owe nothing to the demonstrable cogency of their assertions.

Of those three competitors for our spiritual allegiance, psycho-therapy would appear to suffer a handicap by virtue of its mundane secular character. But this too may be an illusion. Freud put matters backwards when he called the discovery of the unconscious a great blow to human narcissism. As the shrewd if occasionally delirious Jung was quick to perceive, we needn't defer to Rome or the Himalayas to learn about divinity. The gods, Jung told the dissatisfied and yearning Western bourgeoisie, already reside within our heads; they find us quite interesting and lovable; and they are eager to impart their secrets to us. Does mere empirical rationality stand a chance against an appeal that speaks so directly to our needs?

Chapter 14

THE NEW CREATIONISTS AND THEIR FRIENDS

THIS CHAPTER AND THE NEXT WERE ORIGINALLY A TWO-PART ESSAY, "SAVING US FROM DARWIN," IN *The New York Review of Books*, OCTOBER 4 AND 18, 2001. A GOOD IDEA OF THE CONTROVERSY THAT ENSUED, AND OF MY SUBSEQUENT THOUGHTS, CAN BE GAINED FROM APPENDIX A.

I.

It is no secret that science and religion, once allied in homage to divinely crafted harmonies, have long been growing apart. As the scientific worldview has become more authoritative and self-sufficient, it has loosed a cascade of appalling fears: that the human soul, insofar as it can be said to exist, may be a mortal and broadly comprehensible product of material forces; that the immanent, caring God of the Western monotheisms may never have been more than a fiction devised by members of a species that self-indulgently denies its continuity with the rest of nature; and that our universe may lack any discernible purpose, moral character, or special relation to ourselves. But as those intimations have spread, the retrenchment known as creationism has also gained in strength and has widened its appeal, acquiring recruits and sympathizers among intellectual sophisticates, hardheaded pragmatists, and even some scientists. And so formidable a political influence is this wave of resistance that some Darwinian thinkers who stand quite apart from it nevertheless feel obliged to placate it with tactful sophistries, lest the cause of evolutionism itself be swept away.

As everyone knows, it was the publication of *The Origin of Species* in 1859 that set off the counterrevolution that eventually congealed into creationism. It isn't immediately obvious, however, why Darwin and not, say, Copernicus, Galileo, or Newton should have been judged the most menacing of would-be deicides. After all, the subsiding of faith might have been foreseeable as soon as the newly remapped sky left no plausible site for heaven. But people are good at living with contradictions, just so long as their self-importance isn't directly insulted. That shock was delivered when Darwin dropped his hint that, as the natural selection of every other species gradually proves its cogency, "much light will be thrown on the origin of man and his history" (C. Darwin 1993, p. 647).

By rendering force and motion deducible from laws of physics without reference to the exercise of will, leading scientists of the Renaissance and Enlightenment started to force the activist lord of the universe into early retirement. They did so, however, with reverence for his initial wisdom and benevolence as an engineer. Not so Darwin, who saw at close range the cruelty, the flawed designs, and the prodigal wastefulness of life, capped for him by the death of his daughter Annie. He decided that he would rather forsake his Christian faith than lay all that carnage at God's door. That is why he could apply Charles Lyell's geological uniformitarianism more consistently than did Lyell himself, who still wanted to reserve some scope for intervention from above. And it is also why he was quick to extrapolate fruitfully from Malthus's theory of human population dynamics, for he was already determined to regard all species as subject to the same implacable laws. Indeed, one of his criteria for a sound hypothesis was that it must leave no room for the supernatural. As he wrote to Lyell in 1859, "I would give absolutely nothing for the theory of Natural Selection, if it requires miraculous additions at any one stage of descent" (F. Darwin 1897, 2:7).

Darwin's contemporaries saw at once what a heavy blow he was striking against piety. His theory entailed the inference that we are here today not because God reciprocates our love, forgives our sins, and attends to our entreaties but because each of our oceanic and terrestrial foremothers was lucky enough to elude its predators long enough to reproduce. The undignified emergence of humanity from primordial ooze and from a line of apes could hardly be reconciled with the unique creation of man, a fall from grace, and redemption by a person of the godhead dispatched to Earth for that end. If Darwin was right, revealed truth of every kind must be unsanctioned. "With me the horrid doubt always arises," he confessed in a letter, "whether the convictions of man's mind, which has been developed from the mind of the lower animals, are of any value or at all trustworthy. Would any one trust in the convictions of a monkey's mind . . . ?" (F. Darwin 1897, 1:285).

In a sentence that is often misconstrued and treated as a scandal, Richard Dawkins has asserted that "Darwin made it possible to be an intellectually fulfilled atheist" (Dawkins 1996, p. 6). What he meant was not that Darwinism requires us to disbelieve in God. Rather, if we are already inclined to apprehend the universe in strictly physical terms, the explanatory power of natural selection removes the last obstacle to our doing so. That obstacle was the seemingly irrefutable "argument from design" most famously embodied in William Paley's *Natural Theology* of 1802. By showing in principle that order could arise without an artificer who is more complex than his artifacts, Darwin robbed Paley's argument of its scientific inevitability.

With the subsequent and continually swelling flood of evidence favoring Darwin's paradigm, evolutionism has acquired implications that Darwin himself anticipated but was reluctant to champion. Daniel C. Dennett has trenchantly shown that the Darwinian outlook is potentially a "universal acid" penetrating "all the way down" to the origin of life on Earth and "all the way up" to a satisfyingly materialistic reduction of mind and soul (Dennett 1996). True enough, natural selection can't tell us how certain organic molecules first affixed themselves to templates for self-duplication and performed their momentous feat. But the theory's success at every later stage has tipped the explanatory balance toward *some* naturalistic account of life's beginning. So, too, competitive pressures now form a more plausible framework than divine action for guessing how the human brain could have acquired consciousness and facilitated cultural productions, not excepting religion itself. It is this march toward successfully explaining the higher by the lower that renders Darwinian science a threat to theological dogma of all but the blandest kind.

2.

That threat has been felt most keenly by Christian fundamentalists, whose insistence on biblical literalism guarantees them a head-on collision with science. They are the faction responsible for creationism as most people understand the term: the movement to exclude evolution from the public school curriculum and to put "creation science" in its place. The goal of such "young-Earthers" is to convince students that the Bible has been proven exactly right: our planet and its surrounding universe are just 6,000 years old, every species was fashioned by God in six literal days, and a worldwide flood later drowned all creatures (even the swimmers) except one mating pair of each kind.

Creation science enjoyed some political success in the 1980s and nineties, packing a number of school boards and state legislatures with loyalists who then passed anti-Darwinian measures. Clearly, though, the movement is headed nowhere. Its problem isn't the absurdity of its claims but rather their patently question-begging character. "Findings" that derive from scripture can never pass muster as genuine science, and once their sectarian intent is exposed, they inevitably run up against the constitutional ban on established religion.

But the ludicrous spectacle of young-Earth creation science masks the actual strength of creationism in less doctrinaire guises. According to a recent poll, only 44 percent of our fellow citizens agree with the proposition, "Human beings, as we know them today, developed from earlier species of animals" (National Science Board). One of the dissenters may be our current president, who went on record, during the Kansas State Board of Education controversy of August 1999, as favoring a curricular balance between Darwinian and creationist ideas. His administration, moreover, is partial to charter schools, public funding of private academies, and a maximum degree of autonomy for local boards. If creationism were to shed its Dogpatch image and take a subtler tack, laying its emphasis not on the deity's purposes and blueprints but simply on the unlikelihood that natural selection alone could have generated life in its present ingenious variety, it could multiply its influence many fold.

Precisely such a makeover has been in the works since 1990 or so. The new catchword is "intelligent design" (ID), whose chief propagators are Phillip E. Johnson, Michael J. Behe, Michael Denton, William A. Dembski, Jonathan Wells, David Berlinski, Nancy Pearcey, and Stephen C. Meyer. Armed with Ph.D.s in various fields, attuned to every quarrel within the Darwinian establishment, and pooling their efforts through the coordination of a well-funded organization, Seattle's Discovery Institute, these are shrewd and media-savvy people. They are very busy turning out popular books, holding press conferences and briefings, working the Internet, wooing legislators, lecturing on secular as well as religious campuses, and even, in one instance, securing an on-campus institute all to themselves.[1]

The IDers intend to outflank Darwin by accepting his vision in key respects, thereby lending weight to their one key reservation. Yes, most of them concede, our planet has been in orbit for billions of years. No, Earth's ten million species probably weren't crammed into Eden together. And yes, the extinction of some 99 percent of those species through eons preceding our own tardy appearance is an undeniable fact. Even the development, through natural selection, of adaptive variation within a given species is a sacrificed pawn. The new creationists draw the line only at the descent of whole species from one another. If those major transitions can be made to look implausible as natural outcomes, they can be credited to the Judeo-Christian God, making it a little more thinkable that he could also, if he chose, fulfill prophecies, answer prayers, and raise the dead.

This is, on its face, a highly precarious strategy. According to the premises that intelligent design freely allows, speciation *isn't* very hard to explain. If natural selection can produce variations without miraculous help, there is every reason to suppose that it can yield more fundamental types as well. Indeed, Darwin believed, and many contemporary biologists agree, that the very distinction between variation and speciation is vacuous. One species can be distinguished from its closest kin only retrospectively, when it is found that the two can no longer interbreed. The cause of that splitting can be something as mundane as a geographical barrier erected between two groupings of the same population, whose reproductive systems or routines then develop slight but fateful differences. And if one of the sets then goes extinct without leaving traces that come to the notice of paleontologists, the surviving set may not be considered a new species after all, since no discontinuity in breeding will have come to light. The whole business requires a bookkeeper, perhaps, but surely not a God.

In effect, then, the intelligent design team has handed argumentative victory to its opponents before the debate has even begun. As the movement's acknowledged leader, the emeritus UC-Berkeley law professor Phillip Johnson, concedes in his recent book *The Wedge of Truth*, "If nature is all there is, and matter had to do its own creating, then there is every reason to believe that the Darwinian model is the best model we will ever have of how the job might have been done" (P. Johnson 2000, p. 142). Such a weak hand prompts Johnson and others to retreat to the Bible for "proof" that nature is subordinate to God. If scientists can't perceive this all-important truth, it's because their "methodological naturalism" partakes of a more sweeping "metaphysical naturalism"—that is, a built-in atheism. Once this blindness to spiritual factors becomes generally recognized, the persuasiveness of Darwinism will supposedly vanish.

While awaiting this unlikely outcome,[2] however, ID theorists also make an appeal to consensual empiricism. The rhetorically suave Johnson, for example, highlights every disagreement within the evolutionary camp so that Darwinism as a whole will appear to be moribund. There are many such areas of dispute, having to do with morphological versus genetic trees of relationship; with convergent evolution versus common descent; with individual versus group selection; with "punctuated equilibria" versus relatively steady change; with sociobiological versus cultural explanations of modern human traits; and with the weight that should be assigned to natural selection vis-à-vis sexual selection, symbiosis, genetic drift, gene flow between populations, pleiotropy (multiple effects from single genes), structural constraints on development, and principles of self-organizing order. But Johnson misportrays healthy debate as irreparable damage to the evolutionary model—to which, as he knows, all of the contending factionalists comfortably subscribe.

The Wedge of Truth adds nothing of substance to Johnson's four previous volumes in the same vein (P. Johnson 1991, 1995, 1997, 1998). By now, though, his cause has been taken up by younger theorists whose training in science affords them a chance to make the same case with a more imposing technical air. In *Icons of Evolution: Science or Myth?* (2000), for example, Jonathan Wells mines the standard evolutionary textbooks for exaggerated claims and misleading examples, which he counts as marks against evolution itself. His goal, of course, is not to improve the next editions of those books but to get them replaced by ID counterparts.[3] More broadly, he calls for a taxpayer revolt against research funding for "dogmatic Darwinists" and for the universities that house their "massive indoctrination campaign" (Wells 2000, p. 242). What he cannily refrains from saying is that a prior religious commitment, not a concern for scientific accuracy, governs his critique. One must open the links on Wells's website to learn that, having consulted God in his prayers and attended to the direct personal urging of the Reverend Sun Myung Moon, whom he calls "the second coming of Christ," he decided that he should "devote [his] life to destroying Darwinism" (no longer posted).

What is truly distinctive about the intelligent design movement is its professional-looking attack on evolution at the molecular level. Darwin had famously dared his critics to find "any complex organ . . . which could not possibly have been formed by numerous, successive, slight modifications" (C. Darwin 1992, p. 232). Having failed to unearth any such organ, anti-evolutionists have recently turned to the self-replicating cell, with its myriad types of proteins and its many interdependent functions. In *Darwin's Black Box: The Biochemical Challenge to Evolution* (1996), the Catholic biochemist Michael J. Behe has asked whether such amazing machinery could have come into existence by means of "slight modifications." His answer is no: God's intervention within the cell can be demonstrated through the elimination of every possibility other than conscious design. Without waiting to learn what his fellow biologists think of this breakthrough (they have scoffed at it), Behe generously ascribed it to them and called it "one of the greatest achievements in the history of science" (Behe 1996, pp. 232–233).

The heart of Behe's case is his notion of irreducible complexity. Any mechanical or biological system—a mousetrap, say, or a bacterial flagellum—is irreducibly complex if each of its elements is indispensable to its functioning. How could one irreducibly complex system ever evolve into another? According to Behe, any stepwise mutation that altered the original would have rendered it not just clumsy but useless and thus incapable of survival. To maintain otherwise, he urges, would be like saying that a bicycle could grow into a motorcycle by having its parts traded, one by one, for a heavy chassis, a gearbox, spark plugs, and so on, while never ceasing to constitute a maximally efficient vehicle. Since that is impossible, "the assertion of Darwinian molecular evolution is merely bluster" (Behe 1996, p. 186).

The IDers have closed ranks behind Behe as their David to the Darwinian Goliath. His inspiration pervades their manifesto anthology, *Mere Creation: Science, Faith, and Intelligent Design* (Dembski 1998), a triumphalist volume in which the impending collapse of macroevolution is treated as a settled matter. In the view of the editor, William Dembski, Darwinism is already so far gone, and the prospect of reverse-engineering God's works to learn his tricks is so appealing, that "in the next five years [already gone: F.C.] intelligent design will be sufficiently developed to deserve funding from the National Science Foundation" (Dembski 1998, p. 29).

Dembski himself is the author of two books, *The Design Inference: Eliminating Chance Through Small Probabilities* (1998) and *Intelligent Design: The Bridge Between Science and Theology* (1999), that put the case for irreducible complexity on more general grounds than Behe's. The key question about Darwinism, Dembski has perceived, is the one that Paley would have asked: whether natural selection can result in organs and organisms whose high degree of order associates them with made objects (a compass, say) rather than with found objects such as a rock. By applying an algorithmic "explanatory filter," Dembski believes, we can make this discrimination with great reliability. Design must be inferred wherever we find *contingency* (the object can't be fully explained as an outcome of automatic processes), *complexity* (it can't have been produced by chance alone), and *specification* (it shows a pattern that we commonly associate with intelligence). Since living forms display all three of these properties, says Dembski, they must have been intelligently designed.

3.

Working evolutionists, who notice that Behe's and Dembski's "findings" haven't been underwritten by a single peer-reviewed paper, are disinclined to waste their time refuting them. Until recently, even those writers who do conscientiously alert the broad public to the fallacies of creationism have allowed intelligent design to go unchallenged.[4] But that deficit has been handsomely repaired by two critiques published in 1999: Robert T. Pennock's comprehensive and consistently rational *Tower of Babel*, the best book about creationism in all of its guises, and Kenneth R. Miller's *Finding Darwin's God*, whose brilliant first half reveals in bracing detail that intelligent design is out of touch with recent research.

As Pennock shows, Behe's analogical rhetoric is gravely misleading. He makes it seem that *one* exemplar of a molecular structure faces impossible odds against transforming itself into *one* quite different form while remaining highly adaptive. But evolutionary change, especially at the level of molecules and cells, occurs in vast populations, all but a few of whose members can be sacrificed to newly hostile conditions and dead-end mutations. Antibiotic resistance among bacteria and the rapid evolution of the HIV virus are two common examples that carry more weight than any number of mousetraps and bicycles.

Both Pennock and Miller demonstrate that evolution is not a designer but a scavenger that makes do with jury-rigged solutions and then improves them as opportunities and emergencies present themselves.

Typically, the new mechanism will have discarded "scaffolding" elements that were no longer needed. And conversely, a part that may have been only mildly beneficial in one machine can become essential to its successor, which may serve a quite different end. This chain of makeshift solutions is no less true of cilia and flagella than it is of the reptilian jaw that eventually lent two bones to the mammalian middle ear.

Miller's best example is a sequence of experiments run by Barry Hall in 1982. By tinkering with genes, Hall disrupted the mechanism that enables bacteria to make use of lactose as food, whereupon the handicapped cells were challenged to find a way of growing on lactose after all. Before long, and without acts of selection by the experimenter, the bacteria had highjacked another, previously indifferent, gene to serve the missing function, and the entire system then responded with still further adaptations. The result was as irreducibly complex as Behe could have wished, but neither Hall nor God can be regarded as its author.

As for Dembski, his explanatory filter assumes what it is supposed to prove, that natural causes can't have brought about the "complex specified information" characteristic of life-forms. Dembski fails to grasp that Darwinism posits neither chance nor necessity as an absolute explainer of life-forms. Rather, it envisions a continual, novelty-generating disequilibrium between the two, with aleatory processes (mutation, sexual recombination, migratory mixing) and the elimination of the unfit operating in staggered tandem over time. Declaring this to be impossible by reference to information theory, as Dembski does with mathematical sleight-of-hand, is just a way of foreclosing the solid evidence in its favor.[5]

By denying that natural selection can generate specified complexity, theorists like Dembski and Behe saddle themselves with the task of determining when the divine designer infused that complexity into his creatures. Did he do it (as Behe believes) all at once at the outset, programming the very first cells with the entire repertoire of genes needed for every successor species? Or did he (Dembski's preference) opt for "discrete insertions over time" (Dembski 1999, p. 171), molding here a Velociraptor, there a violet, and elsewhere a hominid according to his inscrutable will? Miller and Pennock show that both models entail a host of intractable problems.

The proper way to assess any theory is to weigh its explanatory advantages against those of every extant rival. Neo-Darwinian natural selection is endlessly fruitful, enjoying corroboration from an imposing array of disciplines, including paleontology, genetics, systematics, embryology, anatomy, biogeography, biochemistry, cell biology, molecular biology, physical anthropology, and ethology. By contrast, intelligent design lacks any naturalistic causal hypotheses and thus enjoys no consilience with any branch of science. Its one unvarying conclusion— "God must have made this thing"—would preempt further investigation and place biological science in the thrall of theology.

Even the theology, moreover, would be hobbled by contradictions. Intelligent design awkwardly embraces two clashing deities—one a glutton for praise and a dispenser of wrath, absolution, and grace, the other a curiously inept cobbler of species that need to be periodically revised and that keep getting snuffed out by the very conditions he provided for them. Why, we must wonder, would the shaper of the universe have frittered away some fourteen billion years, turning out quadrillions of useless stars, before getting around to the one thing he really cared about, seeing to it that a minuscule minority of earthling vertebrates are washed clean of sin and guaranteed an eternal place in his company? And should the God of love and mercy be given credit for the anopheles mosquito, the schistosomiasis parasite, anthrax, smallpox, bubonic plague . . . ? By purporting to detect the divine signature on every molecule while nevertheless conceding that natural selection does account for variations, the champions of intelligent design have made a conceptual mess that leaves the ancient dilemmas of theodicy harder than ever to resolve.

4.

In a world where empirical issues were settled on strictly empirical grounds, "intelligent design" would be a doctrine without a future. But scientific considerations can take a backseat when existential angst, moral passions, and protectiveness toward sacred tradition come into play. One doesn't have to read much creationist literature, for example, before realizing that anti-Darwinian fervor has as much to do with moral anxiety as with articles of revealed truth. Creationists are sure that the social order will dissolve unless our children are taught that the human race was planted here by God with instructions for proper conduct. Crime, licentiousness, blasphemy, unchecked greed, narcotic stupefaction, abortion, the weakening of family bonds—all are blamed on Darwin, whose supposed message is that we are animals to whom everything is permitted. This is the "fatal glass of beer" approach to explaining decadence. Take one biology course that leaves Darwin unchallenged, it seems, and you're on your way to nihilism, Eminem, and drive-by shootings.

Crude though it is, such an outlook is not altogether dissimilar to that of prominent American neoconservatives who see their nation as consisting of two cultures, one of which is still guided by religious precepts while the other has abandoned itself to the indulgences of "the sixties." Whatever the descriptive merits of that scheme, it exhibits the same foreshortened and moralized idea of causality that we see among the creationists. If the social fabric appears to be fraying, it's less because objective conditions have changed than because the very principles of authority and order have been gradually undermined by atheistical thinkers from Marx, Nietzsche, and Freud through Herbert Marcuse, Norman Mailer, and Timothy Leary. And Darwin, despite his personal commitment to duty, sometimes makes his way onto the enemies list as well. The most articulate proponent of "two cultures" theory is the distinguished historian Gertrude Himmelfarb, who also happens to be the author of a learned study of Darwin and his milieu, published in 1959.[6] Like her husband Irving Kristol, who has declared "the very concept of evolution questionable" (quoted by K. Miller 1999, p. 83), Himmelfarb showed no patience with natural selection in her book. She aimed to prove that Darwin's "failures of logic and crudities of imagination emphasized the inherent faults of his theory. . . . The theory itself was defective, and no amount of tampering with it could have helped" (Himmelfarb 1996, p. 375). Himmelfarb's *Darwin* remains an indispensable contribution to Victorian intellectual history, but its animus against Darwin and Darwinism makes the book read like a portent of the neoconservatives' realization that, by liberal default, they must be the party of the creator God.

In recent decades both Kristol and Himmelfarb have been ideological bellwethers for the monthly *Commentary*, which, interestingly enough, has itself entered combat in the Darwin wars. In 1996 the magazine caused a ripple of alarm in scientific circles by publishing David Berlinski's essay "The Deniable Darwin," a florid and flippant attack that rehearsed some of the time-worn creationist canards (natural selection is just a tautology, it contravenes the second law of thermodynamics, and so forth) while superadding the latest arguments from intelligent design. And as if to show how unimpressed they were by the corrections that poured in from evolutionists, the editors brought Berlinski onstage for an encore in 1998, this time declaring that he hadn't been taken in by party-line apologetics for the Big Bang, either.[7]

In answering his dumbfounded critics, Berlinski—now a fellow of the Discovery Institute—denied that he is a creationist. What he surely meant, however, was that he isn't a *young-Earth* creationist. His Darwin essay called Paley's 1802 argument from design "entirely compelling," leaving us with no reason to look beyond the following explanation of life: "God said: 'Let the waters swarm with swarms of living creatures, and let fowl fly above the earth in the open firmament of heaven'" (Berlinski 1996, pp. 23, 22). By Phillip Johnson's definition—"A creationist is simply a person who believes that God creates" (Moreland 1994, p. 8)—Berlinski is no less a creationist than every other member of the ID movement.

Commentary is not the only rightward-leaning magazine to have put out a welcome mat for intelligent design. For some time now, Richard John Neuhaus, editor of the conservative religious journal *First Things*, has been using Phillip Johnson as his authority on the failings of natural selection—this despite the fact that Johnson's willful incomprehension of the topic has been repeatedly documented by reviewers. On the dust jacket of *The Wedge of Truth*, furthermore, Neuhaus calls Johnson's case against Darwin "comprehensive and compellingly persuasive," adding, remarkably, that its equal may not be found "in all the vast literature on Darwinism, evolution, creation and theism."

Further: when, in 1995, the neoconservative *New Criterion* sought an appropriate reviewer for Daniel C. Dennett's *Darwin's Dangerous Idea*—a book that rivals Richard Dawkins's *The Blind Watchmaker* as the creationists' most cordially hated text—it was Johnson again who was chosen to administer the all too predictable put-down (P. Johnson 1995b). *The New Criterion*'s poor opinion of evolutionism can be traced to its managing editor Roger Kimball's esteem for the late philosopher David Stove, whose book *Darwinian Fairytales* (1995) is notable for its obtusely impressionistic way of evaluating scientific hypotheses.[8] But since Kimball and *The New Criterion* regularly divide the world's thinkers into those who have and haven't undermined Western ethics, here once again the ultimate source of anti-Darwinian feeling may be moral gloom.

The case of *Commentary* looks more significant, however, because the magazine is published by the American Jewish Committee and is much concerned with defending Jewish beliefs and affinities. In lending their imprimatur to intelligent design, the editors can hardly have been unaware that they were joining forces with Christian zealots like Johnson, who has declared the Incarnation of Christ to be as certain as the proposition "that apples fall down rather than up" (P. Johnson 2000, pp. 161–162), or like William Dembski, whose ultimate thesis is that "all disciplines find their completion in Christ and cannot be properly understood apart from Christ" (Dembski 1999, p. 206). But *Commentary*'s willingness to submerge religious differences for the sake of an imagined solidarity is nothing new. Rallying around both "family values" and the modern state that occupies the biblical Holy Land, the magazine's guiding figures had previously acknowledged that they share some principles with the evangelical right (see, e.g., Kristol 1984). That realignment reached a memorable climax when, in 1995, Norman Podhoretz extended a friendly hand to Pat Robertson despite the latter's authorship of *The New World Order*, a *Protocols*-style tract against "the Jews."⁹

Commentary prides itself on favoring pragmatic realism over wishful thinking; where science and technology are concerned, you can expect its articles to claim the support of authenticated research. But there is one exception: evolutionary biology has been consigned to the Johnsonian limbo of "materialistic philosophy." Such, among those who see themselves as guardians of decency and order, is the power of resistance to the disturbing prospect of a world unsupervised by a transcendent moral sovereign. The result is that *Commentary*, in the company of other magazines that treat natural selection as an illusion, tacitly encourages creationists to advance toward their primary goal: adulterating the public-school curriculum so that children and adolescents will be denied access to an empirically plausible understanding of human origins.

But what about the secular left? Surely, one might suppose, that faction, with its reflexive aversion to "faith-based" initiatives, can be counted upon to come to the aid of embattled evolutionism, and doubly so when some of the attacks are mounted in organs like *Commentary* and *The New Criterion*. This expectation, however, overlooks the anti-scientific bias that has characterized much leftist thought for the past quarter-century.¹⁰

Liberals and radicals who have been taught in college to believe that rival scientific paradigms are objectively incommensurable, that the real arbiter between theories is always sociopolitical power, and that Western science has been an oppressor of dispossessed women, minorities, and workers will be lukewarm at best toward Darwin. It is significant, in this regard, that Phillip Johnson is fond of citing the chief advocates of incommensurability, Paul Feyerabend and Thomas Kuhn, in his own attempts to decertify Darwinism. As he wrote in a newsletter recalling a colloquium with political science professors on one of his campus visits, "I told them I was a postmodernist and deconstructionist just like them, but aiming at a slightly different target" (quoted by Pennock 1999, p. 210).

Matters are not helped, of course, by the fact that Darwin shared the prejudices of his age and allowed some of them to inform his speculations about racial hierarchy and innate female character. Then, too, there is the sorry record of Social Darwinism to reckon with. Insofar as it has become habitual to weigh theories according to the attitudinal failings of their devisers and apostles, natural selection is shunned by some progressives, who are thus in no position to resist the creationist offensive. And while other leftists do broadly accede to evolutionism, much of their polemical energy is directed not against creationists but against Darwinian "evolutionary psychologists," aka sociobiologists, who speculate about the adaptive origins of traits and institutions that persist today.

Political suspicion on the left, fear of chaos on the right. Who will stand up for evolutionary biology and insist that it be taught without censorship or dilution? And who will register its challenge to human vanity without flinching? The answer seems obvious at first: people who employ Darwinian theory in their professional work. But even in this group, frankness is less common than waffling and confusion. The problem, as usual, is how to make room for God. Although Darwin himself was too self-respecting to attempt that compromise, his scruples haven't always been shared by other evolutionists, including some who are personally irreligious. The result in some quarters, as we will see in the next chapter, has been a "defense" of natural selection that robs the theory of its meaning.

Chapter 15

DARWIN GOES TO SUNDAY SCHOOL

This chapter continues the argument of Chapter 14, focusing now not on opponents of natural selection but on some of its champions who seek to make Darwin palatable to religious believers. Again, Appendix A suggests how the essay was received by those whose positions it passes in review.

I.

As even the militant Christian Phillip Johnson concedes, most of our religious sects are formally opposed to the revivified campaign against Darwinism. Various church councils have avowed that evolution poses no threat to supernatural belief, and the same position is eagerly endorsed by scientific bodies.[1] Creationists who read those declarations, however, always notice that a key question has been fudged. What *kind* of God is consistent with evolutionary theory? Theistic evolutionism would seem to demote the shaper of the universe to a *deus absconditus* who long ago set some processes in motion and then withdrew from the scene. And we have already noted that even this faint whiff of divinity is more than the theory of natural selection strictly requires.

Because Americans on the whole profess faith in both science and a personal God, those who experience this conflict are eager to be told that it is easily resolved. The public appetite for such reassurance is never sated. Not surprisingly, then, universities have developed specialties in "science and religion," and one book of soothing wisdom can hardly be scanned before the next entry appears in print. When coldly examined, however, these productions invariably prove to have adulterated scientific doctrine or to have emptied religious dogma of its commonly accepted meaning. And this legerdemain is never more brazen than when the scientific topic is Darwinism.

Take, for example, *The Faith of Biology and the Biology of Faith*, by Robert Pollack, a molecular biologist at Columbia University and the director of its recently founded Center for the Study of Science and Religion. The title of Pollack's book appears to promise a vision encompassing the heavens above and the lab below. By the time he gets to evolution on page 2, however, the project has already collapsed. There he tells us that a Darwinian understanding of the natural world "is simply too terrifying and depressing to me to be borne without the emotional buffer of my own religion" (Pollack 2000, p. 2). By cleaving to the Torah he can lend "an irrational certainty of meaning and purpose to a set of data that otherwise show no sign of supporting any meaning to our lives on earth beyond that of being numbers in a cosmic lottery with no paymaster" (p. 2).

If Pollack's argument had stopped at this point, he could at least be praised for candor about his failure of nerve. But he is determined to place "feelings on a par with facts" (p. 2), and his book is therefore studded with clumsy attempts to make religion and science coincide after all by means of word magic. The rabbi and the molecular biologist, he extravagantly proposes, "share two beliefs founded entirely on faith . . . : that one day the text of their choice will be completely understood and that on that day death will have no power over us" (p. 41). Moreover, he declares that scientific insight comes from "an intrinsically unknowable place" (p. 14)—and who is the Unknowable One, he asks, if not God himself? Hence there is "only a semantic difference between scientific insight and what is called, in religious terms, revelation" (p. 16).

Pollack's half-formed ideas and bumbling prose stand in sharp contrast to the suaveness of John H. Haught, a professor of theology and director of yet another Center for the Study of Science and Religion, this one at Georgetown University. In *God After Darwin: A Theology of Evolution*, Haught acknowledges that the cruel indifference of Darwinian nature ought to jar the complacency of his fellow Catholics. But Haught himself remains unruffled; we need only bear in mind, he says, that our "thoughts about God after Darwin must be continuous with the authoritative scriptural and traditional sources of faith" (Haught

2000, pp. 46–47). In that spirit, Haught blithely assimilates Darwin to "humility theology," a body of thought depicting a God who "participates fully in the world's struggle and pain" (p. 46) and who chose to make himself vulnerable through the Incarnation and Crucifixion.

What God wants from planet Earth, Haught informs us, is "the building of 'soul' in humans" (p. 29). That job requires plenty of agony and death—just what we find, happily, in "the cruciform visage of nature reflected in Darwinian science" (p. 46). Evolution occurs, then, "because God is more interested in adventure than in preserving the status quo" (p. 42). And though the story of speciation and extinction may look rather drawn-out and impersonal from our sublunary point of view, Haught assures us that it's all going to be redeemed: "Everything whatsoever that occurs in evolution—all the suffering and tragedy as well as the emergence of new life and intense beauty—is 'saved' by being taken eternally into God's own feeling of the world" (p. 43).

Not surprisingly, Haught's favorite scientific figure is the long-discredited paleontologist and Jesuit priest Pierre Teilhard de Chardin, who argued, somewhat in Haught's own lofty style, that the evolutionary process is being drawn forward to an "Omega point," a universal acceptance of Jesus Christ as Lord. As Haught remarks, this conception relocates God in the future and depicts him not as a planner but as "a transcendent force of attraction" (p. 83). But it doesn't occur to Haught that such teleology is just what Darwin managed to subtract from science. Whether pushing us or pulling us toward his desired end, the Christian God is utterly extraneous to evolution as Darwin and his modern successors have understood it. Evolution is an undirected, reactive process—the exact opposite of Haught's construal—or it is nothing at all.

Unlike Pollack and Haught, the philosopher of science Michael Ruse, who now teaches at Florida State University, has an expert's understanding of Darwinian theory and a creditable history of standing up to creationists in court testimony. That experience has doubtless shown him how advantageous it is, in God's country, for proponents of evolution to earn the support of religious believers. In *Can a Darwinian*

Be a Christian? the agnostic Ruse contends that only "tensions rather than absolute and ineradicable contradictions" (Ruse 2001, p. 82) subsist between evolutionary and Christian doctrine, and he is sure that those tensions can be eased if both parties resolve to ponder "where and how they might be prepared to compromise . . ." (p. 204). But what gets compromised when Ruse attempts to build this conciliatory case is his own fidelity to the essential features of Darwinism.

Consider the question of original sin. An evolutionist, Ruse concedes, cannot be expected to lend credence to a guilt literally inherited from Adam's primordial transgression. Nevertheless, if we are willing to interpret the concept liberally, "a ready understanding of original sin offers itself" (p. 209). Successful adaptations generally "involve self-interest, if not outright selfishness, with the host of features and attitudes and characteristics that we all find offensive and that the Christian judges sinful" (p. 209). Hence "original sin is part of the biological package" (p. 210).

Can Ruse be serious here? How could the result of fortunate mutations be called a sin? Both "selfishness" and "altruism" are found in nature for the same amoral reason: under given circumstances they yield an adaptive (and eventually reproductive) advantage. Ruse has blundered into gross anthropomorphism, ascribing psychological and moral traits to organisms that were programmed by natural selection to attack, poison, and deceive without cogitation.

And then there is the Darwinian/Christian impasse over miracles. According to Ruse, we needn't suppose that Jesus actually walked on water, produced food from nowhere, and raised the dead. Perhaps "people's hearts were so filled with love by Jesus' talk and presence that . . . they shared" their loaves and fishes (p. 96). Or again, Lazarus may have been in a trance when awakened, and so perhaps was Jesus himself before his alleged resurrection—which, on the other hand, may have been only a metaphor for the "great joy and hope" (p. 96) excited in his followers. On and on plods Ruse, cheerfully turning wonders into banalities. Inside every Baptist, he seems to believe, there is a Unitarian struggling to get free.

In this book, but nowhere else in his soberly rational works, Ruse treats propositions about "God's judgement, the appropriateness of His righteous punishment, and the need and meaningfulness of His grace and forgiveness" (p. 216) as if they carried the same epistemic weight as propositions about the ancestry of birds and dolphins. As he knows full well, it just isn't so. However acrimoniously scientists may quarrel, they subscribe to canons of evidence that refer every dispute to the arbitration of discovered facts, whereas divine judgment, punishment, grace, and forgiveness are *irresolvably* mysterious. Insofar as Ruse tries to put that difference under the rug, he forsakes the empirical tradition that he has elsewhere worked so hard to protect.

The most startling disjunction of sensibility, however—a Jekyll-Hyde metamorphosis between the covers of one book—is manifested in Kenneth Miller's *Finding Darwin's God*, a work whose first half, as I suggested in Chapter 14, constitutes the most trenchant refutation of the newer creationism to be found anywhere. Yet when Miller then tries to drag God and Darwin to the bargaining table, his sense of proportion and probability abandons him, and he himself proves to be just another "God of the gaps" creationist. That is, he joins Phillip Johnson, William Dembski, and company in seizing upon the not-yet-explained as if it must be a locus of intentional action by the Christian deity.

Like the sophists of intelligent design, Miller rounds up the usual atheistic suspects—Dennett and Dawkins, plus Cornell's William B. Provine and Harvard's Edward O. Wilson and Richard Lewontin—and represents them as dangling before us Satan's offer: "Exchange your belief in God for a material theology of disbelief, and complete knowledge will be yours" (K. Miller 1999, p. 209). As always, the choice is stark: we must either surrender to such meretricious temptation or leave some sensible room for theology of the more familiar kind. With Michael Behe and John Haught, Miller wants his biology to sit comfortably with the dogmas of Roman Catholicism—for example, that Jesus was born of a virgin (p. 239). Such a contention, he says, "makes no scientific sense," but that's just the point. "What can science say about a miracle? Nothing. By definition, the miraculous is beyond explanation, beyond our understanding, beyond science" (p. 239).

As Miller realizes, however, an appeal to the ineffable contributes nothing to a project called "finding Darwin's God." His only recourse, if he is to stay faithful to Darwinian theory, is to make a more modest case for a measure of unpredictability that can then be given a theological spin. "What if the regularities of nature," he asks, "were fashioned in such a way that they *themselves* allowed for the divine?" (p. 191). Quantum indeterminacy must have allowed God to shape evolution on the subatomic level "with care and with subtlety" (p. 241), gently nudging matter toward the emergence of "exactly what He was looking for—a creature who, like us, could know Him and love Him, could perceive the heavens and dream of the stars, a creature who would eventually discover the extraordinary process of evolution that filled His earth with so much life" (pp. 238–239).

This case differs only marginally from the intelligent-design argument that Miller decisively refuted in the opening chapters of his book. The distinction is simply that Miller's Darwinian God wouldn't have known in advance that you and I, who have finally pleased him by tumbling to his evolutionary scheme, would emerge from a line of apes. "Theologically," Miller explains, "the care that God takes *not* to intervene pointlessly in the world is an essential part of His plan for us" (p. 241)—or rather, of his plan for some intelligent species that luckily turned out to be us. Now that we're here, though, we humans can regard ourselves as "*both* the products of evolution and the apple of God's eye" (p. 233).

"In each age," Miller writes, God "finds a way to bring His message directly to us" (p. 222). But which divine message, among Earth's thousands, does this writer mean? Although he notes in passing that the Almighty neglected to get his redemptive word out to the Mayas and the Toltecs among others (p. 244), he dismisses that anomaly with an indifferent shrug. By effectively reducing religion to the Western monotheisms and then glossing over *their* differences, he blots from view the world's pantheist gurus, animist shamans, and idol worshipers while making the quarrelsome ayatollahs, cardinals, presbyters, and rabbis look as if they are hearing the same clear voice from above.

Miller doesn't explain how he has been able to delve so unerringly into the Architect's cravings, schemes, and limitations. Nor does he answer the question that he himself crushingly deployed against the ID team: "Why did this magician, in order to produce the contemporary world, find it necessary to create and destroy creatures, habitats, and ecosystems millions of times over?" (p. 128). The God who entrusted his will entirely to mutation and selection can hardly be the one who, as Miller alleges, endowed us with "immortal" souls (p. 222); who presented the ancient Hebrews with an ethical guidebook, "knowing exactly what they would understand" (p. 257); and who, descending from his skybox for a few brief decades, transformed himself into a man so as to settle accounts in a ledger of sin and atonement. As the fruit of a keen scientific mind, *Finding Darwin's God* appears to offer the strongest corroboration yet of William Provine's infamous rule: if you want to marry Christian doctrine with modern evolutionary biology, "you have to check your brains at the church-house door" (quoted by K. Miller 1999, p. 170).

2.

There is, however, one last way of ensuring that Darwinism won't inhibit religious belief and vice versa. It is proposed by America's best-known paleontologist, the late Stephen Jay Gould, whose record of opposition to creationism and to religious interference with scientific research is consistent and unimpeachable. In *Rocks of Ages: Science and Religion in the Fullness of Life*, Gould maintains that the two "magisteria," or domains of authority, will enjoy mutual respect if their adherents refrain from any attempted synthesis. With "NOMA"—that's "non-overlapping magisteria"—kept firmly in mind, scientists and divines can carry out their equally valuable tasks, the investigation of nature and the pursuit of spiritual values and ethical rules, without trespassing on one another's terrain.

Gould's term "magisteria" was inspired by two popes who have issued dictates about evolution. In *Humani Generis* (1950), Pius XII ruled physical evolution to be compatible with orthodox faith but still unproven, and he warned against any supposition that the soul had emerged from natural processes. And in 1996 John Paul II took note of the convergent findings that by then had rendered evolution "more than a hypothesis" —a conclusion that Gould hails as his "favorite example of NOMA" emanating from an unexpected religious source. If this was really the Pope's considered view, says Gould, "we may rejoice in a pervasive and welcome consensus" (Gould 1999, p. 75) between scientists and ecclesiastics.

Regrettably, however, Gould barely hints at a crucial point that ought to have muted his hosanna. John Paul II's position on the supernatural origin of the soul was identical to that of every predecessor pope. "The Church's Magisterium," he wrote in the very statement that Gould hails,

> is directly concerned with the question of evolution, for it involves the conception of man: Revelation teaches that he was created in the image and likeness of God (cf. Gn. 1:27-29). The conciliar Constitution *Gaudium et spes* has magnificently explained this doctrine, which . . . recalled that man is "the only creature on earth that God has wanted for its own sake." . . . Pius XII stressed this essential point: if the human body takes its origin from pre-existent living matter, the spiritual soul is immediately created by God. . . .
>
> Consequently, theories of evolution which, in accordance with the philosophies inspiring them, consider the mind as emerging from the forces of living matter, or as a mere epiphenomenon of this matter, are incompatible with the truth about man. (John Paul II 1997)

This passage shows that the Church, while conceding that evolutionary science can no longer be snubbed, remains intransigently creationist where its own interests are concerned. Nor has Gould been unmindful of that fact. When he broached the NOMA rule in his *Natural History* column of March 1997, he voiced a suspicion that John Paul II's "insistence on divine infusion of the soul" was "a device for maintaining a belief in human superiority within an evolutionary world offering no privileged position to any creature" (Gould 1997). But he backed down at once, pleading in his next sentence that "souls represent a subject outside the magisterium of science." And now in *Rocks of Ages*, borrowing heavily from his *Natural History* piece, he has chosen to omit any mention of his misgivings.

Gould's concordat sounds more reasonable than the pope's until one asks what it might mean in practice. As a paleontologist who was raised without a faith, Gould could be expected to feel more protective of one magisterium than the other. Sure enough, his NOMA forbids the miraculous and, by extension, any idea of divine action within the world: "Thou shalt not mix the magisteria by claiming that God directly ordains important events in the history of nature by special interference knowable only through revelation and not accessible to science" (Gould 1999, pp. 84–85). As Phillip Johnson has understandably complained, "This is 'separate but equal' of the *apartheid* variety" (P. Johnson 2000, p. 99). And John Haught chimes in, "No conceivable theology, by definition, could ever live comfortably with evolution if Gould's claim is correct that Darwin's theory inevitably entails a cosmos devoid of directionality and overall significance" (Haught 2000, p. 26).

Rocks of Ages is an extended effort to soften Gould's peace-on-my-terms through flattery of the pious. The strain is apparent in his uncharacteristically slick and sentimental prose:

> ... science gets the age of rocks, and religion the rock of ages; science studies how the heavens go, religion how to go to heaven. (p. 6)

> I join nearly all people of goodwill in wishing to see two old and cherished institutions, our two rocks of ages—science and religion— coexisting in peace while each works to make a distinctive patch for the integrated coat of many colors that will celebrate the distinctions of our lives, yet cloak human nakedness in a seamless covering called wisdom. (p. 209)

Compare these excerpts, for tone and content, with what Gould spontaneously told a television interviewer in 1998:

> I think that notion that we are all in the bosom of Abraham or are in God's embracing love is—look, it's a tough life and if you can delude

yourself into thinking that there's all some warm and fuzzy meaning to it all, it's enormously comforting. But I do think it's just a story we tell ourselves. (quoted by K. Miller 1999, p. 170)

I am not the first commentator to point out that there is something contradictory about Gould's attempt, in *Rocks of Ages*, to endear himself to believers by praising their "wisdom" while reprimanding atheists for their "aggressive advocacy" (p. 69) of a position scarcely distinguishable from his own.

On one point, however, Gould is perfectly candid. In order to make his "nonoverlapping magisteria" palatable to both parties, he has set aside considerations of truth and followed what he calls a "'Goldilocks principle' of 'just right' between too much and too little. . . . NOMA represents the bed of proper firmness, and the right amount of oatmeal at the right temperature" (p. 210). "Oatmeal," indeed. Instead of grappling with the issues that seriously divide religious and scientific thinkers, as Ruse and Miller at least attempt to do, Gould delivers gratuitous restraining orders to both factions. In exchange for abandoning their immanent God and settling for a watery deism, the religionists get the realm of ethics largely to themselves, while scientists are admonished to eschew "invalid forays into the magisterium of moral argument" (p. 176). But *Rocks of Ages* is itself a moral argument proffered by a scientist and an infidel—and why not?

As Gould maintains, scientific facts and theories don't tell us how we ought to conduct ourselves. This doesn't mean, however, that ethics can be confidently entrusted to shepherds of souls. Undoubtedly, fear of God makes for social cohesion and moral restraint, at least toward those who share our faith; and many noble causes are championed by people who think they are implementing his wishes. But religious certitude can also remain fixated on ancient prejudices and prohibitions that dehumanize outsiders, coarsen ethical calculation, and retard social enlightenment. If he weren't bent on playing the roving ambassador between two wary camps, Gould would be the first person to acknowledge this obvious truth.

Both Gould and his mass readers want to believe that liberty begins where biology ceases to hold sway. We live, he writes, in a universe "indifferent to our suffering, and therefore offering us maximal freedom to thrive, or to fail, in our own chosen way" (p. 207). Ringing words, but what do they mean? The universe is also indifferent to a mouse being tossed and tortured by a cat, but the mouse's freedom is no greater for that. The options we enjoy as a species that has staked its fate on intelligence and foresight are surely a gift of our staggeringly complex neural circuitry, which is natural selection's boldest experiment in trading blind instinct for feedback mechanisms that allow dangers to be consciously assessed and circumvented. By shifting levels of discourse and proclaiming that we acquire our scope for action from a mere absence of interference by "the universe," Gould has momentarily left science behind and become a theologian, albeit an existentialist one.

The evasions practiced by Pollack, Haught, Ruse, Miller, and Gould, in concert with those of the intelligent design crew, remind us that Darwinism, despite its radical effect on science, has yet to temper the self-centered way in which we assess our place and actions in the world. Think of the shadows now falling across our planet: overpopulation, pollution, dwindling and maldistributed resources, climatic disruption, new and resurgent plagues, ethnic and religious hatred, the ravaging of forests and jungles, and the consequent loss of thousands of species per year (Eldredge 2000, pp. 160–161)—the greatest mass extinction, it has been said, since the age of the dinosaurs. So long as we regard ourselves as creatures apart who need only repent of our personal sins to retain heaven's blessing, we won't take the full measure of our species-wide responsibility for these calamities.

An evolutionary perspective, by contrast, can trace our present woes to the dawn of agriculture ten thousand years ago, when, as Niles Eldredge observes, we became "the first species in the entire 3.8-billion-year history of life to stop living inside local ecosystems" (Eldredge 2000, p. 16). Today, when we have burst from six million to six billion exploiters of a biosphere whose resilience can no longer be assumed, the time has run out for telling ourselves that we are the darlings of a deity who placed nature here for our convenience. We are the most resourceful, but also the most dangerous and disruptive, animals in this corner of the universe. A Darwinian understanding of how we got that way could be the first step toward a wider ethics commensurate with our real transgressions, not against God but against Earth itself and its myriad forms of life.

Chapter 16

ZEN AND THE ART OF SUCCESS

THIS REVIEW OF MICHAEL DOWNING'S *Shoes Outside the Door* APPEARED IN THE MARCH 28, 2002, ISSUE OF *The New York Review of Books*. IT AVOIDS PASS- ING JUDGMENT ON ZEN BUDDHISM, TOWARD WHICH I REMAIN IGNORANTLY NEUTRAL, BUT IT DOES REPORT ON WORLDLY TEMPTATIONS THAT TYPICALLY BESET RELIGIOUS MOVEMENTS AND THAT, IN THIS INSTANCE, REFLECT A TIME AND REGION THAT I DO KNOW AT FIRST HAND.

I.

Michael Downing's dramatic and thoughtful *Shoes Outside the Door: Desire, Devotion, and Excess at San Francisco Zen Center* (2001) begins with, and then encircles in widening orbits, a conference held in March 1983 at Zenshinji, or Zen Mind Temple, better known to the world as Tassajara. Tucked narrowly into a canyon of the forbidding Santa Lucia Mountains ten miles east of Big Sur and 150 miles south of San Fran- cisco, Tassajara's hot springs were known to the Esselen Indians for cen- turies before they became, in 1860, Monterey County's earliest resort. In 1966 that isolated, ramshackle, unelectrified property was bought by San Francisco Zen Center and transformed into what Downing calls the first Buddhist monastery established outside Asia in the 2,500-year history of that religion.[1]

Tassajara still welcomes paying visitors, but they don't brave the pre- cipitous, switchbacked, fourteen-mile dirt road from the Carmel Valley simply to bathe in Tassajara Creek or its sulphurous hot springs. Mystic- minded, spiritually restless, or just curious, they come to sample the Zen atmosphere in conditions that are spartan enough to emit a brac- ing whiff of asceticism. But Tassajara in summer sees too much traf- fic to be called a true monastery. Rather, it is part training camp, part profitable tourist enterprise, and part showcase for potential donors

who may be inspired to support Zen Center's instruction in zazen—
the meditative sitting, usually performed in the lotus posture, that was
developed successively in India, China, and Japan, and is now widely
practiced in the West.

Between summers Tassajara is considerably more monastic, though
hardly to the point of celibacy. The cold, the drenching rain, and the
mudslides that sometimes close off the road oblige Zen Center to
restrict Tassajara's population to apprentice monks and priests and to
adepts of *sesshin*, an intensive retreat that can last for a week or more.
Thus the public conference in March 1983 would have been an exceptional gathering even if it hadn't proved to be what some insiders now
call "the Apocalypse."

In Downing's words, Zen Center's abbot Richard Baker

> had invited the most eminent Buddhist teachers, scholars, and poets
> in the Western world to the first Buddhist Peace Conference. Thich
> Nhat Hanh, spiritual pioneer of the Buddhist Mindfulness com-
> munities, was at Tassajara, along with poet Gary Snyder, American
> Zen master and founder of the Diamond Sangha Robert Aitken,
> Esalen cofounder Michael Murphy, former California governor Jerry
> Brown, and most of the senior priests of Zen Center. Richard was
> spending the weekend at the one place on earth where every sentient
> being he passed was bound to recognize him—and to miss him when
> he wasn't around. (Downing 2001, p. 7)

And he *wasn't* around very much. The married Baker spent most of the
weekend in his cabin with the latest of many lovers, and for the first time
ever, he was making no effort to keep the relationship a secret.

One of the things that had set Zen Center apart from earlier Japanese and Japanese-American temples—and Baker himself had strongly
urged this innovation—was its encouragement of women to study and
progress on equal terms with men.[2] But the opportunity cut both
ways. Even before Baker became abbot in 1971, the deference of
female students to his priestly authority gave him easy sexual pickings
in the Northern California world of Zen. Thereafter, as some women

confided to Downing, they had been tapped for bed service in much the same spirit as they might have been called upon to act as one of Baker's personal secretaries or, for that matter, to scrub pots or weed a garden. And understandably, their zazen practice had become hollow or simply impossible once they were made the concubines of their allegedly enlightened master.

This affair, however, was something else again. The shoes outside Baker-roshi's door were those of Anna Hawken, the wife of his best friend Paul Hawken, a wealthy benefactor of Zen Center. And Paul Hawken, amazingly enough, was another stunned guest that weekend. His subsequent threat to hold Zen Center legally accountable for its abbot's misconduct touched off a cataclysm in the Zen community, bringing down Baker-roshi and precipitating an institutional crisis that would finally revolutionize the center's self-image and style of governance.

Starting in 1983, everyone at Zen Center suddenly wanted to air long-standing grievances against Richard Baker. His serial liaisons, hardly unique in the world of high-level American Buddhism, could have been forgiven, but his chronic untruthfulness about them could not. Buddhism of every school, one gathers, readily accommodates behavioral frailty but draws a firm line at hypocrisy. Consider, for example, Chogyam Trungpa Rinpoche, the guru who founded the colorful Naropa Institute in Colorado and who made Tibetan Buddhism fashionable in the U.S. Trungpa was a drunk whose sexual escapades, when he was sober enough to engage in them, were cruder and more ephemeral than Baker's relationships. But unlike Baker, he took no pains to conceal his vices. That made all the difference to his disciples, who considered him "deeply realized."

Baker, by contrast, had wielded the abbot's corrective stick on students who were sometimes guilty of nothing more than flirting with one another. As one of his ex-lovers put it to Downing, "Dick was physically punishing students for behavior that was his for his entire life as a Zen practitioner. Essentially, *I am above the rules. The rules for you do not apply to me*" (p. 97).

A key instrument of progress in the study of Zen is *dokusan*, or the private conference with the master. Typically, it is concerned only with identifying errors in practice and challenging the student to keep on the path of enlightenment. In the years after Baker took over in 1971, however, dokusans at Zen Center gradually became more intimate and less private. Students found that the abbot was leaking their confessions to his inner circle, and some of them inferred that he was collecting evidence that might be used against them later. They also sensed that Baker enjoyed humbling them by scoffing at their professed spiritual gains and thwarting their ambition to advance on the priestly ladder. "There was always this confusion," said one. "Is this Zen practice, or is this just a power trip?" (p. 8). Another aggrieved party reports that Baker used dokusan sessions to convince him that he was incompatible with his wife—who, sure enough, left him for several years and attached herself instead to Baker.

Every school of Buddhism aims at the same characterological goals: self-insight, serene detachment from impermanent objects of desire, apprehension of the underlying unity of all things, compassion toward suffering, reaching out to the needy, and *sangha*, or a loving community of the faithful. In this light Richard Baker presented a disturbingly anomalous model for his flock. He maintained three residences, spent large sums from the general coffers on remodeling, surrounded himself with unpaid student clerks and servants, collected exquisite and expensive works of religious art, traveled widely, and kept company with millionaires and celebrities whose interest in Buddhism was casual at best. His abbacy, Gary Snyder told Downing in disgust, had turned into "an imperial presidency. . . . He had become the Dick Nixon of Zen" (p. 34).

One of Baker's acquisitions stands out as having especially goaded his subordinates. In 1979, four years before the Apocalypse, he cajoled the Abbot's Council—a handpicked body of senior priests that he employed to circumvent Zen Center's legally constituted Board of Directors—into granting him $25,000 for the purchase of a BMW. The car was needed, he said, for his frequent shuttling among

Tassajara, San Francisco, and Green Gulch Farm, a combined organic farm, educational institute, and residential complex for Zen students in western Marin County. But why a BMW, and especially one in the pricey 700 series? A smaller car, Baker pleaded, wouldn't allow him to sit in zazen posture while driving.

Two decades later, speaking more candidly to Downing, Baker admitted that he had entertained other reasons for wanting a sporty Beemer. "I decided I would try to prove that you could be fully a layperson and a monk," he said. ". . . I thought, okay, I'll drive a nice car, and I'll have girlfriends, and I'll go to dinner. . . . I was trying an all-fronts experiment" (p. 37). The experiment might be said to have ended on the day he drove away from the fateful Buddhist Peace Conference. A stickler for ceremony, the roshi generally saw to it that his black-robed students would line up and bow whenever he took his leave. They did so again on that Sunday. But now, appalled by the brazen recklessness of his conduct in Paul Hawken's presence, they saw more clearly than ever that they were bowing not to a custodian of the dharma, the Buddha's sacred teachings, but to a glamorous automobile—Mammon on wheels. In a sense that the Buddhist doctrine of undifferentiation never anticipated, Baker and his BMW had become one.

2.

The consequential fall of Baker-roshi has remained clouded until now by legend, rumors, and smoldering resentments on all sides. With no prior experience as a social historian or a connoisseur of Zen, the novelist Michael Downing has nevertheless proved himself well suited to piecing together the facts and assessing their meaning. He did so chiefly by interviewing more than eighty of the involved figures and weighing each nugget of testimony against the others. The literary result superficially resembles a *Rashomon*-like medley of incommensurate perspectives, but Downing is no relativist. His narrative line, though continually interrupted, is lucid and convincing, and he challenges his interviewees' occasional half-truths with sharp comments and rhetorical questions that bring buried factors into view.

In its assessment of ultimate culpability, however, *Shoes Outside the Door* becomes complex and tentative—and properly so. Downing understands that Richard Baker, for all his faults, was no Jim Jones or David Koresh. The story of the Apocalypse is one of impeaching an errant leader, not of following him over a cliff. As Downing's interlocutors often reminded him, no one was ever coerced into remaining a member of Zen Center. Nor did Baker-roshi play the prophet or insist on eccentric articles of belief. Until that final weekend he was conscientiously working to raise needed funds; to keep Zen Center's multiple enterprises afloat; to conduct sesshins and dokusans; to lecture, interview, and ordain; and to teach proper zazen sitting as he had learned it from masters in the U.S. and Japan.

Baker was a man with a vision; it was, in the words of one still-approving colleague, "to integrate Buddhism into Western society through the arts, business, and politics" (p. 215). That is just what he achieved, in California at least, in the 1970s and early 1980s through intellectual brilliance, charisma, autocratic leadership, and a restless, driving will. Talented architects, artists, and craftsmen were glad to donate their services to his many projects. The center's retail businesses—the Tassajara Bakery, the Green Gulch Greengrocer, the Ayala Stitchery, and Baker's favorite showcase, Greens Restaurant—earned renown as embodiments of the organic, self-sufficient, small-is-beautiful ethic and aesthetic that had emerged from the sixties counterculture.[3] And under Baker's guidance Zen Center developed fertile links with West Coast progressive thought as it was represented by figures as diverse as Stewart Brand, Philip Whalen, Gregory Bateson, and Baker's close friend Jerry Brown, who brought both Zen notions and fellow travelers of Zen Center into the councils of state government.

If Baker's priests and students had been as dazzled by all those famous connections as the lay public was, no sex scandal could have ended his regime. But Downing's interviews show that by 1983, at the apparent height of its glory, the organization was profoundly confused and demoralized. No one lifted a finger to defend the imperiled roshi, because everyone sensed that his pyramiding of highly leveraged properties and his networking with the mighty had been achieved at an intolerable cost—financial, emotional, and spiritual.

But Zen Center may have been headed for trouble before Baker ever took control. The problem can be traced to his predecessor, Shun-ryu Suzuki, the center's nominal founder and now its all but official saint.[4] Impressed by the earnest young dropouts and runaways who had attached themselves to him at Sokoji, his Japanese-American temple in San Francisco, Suzuki had conceived the distinctly naive hope of turning the most dedicated of them into missionaries who might reform the jaded, politically compromised practice of Zen back in Japan. That dream lay behind his wish to establish the training monastery that became Tassajara. But the unworldly Suzuki—who, his wife once reported, would return from a market with the most damaged and wilted vegetables, because he felt sorry for them—failed to anticipate the strains that such a major expansion would produce.

After a typical winter training session at Tassajara, Suzuki's followers naturally wanted to resume their *sangha*, or fellowship, in another residential community. Some of them found it in a new San Francisco institute (City Center), purchased in 1969, that could house seventy students; others moved into subsidized rental quarters or newly purchased buildings in the city; and still others would eventually populate the as-yet-unacquired Green Gulch Farm. In Japan, the counterparts of these communards would have fanned out to become the priests of regional Buddhist temples. But America had no such temples that would accept native-born clergy, and besides, former hippies would hardly have relished doing weddings and funerals for the capitalist bourgeoisie. In the karma-free zone of Zen Center's dormitories they were prolonging a retreat that could last a lifetime. "The Buddha knew his palace was nothing, so he moved out," writes Downing. "Zen Center amassed palaces, and everybody moved in" (p. 147).

Many of these not-quite-monks lacked, or gradually lost, the fervor for zazen that had been shown by Zen Center's earliest members, who had practiced with Suzuki at Sokoji in early mornings before beginning their workdays in ordinary jobs. Furthermore, Buddhists are supposed to devote themselves to the alleviation of suffering; how could that be done in sleepy, pastoral Muir Beach? As for City Center, efforts at outreach to its surrounding black ghetto met with only temporary and limited success.

A more urgent worry, however, was the drain on Zen Center's budget exerted by the housing of so many nonproductive residents. From the day that the mortgage on Tassajara was signed in 1966, the organization could hope to survive only on the kindness of philanthropic strangers. This was the plight inherited by Baker-roshi. He had already shown some talent as an impresario, but his transformation from a conscientious social activist into a hustler with fourteen telephones in his house was set in motion by the overriding need for fund-raising.

In 1970 Baker had become the only American to receive Suzuki-roshi's "dharma Transmission"—the ceremony marking a Zen master's avowal that, through an ineffable "heart-mind" to "heart-mind" understanding, his student has now matched or surpassed him as a worthy carrier of the Buddha's wisdom. By then, Zen Center insiders had already been put off by Baker's ambitious and calculating style. They were dismayed when their adored roshi passed over candidates whose resistance to earthly desire more nearly resembled his own. But in retrospect the choice hardly looks unfathomable. Baker must have struck his teacher as the priest who stood the best chance of holding things together for Zen Center in a period of rapid and taxing change.

Baker's top priority when he became abbot was to press for the costly acquisition of Green Gulch Farm in 1972—a move that appeared to ease Zen Center's housing crunch but actually exacerbated all of the existing tensions. He also began finding more work for his live-in proletariat, partly in staffing the three principal complexes, partly in attending to his own comfort and convenience, and partly in running the various new retail enterprises whose initially low prices, picturesquely shorn and clad employees, and aura of clean-living virtue allowed them to serve as what one shrewd insider called "donative theatres" (p. 284).

A born salesman, Baker at first convinced his charges that they were extending their zazen practice, not sinking into peonage, when they worked without compensation growing potatoes at Green Gulch, peeling them in the kitchen at Greens, or silently presenting them in novel vegetarian entrees at his own San Francisco house as he hosted banquets for the likes of Werner Erhard and Mick Jagger. When the Apocalypse arrived a decade later, the potatoes were still being peeled, but many wielders of the paring knives were by then middle-aged and raising families, having received for their toil neither thanks nor sympathy, not to mention a living wage, health insurance, or Social Security credit. And insofar as these frantically overworked people were gaining business acumen, they were drifting ever farther from the nondualistic "beginner's mind" that Suzuki-roshi had proclaimed as the Zen ideal. They remembered it well enough, however, to pass a sentence of banishment on their arrogant, high-living abbot.

For several years following Baker's departure, Zen Center appeared to be not only ungoverned but ungovernable. Suddenly there were dozens of would-be roshis, united only in their vindictiveness toward the exiled one. "We had meetings," a prominent member recalls, "where people were saying, 'Why should we have to obey the rules?' It became anarchic. City Center became a kind of hotel on Page Street—people were living there and bad-mouthing Zen Center. They had lost their faith in the practice" (p. 145).

The paralysis was such that Baker-roshi's "transmitted" heir apparent, Reb Anderson, had to wait three years before being installed as the next (and last) abbot-for-life, a position he held for only a year before having his powers curtailed by the newly assertive Board of Directors. The precipitating incident was another scandal. Putting Buddha-mind in abeyance, the former boxer Anderson had packed a gun when he went looking for a neighborhood thug who had robbed him, and it turned out that he had lifted that gun, four years earlier, from a corpse he had stumbled across in Golden Gate Park without notifying the police.

Behind the awkward headlines lay nagging, debilitating doubts. Had Anderson really received full Transmission from Baker? (Baker denies it.) What would it mean, anyway, to have acquired the dharma from someone whose callous actions belied his own possession of it? And had zazen sitting and the teaching of resignation, by fostering a docile mentality, undermined the common sense of what one survivor called the "stunningly unaware" Zen Center community? A much-quoted pronouncement by the droll and elfin Suzuki-roshi began to sound all too prophetic: "Establishing Buddhism in a new country is like holding a plant to a stone and waiting for it to take root" (Chadwick 1999, p. 252).

3.

It couldn't have been pleasant for Richard Baker to realize that, with or without his cooperation, *Shoes Outside the Door* was going to be completed and published. Michael Downing finally caught up with him in February of 2000 by driving through a blizzard to remote Crestone Mountain in southern Colorado, where Baker, after several abortive ecclesiastical and commercial ventures in Santa Fe, is now the abbot of a modest training monastery. He refused to discuss his sexual history; instead, he glossed over it in a six-hundred-word document whose sophistries Downing efficiently punctures for us. But Baker did talk about his stewardship of Zen Center, admitting that he had let the operation balloon on a scale that must have been harmful to individual practice. Even so, he remains astounded that the Board of Directors felt itself entitled to strip him of the title *roshi* ("venerable teacher"). That move, he believes, was disastrous for Zen Center and bad for the wider cause of American Zen.

Being an outsider to Buddhism, Downing wisely refrains from dismissing Baker's claim as a mere expression of pique. And in fact there is a serious issue here. In Baker's time at Zen Center it was customary in the U.S. (though not in Japan) to honor as a roshi every "transmitted" Zen adept. But if an elected board could take a vote and declare in effect that someone had been named a roshi in error, wouldn't that also cast into doubt the authenticity of Transmission? Go down that road, Baker believes, and you will lose your awe for a central doctrine of Buddhism: the unbroken lineal descent of the dharma from Gautama Siddhartha, the Buddha, through a chain of enlightened custodians.

Baker may well be right on that score. Yet the early followers of

Suzuki-roshi would have needed only to ponder his conduct in order to acquire a less mystical grasp of Transmission. Suzuki hadn't wanted to be called *roshi*, and he never characterized himself as enlightened. Everything about his ironic manner bespoke a disbelief that one anointed individual can be enduringly more Buddha-like than others. Sheer neglect and then illness, not awe for the unique sacrament of Transmission, prevented him from granting it to anyone at Zen Center except the notably self-interested Baker. And on trips back to Japan, he showed how little Transmission meant to him by conferring it on his own scarcely qualified son and, as a favor to a friend, on another young priest whom he hadn't taught at all.

Nobody, however, seems to have drawn the obvious inference that Transmission must be at least partly a political act. Zen Center's young absolutists, we need to recall, were mostly products of the ingenuous California counterculture, with its psychedelic visions of transcendent reality and its faith in the higher wisdom of Eastern gurus. Suzuki's compromises could have taught them a good deal about the way an established religion has to make its peace with prejudice and privilege, but such "sellout" realism was just what they were seeking to escape through immersion in zazen.

After 1986, with the ascendancy of a more sober generation that had chafed under Baker's dictatorship, Zen Center gradually regained its poise and soldiered on—but in a significantly altered spirit. In addition to closing down or spinning off its business enterprises, reducing its property holdings, and generally trimming its budget, the organization reconstituted itself in a checks-and-balances mode. An authoritarian hierarchy became a dispersed bureaucracy, with multiple advisory boards and committees ensuring that elected officials couldn't make policy on their own.

Now Zen Center appoints rotating co-abbots with fixed terms. In sharp contrast to earlier times, women far outnumber men in positions of responsibility, and they are vigilant against any backsliding into the old patriarchal mode. Already by 1987, for example, a center conference—a "Celebration of Women in Buddhist Practice"—was billed as "entirely a leaderless event," offered with the pointed hope that "such exploration of consensual and horizontal structures will ripple through-out the Buddhist sanghas in America" (Downing 2001, p. 349). There one heard the voice of eighties-style feminism, and it was saying that no more Richard Bakers need apply for starring roles.

Along with egalitarianism came, inexorably, a certain porousness to cultural influences from outside the zendo. According to Down-ing, Zen Center now seeks the advice of secular counselors and group training consultants, and the lingua franca of psychotherapy— *transference, projection, archetypes, addictive behavior*—mingles easily with the ancient religious lexicon. Moreover, the Tassajara guest season, more popular than ever, welcomes citizens who would like to cultivate some Buddhist mindfulness without having to believe in the literal Trans-mission of the dharma, much less in nirvana and reincarnation. Sum-mer visitors can take classes in Judaism and Christianity as well as Buddhism, along with a smorgasbord of peripheral offerings such as yoga, cooking, and bird-watching.

Tassajara's new policy resonates in suggestive ways with *Blue Jean Buddha* (Loundon 2001), a bellwether anthology of personal stories by do-it-yourself Buddhist practitioners now in their twenties and early thirties. Here in the U.S., observes the editor, "all the Buddhist tradi-tions now live side-by-side, colliding and mingling vigorously" (Loun-don 2001, p. 196). Reverence toward roshis has given way to religious comparison shopping by college students who have traveled widely in India, Sri Lanka, Burma, Thailand, and Nepal. "Jew-Bu's" and "UU-Bu's" (Jews and Unitarian Universalists adhering to Buddhist ways) coexist amiably with believers in goddesses and even with one con-tributor who thinks he is a *tulka*, or reincarnated Tibetan monk. The testifiers are, on the whole, socially conscious activists who manifest a cheerful self-satisfaction that would have been rebuked in dokusans with either Shunryu Suzuki or Richard Baker.

Tassajara's current hospitality to such religious eclecticism, however, would appear to be only skin-deep, a matter of balancing the books by marketing insight to a "spiritual" but increasingly nonsectarian public.

The Zen Center's core mission remains the teaching of Soto Zen, purged of its Japanese legacy of racism, sexism, nepotism, and collusion with samurai killers and modern imperialist warlords. And there is no reason to doubt the superior consistency and moral earnestness of such Zen. A practice that is disconnected from civil power and self-restricted to well-meaning liberals can afford to be ideologically pure.

As for the bestowal of dharma Transmission, Yankee fair play has largely supplanted the whims of roshis. Transmission is all but guaranteed to Zen Center students who complete a fixed course of study and remain active within the center beyond ten years. In short, although Zen remains paradoxical at its core, this institution now operates on rationally defensible lines.

Suzuki-roshi has been dead for more than three decades, and few of his disciples remain associated with the center. Troubled fugitives from the America of corporate greed, conformism, race riots, and body bags, they had been drawn to Zen through the person of Suzuki himself, who struck them as radiating an inner peace. He tolerated their wildness while teaching them a way of taming it through rigorous discipline and ritual.

Now Zen Center, deprived of Suzuki's living example but determined to memorialize it, meticulously preserves the formalities he introduced, celebrates his birthday, is readying more of his uncollected lectures for publication, and has erected a shrine in his honor. But is that what the self-effacing Suzuki would have wanted? Can Zen Center promote nonattachment by attaching itself to a legend? Or are we witnessing the coagulation of a passionate, spontaneous, and turbulent movement into a church? "Oh, Americans," Suzuki once confided to Gary Snyder (Downing 2001, p. 126). "They don't have enough sense of humor. They're much too serious."

v.

A Discipline in Crisis

Chapter 17

THE END OF THE POSTSTRUCTURALIST ERA

Here is the revised text of a talk I delivered at a University of Alabama symposium on literary theory in 1992. It subsequently formed a chapter in a collection of the conference papers, *The Emperor Redressed: Critiquing Critical Theory* (1995).

Time is beginning to run out, I believe, for the body of literary theory and practice known as poststructuralism—the discourse that itself reduces all things to discourse according to the models provided by such thinkers as Roland Barthes, Jacques Derrida, Michel Foucault, Jacques Lacan, Louis Althusser, and Julia Kristeva. It has been a long, wild ride, extending from the mid-1970s through the present, and it has altered our intellectual style in ways that will probably linger for generations. Poststructuralists have helped even their adversaries to realize that selfhood is shaped in part by tacit ideology, that "truth" often does the bidding of power, and that we should always ask whose interests are being served by a given claim to intellectual or cultural authority. For reasons that I want to explore, however, the literary inquiries conducted under the banner of this movement appear fated to produce mostly circular and monotonous pseudo-discoveries. Awareness of that fact is already causing dissatisfaction, not just in familiar humanistic quarters, but within the very circles that have hitherto been most hospitable to grand-theoretical speculation of a radical cast. And the dissatisfaction can only redouble as more and more academics from the left end of the political spectrum perceive the connection between flawed methodological premises and hollow and dogmatic findings.

I state this argument so baldly at the outset in order to show that I will not be taking the most commonly heard line of complaint against the discourse theorists. According to that critique, poststructuralism and political correctness are scarcely distinguishable phenomena, since they both seek to undermine the Western values that supposedly shine through our classic literature. I believe, on the contrary, that the relation of poststructuralism to the radical sentiment now dominating "advanced" academic thought is parasitic, replete with ironies, and above all, transitory. To miss that fact is to be abandoned to a quite unnecessary fatalism about the irreversible decline of the humanities, conceived as a steady loss of ground to the joint forces of trendiness and programmatic leftism.

Hence, for example, the unrelenting gloom of Roger Kimball, who takes the very existence of "tenured radicals," with their sinister ethnic and feminist and homosexual concerns, as a sign that the end is near (Kimball 1990). In an article anathematizing the 1990 MLA Convention, Kimball passes in review a rogue's gallery of paper titles— "Reinventing Gender," "New English Sodom," "The Prurient Origins of the American Self," even "The Other Captives: American Indian Oral Captivity Narratives" (Kimball 1992, p. 67)—that supposedly manifest "the substitution of certain political causes for disinterested appreciation" (p. 74). The topics treated in such papers, Kimball declares, are not "the kinds of things that are appropriate subjects for a public scholarly discussion of literature" (p. 73). Which is to say, I suppose, that they might bring a blush to the cheek of a "disinterested" young maiden. For Kimball, then, "an importation of politics into the classroom" is synonymous with the "destruction of academic standards" (p. 83).

Politics, however, have never been absent from the classroom. The ethos of "appreciation" bore a politics of its own, namely, quietism, elitism, ethnocentrism, and a convenient dissociation between the vulgar material realm and the spiritualizing beauties of literature. Today we can easily see the connection between such literary training and the class etiquette of Anglo-Saxon exclusivity. A recognition that *some* politics or other will always be involved in criticism is prerequisite not just to avoiding alarmism about the academy's turn toward social consciousness but also to addressing poststructuralism on its own methodological merits.

There are, of course, academics who share Kimball's nucleus of attitudes: a belief in a small, fixed canon; a wish to restrict critical investigation within the boundaries of "appreciation"; and an untroubled apprehension of selfhood, truth, social decorum, and the appropriate confinement of literary meaning to readily accessible authorial intentions. But Kimball is right to be pessimistic about the likelihood that such innocence will ever again prevail. For now, certainly, there is no sign that literary study has begun to exhaust its recent centrifugal momentum—its enthusiasm for difference, dissent, and decentering. Suspicion of foundationalism, of essentialism, and of transcendental explanatory categories is not waning but continuing to mount—and why shouldn't it?

My concern is not to deplore the skeptical strain in current literary theory but to challenge its monopoly by the poststructuralist camp. For, as I will try to indicate, poststructuralism is not entitled to its vanguard epistemological pretensions. In some respects it has always been a backward-looking and semi-incoherent movement, and the same must be said of the branch of structuralism from which it derived. This is not just my own view of the matter. It has already been ably expounded by such well-informed observers as Vincent Descombes, the late J. G. Merquior, Jacques Bouveresse, Tzvetan Todorov, Luc Ferry and Alain Renaut, John Ellis, Thomas Pavel, Alexander Argyros, Leonard Jackson, Harold Fromm, and Joseph F. Graham among others. Indeed, so devastating *in theory* has been the epistemological critique of poststructuralism that one wonders how the movement has survived as long as it has.

I feel obliged to pause over this question, lest we mistake mere illogicality for a lack of staying power. Poststructuralism would appear to share some of the adaptability shown by two dubious but curiously hardy movements, Marxism and psychoanalysis, that acquired survival value from the passions they aroused and from the pliability of their concepts and propositions. Each has thus constituted what Michael Polanyi once termed a dynamo-objective coupling—that is, a doctrine whose normative claims can always be invoked when its scientific claims appear threatened, and vice versa (Polanyi 1964, p. 230). Poststructuralism from its inception, and notably in the writings of Derrida and Foucault, has played the same shell game, appearing to satisfy the most austerely skeptical intellectual taste while casually introducing propositions of gnomic certitude, prophetic reverberation, and exhilarating historical scope—propositions, for example, about the priority of writing over speech, about the impossibility of objective knowledge, or about the disappearance of man. When those notions come under fire, they can be provisionally brushed aside or even disavowed while the thinker presents himself, or is presented by his offended disciples, as making only local and scrupulous claims. Like Marx and Freud, the prime thinkers of poststructuralism are thus surrounded by unending controversy about what they really meant to say. Scarcely anyone among the faithful pauses to ask if the master shouldn't have taken pains to make himself clear in the first place.

But of course, in a certain sense he *shouldn't* have done so, since it is precisely the master's elusiveness, his rhetorical knack of undetectably segueing between the descriptive and the prescriptive, the analytic and prophetic modes, that has facilitated the satisfying of wildly diverse expectations. Just as Marx and Freud could appear as both objective scientists and social liberators, so Derrida can be seen as a fastidiously rigorous and patient student of small-scale textual cruxes and, alternatively, as a foe of the entire misguided Western tradition; and Foucault, similarly, can be taken either as a skeptical debunker of imperfectly examined notions about historical periods, as a winningly modest activist who eschews the programmatic, or as a visionary who has somehow grasped the inmost workings of all social power, thus rendering up to us history's very engine and essence. Indeed, as many commentators have noted, Foucault and Derrida alike thrive on the paradox of casting doubt on the possibility of any secure knowledge while simultaneously advancing foundational propositions of their own that are to be taken entirely on faith. The contradiction is not bothersome because, quite simply, the loyalists of poststructuralism aren't reading for contradictions. The master's show of extreme vigilance against illusions actually serves as a safe-conduct pass for the new dogmas.

I am aware, of course, that this unflattering account defies a widely held belief that poststructuralism rests on an actual breakthrough in knowledge. Many observers now assume that poststructuralism came into being when certain thinkers perceived a fatal flaw in the structuralists' application of Saussurean linguistics to cultural analysis. Sometimes the flaw is said to have been a weakness in the analogy between linguistics and such fields as anthropology, political economy, and psychoanalysis; at other times the blame is laid on the inability of structuralists to show why certain terms and not others were the essential ones for specifying the underlying pattern of any given myth or poem or network of beliefs and taboos.

These are indeed grave defects in the structuralist tradition, but poststructuralism can hardly be said to have sprung up to remedy them. For, in the first place, the Saussurean linguistic model still dominates poststructuralist thought. We can see that fact not only in such direct instances as Lacan's declaration that the unconscious is structured like a language but also in the pervasiveness within poststructuralism of terms like *sign, text, discourse, signifier, signified, difference*, and *trace* (see Pavel 1989, p. 4). It is precisely the continuing structuralist mindset that induces Foucault, when he recoils from liberal individualism, to discount the active human subject and grant all power to whole regimes or systems.[1] And it is the structuralist affinity for inert and global schematization that renders poststructuralist criticism so clumsy when it attempts to cope with the experienced narrative flow of literature or with the evolving struggles of particular authors to take control of their circumstances and their craft. As for the idea that poststructuralism was founded on a rejection of structuralist overconfidence about truth claims, it leaves us helpless to explain why the founding texts of this later movement feature so many vast pronouncements unaccompanied by anything that might be counted as supporting evidence.

Poststructuralism has been less a reaction against dubious scientific pretensions within structuralism than an accentuation of a grandiose strain that was already discernible in the most influential of French structuralists, Claude Lévi-Strauss. Moreover, by battening on radicalized versions of psychoanalysis even while formally disavowing the essentialism and foundationalism that inhabit the entire psychoanalytic tradition, poststructuralism has manifested a cavalier scientific attitude for which, once again, Lévi-Strauss offered a precedent. His Freudianism aside, Lévi-Strauss's very choice of the Saussurean framework as a model for "the human sciences" was a regressive methodological step—a perverse enshrinement of the static phonological analysis that linguistics had already left behind in its transit from Leonard Bloomfield's research paradigm to Noam Chomsky's and beyond. Yet no critique of structuralism along these inviting lines has been forthcoming from the poststructuralist lawgivers—a symptomatic fact, since their own relation to the rational-empirical ethos represents yet a further decline in rigor.

The extent to which poststructuralism is bogged down in apriorism often goes unappreciated even by opponents of the movement. Listen, for example, to Steven Watts, an Americanist who believes, as I do, that in poststructuralist discourse, typically, "the nature and possibilities of human action are nearly obliterated in a world where discourse is the only reality" (Watts 1991, p. 645). Nevertheless, says Watts, we have to be grateful to the poststructuralists for what they have shown us about American literature:

> Their theoretical insights have forced a reconceptualization of many important topics in the study of American culture. Americanists have been forced to reconsider, for instance, education as a cultural process defining and entrenching certain modes of discourse; gender roles and relationships as cultural formations which pivot on the linguistic constructions of male/female dichotomies; political language and competition as a semiotic battleground for struggles over signification and the privileging of discourse; race as a complex and volatile cluster of signs denoting the myriad binary oppositions of black/white imagery; the visual arts and theater as signs systems which encode certain discursive practices; and literature, both popular and elite, as an interplay of texts, all of which interact with one another in ways that transcend authorial intention, open themselves to fluid and indeterminate meanings. . . . Informing this whole array of

topics . . . is the conviction that *all* American texts and discourses contain within them the seeds of their own destruction. They shelter a
barely hidden instinct for reversibility that can be teased out and liberated by the perceptive critic. (Watts 1991, p. 630)

This handsome concession accurately reflects the political domin-
ion that poststructuralism has carved out for itself in recent years. Yet
the statement goes wrong, I believe, from the very outset in granting
to poststructuralism what the writer calls "theoretical insights." An
insight is presumably an intuitive grasp of something actual that pre-
existed one's consciousness of it. But at issue here is surely not insight
but a threefold *methodological imperative* — namely, to *regard* all social
and critical issues in "discourse" terms as "semiotic battleground[s]";
to *regard* all literary works as "open[ing] themselves to fluid and indeterminate meanings"; and third, to *regard* all texts as "contain[ing] . . .
the seeds of their own destruction." Strictly speaking, no insight about
literature has been mentioned; the sign clusters and subversions are
simply artifacts of the poststructuralist angle of vision.

Watts's unbidden softness toward poststructuralism is especially
apparent in his final sentence, where *texts* are said to "shelter a barely
hidden instinct for reversibility. . . ." Obviously, since they possess neither minds nor bodies, texts cannot nurture instincts of any kind. Yet
from Fredric Jameson's eclectically Freudo-Marxo-poststructuralist
Political Unconscious of 1981 onward, poststructuralist criticism has
indeed treated literature in just this projective anthropomorphizing
spirit, positing, within the bosom of any given work that appears to
endorse majority values, an impish homunculus who, *mirabile dictu*,
agrees entirely with the critic's own opinions. By allowing this sen-
timentality to go unchallenged, Watts gives away precisely the point
about poststructuralism that, in my opinion, needs to be most emphatically made: that findings driven by poststructuralist theory tend to be
willful and largely circular.

Willfulness, of course, is nothing new in literary criticism, and perhaps poststructuralism only lends militancy and an aura of advanced

technique to what used to be known as self-indulgence. Such is John Ellis's harsh view of deconstruction, which, he says, "has given an appearance of theoretical sophistication to what had previously been the more or less incoherent attitudes and prejudices of majority practice" (Ellis 1989, p. 153). But I am not so sure. Criticism in general never played by hermeneutic rules as rigged as those of poststructuralism.

Not long ago, most notably, only Freudians allowed that the absence of a given theme could count, thanks to the handy mechanism of repression, as a sign of its actual ubiquity. Poststructuralism has seized upon this generous rule, correlating it with the determinative function of absence in Saussurean linguistics, and has generalized its application from the individual text and authorial mind to the entire collective mind of a society—so that, for example, the lack of reference to blacks in *The Scarlet Letter* can now be taken without further corroboration to prove antebellum America's all-consuming fear of miscegenation and slave uprisings.

This degree of inferential license would appear to be something new. It bears an affinity, however, to something very old—namely, the style of reading perfected by the fathers of the early Church in their Christianizing of the Old Testament and of Greek and Roman classics. That connection between early medieval and postmodern interpretation, a connection that Jameson openly embraced in *The Political Unconscious* (Jameson 1994, p. 29), is usually obscured from view by the fact that poststructuralists import the absent signified for the sake not of piety but of impiety toward accepted cultural ideals. Yet the homology of method is, as Jameson perceived, far from trivial. In both patristic and poststructuralist interpretation, actual inquiry into as yet unsubdued material is preempted by a display of ideologically circumscribed exegetical inventiveness; in both cases the text gets treated largely as a husk from which an already known truth is to be produced and elaborated.

By now it may be clear why I want to reject John Ellis's proposal that poststructuralism merely theorizes our perennial methodological slackness in "English." Such a notion condemns the best of our practice along with the worst, rendering invisible a key distinction between two kinds of discourse that I will here call the *disciplinary* and the *self-ratifying*. Poststructuralism doesn't so much codify a general laxness in critical inference drawing as it greatly encourages one of our models of professional practice while discouraging and disparaging the other. It is as *an assault on the disciplinary*, I maintain, that American poststructuralism must finally be understood. And when we see it in that light, we will be better able to grasp not only its atavistic status but also its powerlessness to achieve the total hegemony of which its advocates dream, or even to sustain its current glamour as the advancing wing of both theoretical sophistication and political rectitude.

What, then, *is* the disciplinary? Above all, it is the empirical, by which I mean simply the ethic of respecting what is known, acknowledging what is still unknown, and acting as if one cared about the difference. In Paisley Livingston's terms, the disciplinary refers to how people conduct themselves when they place the epistemic goal first (Livingston 1995). But the disciplinary is a collective phenomenon, not just an individual one. In a disciplinary setting, it is taken for granted that all participants prefer empirically defensible assertions to wild ones and that the latter will be vigilantly rebuked. Thus an essential feature of the disciplinary is the give-and-take, largely conducted in journals, between proponents of new hypotheses and possessors of knowledge that may or may not have been successfully accounted for in those hypotheses. For the disciplinary spirit to operate, members of a given intellectual community must read one another's work discriminatingly and try to show, through pointed reference to available facts, that certain apprehensions of those facts are more plausible than others.

Perhaps the surest marker of the disciplinary is the subtle divergence of investigative conventions between one discipline and another. Through the efforts of many persons, over time, to be maximally faithful to the regularities and irregularities of a given subject matter, each discipline will have evolved its own tacit standards of inquiry and reporting. Anthropologists follow one set of intellectual habits and art historians another, not because they differ in their adherence to the disciplinary but precisely because they remain under its sway—so much so that they needn't ever become fully aware of the methodological rules they are observing. It is thus unthinkable, within the disciplinary ethos, that one might suddenly decide to seek enlightenment through whole-sale adoption of the terms and mannerisms of a neighboring discipline, much less those of a pseudoscience or a fad.

Self-ratifying discourse is just the opposite. As the name is meant to convey, it traffics in apriorism and tends to be openly contemptuous toward ideas of truth. Lacking an ethic of appeal to evidential scruples, it focuses only on congenial instances that serve to keep contrary evidence well out of consideration; it tends to supplant measured argumentation with appeals to group solidarity; it indulges a taste for diffusely explana-tory terms such as capitalism, the West, logocentrism, and patriarchy; and it takes a tone of moral absolutism toward the past and, as well, toward the commentator's adversaries, who, instead of being chided for careless reasoning or incomplete knowledge, are typically condemned as harboring an intolerably retrograde social or political attitude. Above all, those who practice self-ratifying discourse are attracted to what they regard as interdisciplinarity, conceived not as the actual practice of a second discipline but as the duty-free importing of terms and concepts from some source of broad wisdom about history or epistemology or the structure of the mind. This is of course not interdisciplinarity at all but *anti*disciplinarity, a holiday from the methodological constraints that prevail in any given field.

It would be a calumny to say that poststructuralists fall entirely within the self-ratifying camp and their traditionalist opponents entirely out-side it. Now that poststructuralist ideas have become conventional wis-dom for much of the literary academy, they can be found within every style of critical discourse; and, conversely, there is no shortage of undis-ciplinary practice by critics who are baffled and annoyed by all literary theory postdating the 1950s. Yet we can hardly overlook the strong cor-relation between explicit poststructuralist advocacy and the symptoms of self-ratifying discourse. Nor is that link at all puzzling, since ideas of rationality, objectivity, and the patient accretion of knowledge are precisely the main targets of poststructuralist iconoclasm.

Thus the success of poststructuralism in American universities points inescapably to a broad (though possibly reversible) weakening of the disciplinary ethos in what might loosely be called the post-Vietnam era. To leave matters there, however, is to overlook the vicissitudes and survival strategies of poststructuralism itself, which has hardly enjoyed the stress-free sway imagined by alarmed nonacademics. Poststructuralism could not have lasted into the 1990s without undergoing an extraordinary mutation that warrants our interest here. I do not mean the retooling of seemingly anti-academic notions to fit the values of the tenure assembly line, though that development is important in its own right. Rather, I have in mind a drastic change of political tone whereby, in an increasingly radicalized atmosphere, a predominantly elitist impulse managed to acquire the protective coloration of egalitarianism.

The passage I quoted from Steven Watts on pages 302–303 shows how one recent adversary of poststructuralism nevertheless assumes that without the contribution of discourse theorists, no headway could have been made against the old academic complacency about race, gender, and class. But despite the apparent exception of Althusser's scholastic Marxism, the most influential poststructuralist doctrines in the American academy—namely, those of Barthes, Derrida, and Foucault—were originally remote from practical sociopolitical concerns. As such, they were prime candidates for rejection when the academy began losing patience with theory that placed linguistic concerns above emancipatory ones. In effect, Americanized poststructuralism spared itself from deportation by entering into a green card marriage with the very party that had begun to spurn it most indignantly.

Watts is too young to remember that the American academy had no need of poststructuralism in order to combat the WASP ethnocentrism, the unreflective sexism, and the nationalistically tinged humanism that still characterized the theory and practice of literary study as late as the 1960s. Poststructuralism was unknown in this country before 1967, and it had little impact before the mid-seventies. But academic radicalism was already robust in the late sixties, when the Modern Language Association was thrown into disarray and subjected to a virtual coup by the New Left, spearheaded by Louis Kampf and Paul Lauter.

I know about those events at first hand because I was myself an antiwar spokesman at the time and was being urged to join the cultural revolution. My ambivalence about taking out a general political frustration on the poor old MLA can be read between the lines of an otherwise radical-sounding paper I gave at the 1969 annual convention, later published in *PMLA* as "Do Literary Studies Have an Ideology?" (Crews 1970). And a subsequent essay I published in 1972, called "Offing Culture: Literary Study and the Movement," emphatically dissociated me from those who wished to trash the entire Western literary heritage in the name of combating the American ruling class. As these recollections help to show, the revolt against Dead White European Males began in the sixties and initially owed nothing to poststructuralism.

Although the New Left as such was falling apart by the early 1970s, activist consciousness within the routine business of the universitites was just getting into gear. The drive for establishing both ethnic studies programs and affirmative action in admissions and hiring had already begun. Before long, ethnic particularism was joined by feminism and then by lesbian and gay studies—movements that by now have made a considerable impact on curricula, appointment practices, and accepted norms of literary-critical discussion. Yet only the last of these movements took shape during the poststructuralist era, and its intellectual and political style was chiefly shaped not by discourse theory but by the two liberationist initiatives that preceded it.

Moreover, when, at the dawn of the seventies, news began to circulate about the novel practice of deconstruction—then the vanguard doctrine of the poststructuralist movement—we heard about it from the least likely of revolutionary headquarters, New Haven, Connecticut. In the hands of critics like Paul de Man, Geoffrey Hartman, J. Hillis Miller, and the early Barbara Johnson, Yale-style deconstruction was as remote as it conceivably could be from the activist spirit. All of those writers were content with the Western canon exactly as they found it. Their manifest aim was not to broaden the literary-critical franchise but on the contrary to bring a spirit of erudite whimsy into the discussion of familiar books, which would be rendered only more endearing by the discovery that their meanings were more multitudinous and undecidable than anyone had yet surmised. As late as 1985, for example, Johnson still presented deconstruction as nothing more ideological than learning how to respond to literature with a fully alert sensibility. "Deconstruction," she explained (in a typically tendentious and coercive formulation), "is a reading strategy that carefully follows both the meanings and the suspensions and displacements of meaning in a text, while humanism is a strategy to stop reading when the text stops saying what it ought to have said" (B. Johnson 1985, p. 140).

What the Yale deconstructionists challenged was not the pernicious social effects of hegemonic texts, much less the quietism of a small professorial elite, but the vulgar earnestness of second-generation New Critics who were toiling away at explication in the academic boondocks and hence, in their classrooms, casting literary pearls before demotic swine. As Hartman memorably phrased it, our classics were "in danger of being routinized or contaminated by endless readings forced out of industrious hordes of students" (Hartman 1980, p. 230). Even deconstructionists, he added with a shudder, were being "tainted by the odor of academic life. . . . For the university has opened its doors" (p. 239).

Understandably, such mandarinism placed deconstruction in peril of being hooted off the academic stage. By the time of Frank Lentricchia's *Criticism and Social Change* and Edward Said's *The World, the Text, and the Critic*, both published in 1983, a full-scale counteroffensive was under way. And by 1986 the game was effectively over, as we can see in J. Hillis Miller's wormwood-flavored presidential address to the MLA— a plaintive exhortation to his "collaborators," as he forlornly called the ascendant academic radicals, to leave a little room in their hearts for deconstruction.

"As everyone knows," Miller conceded, "literary study in the past few years has undergone a sudden, almost universal turn away from theory in the sense of an orientation toward language as such and has made a corresponding turn toward history, culture, society, politics, institutions, class and gender conditions . . ." (J. Miller 1987, p. 283). Deconstruction, he went on, has consequently suffered from "a belief (quite mistaken) that it has become lost in endless sterile concern with the play of language, that it is elite, reactionary, apolitical" (p. 283). But shouldn't Marxists and other concretizers feel at least minimally obliged to deconstruct the material base? "You are my collaborators in a common task," Miller sulked, "even when you attack me or my close associates in ways that seem to me perverse or irrational . . ." (p. 291).

The hollowness of Miller's ecumenical gesture was generally apparent at the time, and it only became more glaring later with the posthumous disgrace of Paul de Man, whom Miller had inadvisedly commended to his MLA audience as having "insisted all along that one cannot fail to be engaged in history and in political action" (p. 284). It was too late, then, for Miller and his generation of deconstructionists to smoke the peace pipe with the left. Yet as we can plainly see in Barbara Johnson's case—just compare her Milleresque *The Critical Difference* of 1980 with her fully ideologized but still Derridean *A World of Difference* seven years later—deconstruction didn't exactly vanish.

Nor did Lacanian psychoanalysis or the Foucauldian archaeology of knowledge. Instead, each branch of poststructuralism that was not already self-identified as politically radical hastened to do so—and, it must be said, with stunning success. Lacanians, for example, weathered the blatant sexism of their dead leader by forging an alliance with radical feminists, who discarded everything uncongenial in Lacan's thought while adapting its thoroughgoing negativity to their own end of "problematizing" bourgeois notions of patriarchal normality. Foucault, for his part, let it be known that he was not just an analyst but a soldier in the trenches against the carceral society. And instead of Derrida the glosser of indeterminacies in metaphysical classics that he had no intention of forsaking, we began to get Derrida the staunch theoretical foe of apartheid and of academic institutionality.

By today, many literary academics are so awed by these hastily assembled activist credentials that they do not even want to contemplate poststructuralism as a distinct movement embodying certain debatable presumptions. Instead, they think approvingly of "theory," a term encompassing all practices that insist on radical reflection about established power and the claims of the marginalized. Thus Gerald Graff recently reported that he had overcome his initial distrust of "theory," since that body of thought now allowed him to perceive such phenomena as the imperialism in "Heart of Darkness" to which he had hitherto been blind (Graff 1992). Graff didn't pause to observe that the Chinua Achebe essay that had affected him so strongly was quite untouched by poststructuralism. On the contrary, he went out of his way to establish precisely that connection—asserting that Achebe's point about contemptuous Western images of Africa "is one that recent literary and critical 'theory' has been making," namely, that texts make a difference in the world, "thereby complicating the problem of truth" (Graff 1992, p. 26).

One cannot disagree with a word of this, but one can note the political camouflage that poststructuralism has acquired since the days when Geoffrey Hartman was portraying the "high-jinks," as he called them, of deconstructionist critics as the most refined literary art of our time. Gerald Graff himself was one of the earliest and most devastating mockers of that effete stand (Graff 1977). What has occurred in Graff's case is a change that has overtaken the profession generally: he, and we, no longer find it feasible to weed out the methodologically dubious from the politically progressive.[2] To attack poststructuralism now is to risk being labeled a right-wing ideologue, a foe not of obscurantist logic chopping but of oppressed people everywhere.

It is important, however, not to exaggerate either the current hegemony of poststructuralism or the willingness of the academy as a whole to be bullied into making specious choices between the disciplinary and the socially conscious. Despite scare talk to the contrary, the roots of American poststructuralism have remained rather shallow and unevenly distributed. Think, for example, of medieval studies, a major field of scholarship and criticism that has, over the past three decades or so, successfully crossed over from the essentializing and nakedly normative orientation of antimodernists who celebrated the supposed medieval worldview to a cannier, more concrete style of research emphasizing the actual social and literary practices rather than the formal doctrines of the period.

That instance is striking because, while research in medieval studies has become markedly less foundational and idealistic in its methodological preferences, it has done so almost entirely without recourse to poststructuralist arguments. Here, in short, is a thriving disciplinary community that has thus far found no need to admit the Trojan horse of poststructuralism within its walls, since its problem-oriented practice is giving it just what it requires: a perpetually fresh set of issues and tools and an enlivening, knowledge-based debate about the field's boundaries and prospects.

If my colleague Anne Middleton is to be believed, moreover, medievalists who have learned to do without patristic exegesis, to say nothing of its deconstructive unraveling, now share a community of interest with students of modern ethnic and colonial literatures over issues of multilinguicity and "vernacular transformations of authority" (Middleton 1992, p. 30). To someone like Roger Kimball, who already knows what "kinds of things . . . are appropriate subjects for a public scholarly discussion of literature," such news must appear as further evidence of the betrayal of the professors. But if we have grasped that the health of literary study resides not in its subject matter or its political leaning but in its disciplinary aspect, we can welcome Middleton's prediction with equanimity. With the waning of poststructuralism, we can expect the study of ethnicity and cultural conflict within any time frame to be guided increasingly by empirical values and practices.

In areas where poststructuralism has become well entrenched, of course, a protracted struggle over method lies ahead. But in no field, including film and ethnic and women's and lesbian and gay studies, does poststructuralism enjoy an uncontested sway. Rather, it is already on the defensive precisely where it seemed to have found a safe haven—namely, in those subdisciplines that bear a manifest liberationist agenda. Activists, after all, are best positioned to see through a formal utopianism—to say nothing of a formal futilitarianism—that regularly overshoots its historical and political targets.

For some time now, feminist thought has been riven by a debate over gender essentialism, a debate whose outcome is already taking shape: the discrediting of the Lacanian identification of the female with pure absence and deprivation. Lesbian and gay critics, meanwhile, are beginning to see that the undifferentiated anti-institutionalism of both Barthes and Foucault left them powerless to champion certain institutional options against others. These critics, too, will be drawn toward the disciplinary, not because they worship academic mores for their own sake but because empirical scrupulousness is the only road to knowledge that can make a real social difference.

The same realization has already overtaken many of the cutting-edge critics in my own field of American literature. When, for example, I open a recent book called *Macropolitics of Nineteenth-Century Literature* (1995), edited by Jonathan Arac and Harriet Ritvo, I find in the introduction a forthright disavowal of Foucault's monolithic conception of power and a contrary determination to explore specific historical interests that clashed with others. And again, in another recent collection, *The New American Studies* (1991), Philip Fisher's introduction takes to task the Foucauldian model, which, Fisher says, may have had some pertinence to absolute monarchies in Europe but is helpless to deal with the quasi-anarchy of the American nineteenth century. Fisher and his contributors are interested not in national myths but in the rhetorics (pointedly plural) of what he calls "regionalisms," or interests that follow their own unique course against the mainstream. Though neither Fisher nor Arac would put it quite this way, they are both feeling the tug of the disciplinary—the ethos that requires us to attune our methods to whatever is problematic and particular in the material with which we are grappling.

Here, surely, we are witnessing the beginning of the end for Foucauldian analysis. As for deconstruction, I note with interest that Fisher discusses it in terms that, though respectful, are elegiacally so. "Deconstruction's most enduring outcome," Fisher states, "has been its powerful analytic techniques in the face of brief crux passages. In this respect, deconstruction extended but did not reverse the techniques of close reading that dominated literary study in the 1950s" (Fisher 1991, p. xxi). The praise, you will note, is distinctly faint; the governing tense in which it is couched is the simple past.

It may well be, as Rodolphe Gasché (1986), Christopher Norris

(1992), and Jeffrey T. Nealon (1992) have all recently urged, that Derrida never sanctioned the professional routinization that took deconstruction, supposedly an attitude of continual questioning, and turned it into a smug technique of critical production whereby undecidability became fetishized as a pervasive meaning in its own right. Yet that is exactly what occurred in American universities, with the foreseeable outcome that deconstructive criticism is now generally perceived to be a bore. Perhaps, as Nealon suggests, it was only the siege mentality of the "theory" faction that kept Derrida in the seventies and eighties from publicly rebuking the guildlike adaptations of Professors Hartman, Miller, de Man, and Culler (Nealon 1992, p. 1276). As I write, admirers of Foucault are doubtless fashioning parallel exculpations of their idol from the interpretative banalities that have been committed in his name.

Whether the twin giants of poststructuralism can thereby be spared the coming fate of their movement remains to be seen, but the question is hardly of monumental interest. What does matter is that the discipline, never as severely weakened as either its detractors or its proponents have allowed themselves to believe, is poised to reoccupy the contested intellectual space from which poststructuralism will inevitably be expelled, even while the democratizing impulse in academic discourse and conduct continues to expand. More guardedly stated, literary study can renew its disciplinary commitment *if we so choose*. My only wish, at such a promising moment, is that our allegiance to empirical values be made as explicit and unabashed as possible, lest the literary academy be allowed to fall directly, as well it might, from one mode of self-ratifying discourse into yet another.

Chapter 18

KAFKA IN THE CLOUDS

This chapter, originally published in the January 21, 2005, issue of *The New York Review of Books*, discusses recent studies of Franz Kafka and considers the major shifts in our perception of the writer, especially since the rift between deconstructive and "cultural studies" schools of criticism a generation ago. In showing that sociopolitical analysis isn't necessarily in conflict with close reading and literary appreciation, this essay points toward the resolution, or at least the subsidence, of current academic disputes.

I.

When Franz Kafka died of tuberculosis in 1924 at age forty-one, he enjoyed a modest and largely local reputation. With the exception of a few renderings from German into Czech by his sometime lover Milena Jesenská, for example, not one of his works had been translated into any language. Things began to change, but still slowly, when his friend and literary executor Max Brod, making bold guesses about the intended shape and meaning of the three unfinished novels, launched *Der Prozeß* *(The Trial)* into print in 1925, followed by *Das Schloß (The Castle)* and *Amerika* in the next two years. When Willa and Edwin Muir began their influential English translations of the Brod texts with *The Castle* in 1930, Edwin could still report in his introduction that "Franz Kafka's name, so far as I can discover, is almost unknown to English readers." (Murray 2004, p. 387).

A number of factors converged in the 1930s and thereafter to transform Kafka into the preeminent modernist and a giant of world literature. "The Kafkaesque," a distinctive sense of helplessness before remote and absurdly arbitrary powers, spoke to the experience of many readers who had felt the dehumanizing effects of corporate, bureaucratic, and totalitarian structures of authority. The portentousness of that impression, however, was greatly magnified by Brod's and the Muirs' emphasis on metaphysical significance. For Brod, the author of such works as *Paganism, Christianity, Judaism: A Confession of Faith*, Kafka was a modern saint who, torn between belief and unbelief, "sought God" throughout his later writings and hoped to advise his readers about how to conduct the ethical life.

That conception would fit neatly with the future vogue of existentialism, with ethnicity-effacing liberalism, and with Cold War ideology, which placed a premium on universal values that the atheistical and class-conscious Marxists had spurned (Dowden 1995). The puppet regime of Sovietized Czechoslovakia underlined that contrast by banning Kafka's works and airbrushing him from the state's literary prehistory. Meanwhile, emergent knowledge about the Holocaust, which had annihilated all three of Kafka's sisters, his correspondent Grete Bloch, and Milena Jesenská herself, imparted further poignancy to his writings, which could now be seen as anticipations of the Nazi terror.

In Brod's interpretation, advanced through editorial commentary and a biography, *The Castle* was a religious allegory, and the castle itself stood baldly for "divine guidance." Accordingly, the Muirs chose language that rendered K., the protagonist, not as the obtuse and selfish two-dimensional figure Kafka had devised but as an authorial surrogate, a sympathetic pilgrim on a grand spiritual quest. And as a corollary, Kafka's ridicule of labyrinthine bureaucracy, a phenomenon he had wryly studied every weekday in his executive role at the Workers' Accident Insurance Institute for the Kingdom of Bohemia in Prague, became harder to enjoy or even perceive. So did the impishness with which, in both *The Trial* and *The Castle*, he courted contradictions; shifted abruptly among violence, slapstick, and hairsplitting debate; and danced away from his own hints of theological and mythic significance.

In emphasizing solemn themes and prophetic insight, Kafka's early admirers courted a backlash, and it arrived in the form of a challenge by Edmund Wilson in a *New Yorker* essay of 1947 (Wilson 1962). Wilson argued that the Kafka cult was being promulgated by weak and self-hating intellectuals who resembled Kafka himself in that regard. It was strange, he wrote, that a so-called master novelist hadn't completed a single novel or indicated how the structural dilemmas in his uneven fragments could have been resolved even in principle. And he concluded: "What [Kafka] has left us is the half-expressed gasp of a self-doubting soul trampled under. I do not see how one can possibly take him for either a great artist or a moral guide" (Wilson 1962, p. 97).

Kafka would probably not have disputed Wilson's assessment. Although "The Judgment" had virtually composed itself in one fevered night, leaving him with a sense of great creative power, that mood didn't return. "I have never been the sort of person who carried something out at all costs," he lamented to Brod in 1912; ". . . What I have written was written in a lukewarm bath. I have not experienced the eternal hell of real writers . . ." (Kafka 1977, p. 82).

One of Kafka's most astute scholar-critics, Malcolm Pasley, has shown that in a number of shorter works the writer was playing what Pasley calls "semi-private games," turning his plots into extended puns and alluding hermetically to other writings of his own and to circumstances of his life that he never expected to be memorialized by biographers (Pasley 1977). Not only was he content to leave the public in the dark; he seems to have relished the role of trickster, seeding apparent clues that led nowhere and marshaling one set of symbolic associations against an equally seductive but thematically contrary set. As another critic, doubtless thinking of the lengthy bill of grievances in Kafka's "Letter to the Father," has plausibly speculated, "the inclusion of spurious and obscure items may well have given him that sense of mastery over the text—and his reader—which he felt his own father exercised over him" (Hutchinson 1977, p. 214).

If this was indeed Kafka's usual way of working, it hardly constitutes a refutation of Wilson's critique. That essay, however, had no dissuasive impact on the growth of Kafka studies, which now rested on a received view of the author as the "representative man" of his century. Insofar as critics of the forties, fifties, and sixties detected indeterminate elements in his texts, they tended to correlate them with profound thoughts about the moral maze we all inhabit after the death of God. More often, however, the ambiguities simply went unnoticed, because the critics had been primed to excavate messages and patterns, not elements of discontinuity and blockage.

This yen for closure survives even today as some critics labor to rectify disproportions and resolve mysteries that Kafka himself evidently wanted to maintain. Thus we still see articles and books declaring why it is fitting, on grounds of the protagonist's grave personal flaws, that Josef K. get arrested and put to death, or that Gregor Samsa be turned into a repulsive bug, or that K. be denied access to the castle. In supplying a poetic justice that Kafka himself disdained, such commentators spare themselves from the most constant, and possibly the most significant, aspect of his fictional universe: its strict amorality, or the absence of any means by which human beings can appease either heaven or the state by manifesting virtue.

2.

By now many professional students of Kafka's work do regard the moralizing tendency as an atavism held over from a relatively primitive state of biographical knowledge about him.[1] Meanwhile, objective research into every significant aspect of his life and context has proved greatly fruitful, and reliable new editions of his writings have corrected many misjudgments.[2] But this is not to say that critics are converging toward agreement about how his fiction ought to be approached. On the contrary—and not surprisingly, after all—Kafka studies during the past three decades have played out the same dispute between deconstructive formalism and sociopolitical engagement that has divided academic literary criticism at large.

For a long while now, Stanley Corngold of Princeton has been regarded as the dean of American Kafka experts. His *Franz Kafka: The Necessity of Form*, written before the disclosure of Paul de Man's early collaborationist journalism and published shortly thereafter in 1988, represented the deconstructive attitude in its last moment of undefensive self-assurance. So far as Corngold was concerned, de Man had shown that literary history, along with every other kind of history, is an illusion, because apprehended "reality" itself consists entirely of discourse. "As the world and the text are both fictions," Corngold paraphrased de Man as saying, "the ontological status of both remains suspended. Both fall away in their being to a vanishing point of interminable self-difference . . ." (Corngold 1988, p. 146). This was Corngold's warrant for declaring that Kafka's life "has no other story to tell than the search for circumstances propitious for the leap out of it into the uncanny world of writing" (p. 6).

Features of Kafka's practice that we have already noted—his sly punning, his planting of false leads, his preference for quandaries over neat resolutions, his buried allusions to his own previous work—all lent themselves handily to Corngold's view of him as a deconstructionist *avant la lettre*. The less Kafka's writings had to say about "reality," the more congenial he appeared to be. Thus "The Judgment," for Corngold, was really about its own "undecidability" (Corngold 1988, p. 44). "In the Penal Colony," he wrote, "is not about experience but about writing" (p. 247); in fact, it is about the writing of *The Trial* (p. 229), which is in its own turn a novel about writing. The vermin that used to be Gregor Samsa "is not a self speaking or keeping silent but language itself (*parole*)—a word broken loose from the context of language (*langage*), fallen into a void the meaning of which it cannot signify, near others who cannot understand it" (p. 76). And so forth.

Many of the same interpretations reappear, with variations that are by no means clarifying, in Corngold's new book, *Lambent Traces: Franz Kafka*. When Kafka decides to have Josef K. executed in *The Trial*, for example, he "implicitly sentences his authorial personality to death as K.'s guilty executioner" (Corngold 2004, p. 64). And the actual death sentence in "In the Penal Colony" is now said to be the author's self-fatwa for "not knowing or no longer knowing—disowning, forgetting—[his] story 'The Judgment'" (p. 14). Corngold issues such capital decrees with an alacrity matched only by the Red Queen in *Alice in Wonderland*, and the results are equally phantasmagorical.

As Corngold grudgingly admits, however, deconstruction has lost its

éclat in recent years. His new book reflects this altered climate by somewhat confusedly welding an old-fashioned intentionalist argument to
his de Manian emphasis on writing-about-writing. This move, however,
leaves Kafka looking more ethereal than ever. Corngold's idea—by no
means original, and already considered by knowledgeable scholars to
constitute a dead end—is that Kafka was a gnostic dualist who rejected
the entire realm of the senses as demonic and meant his literary works
to be acts of communication with a realm of transcendent essence.[3]

A handful of Kafka's scattered remarks, which Corngold is obliged
to keep repeating because of their scarcity, do point in this direction. Kafka deplored scientific materialism; theosophy was among his
occasional interests; and he did aspire at times to draw immutable and
unmimetic art, and deep truth as well, from what he called "the indestructible" and "the decisively divine" within his soul. Nevertheless,
there are three crippling problems here.

First, although Kafka's library contained one book about gnosticism,
neither he nor any members of his immediate circle are known to have
expressed sympathy for any gnostic movement, ancient or contemporary. Second, the great majority of his religious references, including his
very skeptical ones, have a traditional Jewish cast. As many scholars have
shown, Kafka concerned himself with a single creator God who, though
now absconded if not downright mythical, nevertheless was unmistakably the Jehovah who wanted his people to thrive on this imperfect
earth and who exacted ethical obligations from them—obligations that
Kafka took seriously, as a gnostic dualist would not.[4] And third, however strongly Kafka yearned to leave flesh and property behind, his
works are not ecstatic but consistently ironic, turning every lunge
toward the absolute into a pratfall. As Robert Alter, citing the shared
perception of Walter Benjamin and Gershom Scholem, has said, Kafka
is notable for his "ruthless satiric exposure of pretenses to the transcendent" (Alter 1991, p. 112).

The literary Kafka whom most of us cherish is the one who, con-
templating the awesome legend of Abraham and Isaac, wrote sardonically that he could conceive of several alternative Abrahams. One in

particular, he imagined, "would never have gotten to be a patriarch or even an old-clothes dealer—[he] was prepared to satisfy the demand for a sacrifice immediately, with the promptness of a waiter, but was unable to bring it off because he could not get away, being indispensable" (quoted by Alter 1991, p. 73). The tone here is more evocative of Mel Brooks than of some moonstruck heretic. In suppressing the sad-but-hilarious whimsy of a writer who smilingly told his best friend that the Lord of Lords was "having a bad day" when he fashioned humankind (quoted by Murray 2004, p. 289), Corngold misrepresents the uniquely Kafkan vision he set out to champion.

3.

Stanley Corngold puts a gun to our head. If we Kafka lovers don't opt for deconstruction and gnostic theology, he implies, our author will be left at the dubious mercy of literature-hating "cultural studies" thugs. He has two cautionary examples in mind: Elizabeth Boa's *Kafka: Gender, Class, and Race in the Letters and Fiction* (1996), which allegedly demeans Kafka as an antifeminist, and Sander L. Gilman's *Franz Kafka: The Jewish Patient* (1995). If Corngold is to be believed, Gilman hits bottom by charging Kafka, amazingly, with not having been "anti-Semitic enough" (Corngold 2004, p. 200).

That is a vicious slur and nothing more. But in other passages Corngold does point to a real weakness in *The Jewish Patient*. Gilman can perceive only the shamed, negative side of Kafka's identity as a Jew. His Kafka is a would-be assimilator who does everything except get himself baptized in order to efface his stigmatized characteristics, but his attempts at passing are torpedoed by his unconscious incorporation of the slanders circulated by racist gentiles. Accordingly, Gilman sees Kafka's writings in symptomatic terms as displaying a return of the repressed—an obsession with the very traits, physical and behavioral, that he was hoping to disown.[5]

There is surely a grain of truth here. But if Kafka was merely running from his ethnicity on Gilman's Freudian treadmill, one must wonder why he took an open interest in such causes as Yiddish language and theater, a Jewish relief charity, Zionism, and Hebrew study. Following Gilman's reading, moreover, we would find it hard to fathom why Kafka went out of his way to invent easily identifiable "crypto-Jewish" heroes, from Georg Bendemann of "The Judgment" and Gregor Samsa of *The Metamorphosis* through the misunderstood hunger artist and the suppli- cant "man from the country" in "Before the Law" who waits a lifetime until he is told that the open but guarded door to justice, reserved for him alone, is now being closed.

Corngold finds it especially urgent to warn us away from Boa's femi- nist study. According to him, she awards Kafka's self-incriminating let- ters to his two-time fiancée Felice Bauer and to Milena Jesenská "the same or higher rank than the fiction" (Corngold 2004, p. 196), and she treats that fiction as unmediated "plagiarism" of "the allegedly wider social text" (p. 197). Boa's pathetically inert Kafka, taunts Corngold, "just went slack and ruptured, he took in the collapsing patriarchal . . . order as the flailing swimmer takes in the water in which he drowns" (p. 197). Clearly, then, no enlightenment can be expected from Boa's forbiddingly titled polemic.

The reader who ignores these animadversions and opens Boa's book, however, will learn that all of Corngold's charges are false. Boa devotes most of her pages to close analysis of Kafka's fiction, in which she takes open delight, and she comes to grips with its formal idiosyncrasies. Furthermore, her Kafka is no passive cultural sponge. Although Boa is unsparing in scrutinizing the writer's psychosexual oddities and relating them to ideological currents in his day, she also credits him with con- siderable acuteness in self-observation—a trait, she shows, that enabled him to satirize his own recognized deficiencies of attitude.

As a feminist, Boa inevitably wants to study how female figures were treated both in Kafka's fiction and in his life. Too often his women have been slighted as mere sirens whose base enchantments jeopardize the hero's path to acquittal (for Josef K.) or his incorporation into an all- male ruling order (for K.) or his artistic immortality (for Kafka him- self). Boa shows that his fictive women evolve, in parallel with his own growing capacity for empathy, from merely contrastive symbolic functions—think of Gregor's nubile sister Grete, stretching her budding body as memory of the dead insect fades—to having quasi-independent voices of their own—think of Frieda, Amalia, and Olga in *The Castle*.

Boa's concluding chapter on the "dystopian pastoral" of *The Castle* shrewdly relates the sexual politics of Kafka's era to that novel's social order, in which young women, having been seduced into marriage by the false promise of bourgeois romance, grow into petty matriarchs who then uphold the privileges of the castle autocrats. Those old boys need never articulate their governing rules, because the castle itself is nothing other than "an externalization of the customary practices in village life and their imaginary heightening in village minds" (Boa 1996, p. 261). In mapping the caste exclusions of this Lilliputian society, Boa convincingly argues, Kafka acknowledged the limits of female emancipation in his own imperfectly modernizing world.

When Boa's monograph is compared with Gilman's, it becomes clear that there is no such thing as "the" cultural studies attitude toward Kafka or any other writer. Nor should a frank declaration of sociopolitical interest be automatically regarded as a barrier to objectivity. Kafka criticism, we have seen, has been ideological from the outset, not excepting Stanley Corngold's quietistic epiphanies. Boa's feminist agenda doesn't inhibit her from shuttling deftly between social and literary analysis—as Gilman has some trouble doing and as Corngold won't even try—without ever mistaking one kind of investigation for the other.

4.

Most people who love Kafka are less interested in the quarrels of the literature departments than in immediate encounters with the life of his disorienting texts. This is one reason why advance notice of Roberto Calasso's *K.*—elegantly translated from the 2002 Italian edition by Geoffrey Brock—has aroused much interest and hope. The erudite and sophisticated Calasso belongs to no academic faction. He is the publisher of Adelphi Edizioni in Milan and the author of stunningly brilliant books about Greek and Hindu religious myths (*The Marriage of Cadmus and Harmony* and *Ka*, respectively), about literary uses of myth (*Literature and the Gods*), about the premises and the ultimately sinister evolution of European modernity (*The Ruin of Kasch*), and about authors who have risked incomprehension and madness for the sake of pressing beyond the arbitrary categories of Western thought (*The Forty-nine Steps*). No one could bring more intelligence and cultural range to a fresh encounter with Kafka.

Calasso's habit is to pass lightly over controversies and to delve directly into an issue so huge and fundamental that specialists rarely perceive it at all. This is the question of how experience feels to people—and what they are accordingly incapable of feeling—when they reside within one or another metaphysical mindset, whether archaic-demonic, polytheistic, monotheistic, or rationalist-materialist. From this standpoint, Kafka has always struck Calasso as a fascinating throwback who, unlike other atheistical writers, eschews skeptical secularism and puts his characters' fates in the hands of an awesome "prereligious" power, unknowable and indifferent to prayer and sacrifice.

Calasso does not want his *K.* to be regarded as one further interpretation of Kafka's fiction; indeed, he finds interpretation tiresome and symptomatic of a fussy, logic-chopping age. He is making a bold attempt to "inhabit" Kafka's work empathetically, with prime stress on *The Trial* and *The Castle*, and thereby to make the unique qualities of those works patent without falling into discursiveness. And because he is himself a master stylist, he does succeed in evoking the atmosphere of both novels as it is manifested in endless "proceedings" that go nowhere, in pseudo-clever stratagems to placate a system that welcomes bribes but gives nothing in return, and in an array of "subordinate, erotic" women who seem, uncannily, to have "always inhabited some niche in [the protagonists'] minds" (Calasso 2005, p. 67).

But Calasso isn't just paying tribute to Kafka's art. When Kafka suffered a brief nervous collapse in 1922, his thoughts turned to his own works as an attempted "attack on the frontier" of human experience—a project that, he told himself, could have "developed into a new secret doctrine, into a Kabbalah," if distractions hadn't intervened (quoted by Calasso 2005, p. 122). Since the original Kabbalah consists of esoteric commentaries that purport to disclose hidden meanings in scripture, Kafka appears to have been hinting at intuitive lore that might have been revealed to him through a shattering of his rational ego. Calasso, one of whose book titles, *The Forty-nine Steps*, also alludes to the Kabbalah, evidently believes in just such wisdom himself.

In one way or another, all of Calasso's writings have waged a guerrilla war against the Western logos. He has never forgiven Plato for disparaging Homer's world of luminous amoral fatality, and he regards theology as a decadent form of reflection, one that already at its origin was headed downhill toward the modern wasteland of denatured "facts," algorithms, and the banalities of "public opinion." This is why he has been drawn to Kafka, whose own philosophical clock, Calasso suspects, has been turned all the way back to animism, before a sense of the undifferentiated power of the cosmos was precipitated into tales about gods and demons. And so Calasso sees the plot of *The Castle* unfolding at "the dividing line between *vyakta* and *avyakta*," early Hinduism's "manifest" and vastly larger "unmanifest," or imperceptible, portions of reality (pp. 47, 49).

What Calasso has in mind may sound much like Stanley Corngold's gnosticism, but there is an important difference. In Calasso's version, Kafka never writes directly about a transcendent state. Instead, his two major novels simulate a mad chase "away from humanity" (Kafka's phrase) toward a receding otherness that can be intimated only through images, one succeeding another without progress or exit. That labyrinth, Calasso implies, is Kafka's literary home, and it is bodied forth in Josef K.'s attempts to influence a rigged justice system and in K.'s one step forward, two steps back as he vies for the favor of *The Castle*'s indifferent and withdrawn authorities.

Where, then, has the primordial "unmanifest" gone? In a post-Enlightenment condition, says Calasso, it has supposedly been banished, but that is a secularist illusion; the unmanifest has actually migrated into "society," which then takes on an ersatz aura of divine sanction. Yet "the majesty and the articulations of the old order are retained even as the memory of it is erased" (p. 23). And so, in Kafka's world, "beyond the windows, the air teems with the tribes of the invisible" (p. 30).

But does it, really? Who has placed those tribes just out of sight, Kafka or his exegete? One longs to see some evidence here, not just assertion; but evidence, as we can gather from Calasso's other writings, is one of those soulless notions that he considers inferior to "metamorphic knowledge, all inside the mind, where knowledge is an emotion that modifies the knowing subject . . ." (Calasso 2001, p. 262). And so we must take it on faith that in writing *The Trial* and *The Castle*, Kafka was steering by the same star that now guides Calasso.

Despite Calasso's distaste for interpretations, his book amounts to one, and the question to be asked of any interpretation is how much it can and can't explain. The strangeness of Kafka's novels may derive simply from allegorical intent—the desire to implicate ideas by assigning discontinuous and antirealistic narrative devices to them—rather than from a vision of hidden noumenality. In both *The Trial* and *The Castle*, and in *Amerika* as well, the protagonist is subjected to a battery of farcical predicaments that appear designed to reveal deficiencies of awareness or attitude on his part. These plots acquire their coherence, such as it is, not from verisimilitude but from the reader's translation of each discrete episode into the moral or psychological point it was meant to illustrate. Such schematism would seem to discourage the positing of spiritual agents not actually represented yet somehow entailed in the world of *The Castle*.

Calasso never allows himself to entertain that potentially deflating hypothesis. Moreover, he appears to have understated the thoroughgoing drabness and sordidness of Kafka's represented world. There is no "majesty" to be discerned in a court that holds its unruly sessions in slum dwellings and condemns its victims without disclosing why, nor in a dilapidated rural castle whose officials are good for nothing but sexual predation and the smoking of cigars.

Surely we ought to relate such corruption to the conditions in which Kafka actually lived. He suffered through the decay and eventual demise of a quite uninspiring order, the pompous and dubiously legitimate Habsburg empire, whose "equal rights" for its member states were a sham and whose dim afterlife in the Czech Republic continued to tax him with indignities as a Jew. And as Calasso himself recognizes, both novels evoke Jewish themes of persecution, unequal justice, denied recognition, and ostracism, none of which seem to fit very well with a sacral emphasis.

When Kafka gave an oral reading from the supposedly anguish-ridden *Trial* for a group of friends, he was repeatedly interrupted by his own uncontrollable laughter. Those friends were all Prague Jews like himself, and it seems reasonable to infer that the absurdism of his plot spoke to a shared sense, at once desperate and funny, that the Habsburg system held little in store for them but oppression and a legalistic run-around. Calasso takes note of the manically farcical element in both *The Trial* and *The Castle*, but, once again, he is unable to fold it into his supernaturalism. Like a preceding regiment of tenure-seeking critics whom he wouldn't care to meet, he may have apprehended these books with more sobriety than Kafka exercised in writing them.

Roberto Calasso always repays close study, his prose is a marvel, and *K.* makes for an exhilarating adventure. But Calasso's cordial embrace of Kafka, like Heidegger's of Nietzsche, threatens to suffocate the admired party. From Brod to Corngold and now Calasso, the transcendentalizing impulse has tended to efface the one truly obvious fact about Kafka's writing, its wry and surreal reference to the circumstances of his own life. As Edmund Wilson already put it in 1950, some of Kafka's critics have been turning him, unnecessarily, into "a human shadow thrown on the mist in such a way that it seems monstrous and remote when it may really be quite close at hand" (Wilson 1962, p. 91).

Chapter 19

CALL ME LIBERAL

THIS IS AN EXPANDED VERSION OF AN ESSAY THAT APPEARED IN *The New York Review of Books*, DECEMBER 1, 2005.

I.

It ought to be easy by now to get a clear general view of Herman Melville, whose reputation has long been unsurpassed among American authors. Although he left relatively few documentary traces and went unnoticed through the last three-quarters of a literary career that began in the 1840s and extended all the way to his death in 1891, herculean scholarly efforts by Harrison Hayford, Jay Leyda, Henry A. Murray, Hershel Parker, and others have unearthed more than enough facts to establish how his social station plummeted when, at age eleven, he endured his father's business failure and sudden death; how his sea voyages and his omnivorous reading vastly broadened his outlook; how, after much effort in subsequent novels, tales, and sketches, he gave up trying to retain the admiration of readers who had welcomed such early adventure novels as *Typee* (1846), *Omoo* (1847), *Redburn* (1849), and *White-Jacket* (1850); and how he eventually became a reclusive poet, an ill-paid customs inspector, and an unhappy husband and father whose domestic life was punctuated by horrors—the suicide of one son and the early death of another—that reinforced his already pronounced susceptibility to depression.

Notoriously, however, nothing close to agreement prevails about the intent behind the two great works that have fascinated the public and preoccupied the critics, *Moby Dick* (1851) and *Billy Budd* (1924; corrected edition 1962).[1] Nor is anyone content merely to say that those fictions must be ambiguous at their core. Since the 1920s each new American generation has wanted a Melville of its own, and the figure served up by the critics in one era always looks like an artifact of those critics' pretensions and illusions when a new cohort takes its turn.

Once Melville studies became an ever-expanding industry in the 1940s, the very traits that had rendered *Moby Dick* unreadable in the nineteenth century—its boisterous raids on history, ethnography, zoology, mythology, and religion; its abrupt shifts of register and perspective; its transmutation of natural and artifactual objects into portentous symbols; and its apparent wavering between sympathy for Captain Ahab and condemnation of his hubris—turned that novel into the premier hunting ground for Americanists in search of suitably complex projects. But all of those thematic inquiries resulted, collectively, in a loss of feeling for the immediate texture of Melville's prose and a widening of the gap between specialists and amateur readers.

By 1962 one Harvard professor, Warner Berthoff, felt that it was time for the academics themselves to be reminded of why Melville is widely cherished. It isn't, he wrote in *The Example of Melville*, because the author possessed great notions or a stoic attitude or a symbolic imagination or some ineffable "Americanness," but because he commanded a sentence-by-sentence authority, a "plenitude of released and extended power," that bespoke a unique combination of energy, intelligence, and magnanimity, along with a "thrust toward explication" that would settle for nothing less than "an entire explicitness" (Berthoff 1962, pp. 206, 208).

Berthoff's argument was refreshing, but it was also tilted toward a phase of Melville's career that ended with *Moby Dick*. *Pierre*, "Bartleby, the Scrivener," "I and My Chimney," "The Piazza," "The Paradise of Bachelors and the Tartarus of Maids," "Benito Cereno," *The Confidence-Man*, and *Billy Budd* do not drive toward full explication but slyly withhold it; they are as pregnant with unspecified discontent as *Moby Dick* is (deceptively) hearty. And when Melville seems most explicit, he may be merely toying with a hypothesis or representing a literal-mindedness that is inadequate to the horror or the moral scandal at hand.

In any event, Berthoff's one-man campaign didn't alter the headlong course of academic Melville studies—"psychological, mythic, ideological, social, ethical, epistemological, linguistic, metaphysical," as one observer has noted—even for a moment (Gunn 2005, p. 11). And we will see that when criticism changed direction again in the 1980s, it moved still farther from Berthoff's mode of assessment. His cause, however, has found a new and formidable champion in Andrew Delbanco. If any one volume stands a chance of satisfying the lay public without oversimplifying the current state of knowledge, Delbanco's *Melville: His World and Work* (2005) is that book.

Like Berthoff, Delbanco speaks up unabashedly for sheer literary quality and its ultimate source in a writer's character. "It was his *words*," he writes of Melville, "that seized and dazzled us" (p. xxiii), and he wants us to bear in mind D. H. Lawrence's observation that Melville "wrote from a sort of dream-self, so that events which he relates as actual have indeed a far deeper reference to his own . . . inner life" (p. xxiii). That inner life is just what Berthoff meant to designate through quotation and analysis of passages representing Melville's most exuberant manner. Delbanco, however, is mindful of the stylistic break that occurred in the early 1850s, leading eventually to the coldly formal, halting, unpictorial prose of *Billy Budd*. And he knows that the break didn't occur within any dream-self but in the shaken mind of a man who was wrestling with his own volatile temper, with vexations and debts, with the incomprehension of reviewers and readers, with sexual confusion, and with the cooling of the one relationship (with Nathaniel Hawthorne) in which he had rashly invested all of his hopes for close brotherhood.

Delbanco wants to tell that story and many others besides, not for their own sake but because he takes solace from the way a great artist can "make something beautiful and enduring out of the recalcitrance and fleetingness of life" (p. xxi). And so he has written a mid-sized biography that restores Melville's literary achievements to their original setting: the writer's physical and intellectual adventures, his relation to predecessors and contemporaries, and, most generally, the social development, politics, and culture of an America that was convulsed and utterly transformed during his lifetime.

Among recent lives of Melville, this one has no peer for grace of style, vividness of historical evocation, and sympathy for a subject whose flaws and prejudices are nevertheless kept in view. One never feels that Delbanco is shuttling routinely between "influences" and their mechanically produced effects in Melville's fiction and poetry. Instead, with a tact born of respect for genius, he indicates in a looser, more suggestive way how the autodidact Melville seized on elements of his experience and transformed them into a new manner of thinking in images.

Take, for example, Delbanco's exposition of the strong effect that was exerted on the writer's style and thought by his several years of residence, in the late 1840s, in New York—already the most bustling, polyglot, and liberated of American cities. Melville wrote little about Manhattan itself, but the brashness of its journalism and the rhythm of its daily life, Delbanco finds, were reproduced in his sentences. "Moving clause by clause through Melville's New York prose," he says,

> is like strolling, or browsing, on a city street: each turn of phrase brings a fresh association; sometimes we are brought up short by a startling image requiring close inspection; sometimes a rush of images flickers by; but there is always the feeling of quickened pulse, of some unpredictable excitement, in aftermath or anticipation. And if New York broke open Melville's style, it opened his mind as well to the cosmopolitan idea of a nation to which one belongs not by virtue of some blood lineage that leads back into the past, but by consent to the as-yet-unrealized ideal of a nation comprehending all peoples . . . in a future of universal freedom. New York was the birthplace of Melville's democratic imagination—both in substance and style. (p. 119)

This is Warner Berthoff's intuitive and great-hearted Melville—the one who was replaced in the early 1850s by a warier man who had learned how to satisfy magazine readers with well-wrought tales and sketches that exposed as little as possible of his wounded self. Delbanco is acute in characterizing, if not in fully explaining, that withdrawal into canny professionalism and then the more drastic retreat into isolation and verse. And because he stays primarily attuned to language, not to themes, he can't join some other recent Melvilleans in elevating the 18,000-line meditative poem *Clarel* (1876) to parity with the novels. *Clarel* abounds in discussable ideas, but Delbanco insists that its mostly prefabricated "poetical" language bespeaks a loss of the reckless agility of mind that allowed Melville at midcentury to tease out an observation or a figure of speech until it yielded some unforeseen and liberating insight.

Among nonacademic readers of Delbanco's *Melville*, perhaps the only ones who will be disappointed are those expecting to find pat interpretations of what each studied work "means to say." Delbanco refers to many such readings, but, with one controversial exception that I will challenge later, he doesn't feel a need to choose among them. It isn't modesty, I gather, that motivates this discretion, but rather a belief that the capacity of Melville's strongest writings to generate and sustain rival notions of meaning attests to their classic standing.

2.

Delbanco, then, has written an eclectic, humane, historically grounded tribute to Melville's best achievements and a moving account of the troubles that closed in on him, all but snuffing out the creativity that he summoned for one last triumph in *Billy Budd*. Whether this study will have any more effect on academic Melville criticism than Berthoff's *The Example of Melville* did in 1962, however, is another matter. Although history is the watchword of nearly all work in American studies these days, and although Delbanco's command of Melville's life and times is impressive, his book quietly but knowingly goes against the academic grain.

Two earlier essays by Delbanco make it clear that his *Melville* is meant to exemplify principles that are honored only spottily in contemporary academic work. One of those pieces (Delbanco 1999a), attempting to account for the low esteem in which English departments are now held, puts much of the blame on a lapse of dedication to the idea of introducing students to works whose complexity and amplitude of spirit can dislodge their prejudices and draw them into imaginative sympathy with other minds and eras. Instead, wrote Delbanco, the professors have turned to epistemic relativism, pop-cultural leveling, radical proselytizing, and the tunnel vision of "subject positions," or reading solely for the reinforcement of group identity. For Delbanco now to put forward Melville's major writings on the basis of their objective (not their "socially constructed") greatness thus constitutes a deliberate reassertion of a traditionalist perspective.

Just how Delbanco's critique of "English" relates to Melville studies can be discerned by consulting his earlier article evaluating works in that subfield that were published in the 1980s. Echoing the novelist Dan McCall, whose book *The Silence of Bartleby* struck him as "the single most sensitive response to Melville's genius since Warner Berthoff's *The Example of Melville*," Delbanco referred demeaningly to "prosecutorial" books and articles that "have the quality of a belated inquest convened not to determine if a crime took place—the crime is called culture—but to determine the degree of Melville's complicity in it" (Delbanco 1992, pp. 710, 711, 715).

Delbanco's quarrel was with a circle of angry "post-Vietnam" academics whose influence in American studies remains strong if somewhat diminished today.[2] Their ruling premise is that the U.S. has always been a racist, sexist, anti-labor, genocidally expansionist nation whose philosophers and literary pundits have facilitated oppression by promoting "consensus values," such as freedom and independence, that put socially divisive issues under the rug. Declamatory prose in Melville's era about spreading liberty across the American landscape, they maintain, was largely window dressing for an agenda of displacing and slaughtering Native Americans, seizing Mexican territory, and extending the sway of slavery. Melville himself had written just such prose,[3] and even when he voiced opposite sentiments, warning against nationalistic hubris, he did so in tones of flamboyant Emersonian individualism—an attitude that was now, post-Vietnam, stigmatized as the mark of an imperialist mentality.

In his *American Renaissance* of 1941, F. O. Matthiessen had ushered five white males—Emerson, Thoreau, Hawthorne, Melville, and

Whitman—into a mid-nineteenth-century pantheon whose criteria for entry were a democratic spirit on the one hand and a fine literary complexity on the other. To the revisionist or "dissensus" school forty years later, the Matthiessen canon amounted to an aestheticizing of the authors' political evasions. Why admire Hawthorne's prim formal effects if they served as a distraction from his shocking complacency about slavery? And as for Melville, his father-in-law and his chief stay against bankruptcy was Lemuel Shaw, chief justice of the Supreme Judicial Court of Massachusetts, an adamant if conflicted upholder of the Fugitive Slave Law. Thus, in the eyes of some revisionists, Melville's curious silence about abolition bore an appearance of self-interested family solidarity.

Inevitably, the principal text that called for revisionist scrutiny was *Moby Dick*. Matthiessen had chosen the figure of Ishmael to personify the democratic impulses that had to be defended from Hitler in the 1940s. For the dissensus academics of the 1980s, such rallying around the flag recalled the political hypocrisies of Melville's own day and anticipated the "free world" propaganda of the Cold War. Recoiling in disgust, one revisionist, Donald E. Pease, maintained that Ishmael's fixation, as controlling narrator, on an "endless proliferation of possible deeds" is itself latently totalitarian. For Pease, Ahab was merely "a product of one of Ishmael's rhetorical exercises," and the only safe answer to Matthiessen's implicit demand that we choose between those two models of character was a Bartlebyesque "I prefer not" (Pease 1985, pp. 147, 149, 153).

Some radical critics, including Pease himself, have eventually found ways to rehabilitate Melville as a wholesome outsider. Their aversion to power in any form, however, makes this a delicate task. Thus William V. Spanos, in a theory-laden study of 1995, strains to reconceive *Moby Dick* in terms so resistant to co-optation that they may offer us "a context for the articulation of a counterhegemony that is not *essentially* hegemonic." Spanos pins his hopes for this phantasmal result on Ishmael after all, not as a model democrat but as Melville's instrument for undermining all metaphysical "presence" and "determinate

meaning." Melville is thereby absolved not just of Jacksonian bump-
tiousness but of any ideas whatsoever that might, on vigilant interrogation, have suggested an awkward kinship with the wicked Uncle
Sam (W. Spanos 1995, pp. 45, 60).[4]

Whether indicting or acquitting Melville, the revisionists were still
judging him against the standards of their own modern leftism and
allowing for no middle ground between total condemnation and total
vindication of his views. Such latter-day Puritanism is anathema to
Delbanco. "Herman Melville," he asserts in his new study, "was one
of those writers whom Lionel Trilling described as 'repositories of the
dialectics of their times' in the sense that they contain 'both the yes and
no of their culture'" (p. 16).

Delbanco's invocation of Trilling may not have been expressly
designed to infuriate his remaining "dissensus" peers, but it will surely
have that effect. The sententiously liberal Trilling, far more than the
anguished socialist F. O. Matthiessen, has been the bête noire of the
academic radicals, who regard him as having been all too quick to subli-
mate sociopolitical struggle into Arnoldian detachment and an aestheticizing "tragic consciousness." But Delbanco, while acknowledging a
certain pomposity in his predecessor on the Columbia faculty, has taken
substantial inspiration from him. Trilling helped to shape his pedagogical ideal; he served as the model critic in another book of Delbanco's,
Required Reading, about the capacity of major American authors to sur-
mount limitations of class (Delbanco 1997, pp. x–xi); and Delbanco is
reciting his own credo when he says that Trilling stood for "the idea of
living self-critically with respect but without idolatry toward standards
inherited from the past" (Delbanco 2001, p. 41).[5]

Respect for the past, in Delbanco's case, includes eschewing the revisionists' "gotcha!" approach to a dead author's limitations and instead
trying to re-create the dilemmas that he faced. On the pivotal issue of
abolitionism, for example, Delbanco doesn't buy the crude idea that
Melville's reluctance to become an activist was motivated by a wish to
avoid offending his benefactor and kin, Judge Shaw. No one in Melville's day could envision how the slaves might be emancipated without

triggering secession. Although the novelist made it plain that he detested slavery, he joined the great majority of his Northern compatriots in hoping to avoid the gruesome war that would soon cost over 600,000 American lives. To condemn him with the hindsight of 150 years, Delbanco would doubtless say, is simply to reveal one's own failure of historical imagination.

Because Delbanco is comfortable dealing with a writer who sensed an impasse between his gut sympathy and his fear of a holocaust, he is well equipped to illuminate what has become, "in our own time of terror and torture, . . . the most salient of Melville's works" (p. 231), "Benito Cereno." According to one recent revisionist analysis, Myra Jehlen's, that story of a slave uprising at sea is to be deplored for its racist demonizing of the rebel leader, Babo, who, unforgivably, "remains locked inside the limits of his own perspective" and thus isn't accorded the same respect that Melville elsewhere grants to the Caucasians Ahab and Ishmael (Jehlen 2005, p. 100). But Delbanco shows that "Benito Cereno" gained artistic power precisely by refusing the agreeable expedient of turning Babo into a hero.

Melville's emphasis in the story, Delbanco points out, falls on two representative instances of white "race psychology": the haunting of a traumatized Spaniard, Cereno, by his own devilish idea of "the negro," and the inability of a cheerful, shallow, obtusely benevolent Yankee, Amasa Delano, to clear his mind of a contrary Uncle Tom stereotype. In the latter case, as Delbanco puts it, Melville captured "the kind of moral opacity that still seems to afflict America as it lumbers through the world creating enemies whose enmity it does not begin to understand" (p. 240). As Ralph Ellison surely realized when he took his epigraph for *Invisible Man* from "Benito Cereno," no such reverberating significance would have been possible if Melville had refrained from imparting a devilish aspect to Babo.

In the fifteen years since Delbanco began work on his *Melville*, the "post-Vietnam" mood in literary criticism has considerably eased, and now it is Jehlen rather than Delbanco whose reproachful view of "Benito Cereno" appears dated.[6] Nevertheless, Delbanco's hybrid intention—to render Melville and his writings as they were shaped by their own age but also to establish where his permanent excellence lies—will cause uneasiness in some academic circles. Most Americanists now feel that nothing but ideologically blinkered anachronism can result from treating one's own artistic criteria as if they were exempt from historical contingency. And, indeed, they won't be reassured by Delbanco's efforts in that vein.

Not entirely unlike Lionel Trilling, Delbanco has a Whiggish tendency to treat "modernity," with its confronting of mass atrocity and its deep psychoanalytic insights, as the most developed and disenchanted stage of Western consciousness and art.[7] As a result, he thinks he is paying Melville a compliment when he asserts, without sufficient reason, that *Moby Dick* is "the work of a twentieth-century imagination" (p. 175). In illustration, he cites the fact that when Melville decided to eliminate from his plot a seemingly important character, the noble mariner Bulkington, he didn't efface what he had already written in an early chapter but simply added another brief chapter announcing that nothing further would be seen of Bulkington. Thus, according to Delbanco, Melville left "what Freud calls a 'memory-trace'" in his text, thereby rendering *Moby Dick* a "protomodernist" work in the vein of James Joyce and Virginia Woolf (p. 148).

Neither Joyce nor Woolf, however, would have found anything in Melville's Rabelaisian extravagance and oracular soliloquizing to remind them of their own meticulous, coldly calibrated fiction, which doesn't break decorum through authorial confidences or shards of superseded drafts. Melville's casual farewell to Bulkington, calling attention to himself as the stage manager of his characters, aligns him less with any modernist than with, say, Henry Fielding.[8] And more generally, it is neither necessary nor advisable to validate Melville's stature by pushing him forward in time, as if the passage from Romanticism to modernism should be seen as qualitative progress rather than as a mere difference in aesthetic premises.

3.

Delbanco's attempts at modernizing Melville appear just often enough to raise another doubt about his assimilation of the writer to values of his own. Although the chapter-by-chapter excellence of his biography can hardly be faulted, his concluding summary of Melville's evolving political attitudes appears to be a contemporary lesson in the virtue of looking beyond particular causes to the preservation of basic social order. It is clear that the lesson matters intensely to Delbanco, but less clear that it has anything much to do with Melville.

For the late Melville, Delbanco writes, "our fate as human beings is to live by norms that have no basis in divine truth, but that have functional truth for the conduct of life" (p. 311). He continues:

> As a young man, Melville had pushed against the norms in order to expose them as provincial and suppressive contingencies. . . . But in the works of his maturity—*Moby-Dick*, *Pierre*, "Bartleby," *Benito Cereno*—Melville wrote more and more about the cost of overturning the norms. . . . By 1850 he already had become a reformed, if not repentant, romantic, who saw the fragility as well as the deformity of culture; . . . [and] by the time he composed *Billy Budd*, he was not so much outraged as resigned to the disjunction between law and justice. *Billy Budd* was his farewell to what he had called, in *Pierre*, "the beautiful illusions of youth." (p. 312)

This passage is oddly discordant with Delbanco's previous discussions of the works cited here. Didn't Melville share in Ahab's rage against the world's savagery, and isn't Ishmael still a free anarchistic spirit, if a more haunted one, at the end of *Moby Dick*? Where is the surrender to "norms" in the frenetic, pugnacious, self-lacerating *Pierre*, whose characters, as Delbanco has already reported through John Updike's words, "are jerked to and fro by some unexplained rage of the author's" (p. 180)? Does Melville's main emphasis in "Benito Cereno" and the Dickensian "Bartleby" really fall on the cost of overturning norms? (Norms of slavery? Of dead-end alienated labor?) And where, we might add, does the sardonically cynical *The Confidence-Man* (1857)—a book that Delbanco has earlier called "bilious" and "half-deranged" (pp. 250, 246)—fit into the picture of social reconciliation?

It is true enough that the young Melville "pushed against the norms," if by norms we mean flogging in the navy, prejudice against nonwhites at home and abroad, indifference to starvation in the streets of Liverpool, devastation of South Pacific tribes by gunboats and missionaries, and the sexual poverty of straitlaced bourgeois marriage. The question, however, is whether he ever backed off from any of those convictions. Nothing in Delbanco's biography points to such a change.[9] What did vanish was Melville's once cheerful belief in the possibility of social and political reform—a belief that was doomed by personal disappointments and by a subsequent disgust with the crudity of vindictive Reconstruction, the resurgent oppression of blacks, and the raw greed of the Gilded Age.

Robert Milder, among others, has detected a socially revolutionary, though nonviolent, strain in Melville that fortified him against the materialism and timid conventionality of his era. The writer believed in a genial, democratic, anti-Calvinist and anticapitalist, homoerotically tinged humanism, melding Western sophistication with Polynesian spontaneity and sensuousness. However naively, he meant to commend that model of a new dispensation to his Bible-clutching countrymen by means of *Moby Dick*, and more particularly through the seriocomic "marriage" of Ishmael and Queequeg. Although he became permanently embittered when his oblique advocacy was ignored, there is no evidence to indicate that he lost faith in the fundamental rightness of his ideal. Milder, for one, is sure that he clung passionately to his fraternal "paradise to be regained, whether in some distant historical time or in the atemporal reconciliations of art."[10]

As always in controversy over Melville, the question of continued defiance versus acquired resignation comes down to alternative readings of *Billy Budd*, a story of the execution at sea of an angelic youth who has accidentally killed a persecutor who was himself tormented by "the handsome sailor's" grace of form and ingenuousness of mind.

Here, no doubt in order to support his thesis about Melville's growth toward accommodation, Delbanco departs for once from his reluctance to choose between rival readings. According to the interpretation that he favors, the novella, by representing an unavoidable, tragic clash between sympathy and duty, dramatizes Melville's agreement with the anti-Jacobin Captain Vere that "forms, measured forms" must be preserved at all cost (Melville 1962, p. 128).

"Why must Billy die?" asks Delbanco. The simple answer, he asserts, is to be found in the Royal Navy's Articles of War, which prescribed capital punishment for any sailor convicted of striking a superior for any reason (Delbanco 2005, p. 309). "These norms are the grammar of culture," Delbanco writes, "and the culture Vere has sworn to defend is that of the Royal Navy in time of war. Billy killed an officer. Billy must hang" (pp. 311–312).

As many dissenting critics have noted, however, the article's strict or merciful application to Billy's unusual case could have been determined by a properly convened panel on land at a later date. All of Vere's subordinate officers and the ship's surgeon are flabbergasted by his refusal to adopt that "way dictated by usage" (p. 101)—in other words, by his flouting of the norm. Melville underscores Vere's *preemption* of correct procedure through nervous actions that cause the surgeon, for one, to suspect that he has become unhinged.

Although Melville was still altering *Billy Budd* at the end of his life, his latest draft leaves no room for doubt that Vere's legalistic rigging of the hastily convened trial, immediately prompted by his fear of mutiny, is ultimately rooted in self-mistrust. Billy must die as soon as possible because the ambitious but colorlessly "bookish" and "pedantic" Vere (p. 63) knows that he can't command intuitive loyalty from his crew in the manner of Lord Nelson. And as if he wished to head off just such a tragic/heroic reading as Delbanco's, Melville ended his tale by recounting an uncathartic flurry of rumors, lies, nasty innuendoes, and false recollections manifesting the unreformed social order's distortion and disposal of Billy's judicial murder without being discommoded by it in the slightest degree.

When Delbanco, back in 1992, was surveying Melville criticism from the previous decade, he reserved his sternest reproval for those commentators whose distrustful minds couldn't grasp that *Billy Budd* is "a story about the agony of a man who has discovered, after long resistance, the incompatibility of love and innocence with culture itself..." (Delbanco 1992, p. 718).[11] That is just what Lionel Trilling, who always preferred the larger picture and who took seriously the portentous banalities of *Civilization and Its Discontents*, might have said about *Billy Budd*. As Robert Milder observes, however, Melville's unforsaken vision of a better society had less in common with Freud, who maintained that all civilization must be founded on repression, than with Herbert Marcuse, "who distinguished 'civilization' from a particular historical *form* of civilization and who regarded capitalist social, economic, moral, and sexual organization as excessively denying" (Milder 2005, p. 23).

In this light, it is the post-Vietnam revisionists who have most ironically misconstrued Melville. They are the ones who were reading Marcuse at the height of our campus troubles in 1968, when the crestfallen Trilling repented that he had ever called students' attention to subversive modern texts. When those New Leftists later took to their fantasy battle stations in the English departments, they held Melville and the other literary giants of antebellum America to be guilty until proven innocent of ideological corruption. And so they failed to notice that in this writer's case they were dealing with a persistent radical whose commitment to equality was more reflective, more intimate, and altogether more genuine than their own.

The revisionists have been right, however, on one point that Delbanco doesn't seem to have grasped: liberal disinterestedness is itself an interest, and one that can leave a critic overeager to believe that a great writer has transcended political passions and arrived at a generous encompassing wisdom. Melville's actual development, in contrast, appears to have been toward greater misanthropy. Already in 1851 he recognized that his commitment to "unconditional democracy" was combined with "a dislike to all mankind—in the mass" (Melville 1993, p. 191). And instead of subsequently acquiring a worry about "the fragility of culture," as Delbanco alleges, he hardened his heart against the one culture, his own, whose predatory ways infuriated him.

The following lines from *Clarel* (1876), spoken by one character among many but conveying a sentiment that had been festering in Melville ever since *Omoo* in 1847, capture his late extremity. And in the bargain they suggest why, in the early twenty-first century, that extremity needs no apology or softening:

> The Anglo-Saxons—lacking grace
> To win the love of any race;
> Hated by myriads dispossessed
> Of rights—the Indians East and West.
> These pirates of the sphere! grave looters—
> Grave, canting, Mammonite freebooters,
> Who in the name of Christ and trade
> (Oh, bucklered forehead of the brass!)
> Deflower the world's last sylvan glade!
>
>   (Melville 1991, p. 413, 4.9.117–125)

Appendix A

COMPROMISES WITH CREATIONISM

THE FIRST PUBLICATION OF THE ESSAY THAT BECAME CHAPTERS 14 AND 15 ELIC-
ITED STRONG RESPONSES, SOME OF WHICH ARE DISCUSSED IN THIS INTERVIEW
WITH GLENN BRANCH. THE INTERVIEW APPEARED IN THE NOVEMBER–DECEMBER
2002 ISSUE OF *Reports of the National Center for Science Education*. BRANCH IS THE
CENTER'S DEPUTY DIRECTOR.

GB: First of all, I understand that congratulations are in order: "Saving Us from Darwin" is slated to appear in *The Best American Science and Nature Writing 2002* (edited by Natalie Angier; New York: Houghton Mifflin, 2002).

FC: Thanks! No one could have been more surprised by that honor than I was. I have no practical scientific aptitude or training; I'm just a literary critic with a commitment to empirical inquiry and a nose for controversy. And my essay wasn't really "science writing" but a survey of recent attempts, from opposite standpoints, to deal with the challenge that Darwinism poses to traditional religious belief.

GB: In the case of psychoanalysis, your critique was from the position of a lapsed adherent who eventually realized that his former beliefs were untenable. But I take it that you are not a recovering creationist, so to speak. What spurred your interest in creationism? Was it in part the fact that two of the foremost proponents of "intelligent design," Phillip Johnson and Jonathan Wells, were connected with Berkeley?

FC: I had never heard of Jonathan Wells when I began working on that piece. Phillip Johnson is another matter, as I'll explain later. But no, his presence at Berkeley had nothing to do with my essay.

"Saving Us from Darwin" began in a way that's typical for me. I've been contributing to *The New York Review of Books* since the mid-1960s. Usually at the editor's suggestion, but sometimes on my own, I start considering a recent or forthcoming book or two. But because I always work very slowly, trying to bring my background knowledge up to date, several other relevant books usually come to notice and get added to the assignment, and sometimes a full-blown essay takes shape. That's how "The Unknown Freud" came to pass, and the same is true of "Saving Us from Darwin."

When I began distancing myself from Freudianism around 1970, it was because of a growing, and personally vexing, sense that psychoanalytic "knowledge" is acquired and certified by fatally lax means. I realized at that juncture that my deepest loyalty was not to any particular doctrine but to empirical rationality itself—the ethos that characterizes not just science but every investigative discipline worthy of the name. Ever since then, I've been fascinated by irrationalist movements that make a strong appeal to educated people who ought to know better.

Here is where intelligent design comes in. I had been aware in a general way that young-Earth creationism, having been stymied in the courts, was being largely supplanted by a new approach that steered clear of biblical revelation and challenged Darwinism on its own scientific turf. What really caught my eye, though, was the fact that ID, using arguments that look good only at first glance, had gotten its foot through some important doors. Organs of opinion such as *Commentary*, *The New Criterion*, and *First Things* were treating ID as having refuted evolution; members of Congress had been successfully recruited to its cause; and its evangelism in the universities was making converts as well.

This phenomenon seemed important enough to make me want to address it after bringing myself up to speed with an educated layman's understanding of the issues. Actually, it took me an entire year before I could be satisfied that I wasn't making fundamental scientific blunders. In this regard, by the way, our mutual friend Kevin Padian was an invaluable resource.

As I got more deeply into the anticreationist literature, I began to notice that much of it seemed to be soft-pedaling Darwin's theory. The reason in some cases was obvious and forgivable. People who serve the cause of science education by repeatedly testifying against creationist initiatives come to understand that they can't succeed without support from other, less dogmatic, Christians; but the unvarnished Darwinian vision isn't reassuring to even the mildest supernatural belief. My own predilection is for being frank about conflicts, however troubling. Hence the second part of my essay, which left the IDers behind and asked whether some prominent defenders of evolution have been diplomatically overstating the theory's hospitality to faith.

GB: Phillip Johnson posted a reaction to the first half of "Saving Us from Darwin" on the Access Research Network website the day after he received the issue of *The New York Review* in the mail. Amid the usual Johnsonian rhetoric was what I thought was a fair question: "Why didn't the *[New York] Review* assign the demolition job to one of its regular science writers, such as Richard Lewontin, Stephen Jay Gould, or Steven Weinberg?"

FC: If Johnson had waited for Part II to appear, he could have answered his own question. Gould was one of the staunch Darwinians I criticized for having proposed a facile and not altogether sincere entente with religion. And though no one admires Steven Weinberg more than I do, there's a simple reason why the *Review* didn't tap him or Lewontin for that assignment. It wasn't an assignment at all but a direct proposal from me. Even so, I did volunteer to step aside if Weinberg wanted to address the topic.

Phillip Johnson and I are acquainted, though it has been a long while now since we've had any personal dealings. He sought me out, in his famously cordial way, in the early 1980s, because he was impressed by my work on Freud. Would I, he asked over lunch, like to turn the same unsparing critical attention to Darwin?

In Johnson's view, Freud and Darwin alike had been prisoners of metaphysical naturalism—that is, the belief that nothing in our universe requires a nonmaterialistic explanation. That position, Johnson asserted, lies beyond any possibility of scientific proof. I readily agreed that there is no way of determining for certain that the world isn't governed by hidden spiritual forces. But I also told Johnson that my objections to Freud resided entirely within a provisional materialistic framework—namely, the ground rules of science, which require that competing hypotheses be tested for their relative adequacy to accessible, neutrally presented data. And I added that, so far as I knew, Darwin's work met those same criteria with overall success.

Johnson's interest in me lapsed at that point and has only recently been revived. No more Mr. Nice Guy! On his website he refers disdainfully to my "obsessive crusade against psychoanalysis" and suggests that I didn't even read the books discussed in my Darwin essay.

GB: The first part of "Saving Us from Darwin" won general praise, except, of course, from creationists and their fellow travelers. In addition to the response from Johnson, a letter from Alvin Plantinga was published in the November 29, 2001, issue of *The New York Review*; an effective feature of your reply to Plantinga was your exposing him as a creationist. Were there any other creationist responses of interest that *The New York Review* was unable or unwilling to print?

FC: No. The few hostile critiques that I've seen all appeared elsewhere, in "home team" venues: *Commonweal, First Things,* and *The Christian Century.* And it is easy to guess why. The consistently expressed objection to my essay was that, once again, it manifested metaphysical naturalism or materialism; but most readers of *The New York Review* wouldn't register the necessary horror at that charge even if it were substantiated.

GB: In the second half of "Saving Us from Darwin," you criticize the attempts of John F. Haught, Michael Ruse, Kenneth Miller, and Stephen Jay Gould to reconcile evolution with religion. Your criticism, in brief, was that "these productions almost invariably prove to have adulterated scientific doctrine or to have emptied religious dogma of its commonly accepted meaning." I know that both Haught and Ruse have publicly replied; did Miller or Gould privately reply?

FC: I received a friendly and generous e-mail message from Kenneth Miller, who apparently enjoyed my essay simply as a piece of brisk rhetoric. Although he and I will always disagree on a number of points, I was relieved to note that he didn't object to my handling of the scientific issues. There is no more powerful refutation of ID claims than the first half of his *Finding Darwin's God.*

Gould didn't reply, but he couldn't have been pleased. His *Rocks of Ages* constitutes the clearest possible illustration of the point you have cited, which was indeed the thesis of my Part II. Needless to say, however, everyone who cares about defending the cause of evolution will miss Gould's tireless and eloquent advocacy.

GB: Writing in *Commonweal,* January 25, 2002, Haught complained that you are as ideologically motivated as the proponents of "intelligent design" that you criticize: "Throughout his articles he enfolds his own understanding of evolutionary science within an avowedly materialist belief system." I take it that you disagree, at least with the claim that methodological naturalism is on a par with the metaphysical presuppositions of Phillip Johnson and his coterie.

FC: Haught subscribes to Father Pierre Teilhard de Chardin's long-discredited theory of "creative evolution," an insubstantial soufflé concocted from equal parts of Catholic theology and mystified science. As the name implies, creative evolution is a stealth version of creationism. According to Teilhard and Haught, the universe, continuously "emerging into being" in ways unfathomable to man, is actually being drawn ahead by God toward a general redemption. As Haught says in his *Commonweal* article, it may well be that "the final truth beneath Darwinism is a world open to the coming of God." But Darwin, we can be sure, would have considered this fantasy to be 180 degrees opposed to his theory, which was precisely an attempt to account for biological processes and outcomes without reference to goals and plans.

Rather than address my criticism of his position, Haught has borrowed a page from Phillip Johnson and attacked my own philosophical premises as he (mis)understands them. His article abounds in references to Crews's "directives for getting to the ultimate truth about the universe." But "truth" is his term, not mine; it appears in my essay only when I am characterizing religionists like himself who think they possess a special revelation independent of the senses.

I am not a metaphysician but simply a skeptic—someone who tries to refrain from affirming propositions until he has been shown adequate grounds for doing so. Skepticism leaves me light-years removed from "ultimate truth." Haught, in contrast, maintains in his *Commonweal* article that theology—by which he means the supernatural teaching of his own church—"is wide and deep enough to embrace coherently all of the relevant scientific information . . . , while at the same time allowing logical space for a God who makes promises to be the *ultimate* explanation of evolution" (italics as found).

A skeptic must ask on what grounds an outsider is supposed to choose between Catholic dogmas and those of innumerable rival sects. Indeed, how can theology be considered knowledge at all, when the myriad intuitive knowers lack any way (short of persecution and murder) of resolving their differences? Moreover, where is that "logical space" in which the bleak Darwinian vista of wasteful, indifferently cruel speciation and extinction can be reconciled with divine promises to certain approved members of one latecomer species? Haught's strategy, in *God After Darwin*, for making these antagonistic paradigms look compatible is to cover them in a blizzard of fluffy, soothing phrases.

All of my religious critics, including Haught, have portrayed my essay as a deductive exercise: from my initial metaphysical naturalism I supposedly derive an idiosyncratic reading of evolution as proof of God's nonexistence. The essay itself is very different. It begins from the effect that Darwin's theory has *actually, historically*, exerted on religious believers and waverers, and it proceeds to examine how some recent authors have been coping with that continuing effect.

As is well-known, the cultural shock that radiated from *The Origin of Species* was—and still is—the strongest challenge to human vanity since Copernicus, and possibly ever. Our kinship with apes, left implicit until *The Descent of Man*, was only the most sensational feature of the theory; more deeply troubling was its sheer explanatory success in obviating the need to invoke a supernatural designer of biological forms, including our own. As Alvin Plantinga recently put it in a moment of unwonted candor, "as science explains more and more, the scope for God's activity is less and less;

it is in danger of being squeezed out of the world altogether, thus making more and more tenuous one's reasons (on this way of thinking) for believing that there is such a person as God at all." My essay is about the various measures—"scientific" denial, prettification of the theory, dubious overtures of peace—that some worried writers have adopted in the face of this perceived threat.

GB: On March 3, 2002, *Encounter*, a radio program about religious issues produced by the Australian Broadcasting Corporation, broadcast a show about "intelligent design" in which "Saving Us from Darwin" featured prominently and in which you, as well as several of the people whose books you reviewed, were interviewed. I noticed that Michael Ruse complained there, "it seems to me that neither Dawkins nor Crews, nor any of the others who take this line of argument, have bothered to look at any Christian theology whatsoever." Is there any justice to his complaint?

FC: I would never read theological tracts for pleasure, improvement, or uplift; give me the great outdoors instead. But I am familiar with the major Christian dogmas, and I rather doubt that Ruse, who is no more a believer than I am, has registered their full impact. Surely, for example, the stern and horrific concept of original sin is travestied when Ruse finds it exemplified in biological adaptations, which "involve self-interest, if not outright selfishness, with the host of features and attitudes and characteristics that we all find offensive and that the Christian judges sinful." Jonathan Edwards, for one, would have given that hermeneutic effort a failing grade—and so would Darwin.

GB: Admonishing Haught in "Saving Us from Darwin," you wrote, "[e]volution is an undirected, reactive process . . . or it is nothing at all." I was reminded of the furor over the National Association of Biology Teachers' definition of evolution, which originally (in 1995) defined evolution as "an unsupervised, impersonal, unpredictable and natural process of temporal descent with genetic modification that is affected by natural selection, chance, historical contingencies and changing environments." Due in part to a recommendation by Alvin Plantinga and Huston Smith, and with the blessing of NCSE's Eugenie C. Scott, the words "unsupervised" and "impersonal" were removed (in 1997) as inessential and needlessly prone to misinterpretation. Do you think the removal was a bad idea?

FC: As a paid-up member of NCSE and a strong admirer of its work, I am taken aback by this news. First of all, the omitted words go straight to the heart of evolutionary theory; their deletion would seem to constitute an opening to the idea of miraculous intervention, which Darwin rightly judged to be antithetical to descent with modification. Second, it is hard to fathom why the spiritualizing Plantinga and Smith were rated by NABT as scientific experts. This would be like—what? Consulting Madeleine Albright on revision of the infield fly rule?

I can understand why NCSE might have felt obligated to stomach this intellectually indefensible compromise. NCSE is like a volunteer fire department for the town of Evolution; when a creationist blaze breaks out, everyone who isn't an outright arsonist must be welcome to lend a hand. As I remarked earlier, the anticreationist cause in the U.S. would be doomed without the help of Christians who are favorably inclined toward the teaching of evolution. And the center's outstanding record of success speaks for itself.

Nevertheless, a question does arise: at what point of accommodation has "science education" been stripped of too much meaning? I hope that NCSE's own account of evolutionary theory is free of censorship.

GB: Let me follow up with a further question about the political arena. Michael Ruse told *Encounter* that he thought that your line of argument in "Saving us from Darwin" was not only insufficiently attentive to Christian theology but also tactically unwise: "It's all very well for Crews to say, 'Don't have anything to do with them [Christians], and people like Ruse who do are just selling out.' Well, if Crews doesn't mind his grandchildren being taught creationism in their biology classes, so be it. I do."

FC: I didn't suggest that Ruse was selling out. I merely indicated that, despite his "expert's understanding of Darwinian theory and a creditable history of standing up to creationists in court testimony," he painted himself into some awkward corners in *Can a Darwinian Be a Christian?* The same point, by the way, was later established in more detail by Jerry Coyne in *The London Review of Books*, May 23, 2002.

Although Ruse's book was meant to ease tensions and thus can be regarded as a tactical undertaking, his argument was not tactical but substantive: he contended that the Darwinian and Christian worldviews can be readily reconciled. Such a thesis is either going to be well supported or not. I hope that Ruse's complaint on the radio wasn't meant to imply that a pro-Darwinian reviewer should have given his book a free pass for political reasons.

This whole fear of alienating believers, I must say, strikes me as overblown. Although the intellectual barriers to mixing Darwinism and theology are formidable, very few people think like intellectuals. Most of us feel pressure from one side and another and respond by just muddling through.

The best way to make evolution palatable to open-minded churchgoers isn't to Christianize the theory but simply to keep reporting on its consilience with new findings. Ruse is quite good at doing that, and I encourage him to keep it up.

GB: Are we going to see a further installment of "Saving Us from Darwin"?

FC: No, because I have said my piece and reached the limit of my grasp of biology. Let me add that I was careful, in that essay, to skirt controversies that are internal to the evolutionary camp; I lack the expertise to take sides.

In contrast, I felt confident about the standing of evolution and natural selection as such. Despite Phillip Johnson's repeated prediction, for more than a decade now, that Darwinism will soon collapse, the theory at large, reinforced by new findings in genetics and other disciplines, is more firmly established than ever. The convergence of evidence from all sides attests not only to the theory's power but also to the methodological soundness of science itself, which needn't be supplemented or trumped by a higher order of explanation.

Appendix B

FREUD, LACAN, AND THE
PSEUDOSCIENTIFIC ACADEMY

IN THE AFTERMATH OF A LECTURING VISIT TO THE UNIVERSITY OF REGINA, SASKATCHEWAN, IN 2004, I WAS INTERVIEWED VIA E-MAIL EXCHANGES BY THOMAS CHASE, AN ENGLISH PROFESSOR AND ASSOCIATE DEAN IN THE FACULTY OF ARTS, AND SHADIA DRURY, CANADA RESEARCH CHAIR IN SOCIAL JUSTICE AND A PROFESSOR IN THE DEPARTMENT OF PHILOSOPHY AND CLASSICS. A LONGER VERSION OF THIS TEXT HAS BEEN PUBLISHED IN *The Wascana Review*, 38:2 (WINTER 2005).

SD: The concept of repression is central to psychoanalysis. Yet there is a great deal of ambiguity about that concept. On one hand, Freud considers the repression of traumatic experiences into the unconscious to be the cause of neuroses and claims that these repressed memories have to be fished out and brought before the patient through analysis so that they can be "properly" dealt with—whatever that means. On the other hand, Freud follows Nietzsche in thinking that forgetfulness, especially of dreadful events and humiliations, is a sign of mental health and strength. Some commentators on Freud claimed that in his later work, Freud distinguished between repression and suppression and considered one to be a source of health and the other to be a source of neurosis. But which is which? When is forgetfulness the source of disease, and when is it the source of health? Can you clear this up for us?

FC: Although your questions are eminently reasonable, they admit of no clear answer, because Freud himself never troubled to remove inconsistencies from his doctrine. His unclarity about repression is more significant than one or another delimited construal of the concept. What must be understood is that vagueness served his purposes better than definiteness. As a pseudoscience resting on no evidential base, psychoanalysis has been necessarily more oriented to confounding its critics than to putting forward risky propositions in the Popperian sense. If repression can, in defiance of logic, be either conscious or unconscious, salutary or pathogenic, normal or deviant, then no one will be able to refute its existence; any seeming prediction entailed by the concept can be temporarily withdrawn if unfulfilled and replaced by an opposite one. This is a scientific disgrace but a successful recipe for indefinitely postponing the demise of the psychoanalytic movement.

Matthew Erdelyi is the Freudian commentator who has most fully expounded the fact that Freud sometimes treated repression as a conscious mechanism and at other times as an unconscious one. For Erdelyi, such wavering shows an admirable flexibility on the master's part. On the contrary, it illustrates Freud's habitual recourse to ad hoc tinkering with his system of thought.

What Freud cared about wasn't determining just how repression operates but invoking the notion whenever he wished to negate a common-sense view. "Little Hans," for example—the son of one of Freud's enthusiastic disciples—saw a carriage horse fall to the street and immediately developed a fear of horses. Common sense would suggest a direct causal relation between the two facts, but Freud preferred to think that Hans was really afraid of being castrated by his father for his (wholly unproven) sexual designs on his mother. Repression came to the rescue; by invoking it, Freud could sweep away the "superficial" interpretation and replace it with his own far-fetched, dogmatic one.

Was Hans's alleged repression, then, to be regarded as conscious, or as unconscious? Freud didn't care. He thought about such dilemmas only when pressed by skeptics, whose criticism could be parried by expanding the scope of a given concept or by opportunistically redefining an ordinary term. In *Freud Evaluated: The Completed Arc* (1997)—the single most important book about Freud's ideas—Malcolm Macmillan has shown that the chronic application of such expediency to many threatened concepts, over several decades of cavalier improvisation, produced a jumble of contradictions that subsequent psychoanalytic theorists have not succeeded in untangling.

Note that one such instance of fudging with regard to repression lay at the very foundation of psychoanalysis as we know it. Originally, repression applied only to memories of actual events. When Freud's "seduction theory" of hysteria formation collapsed, he decided that repression would now cover fantasies as well as memories. No clinical discoveries dictated this fateful change; it was simply a matter of salvaging a discredited idea (along with Freud's reputation and his candidacy for a professorship) by arbitrarily doubling its area of reference.

One of Freud's especially quaint ideas was that the course of civilization has shown a steady increase in the level of repression as libido has been increasingly invested in (all-male) projects of intellectual and artistic achievement, resulting, therefore, in ever more neurosis, pallid misery, and flight from sexual enjoyment. This is the thesis of what I have called the most overrated book of all time, *Civilization and Its Discontents*. If Freud were right, latecoming centers of cultural achievement such as Paris and San Francisco ought to manifest an especially weak interest in erotic matters, while such ancient societies as Sparta and Israel ought to have been notably sportive and libertine. The idea is self-refuting.

Finally, is there such a thing as repression at all? Testimony to its actuality is typically retrospective; people who have been convinced, usually through therapy, that they once repressed something are happy to tell us about it, paraphrasing their doctors. But the only proper test of the mechanism is *prospective*: taking a population of victims of a known traumatic event, such as the Holocaust or a mass abduction or the sadistic treatment of war prisoners, and inquiring whether those victims ever lost their capacity to remember their ordeal. The Harvard psychologist Harrison G. Pope, Jr., and his colleagues have assessed all known studies of this kind, weeding out those with obvious methodological flaws. What remained was approximately 10,000 reported cases of well-remembered trauma and zero cases of repression—not a single one. Does this prove that repression is nonexistent? In strict logic, no—but it shows that no basis has been found for continuing to invoke the term.

TC: As one with a great interest in the phenomena of linguistic difficulty, obscurity, and obscurantism, I'm struck by your description of Freud as "the most cunning of rhetoricians." Where do you locate the sources of Freud's rhetorical power? How does he use language so effectively to persuade, dazzle, and mislead his readers both lay and professional? How much of his hieratic status rests on his manipulation of language? More bleakly, why do so many of us like to be dazzled?

FC: Freud is often characterized as "more a literary figure than a scientist," and those of us who skeptically examine his ideas are consequently rebuked for our lack of aesthetic sensibility. The fact that the great storyteller won the Goethe Prize for literary achievement is regularly cited in this connection. How can we be so literal-minded and "positivistic" in the presence of consummate verbal art?

That question, however, reflects a fundamental misunderstanding of Freud's enterprise. In no sense was he aiming directly at imaginative fiction, acknowledged to be such. Although he was indeed a brilliant writer, his art was that of self-interested rhetorical seduction. His entire career as a psychoanalytic author was directed to a practical end: persuading his readers to endorse his self-image as a trustworthy reporter, a fearless investigator, an ingenious detective, a benevolent doctor, and a great scientific pioneer.

Recognizing this fact is the essential step that must be taken by any reader who wants to graduate from being a charmed consumer of Freud's literary ploys to being a well-equipped analyst of them. Freud didn't set out to be a rhetorician; he expected to become the Copernicus or Darwin of the mind. But as Macmillan has shown with exemplary patience, not a single one of Freud's continually shifting theoretical expectations was corroborated by his clinical work. All of his rhetorical maneuvers were dictated by his decision to insist on the significance of his scientific breakthroughs in the absence of any supporting evidence for them. Hence, for example, his dictum that no one other than a psychoanalyst was qualified to pass judgment on psychoanalytic assertions, his declaration that opponents of his doctrine were suffering from the very repression that was centrally featured in that doctrine, and his stigmatizing of dropouts from his movement as having fallen into psychosis. Psychoanalysis had, by default, to become a self-validating theory, and Freud then had to bend his main effort to dissuading readers from coming to grips with that fact.

One might think it would be easy to see through such verbal coercion, which we certainly wouldn't tolerate from any other scientific claimant. But no one else has matched Freud's skills in self-glorification. Note, in the first place, his reliance on sheer brazen falsehood. Over and over he tells us that his patients have presented him with irrefutable evidence of mechanisms whose operation he has been reluctantly compelled to recognize. The show of reluctance is a key ingredient here. With brilliant cunning, Freud anticipates and "identifies with" his readers' repugnance at being told, for example, that we all want to fornicate with one parent and murder the other.

It was only gradually, says Freud, thanks to my ascetic devotion to scientific ideals, that I myself was compelled to reach such conclusions. Thus we readers are offered a flattering reward: if we respond favorably to Freud's appeal and agree that we must be, in our repressed unconscious minds, oedipal monsters, we thereby become courageous vicarious discoverers, mini-Freuds who stand out from our timid, convention-bound neighbors. That is an attractive prospect for anyone, and for spite-filled literary intellectuals it has proven irresistible.

If Freud had ever admitted that his propositions were airy deductions and uncited borrowings from other theories as opposed to inferences from painstaking clinical induction, or that he had never cured anyone of any ailment, or that, far from listening attentively to his patients, he had typically hectored them into agreeing with his a priori formulations about their hidden desires, the whole game would have been over. Instead, he kept the ball in the air by continuing to dramatize the choice, which he personified in his own faked history, between facing and fleeing from the awful truth of the psyche.

Meanwhile, Freud wasn't naive enough to suppose that his readers would remain utterly unconcerned about evidence. At carefully spaced intervals he himself raised the very doubts that would be going through a reader's mind. He met those doubts by claiming to have shared them himself until "psychoanalytic findings" had overwhelmed his skepticism. And, counting on our inattentiveness, he assured us that the proof in question had been supplied earlier in his text or would soon be forthcoming. Of course it is to be found nowhere in his collected works—but how many people have read through them in a spirit of sober inquiry?

Finally, let me mention Freud's consummately skillful recourse to false modesty. He often "humbled himself" before his readers, admitting to an earlier mistake that had now been corrected, confessing to having been held back by his plodding scientific scrupulosity and his bourgeois squea-mishness about sexual weirdness, alluding to puzzles (such as the whole of female psychology) that remained to be satisfactorily solved, deferring to great writers who had anticipated his discoveries through intuitive powers that he could only envy, predicting that neurology would one day replace the (for now indispensable) formulations of psychoanalysis, and even confessing, in a safely late phase of his career, that he couldn't cure neuroses after all.

What a splendid fellow, shrinking from his own manifest greatness! But in each instance a cool rhetorical analyst will find that Freud has made a favorable trade, strengthening his scientific authority by detaching it from announced human failings that were, in fact, just as phony as his alleged accomplishments. The intended message is always that psychoanalysis, despite its imperfections and Freud's own, is still the very best that psychological science can put forward for now.

SD: Much of Freud's popularity these days has to do with his appropriation by the postmodernists, especially by Jacques Lacan. Freud appeals to the suspicious and conspiratorial nature of the postmodern mind, which tends to assume that nothing is what it appears—and Freud has taught that beneath all conscious actions and claims are unconscious desires and motives that can be unmasked. The project of unmasking or unveiling is the supreme project of postmodernism, even if postmodernists are not always sure that there is anything behind the mask or the veil to discover. What is puzzling about Lacan's appropriation of Freud is that he abandons the most central assumption that Freud makes—namely that the structure of the psyche is given and that civilization acts upon it, primarily by repressing or sublimating its destructive instincts. But Lacan sees the psyche as a porous entity whose inner structure is not given but determined by social conditions and expectations. In view of this, can Lacan be considered a Freudian in any meaningful sense?

FC: The vogue of Lacan, which in my country is largely restricted to feminist academics harboring a radical agenda, is instructive on grounds that I will set forth after some necessary general exposition.

Whereas Freud went through an elaborate charade of having derived his findings from sober clinical work, Lacan made no such hypocritical bow toward empiricism. His doctrine was manifestly a recasting of Freud's own to achieve ideological consistency. He wanted to excise the socially conformist, "bourgeois" component of psychoanalysis, leaving only a drastic picture of how children's personalities are warped by pressures that force them into predestined complexes. Lacan's conceptual innovations—an unconscious that is "structured like a language," the intimidating "Name-of-the-Father," the progression from a "mirror stage" to "the symbolic" to "the real," and so forth—were all dogmas bearing no connection with independent research. In this sense Lacan was indeed more Freudian than Freud: he dispensed with the pretense of scientific accountability.

The stages of childhood transformation were no less fixed in Lacan's system than in Freud's. Moreover, Lacan actually outdid Freud's notorious male-centeredness, devoting nearly all of his attention to the psychologically bombarded little boy. The latter allegedly suffers a "linguistic" version of the Freudian castration complex, and he is permanently haunted by loss of oneness with his mother and by the specter of female "lack" in general.

Ironically, however, it is just this gender asymmetry that explains Lacan's attractiveness to some feminists. He is embraced as a theorist of patriarchal oppression, a phenomenon that is thought to result from men's panic over separation from an undifferentiated female matrix. Lacan knew so little about women that he could think of them only as a principle in the mental economy of the other sex. As such, however, they were sympathetically reconceived as voiceless, helpless objects of persecution. And that image has suited the purposes of radical feminists who are themselves far from voiceless or helpless. If they really sought gender equality, they would be mortified by Lacan's depiction of female incapacity. Instead, they seek a total exposé of the fearfully aggressive male psyche, and Lacan provides an avenue, however chimerical, to that end. So strong is his doctrinal charm in this regard that the egregious sexism of his personal behavior is left entirely out of account.

Few of Lacan's disciples have cared that he himself was at best a pseudo-egalitarian who had no revolutionary prescription in mind. He thrived within a conservative dispensation that allowed him to behave like a little emperor or pope, surrounding himself with flatterers, excommunicating doubters, and issuing edicts with an air of sublime infallibility. One must wonder, inevitably, whether this side of Lacan goes unrebuked because it speaks to a comparable strain of authoritarianism in his admirers.

You have asked whether there is anything truly Freudian about Lacan's version of a psyche wholly "determined by social conditions and expecta-tions." But Freud's more biologistic conception, so different in appearance from Lacan's obscurantist recourse to the once-fashionable linguistics of Saussure, already contained that potentiality. To be sure, Freud emphasized allegedly universal as opposed to culturally unique features of social con-trol over impulse. In doing so, he engaged in "armchair anthropology" of an aprioristic kind that everyone now considers unacceptable. Yet Freud and Lacan, who was himself no student of diverse practices of socialization, occupy a continuum of emphasis on the forcible, often pathogenic thwart-ing of the wishes that children bring into the world.

All that Lacan did, one might say, was to highlight a half-hidden strain of rebellion in Freud's thought that was already seductive to Freudo-Marxists in the 1930s and that still speaks to their remnant (such as Eli Zaretsky) today. The root idea is this. If we conceive of humans, in their essential being, as presocial creatures who learn to "behave themselves" only through traumatic crises in childhood, then the prospect arises of improving "human nature" by overturning or at least modifying the adult value system.

Much twentieth-century advice about child rearing and education stemmed from a mild neo-Freudian construal of this notion. See, for example, the early editions of Benjamin Spock's influential handbook. If you accept the little boy's Oedipus complex as normal, suggested Dr. Spock, he will be less likely to be scarred by his terror of punishment for it. By rendering adults more liberal through psychoanalytic enlightenment, we allow their children to become more comfortably "adjusted."

"Sixties" enemies of social control such as R. D. Laing went a step fur-ther and inverted the entire hierarchy between sanity and insanity. Now society itself was seen as the deranged party, and schizophrenia reacquired the air of holiness it had sometimes possessed in the Middle Ages. Laing, too, was Freud's heir, though Freud would have wanted no credit for having inspired him.

In the light of such actual, acted-out radicalism as Laing's, Lacan appears rather tame after all. Were it not for his poststructuralist idiom and his picture of womankind as victimhood personified, he probably wouldn't have attracted much notice. What remains interesting is not his wholly unsupported account of the psyche but his ongoing sway in universities, where, supposedly, we are all engaged in the common pursuit of truth.

TC: Your mention of Lacan's "obscurantist recourse to the once-fashionable linguistics of Saussure" and your evocation of the enduring hold of Lacanian and other dogmatic stances in the contemporary academy raise fundamental questions about language and clarity. One of the more visible characteristics of theoretical work in the humanities and social sciences during the second half of the twentieth century was an eagerness to invoke the authority of a distant academic field (e.g., set theory or quantum mechanics) as a bolster for vague theorizing in another. Lacan was no stranger to this rhetorical tactic, and indeed made frequent recourse to areas such as mathematical topology in order to support his views. The problem, however, is that mathematicians and physicists such as Alan Sokal and Jean Bricmont have demonstrated that Lacan's understanding of topology and other scientific areas was both incomplete and faulty. Why, after throwing off during the nineteenth and early twentieth centuries much of the authoritarianism of ideologies such as Christianity, did many intellectuals fall prey to the intentionally obscurantist and hieratic language of Lacan and others like him?

FC: I rejoice in your citation of Sokal and Bricmont, whom I know not only through their spirited writings but also through cordial e-mail exchanges and one personal meeting with Sokal. His mock paper on deconstruction and quantum gravity, which he shared with me long before it was smuggled into the alien pages of *Social Text*, is surely the finest travesty of academic irrationalism ever written. And I borrowed some material from Sokal and Bricmont's incomparably damning, and very funny, *Fashionable Nonsense* (originally *Impostures Intellectuelles*) when preparing my own *Postmodern Pooh*.

In the 1960s Ferdinand de Saussure's largely forgotten theory of language was resuscitated and adapted (or adulterated, as some observers believe) by structuralist thinkers who were not ideologues but serious

philosophical linguists. Structuralism, however, proved to be a hermeneutic game that any number might play without encountering a satisfac-
tory means of choosing between proliferating patterns of meaning. Some
of the brightest young structuralists, such as Tzvetan Todorov, backed off
from the theory when they were stymied by such "undecidability."

But a new school of poststructuralists, including Derrida, Foucault,
Deleuze, Kristeva, Althusser, and Lacan, saw in undecidability a potent
weapon against conventional "absolutes" and "universals," the philosophical props of Western hierarchical order. And although those glamorous
authorities harbored diverse feelings about the convulsion of Paris 1968,
the student revolutionaries of that moment and thereafter welcomed all
of them as liberators who had exposed the arbitrariness of Enlightenment
rationality and its most admired product, modern science.

As leftist fortunes then slid into a long and bitter decline, poststructuralism continued to gain adherents. It offered a shadow revolutionism whose
very abstruseness insulated it from the real-world shocks being endured
by Marxist regimes and movements. And while the radical students of '68,
in both Europe and North America, were becoming the professors of the
1980s, an antiscience attitude, formerly associated chiefly with the reactionary religious right, established a broad sway throughout the humanities on both sides of the Atlantic.

As Sokal and Bricmont have shown, however, overt rejection of science
is less useful, rhetorically, than specious appropriation of a few radical-
looking notions such as relativity, quantum "strangeness," and the uncertainty principle. What is missing here isn't just a correct understanding of
the concepts in question. More fundamentally, it is the whole spirit of scientific investigation, which eschews ideological clichés, welcomes discon-
firming as well as corroborative evidence, and seeks to adjudicate between
competing explanations on demonstrable objective grounds.

That entire ethos is now dismissed as naïve, as humanists eagerly cite
Feyerabend, Kuhn, and others in an attempt to show that undecidability prevails within science itself. Scientific theories, they say, are really
established by social and political power, and their purpose is to reinforce
that very power. Why not, then, choose one's own convenient scientific
verities—for example, certain dogmas advanced by Freud and Lacan—and
give them a spin to the left?

TC: Jeffrey Williams and others have argued that among the reasons
for the "rise of theory" in the seventies and eighties was an economic
one. Specifically, the dominance of the science-engineering axis within the

post–World War II academy led to a devaluing of humanities research, and a corresponding drop in the resources allocated to it (to say nothing of the prestige of its practitioners). Eagerly adopting the trappings of high theory was, in this view, one way to impart to the humanities and social sciences a level of difficulty, a cachet, a claim to high epistemic value, that would go a long way toward reversing this marginalization. But most observers would agree that this project failed and that these disciplines remain, to a greater or lesser degree, peripheral rather than central.

What do you, as a lifelong student of language and literature, see as the way forward? What epistemologies do we need to ensure a future for our disciplines?

FC: In general, I agree with Jeffrey Williams's analysis. However, it is always a good idea to ask where and how a movement got going and whether it then borrowed strength from factors that weren't necessarily operative at its birth. Let me give this a try.

"High theory," when it took shape in France after the waning of existentialism, phenomenology, and classical structuralism, had more to do with anthropology, psychology, philosophy, and politics than with literary criticism. (Roland Barthes was exceptional in this regard.) But when poststructuralism caused a buzz at a Johns Hopkins conference in 1967, setting off the American craze for theory, the sensation was felt almost exclusively by professors of literature. Why?

The answer, I believe, is that this field of study found itself in a unique state of stagnation and crisis. New Critical formalism had ruled in the academy for a quarter-century, extracting "organic unity," ironies, paradoxes, and tame moral lessons from an Anglo-American canon that was scarcely expanding at all. Since World War II, however, the universities themselves had grown at a great rate, first thanks to the returning GIs and then again in the post-Sputnik era of the later fifties and early sixties, when a sense of emergency about education in science and technology brought not just new laboratories and institutes but also vast sums of governmental research money, some of which trickled down to the formerly penurious humanities. Thus, in literature departments, we had more graduate students to teach and more young professors seeking promotion, but precious little that remained to be said, along formalist lines, about fixed national canons. The currency of advancement was felt to be in desperately short supply.

Poststructuralism, with its aura of novelty, thus appeared to be a godsend for the not yet tenured. In its early applications on elite campuses such as

Yale and Cornell, it recommended itself not on political grounds but as a more refined and sophisticated variant of New Criticism. We could still natter about the classic texts, whose overriding claim on our attention wasn't yet doubted, but now those texts were seen to be "disseminative," or indefinitely fertile in meanings that departed from what the authors had thought they were saying. If each text had only one manifest thematic core—a claim that poststructuralists never bothered to dispute, because they wanted texts to look boringly simple prior to their exciting deconstruction—there were any number of potential "margins" to be exposed.

This was just another hermeneutic game, played, like New Criticism itself, for the sake of displaying a subtlety beyond the reach of the uninitiated, but now without even a pretense of uplifting mass literacy. Soon, however, this heightened elitism began looking like a scandal. First a revived Marxism, then agitation for the establishing of ethnic studies departments, then a powerful upsurge of feminist consciousness, and finally the cause of lesbian and gay liberation all promoted an activist spirit that appeared antithetical to New Haven–style deconstruction. But in the 1980s, high theory itself, thanks to its potential for undermining "discourses" that were presumed to have upheld the ruling order in any given age, adapted to the new climate and became egalitarian in tone. The literary margins, it was suddenly perceived with relief, were occupied by none other than "the marginalized."

Since, however, this egalitarianism was couched in terms that only a minority of academics and no one else could understand, there was no chance that it would have liberating reverberations beyond the campuses. Quite the reverse, in fact, was true. Thanks to public alarm over subversive-sounding theory, conservative ideologues such as William Bennett and Lynne Cheney could wage an effective "culture war" against the radicalized humanities, recruiting adherents to the Republican Party by vilifying an academic left that could now be plausibly called at once antitraditional, unpatriotic, intolerant, entrenched, and obscurantist. Like my own campus's famous free speech movement, which I gladly supported in 1964–1965 but whose main achievement was to propel Ronald Reagan into the governorship of California, politicized high theory has proved to be a handsome gift to the right.

I have strayed from your questions, but I haven't lost sight of them. As you can gather, I don't agree that the post–World War II surge in emphasis on science and engineering took resources away from the humanities. The latter had previously existed in genteel poverty—the patched elbows of the faded corduroy blazer and all that. Government-sponsored research now produced boom times all around, with plenty of money for new appointments, humanities centers, and international conferences dominated by a new breed of overpaid superstars whose teaching loads had been negotiated downward toward zero.

For a while in the sixties and seventies, politicians who controlled the purse strings continued to leave uncriticized the quaint idea that the humanities, with their noble adherence to universal values and the Western canon, were marching arm in arm with science in the anti-Soviet crusade. But when right-wing intellectuals and journalists began publicizing the actual goings-on at the annual Modern Language Association meetings and other gatherings of the theory class, the public mood changed to puzzlement, disillusionment, and finally disgust. When economic recessions then required belt tightening, the humanities were first in line for cutbacks. And when the recessions ended and tax dollars were once again plentiful, pleas for restoration of the status quo ante fell on deaf ears. The tenured radicals, as Roger Kimball dubbed them, could now walk, not fly, to their anti-American conclaves.

It may appear to you that I am siding with the reactionaries here. If only our humanists had kept waving the national flag and celebrating the "democratic values" that have inhered in our tradition from the Greeks through Shakespeare to Melville and Mark Twain . . . ! Not so. The purpose of the humanities is not to support any socioeconomic order but to study cultural products in a way that will yield accurate knowledge about them. If that knowledge leads to a sweeping reassessment of the West, calling its official pieties into question, so be it. Our society will probably be stronger for having been shaken from its self-congratulatory mood and rendered more inclusive than it was when "democratic values" were the preserve of heterosexual white men with English-sounding names. But it won't be stronger if the idea of objective truth gets discarded along with more dispensable prejudices.

I think that I have tacitly addressed your final question—what should be the epistemology of the humanities?—but I will make my answer explicit. The human race has produced only one successfully validated epistemology, characterizing all scrupulous inquiry into the real world, from quarks to poems. It is simply empiricism, or the submitting of propositions to the arbitration of evidence that is acknowledged to be such by all of the contending parties. Ideas that claim immunity from such review, whether because of mystical faith or privileged "clinical insight" or the say-so of eminent authorities, are not to be countenanced until they can pass the same skeptical ordeal to which all other contenders are subjected.

In a university honoring the empirical ethos, each discipline will have its own conventions and practices suited to its style of research, and disciplines will of course vary in the degree of certainty that can be attached to their conclusions. Nevertheless, they will share the essential common feature that vouches for their authenticity as legitimate fields of inquiry—namely, a care to maintain a sharp separation between hypotheses and evidence. When, in contrast, conclusions are built into the questions that are posed, and when the marshaled "evidence" is really just the illustration of prior beliefs, knowledge is no longer being sought. We shouldn't be surprised or even disappointed when public support for such activity is withdrawn.

NOTES

I. THE ANTISCIENCE
Chapter 1: The Unknown Freud

1 "I should without question consider a person hysterical," writes Freud
about the fourteen-year-old girl who had been grabbed and kissed in a
darkened room by her family's married friend, "in whom an occasion for
sexual excitement elicited feelings that were preponderantly or exclusively
unpleasurable . . ." (Freud 1953–1974, 7:28). Apart from its sheer dement-
edness, this statement is of interest for the light it throws not just on
Freud's conception of female psychology but also on the itchiness of his
diagnostic trigger finger. No wonder that he decided, in the critical year
of 1897, that several of his sisters, his brother, and he himself were all hysterics, or that people who disagreed with him, including Fliess, Adler, and
even Jung, were suddenly found to be paranoiacs.

2 See also Schatzman 1992 and Israëls & Schatzman 1993.

3 Freud's early papers make it clear why he felt entitled to dictate what must
have happened to his patients decades earlier. For him, each presented
symptom bore a message about a homologous sexual trauma. Thus, vom-
iting pointed infallibly to oral violation, painful defecating to anal violation, and so on (e.g., 3:214). This allegorizing tendency, whereby a symptom is regarded as the charade of an unconscious memory, survived the
seduction theory and found a happy home within psychoanalysis; it is, for
example, a prominent feature of the Dora case.

4 See also Grosskurth 1991.

5 Spielrein began to come into modern historical focus with the publication of the Freud-Jung letters in 1974, and much of her importance was
grasped by Carotenuto 1983. Since then, however, two further discoveries of unedited documents have permitted the fuller understanding that is
registered in *A Most Dangerous Method*.

6 Given the norms of conduct in Freud's circle, however, he could hardly
have been morally outraged by the news. As Kerr relates, "Gross's exploits
were legendary, Stekel had long enjoyed a reputation as a 'seducer,' Jones
was paying blackmail money to a former patient, and even good Pastor
Pfister was lately being entranced by one of his charges. Indeed, the most
extraordinary entanglement was Ferenczi's, the amiable Hungarian having taken into analysis the daughter of the woman he was having an affair
with and then falling in love with the girl."

7 See, e.g., Kerr's recounting of how Freud vindictively leaked Fliess's

unpublished theory of bisexuality to Otto Weininger, who mysteriously committed suicide after pirating that theory in his international best seller, *Sex and Character* (1903). Freud lied to Fliess in denying his own instigation of the plagiarism, but by 1903, thanks to a widely publicized lawsuit, his true role in the affair was common knowledge.

Chapter 2: Freudian Suspicion versus Suspicion of Freud

1 Lear's recourse to interpretive truth rests on a fundamental confusion of categories that will be addressed in Chapter 3. Although interpretation is prominent within the analytic hour, the claims of psychoanalytic theory are not interpretations but determinate propositions about how the mind regularly works. Those propositions have to do, for example, with the function and meaning of dreams, the nature of drives, the defense mechanisms, the fantasies of the nursing infant, and the ubiquity of the Oedipus complex—all of which folklore is treated as established fact in Lear's vitalistic *summa Freudiana* of 1990, *Love and Its Place in Nature*.

2 A later reprint of my Hawthorne book (Crews 1989) afforded me the opportunity to add an afterword detailing the respects in which the historical dimension of my argument had been cramped by its Freudian premises.

3 Another such model was the Antichrist, who must have been rendered attractive to Freud by a bolder rebel than himself, Nietzsche. See Swales 1983 and Vitz 1988, pp. 161–165.

4 Goodheart doesn't explain where he acquired his affinity for psychoanalysis, but his autobiography leads one to believe that the source was Trilling, his favorite professor at Columbia (Goodheart 2001, p. 51).

Chapter 4: Unconscious Deeps and Empirical Shallows

1 Michels's hypothesis about the superior effect of his theory-based interpretations would not be testable unless, at a minimum, he and many other therapists of different schools, under strict experimental controls and close observation by non-Freudian evaluators over a period long enough for the improvement, deterioration, or unchanged condition of the patient-volunteers to be reliably ascertained, were all to impart, to socioeconomically comparable sets of clients harboring the same complaints with the same level of gravity, the theoretical mumbo-jumbo in which those therapists variously believed. But even then, there would be no way of ascertaining that the concepts and supposed laws themselves, and not some other feature of treatment, had been responsible for the differential results.

2 A fine example was provided, in the second day at Yale, by Arnold M. Cooper, a past president of the American Psychoanalytic Association. He asserted that the hypothesis of a dynamic unconscious is "now evidentially

well founded" and that Freud's basic method of "free association and analytic listening" has amply proven its worth. Using those tools, Cooper added, "we have moved very far" from Freud's single model of the mind. Indeed we have. Now we are faced with an ever-expanding number of conflicting models and no agreed-upon way of choosing among them. Is that progress, or does it constitute an indictment of the very tools that Cooper regards as having been vindicated?

II. MODERN DEVILTRY
Chapter 5: The Revenge of the Repressed, Part I

1 On this point, see Erdelyi 1990. Remarkably, Erdelyi welcomes Freud's unclarity as providing a sound basis for integrating the "dynamic" with the cognitive unconscious. The idea is that since Freud didn't really know what he meant by repression, we are free to bring the concept into alignment with current research while still thinking of ourselves as Freudians.

2 Whether Terr had actually detected anything is open to doubt. The upsetting death of King's boyhood friend was already familiar to her from King's autobiography—where, however, King reports that, so far as he knows, he did not witness the accident in question. Thus Terr's courtroom example of trustworthy clinical reasoning—proceeding from obsessive themes in King's eventual artistic productions to a "repressed" fact about one early day in his life—actually dealt with a still uncorroborated detail superadded to a story in the public domain. Insofar, then, as the Franklin trial hinged on Terr's testimony about Stephen King, it appears that one no-evidence case was decided on the basis of another.

3 Eileen Lipsker's problems with memory are echoed by Terr's own in her capacity as storyteller. Eileen never testified about seeing what Terr calls "white socks and white child-size underwear" in the rape scene, but only something white. And Terr, bent upon condemning George Franklin as a rapist, subsequently provided the useful "fact," which is false, that semen was found in the dead Susan Nason's vagina.

4 As for anomalies, why did George Franklin take his daughter along to watch the rape and murder of her dearest friend? How could he not have expected to be found out? Why would he then make Eileen witness another killing? Why did no one in a crowded living room notice George inserting his finger in Eileen's vagina? Etc.

5 Lipsker quickly became a heroine in psychotherapeutic circles, appeared on *Sixty Minutes*, collaborated on an as-told-to book, and found herself flatteringly portrayed by Shelley Long in a made-for-TV movie about the case. Her book and movie contracts, negotiated by a Hollywood entertainment lawyer, were signed before the case had gone to trial.

6 One month before Paul Ingram was summoned to police headquarters

for his first grilling, the Ingram family sat down to watch Geraldo Rivera's prime-time special, *Devil Worship: Exposing Satan's Underground*. The previous day's program, which they may or may not have seen, was called *Satanic Breeders: Babies for Sacrifice*.

7 Ingram himself learned, pathetically, how to talk the self-pitying lingo of recovered memory. "I have also been a victim since I was five years old," he told an interrogator, "and I learned very early that the easiest way to handle this was to hide it in unconscious memory. . . " (p. 173).

8 For a reliable account of the way that the mania over "Satanic ritual abuse" has blended with recovered memory, see Victor 1993. For the FBI's inability to locate any such abuse, see Lanning 1989. Among the books under review, the question of Satanism is most fully covered by Pendergrast.

Chapter 6: The Revenge of the Repressed, Part II

1 Controlled research indicates that there is nothing easy about identifying incest victims from their symptoms. See, e.g., Horner 1993, who found that forty-eight experts, all examining the same material, could reach no significant agreement as to whether a child had been molested by her father.

2 Renee Fredrickson goes a step farther, remarking that patients may not notice any symptoms at all "until they are immersed in the process of deal-ing with their memories" (Fredrickson 1992, p. 36). Then the torment begins.

3 See Yapko 1994; Wakefield & Underwager 1994; Wassil-Grimm 1995; and Kelley & Kelley 1994. Earlier important books include Goldstein & Farmer 1992, 1993.

4 Earlier in 1994, Gary Ramona of Petaluma, California, was awarded a settlement against a therapist, a psychiatrist, and a hospital for their role in bringing about his daughter Holly's "memory" that he had molested her. Sued by Holly, Ramona had countersued the other parties for com-pensation of the loss of his job, marriage, and reputation. (Lenore Terr, incidentally, put in her customary court appearance, offering an expert opinion that Holly Ramona's current aversion to pickles and bananas con-firms her childhood trauma of forced oral sex.) An excellent later study of the Ramona case is Johnston 1997.

5 See Freud 1985, pp. 220, 223; Freud 1953–1974, 3:215.

6 It must be admitted, however, that no one has yet approached Freud's level of ingenuity in turning his own punning associations into knowledge about his patients' histories. See, e.g., the letter of 1899 in which he tells Fliess about a patient who "deflowers" women because he failed botany and who, as a teenager, once masturbated in a contorted position so that he

could keep the Jungfrau in view (Freud 1985, p. 346). As Robert Wilcocks remarks, "Surely only Freud (or perhaps Alfred Jarry?) could have imagined a 14-year-old boy masturbating with a view of that massive rugged rockpile, his adolescent ardor aroused to ejaculation by the provocative mountain because its name means 'virgin'" (Wilcocks 1994, p. 198).

7 "I believe that the pervasive Freudian transformation of our modern working conception of the self is evidence of the validity of his attempt to extend the psychological far beyond its conscious base. Common sense has in fact expanded to include parts of Freudian theory. This in turn makes it credible that more extensive and systematic insights of the same type can be developed by analysts who probe far more deeply and uncover far more material for interpretation" (Nagel 1994, p. 36).

Chapter 7: Demonology for an Age of Science

1 Under "suggestion" I also mean to include *autosuggestion*, which doesn't require the physical presence of the influencing party. This distinction is important because the mass media can now exercise a quasi-hypnotic function in diffusing both misconceptions and panic.

2 See, e.g., Harris 1996; Pope & Brown 1996; J. Freyd 1996; and for commentary, Crews 1996.

3 For this failure on Janet's part, see Hacking 1995. As for Freud, his own critique of his faulty "seduction" logic (Freud 1985, pp. 264–265) ought to be caution enough against our taking his cases of the mid-1890s at face value.

4 See, e.g., Masson 1992; Herman 1992. Masson's new preface is notable, incidentally, for its righteous reaffirmation of the defendants' guilt in the granddaddy of daycare scandals, the McMartin affair.

5 See, e.g., Lear 1996; Michels 1996.

6 See Masson 1992; Harris & Aron 1993; and especially Fortune 1993.

7 In hypnotherapy, the patient is expected to be free of the symptom upon returning from the trance in which the therapist urges that result. The treatment works marvelously if, as with "hysteria," the symptom itself has been produced by the suggestive therapeutic context.

8 The following discussion is heavily indebted to Swales 1989a, 1989b.

9 Freud's interest in Weier was evidently derived from a book of Hippolyte Bernheim's on hypnotism, suggestion, and psychotherapy that he translated in 1892; see Swales 1988, p. 154.

10 See Swales 1982b; Wilcocks 1994; Borch-Jacobsen 1996a.

Chapter 8: The Trauma Trap

1 The fullest treatment of the recovered memory episode and its historical antecedents is Pendergrast 1996. For a concise and pointed account of the

multiple personality fad, see Acocella 1999. The best extended discussion is Spanos 1996. On Satanic abuse, see Victor 1993 and Nathan & Snedeker 1995. The plight of daycare workers who remain imprisoned even today is treated by Rabinowitz 2003.

2 For the current state of knowledge about "Sybil," see Borch-Jacobsen 2002, pp. 111–168.

3 For Masson's errors about Freud's "seduction" phase, see Esterson 1998, pp. 1–21. In his preface to the most recently reprinted edition of *The Assault on Truth* (2003), Masson at last concedes that Freud's patients in 1895–1896 resisted the incest stories that he tried to force upon them. Bizarrely, however, Masson still counts those patients among the likely victims of sexual abuse in Freud's day.

4 See, in this connection, the final chapter of Leys 2000.

5 In one paper, for example, Scheflin and Brown addressed the problem of patients' suggestibility, but the danger they envisioned from that quarter was only "false litigant syndrome," or surrender to "pro-false-memory suggestive influences" emanating from "plaintiffs' attorneys and expert witnesses" brought into malpractice suits against their former therapists (Scheflin & Brown 1999). This same argument surfaces in *Memory, Trauma Treatment, and the Law*, which states that pressures exerted in therapy "pale in comparison" (p. 398) with those that can turn a patient into a litigious ingrate.

6 Scheflin 1995. Transcripts of the Texas conference proceedings have been available from Toronto radio station CKLN. See also Harrington 1996.

7 "I think it's time somebody called for an open season on academicians and researchers," Hammond said in 1997; ". . . it's time for clinicians to begin bringing ethics charges for scientific malpractice against researchers and journal editors" who disparage recovered memory theory (Hammond 1997).

8 Understandably, tapes of this talk have been withdrawn from sale, but a transcript, which repays reading from start to finish, can be found at www. heart7.net/mcf/greenbaum.htm.

9 Patients of hypnosis-wielding MPD enthusiasts really have acquired crippling beliefs about their cult participation. That is why Bennett Braun, in 1997, had his license to practice suspended and why his insurers paid one of his tormented ex-patients a sobering malpractice settlement of $10.6 million.

10 See, e.g., Crews et al. 1995, pp. 15–29; Crews 1996; and Crews 1998, pp. x–xi. The special number of *Psychoanalytic Dialogues* containing Crews 1996 became a book edited by Richard B. Gartner (1997). My contribution, however, was excised and replaced by an attack on my earlier criticisms of psychoanalysis.

11 On this last point, see Simon 1992.

12 A welcome new critique of fad therapies is Lilienfeld et al. 2003.

13 On this point see Dawes 1994, especially pp. 10–22.

14 See especially Young 1995 and Kutchins & Kirk 1997.

15 As the Pied Pipers of recovered memory, Ellen Bass and Laura Davis, told prospective survivors in 1988, "When you first remember your abuse or acknowledge its effects, you may feel tremendous relief. Finally there is a reason for your problems. There is someone, and something, to blame" (Bass & Davis 1988, p. 173).

III. MORE DIAGNOSTIC FOLLIES
Chapter 9: Keeping Us in Hysterics

1 For example: "The feminist classroom is the place to use what we know as women to appropriate and transform, totally, a domain which has been men's. . . . Let us welcome the intrusion/infusion of emotionality—love, rage, anxiety, eroticism—into intellect as a step toward healing the fragmentation capitalism and patriarchy have demanded from us" (Culley et al. 1985, p. 19).

Chapter 10: Out, Damned Blot!

1 James M. Wood and M. Teresa Nezworski are associate professors of psychology at the University of Texas at El Paso and Dallas, respectively; Scott O. Lilienfeld is associate professor of psychology at Emory University; and Howard N. Garb, formerly clinical associate professor of psychiatry in the University of Pittsburgh's School of Medicine, is now at Wilford Hall Medical Center, Lackland Air Force Base. Since all but one of the book's twelve chapters were drafted by Wood, I will usually write "Wood" when designating the authors collectively. No slight to the other collaborators is intended.

2 See Rorschach 1975, pp. 96–97, 102, 107, 112. With the assistance of prominent American Rorschachers, a Columbia Ph.D. candidate followed Rorschach's lead in 1939, using test results to suggest that "the White race," sampled in one of its typical habitats, Columbia Teachers College, is more introversive on the whole than "the Negro race," sampled in Harlem. See Sicha 1939, pp. 40, 56.

3 The struggle between romantic and empiricist tendencies in modern psychology is highlighted in McHugh 1994.

4 Respect for colleagues has impelled Wood et al. to omit images of the cards, whose (already debatable) effectiveness could be jeopardized if they were made too accessible. But several other books do reproduce the cards, and anyone with Internet access can easily find depictions of them.

Chapter 11: The Mind Snatchers

1　The logistical difficulties surrounding the UFO thesis, it should be noted, do not extend to the interception of (as yet undetected) radio signals from remote civilizations. In this connection, see Lemonick 1998 and Parker 1998.

2　For cogent discussion of the Roswell matter, see Klass 1997 and Frazier et al. 1997. Sensible broader studies are Klass 1988 and, largely prior to the abduction fad, Menzel & Taves 1977.

3　Mack 1984, p. 484. Mack 1994 was his chief contribution to the abduction debate.

4　*The UFO Incident* founded the abduction craze by purporting to relate the true vicissitudes of Barney and Betty Hill, who had supposedly been kidnapped by ETs in 1961. NBC's light regard for facts is explored in Klass 1988 and Menzel & Taves 1977.

5　Strieber's abduction series thus far includes, between *Communion* and *Confirmation, Transformation* (1998a), *Breakthrough* (1995), and (with Ann Strieber) *The Communion Letters* (1997).

6　In yet another coup, Strieber has been permitted to include in *Confirmation* an interview conducted by the UFO visionary Michael Hesemann, with Monsignor Corrado Balducci, a member of the Curia of the Roman Catholic Church, a noted authority on demonology, and a practicing exorcist. The Monsignor declares the evidence for UFOs to be overwhelming, and he speculates that "these extraterrestrials—if that is what they really are, rather than angels— . . . are very good beings who aim to bring us nearer to God" (Strieber 1998b, p. 273).

7　For a sense of the fringe beliefs attending UFO interest, see the credulous but wide-ranging final chapter of C. D. B. Bryan's *Close Encounters of the Fourth Kind* (1995) and Phil Patton's more consistently reportorial *Dreamland* (1998).

8　See, e.g., Spanos 1993 and Parnell 1988.

9　Mack 1994, p. 12. It should also be mentioned that Barney and Betty Hill (see note 4 above), the Adam and Eve of abduction legend, did not come to believe in their own alien kidnapping until they, too, were hypnotized. In their case, however, even the hypnotist remained unconvinced; see Klass 1988, pp. 7–13.

10　See, in this connection, Blackmore 1998.

IV. THE WILL TO BELIEVE
Chapter 12: The Consolation of Theosophy

1　This discussion, including the quotations from Yeats, his father, and Pound, is indebted to Murphy 1995, pp. 369–389. See also the classic account in Ellmann 1948, passim.

2 Some definitions are called for here. I will treat *occultism* as the belief that nature possesses secret properties contradicting the presumed laws of science; a dedicated occultist believes that those properties can be manipulated through adept exercises of *magic*. *Esotericism* is the broader project that weds occultism to self-transformation. *Spiritualism* is the attempted practice of communicating with the dead through séances. *Mysticism* purports to bring the seeker into direct experience of, even merger with, a transcendent deity. *Gnosis*, broadly conceived, is the intuitive apprehension of deep truth without a felt need for corroborating evidence. Uncapitalized, *theosophy* is gnostic and esoteric lore that relates human destiny to speculation about the origin, nature, and governance of the universe. Finally, in its capitalized form *Theosophy* refers to the specific theosophical doctrines and organizations launched by Madame Blavatsky and her successors.

3 I take it as axiomatic that in assessing paranormal claims, we ought to be guided by Hume's sturdy principle for authenticating miracles: that the testimony to establish a given miracle be so credible that its falsehood would be more miraculous than the alleged phenomenon itself. Thus the possibility of fraud or self-deception (neither of which defies common sense) deserves priority over the hypothesis that a reported wonder, such as the receipt of psychic e-mail or the appearance of an adept in two places at once, has somehow slipped the hold of known physical laws.

4 That Gurdjieff was deeply strange is not in dispute. Washington cites one occasion when "a party of rich and respectable New Yorkers dining with Gurdjieff were shocked by a recital of his most obscene stories, liberally decorated with four-letter words. Nevertheless, they gradually succumbed to his power of suggestion and threw themselves into an orgy under Gurdjieff's direction—until violently and humiliatingly interrupted by his harangue on the slavery of all Americans to the sex instinct" (p. 284).

5 Look, for example, at one of Wallace's so-called guru letters to his fellow Theosophist Nicholas Roerich—letters whose rumored existence probably doomed his renomination as vice president, and whose later authentication by the journalist Westbrook Pegler finished off his already hopeless campaign for the presidency:

Dear Guru,

I have been thinking of you holding the casket—the sacred most precious casket. And I have thought of the New Country going forth to meet the seven stars under the sign of the three stars. And I have thought of the admonition "Await the Stone."

We think of the People of Northern Shambhalla and the hastening feet of the successor of Buddha and the Lightning flashes and the breaking of the New Day. (Maze & White 1995, p. 65)

This is wonderfully daffy prose, but the greater wonder is that if FDR had died one year earlier than he did, the awaiter of the Stone would have become our chief executive.

Chapter 13: The Esoteric Unconscious

1 See, e.g., Ellenberger 1970; Macmillan 1997; and Crabtree 1993. Unfortunately, Crabtree's book fails to take cognizance of the methodological excesses that characterize the entire Mesmeric tradition.

2 See, e.g., Freud 1987, especially the editor's discussion on pages 75–107.

Chapter 14: The New Creationists and Their Friends

1 I refer to Baylor University's Michael Polanyi Center, whose founding director was William Dembski. Despite its Baptist affiliation, however, Baylor has not proved quite ready for intelligent design. Soon after the center was established without faculty consultation, scientists on the campus called for its dissolution. Though it remains in existence, the openly evangelizing Dembski was relieved of his directorship in October 2000. The new director, Bruce Gordon, has been at pains to characterize intelligent design as a research paradigm, not an established fact.

2 We can be quite sure that science will never become spiritual in Johnson's sense—not because scientists are committed atheists but because their job is to test theories against the real-world consequences that those theories entail. An immaterial factor such as God's will can't figure in a successful empirical argument, because it is compatible with every physical state of affairs.

3 One such book, cleverly crafted to pass constitutional review, already exists: Percival Davis and Dean H. Kenyon, *Of Pandas and People* (Davis & Kenyon 1993). The educational strategy for getting similar works into the classroom is set forth in DeWolf et al. 1999.

4 Thus the paleontologist Niles Eldredge, in an otherwise excellent book published in 2000, offered no index entry for intelligent design, devoted only a handful of paragraphs to its adherents, and declared, mistakenly, that "there is literally nothing new in their antievolutionary rhetoric" (Eldredge 2000, p. 13).

5 Dembski reasons that information can only diminish when acted upon by chance processes. But he has confounded two notions, "Shannon information," or reduction of uncertainty, and complexity proper. For an account of his error, see Roche 2001.

6 See Himmelfarb 1994, 1995, 1996, 2001.

7 Berlinski 1998. In a more recent piece for *Commentary* (2001), Berlinski quietly backed off from his opposition to the Big Bang but resumed his emphasis on the inability of science to cope with the ultimate mystery of existence and life.

8 See Kimball's introduction to Stove 1999.
9 Podhoretz 1995. For discussion of *The New World Order*, see Lind 1995.
10 See Gross & Levitt 1996; Koertge 1998; Levitt 1999.

Chapter 15: Darwin Goes to Sunday School

1 A sampling of these statements can be found in Appleman 2001, pp. 525–
   533, 613–623. This volume is the most convenient collection of readings
   surrounding Darwin's career and its significance.

Chapter 16: Zen and the Art of Success

1 San Francisco Zen Center operates at three sites: Tassajara, City Center,
   and Green Gulch Farm in western Marin County. They were acquired,
   respectively, in 1966, 1969, and 1972. ("Zen Center" in this chapter always
   refers to the organization as a whole.) Japanese Zen Buddhism possesses
   two major schools, the Rinzai and the Soto. Rinzai Zen relies on the study
   of paradoxical koans, with emphasis on the attainment of *kensho* (satori), or
   enlightenment. Soto Zen, the tradition from which Zen Center emerged,
   is focused chiefly on zazen sitting, the correct performance of which is
   considered spiritually sufficient. Individual masters, such as Zen Center's
   first abbot, Shunryu Suzuki, tend to draw from both traditions, but with
   a bias toward the school in which they were trained.
2 Zen Center was by no means the first organization of its kind in the United
   States or even in San Francisco. Nyogen Senzaki had established a "floating zendo" there in 1927 before moving on to a temple in Los Angeles, and
   Sokei-an Sasaki had founded the First Zen Institute of America in New
   York as early as 1930. Zen Center itself began as a guest operation within
   Sokoji, the Soto Zen Mission, which had been functioning on Bush Street
   since 1934. And by the sixties there were mixed-nationality Zen groups in
   New York, Rochester, Boston, rural Maine, Philadelphia, Chicago, Washington, Los Angeles, and Maui. For this background, see Fields 1992.
3 Of those undertakings, only Greens survives; it has gone upscale and is no
   longer staffed by Zen Center students. Its vegetarian chefs in Baker-roshi's
   day, Deborah Madison and Annie Somerville, are the authors of outstanding and still widely consulted cookbooks, as is Edward Espe Brown, who
   ran the admired Tassajara Bakery.
4 Suzuki (no relation to D. T. Suzuki, an important early spokesman for
   Zen in America) is the subject of an affectionate biography, David Chadwick's *Crooked Cucumber* (1999). His talks and comments, liberally rendered into more idiomatic English, are sampled in Suzuki 1970 and Chadwick 2001.

IV. A DISCIPLINE IN CRISIS

Chapter 17: The End of the Poststructuralist Era

1 On this point see McCarthy 1978, p. 56. As Christopher Norris (1992, pp. 100–110) recognizes, Foucault's later turn toward the local-scale activism of the "specific intellectual" represents, on the plane of theory, a very imperfect restoration of the human agent, who is still denied the perspective and moral authority of the spurious "universal intellectual" who dares to consult his conscience.

2 Graff, of course, recognizes differences between current critical doctrines; his pedagogical suggestion is that we pit them against one another in the classroom, thus refreshing and empowering students by letting them share our intellectual struggles (Graff 1992). The idea is attractive, but it presupposes something I am unwilling to grant: an equivalence between theories that advance the cause of careful research and those that make a mockery of it. Of course one could raise this very point in one's theoretical innings, but the recent history of the academy suggests that in the short run, empirically grounded theories stand little chance against aprioristic ones if the latter also happen to be politically fervent.

Chapter 18: Kafka in the Clouds

1 An excellent new biography—judicious, well proportioned, lively, and fully conversant with the current state of research—is Nicholas Murray's *Kafka* (2004).

2 The leading Kafka scholar has been Hartmut Binder, whose two-volume collaborative *Kafka-Handbuch* (1979) is invaluable. Two ongoing "manuscript" editions now compete to be recognized as definitive: Kafka 1982– and Kafka 1995–. English versions profiting from the newer scholarship include translations of *Amerika* by Michael Hofmann (2002), of *The Trial* by Breon Mitchell (1998), and of *The Castle* by Mark Harman (1998).

3 See, for a statement of the thesis, Sokel 1985; and for a penetrating critique, Robertson 1994, especially pp. 118–120.

4 Kafka's ties to Jewishness, in the broad sense of *Judentum*, are the subject of many valuable studies by Giuliano Baioni, Jean Jofen, Mark Anderson, Régine Robin, and Karl Erich Grözinger, among others. The fullest study in English is Robertson 1985.

5 Despite his belief that Freud's work, too, grew out of Jewish self-loathing, Gilman subscribes to psychoanalytic categories of explanation. See Gilman 1993b.

Chapter 19: Call Me Liberal

1 I agree with those scholars who think that the hyphen on the title page of Melville's first American edition was a mistake or editorial arrogation that

needn't have been perpetuated. "Moby Dick" is unhyphenated through-out the printed text (including a chapter title) and in a surviving letter to Sophia Hawthorne in Melville's hand.

2 Some of the more militant of these critics gladly adopted the name "New Americanists" after I myself bestowed it on them (Crews 1988). By now, however, the term "new" is hardly appropriate.

3 E.g.: "We are the pioneers of the world; the advance-guard, sent on through the wilderness of untried things, to break a new path in the New World that is ours . . ." (Melville 1983, p. 506).

4 When other Americanists discuss the revisionist school, debating whether its accusatory conception of the national destiny is bracingly realistic or too unrelievedly negative in its determinism, one virtue is always con-ceded: these desublimators of accepted myths are wholeheartedly devoted to accurate reconstruction of the past. But are they? "I do not quite wish to recover the scene of cultural persuasion at the time of the publication of *Moby Dick*," wrote Donald Pease in the eighties, "but to recover from the scene of persuasion, the Cold War drama, that has appropriated it" (Pease 1985, p. 117). And still more drastically, William Spanos now feels compelled to dissociate himself from "the violent interest inscribed in the disinterested discourse of truth" (W. Spanos 1995, p. 27).

5 Delbanco's writings also include two books (1995, 1999b) that bring Trill-ing to mind in their urging of secular liberals to cultivate a sense of moral complexity.

6 Delbanco's analysis closely resembles that of Eric J. Sundquist's *To Wake the Nations* (1993, pp. 135–189), a book that typifies recent studies in applying skeptical attention to ideological issues while shying away from the dis-sensus school's accusatory moralism. See also, in this connection, Samuel Otter's *Melville's Anatomies* (1999), which explores "a Melville who analyzes the forces that move him to feel" and whose fiction thus registers "an inside sense of the power of ideology, its satisfactions and its incarcerations" (pp. 4, 7).

7 On numerous occasions Delbanco strains to award Melville points for hav-ing anticipated Freud. Thus he asserts that Melville was aware, "as Freud later puts it, that 'in mental life nothing which has once been formed can perish'" (p. 146), and he characterizes Mrs. Glendinning in *Pierre* as "a model of the overbearing mother whom Freud blames for homosexual tendencies in boys" (p. 183). Freud happened to be disastrously wrong on both points, neither of which, besides, can be matched with anything said or implied by Melville.

8 Attention to eighteenth-century precedents could also have forestalled Delbanco's strange assertion that the following passage from *White-Jacket* "creates a seesaw feeling not very different from what one feels when

reading a late twentieth-century postmodern writer like Jacques Derrida or Paul de Man":

> [Wooloo] seemed a being from some other sphere. His tastes were our abominations: ours his. Our creed he rejected: his we. We thought him a loon; he fancied us fools. Had the case been reversed; had we been Polynesians and he an American, our mutual opinion of each other would still have remained the same. A fact proving that neither was wrong, but both right. (p. 55)

This could easily be Addison, Steele, or Samuel Johnson, but never de Man or Derrida.

9 To be sure, Delbanco is justified in noting a conservative side to the very complex and ambivalent Melville. Agitators, mobs, and violent European revolutionaries elicited nothing but scorn from him. The trouble is, however, that Melville didn't gradually acquire that distaste as a result of personal setbacks. As Delbanco's own biographical narrative shows, he never held any different opinion of those who would force their ideas upon others.

10 Milder 2005, p. 23. See also Milder 2000.

11 Interestingly, Delbanco echoes Warner Berthoff in treating *Billy Budd* almost exclusively as the story of Vere's tragic anguish. Berthoff, who *thought* he was immune to the thematic appeal of "Americanness," had absurdly recruited a fictive British aristocrat to the cause of demonstrating "greatness of mind and spirit in a mass society" (Berthoff 1962, p. 194). Delbanco evidences a comparable amnesia in asserting that Vere has to "discover, after long resistance," what he was surely raised from childhood to believe about saving class privilege from such rabble as the subproletarian Billy and his restive but easily manipulated shipmates. Both critics could have profited from recalling that the novella is called *Billy Budd, Sailor*, not *Captain Vere*.

WORKS CITED

Acocella, Joan. 1999. *Creating Hysteria: Women and Multiple Personality Disorder.* San Francisco: Jossey-Bass.

Alpert, Judith L., Laura S. Brown, and Christine A. Courtois. 1996. "Symptomatic Clients and Memories of Childhood Abuse: What the Trauma and Child Abuse Literature Tells Us." In *Final Report of APA Working Group on Investigation of Memories of Childhood Abuse.* Pp. 15–105. Washington, DC: American Psychological Association.

Alter, Robert. 1991. *Necessary Angels: Tradition and Modernity in Kafka, Benjamin, and Scholem.* Cambridge, MA: Harvard University Press.

Anzieu, Didier. 1986. *Freud's Self-Analysis.* London: Hogarth Press.

Appleman, Philip (Ed.). 2001. *Darwin: A Norton Critical Edition.* 3rd ed. (1970). New York: Norton.

Arac, Jonathan, and Harriet Ritvo (Eds.). 1995. *Macropolitics of Nineteenth-Century Literature: Nationalism, Exoticism, Imperialism.* (1991). Durham: Duke University Press.

Aron, Lewis, and Adrienne Harris (Eds.). 1993. *The Legacy of Sándor Ferenczi.* Hillsdale, NJ: Analytic Press.

Balt, John. 1967. *By Reason of Insanity.* London: Hutchinson.

Bass, Ellen, and Laura Davis. 1988. *The Courage to Heal: A Guide for Women Survivors of Child Sexual Abuse.* New York: Harper & Row.

———. 1992. *The Courage to Heal: A Guide for Women Survivors of Child Sexual Abuse.* 2nd ed. New York: HarperPerennial.

———. 1994. *The Courage to Heal: A Guide for Women Survivors of Child Sexual Abuse.* 3rd ed. New York: HarperPerennial.

Behe, Michael J. 1996. *Darwin's Black Box: The Biochemical Challenge to Evolution.* New York: Touchstone.

Berlinski, David. 1996. "The Deniable Darwin." *Commentary,* June, pp. 19–29.

———. 1998. "Was There a Big Bang?" *Commentary,* February, pp. 28–38.

———. 2001. "What Brings a World into Being?" *Commentary,* April, pp. 17–23.

Berthoff, Warner. 1962. *The Example of Melville.* Princeton: Princeton University Press.

Binder, Hartmut. 1979. *Kafka-Handbuch.* 2 vols. Stuttgart: Alfred Kröner.

Blackmore, Susan. 1998. "Abduction by Aliens or Sleep Paralysis?" *Skeptical Inquirer,* 22 (May/June): 23–28.

Blume, E. Sue. 1990. *Secret Survivors: Uncovering Incest and Its Aftereffects in Women.* New York: Wiley.

Boa, Elizabeth. 1996. *Kafka: Gender, Class, and Race in the Letters and Fictions.* Oxford: Clarendon Press.

Borch-Jacobsen, Mikkel. 1996a. "Neurotica: Freud and the Seduction Theory." *October,* 16:15-43.

———. 1996b. *Remembering Anna O: A Century of Mystification.* Trans. Kirby Olson in collaboration with Xavier Callahan and the author. (1995). New York and London: Routledge.

———. 2000. "How to Predict the Past: From Trauma to Repression." *History of Psychiatry,* 11:15–35.

———. 2002. *Folie à plusieurs: De l'hystérie à la dépression.* Paris: Les Empêcheurs de penser en rond/Le Seuil.

Bornstein, Robert F. 2001. "The Impending Death of Psychoanalysis." *Psychoanalytic Psychology,* 18:3–20.

Bouveresse, Jacques. 1995. *Wittgenstein Reads Freud: The Myth of the Unconscious.* Trans. Carol Cosman. Princeton: Princeton University Press.

Bradshaw, John. 1992. "Incest: When You Wonder If It Happened to You." *Lear's,* Aug., pp. 43–44.

Brenneis, C. Brooks. 1996. *Recovered Memories of Trauma: Transferring the Present to the Past.* Madison, CT: International Universities Press.

Brooks, Peter, and Alex Woloch (Eds.). 2000. *Whose Freud? The Place of Psychoanalysis in Contemporary Culture.* New Haven: Yale University Press.

Brown, Daniel, Alan W. Scheflin, and D. Corydon Hammond. 1998. *Memory, Trauma Treatment, and the Law.* New York and London: Norton.

Bryan, C. D. B. 1995. *Close Encounters of the Fourth Kind: Alien Abduction, UFOs, and the Conference at M.I.T.* New York: Knopf.

Calasso, Roberto. 2001. *The Forty-nine Steps.* Trans. John Shepley. (1991). Minneapolis: University of Minnesota Press.

———. 2005. *K.* Trans. Geoffrey Brock. (2002). New York: Knopf.

Carotenuto, Aldo. 1983. *A Secret Symmetry: Sabina Spielrein Between Freud and Jung.* (1982). New York: Pantheon.

Ceci, Stephen J., and Maggie Bruck. 1995. *Jeopardy in the Courtroom: A Scientific Analysis of Children's Testimony.* Washington, DC: American Psychological Association.

Chadwick, David. 1999. *Crooked Cucumber: The Life and Zen Teaching of Shunryu Suzuki.* New York: Broadway Books.

——— (Ed.). 2001. *To Shine One Corner of the World: Moments with Shunryu Suzuki.* New York: Broadway Books.

Cioffi, Frank. 1972. "Wollheim on Freud." *Inquiry,* 15:171–186.

———. 1974. "Was Freud a Liar?" *The Listener,* 91:172–174.

———. 1988. "'Exegetical Myth-Making' in Grünbaum's Indictment of Popper and Exoneration of Freud." In *Mind, Psychoanalysis, and Science,* ed. Peter Clark and Crispin Wright. Pp. 61–87. Oxford and New York: Blackwell.

————. 1998. *Freud and the Question of Pseudoscience*. Chicago: Open Court.

Clancy, Susan A. 2005. *Abducted: How People Come to Believe They Were Kidnapped by Aliens*. Cambridge, MA, and London: Harvard University Press.

CNN Interactive. 1997. "Poll: U.S. Hiding Knowledge of Aliens." June 15: http://www.cnn.com/US/9706/15/ufo.poll/index.html.

Corngold, Stanley. 1988. *Kafka: The Necessity of Form*. Ithaca: Cornell University Press.

————. 2004. *Lambent Traces: Franz Kafka*. Princeton: Princeton University Press.

Crabtree, Adam. 1993. *From Mesmer to Freud: Magnetic Sleep and the Roots of Psychological Healing*. New Haven: Yale University Press.

Crews, Frederick. 1966. *The Sins of the Fathers: Hawthorne's Psychological Themes*. Princeton: Princeton University Press.

————. 1970. "Do Literary Studies Have an Ideology?" *PMLA*, 85:423–428. Reprinted in Crews 1975, pp. 105–120.

————. "Offing Culture: Literary Study and the Movement." *Tri-Quarterly*, 23/24 (Winter/Spring), pp. 34–56. Reprinted in Crews 1975, pp. 121–144.

————. 1975. *Out of My System: Psychoanalysis, Ideology, and Critical Method*. New York: Oxford University Press.

————. 1986. *Skeptical Engagements*. New York: Oxford University Press.

————. 1988. "Whose American Renaissance?" *New York Review of Books*, Jan. 19, pp. 68–71. Reprinted in Crews 1992, pp. 16–46.

————. 1989. *The Sins of the Fathers: Hawthorne's Psychological Themes*. 2nd ed. Berkeley and Los Angeles: University of California Press.

————. 1992. *The Critics Bear It Away: American Fiction and the Academy*. New York: Random House.

————. 1996. "Forward to 1896? Commentary on Papers by Harris and Davies." *Psychoanalytic Dialogues*, 6:231–250.

———— (Ed.). 1998. *Unauthorized Freud: Doubters Confront a Legend*. New York: Viking.

Crews, Frederick, et al. 1995. *The Memory Wars: Freud's Legacy in Dispute*. New York: New York Review Books.

Culley, Margo, et al. 1985. "The Politics of Nurturance." In *Gendered Subjects: The Dynamics of Feminist Teaching*, ed. Margo Culley and Catherine Portuges. Pp. 11–20. Boston: Routledge and Kegan Paul.

Darwin, Charles. 1993. *The Origin of Species by Means of Natural Selection: Or The Preservation of Favored Races in the Struggle for Life*. (1859). New York: Modern Library.

Darwin, Francis (Ed.). 1897. *The Life and Letters of Charles Darwin: Including an Autobiographical Chapter*. 2 vols. New York: D. Appleton.

Davies, Jody Messler. 1994. *Treating the Adult Survivor of Childhood Sexual Abuse*. New York: Basic Books.

————. 1996. "Dissociation, Repression and Reality Testing in the

CounterTransference: The Controversy over Memory and False Memory in the Psychoanalytic Treatment of Adult Survivors of Childhood Sexual Abuse." *Psychoanalytic Dialogues*, 6:189–218.

Davis, Percival, and Dean H. Kenyon. 1993. *Of Pandas and People: The Central Question of Biological Origins*. Dallas: Haughton.

Dawes, Robyn M. 1994. *House of Cards: Psychology and Psychotherapy Built on Myth*. New York: Free Press.

Dawkins, Richard. 1996. *The Blind Watchmaker: Why the Evidence of Evolution Reveals a Universe without Design*. (1986). New York and London: Norton.

Dean, Jodi. 1996. *Solidarity of Strangers: Feminism After Identity Politics*. Berkeley and Los Angeles: University of California Press.

——— (Ed.). 1997. *Feminism and the New Democracy: Re-siting the Political*. Thousand Oaks, CA: Sage.

——— . 1998. *Aliens in America: Conspiracy Cultures from Outerspace to Cyberspace*. Ithaca, NY: Cornell University Press.

Delbanco, Andrew. 1992. "Melville in the '80s." *American Literary History*, 4:709–725.

——— . 1995. *The Death of Satan: How Americans Have Lost the Sense of Evil*. New York: Farrar, Straus & Giroux.

——— . 1997. *Required Reading: Why Our American Classics Matter Now*. New York: Noonday Press.

——— . 1999a. "The Decline and Fall of Literature." *New York Review of Books*, Nov. 4, pp. 32–38.

——— . 1999b. *The Real American Dream: A Meditation on Hope*. Cambridge, MA, and London: Harvard University Press.

——— . 2001. "Night Vision." *New York Review of Books*, Jan. 11, pp. 38–41.

——— . 2005. *Melville: His World and Work*. New York: Knopf.

Dembski, William A. (Ed.). 1998. *Mere Creation: Science, Faith & Intelligent Design*. Downers Grove, IL: InterVarsity Press.

——— . 1999. *Intelligent Design: The Bridge between Science and Theology*. Downers Grove, IL: InterVarsity Press.

Dennett, Daniel C. 1996. *Darwin's Dangerous Idea: Evolution and the Meanings of Life*. (1995). New York: Simon & Schuster.

DeWolf, David K., Stephen C. Meyer, and Mark E. DeForrest. 1999. *Intelligent Design in Public School Science Curricula: A Legal Guidebook*. Richardson, TX: Foundation for Thought and Ethics.

Dolnick, Edward. 1998. *Madness on the Couch: Blaming the Victim in the Heyday of Psychoanalysis*. New York: Simon & Schuster.

Dowden, Stephen D. 1995. *Kafka's Castle and the Critical Imagination*. Columbia, SC: Camden House.

Downing, Michael. 2001. *Shoes Outside the Door: Desire, Devotion, and Excess at San Francisco Zen Center*. Washington, DC: Counterpoint.

Eddins, Dwight (Ed.). 1995. *The Emperor Redressed: Critiquing Critical Theory.* Tuscaloosa: University of Alabama Press.

Edmunds, Lavinia. 1988. "His Master's Choice." *Johns Hopkins Magazine,* 40 (April): 40–49.

Eldredge, Niles. 2000. *The Triumph of Evolution and the Failure of Creationism.* New York: W. H. Freeman.

Ellenberger, Henri F. 1970. *The Discovery of the Unconscious: The History and Evolution of Dynamic Psychiatry.* New York: Basic Books.

Ellis, John M. 1989. *Against Deconstruction.* Princeton: Princeton University Press.

Ellmann, Richard. 1948. *Yeats: The Man and the Masks.* New York: Macmillan.

Erdelyi, Matthew H. 1990. "Repression, Reconstruction, and Defense: History and Integration of the Psychoanalytic and Experimental Frameworks." In Singer 1990, pp. 1–32.

Erikson, Erik H. 1962. "Reality and Actuality." *Journal of the American Psychoanalytic Association,* 10:451–474.

Erwin, Edward. 1996. *A Final Accounting: Philosophical and Empirical Issues in Freudian Psychology.* Cambridge, MA: MIT Press.

Esterson, Allen. 1993. *Seductive Mirage: An Exploration of the Work of Sigmund Freud.* Chicago: Open Court.

———. 1998. "Jeffrey Masson and Freud's Seduction Theory: A New Fable Based on Old Myths." *History of the Human Sciences,* 11:1–21.

Eysenck, Hans J., and Glenn D. Wilson. 1973. *The Experimental Study of Freudian Theories.* London: Methuen.

Faivre, Antoine. 1994. *Access to Western Esotericism.* Albany: State University of New York Press.

Ferenczi, Sándor. 1988. *The Clinical Diary of Sándor Ferenczi.* Ed. Judith Dupont. Trans. Michael Balint and Nicola Zarday Jackson. Cambridge, MA: Harvard University Press.

Fields, Rick. 1992. *How the Swans Came to the Lake: A Narrative History of Buddhism in America.* (1981). Boulder, CO: Shambhala.

Fisher, Philip (Ed.). 1991. *The New American Studies: Essays from "Representations."* Berkeley: University of California Press.

Flores, Angel (Ed.). 1977. *The Kafka Debate: New Perspectives for Our Time.* Staten Island, NY: Gordian Press.

Fortune, Christopher. 1993. "The Case of 'RN': Sándor Ferenczi's Radical Experiment in Psychoanalysis." In Aron & Harris 1993, pp. 101–120.

Frazier, Kendrick, Barry Karr, and Joe Nickell (Eds.). 1997. *The UFO Invasion: The Roswell Incident, Alien Abductions, and Government Coverups.* Amherst, NY: Prometheus.

Fredrickson, Renee. 1992. *Repressed Memories: A Journey to Recovery from Sexual Abuse.* New York: Simon & Schuster.

Freud, Ernst, Lucie Freud, and Ilse Grubrich-Simitis. 1978. *Sigmund Freud: His Life in Pictures and Words*. Trans. Christine Trollope. New York: Harcourt Brace Jovanovich.

Freud, Sigmund. 1953–1974. *The Standard Edition of the Complete Psychological Works of Sigmund Freud*. 24 vols. Trans. James Strachey. London: Hogarth Press.

———. 1954. *The Origins of Psycho-Analysis: Letters to Wilhelm Fliess, Drafts and Notes: 1887–1902*. Ed. Marie Bonaparte, Anna Freud, and Ernst Kris. Trans. Erich Mosbacher and James Strachey. New York: Basic Books.

———. 1985. *The Complete Letters of Sigmund Freud to Wilhelm Fliess, 1887–1904*. Trans. and ed. Jeffrey Moussaieff Masson. Cambridge, MA, and London: Belknap Press of Harvard University Press.

———. 1987. *A Phylogenetic Fantasy: Overview of the Transference Neuroses*. Ed. Ilse Grubrich-Simitis. Trans. Axel Hoffer and Peter T. Hoffer. Cambridge, MA: Belknap Press of Harvard University Press.

Freyd, Jennifer J. 1996. *Betrayal Trauma: The Logic of Forgetting Childhood Abuse*. Cambridge, MA: Harvard University Press.

Gartner, Richard (Ed.). 1997. *Memories of Sexual Betrayal: Truth, Fantasy, Repression, and Dissociation*. Northvale, NJ: Jason Aronson.

———. 2005. *Beyond Betrayal: Men Cope with Being the Victims*. New York: Wiley.

Gasché, Rodolphe. 1986. *The Tain of the Mirror: Derrida and the Philosophy of Reflection*. Cambridge, MA: Harvard University Press.

Gay, Peter. 1988. *Freud: A Life for Our Time*. New York: Norton.

Gellner, Ernest. 1996. *The Psychoanalytic Movement; or The Cunning of Unreason*. (1985). Evanston, IL: Northwestern University Press.

Gilman, Sander L. 1993a. *Freud, Race, and Gender*. Princeton: Princeton University Press.

———. 1993b. *The Case of Sigmund Freud: Medicine and Identity at the Fin de Siècle*. Baltimore and London: Johns Hopkins University Press.

———. 1995. *Franz Kafka: The Jewish Patient*. London: Routledge.

Glenn, David. 2003. "Nightmare Scenarios." *Chronicle of Higher Education*, Oct. 24, pp. 14–17.

Godwin, Joscelyn. 1994. *The Theosophical Enlightenment*. Albany: State University of New York Press.

Goldstein, Eleanor, and Kevin Farmer. 1992. *Confabulations: Creating False Memories, Destroying Families*. Boca Raton, FL: SIRS Books.

———. 1993. *True Stories of False Memories*. Boca Raton, FL: SIRS Books.

Goodheart, Eugene. 1984. *The Skeptic Disposition in Contemporary Criticism*. Princeton: Princeton University Press.

———. 1995. "Freud on Trial." *Dissent*, 42:236–243.

———. 2001. *Confessions of a Secular Jew: A Memoir*. Woodstock, NY: Overlook.

Goodrick-Clarke, Nicholas. 1991. *The Occult Roots of Nazism: Secret Aryan Cults and Their Influence on Nazi Ideology: The Ariosophists of Austria and Germany, 1890–1935.* (1985). New York: New York University Press.

Gould, Stephen J. 1997. "Nonoverlapping Magisteria." *Natural History,* 106:62.

———. 1999. *Rocks of Ages: Science and Religion in the Fullness of Life.* New York: Ballantine.

Graff, Gerald. 1977. "Fear and Trembling at Yale." *American Scholar,* 46:467–478.

———. 1992. *Beyond the Culture Wars: How Teaching the Conflicts Can Revitalize American Education.* New York: Norton.

Gross, Paul R., and Norman Levitt. 1998. *Higher Superstition: The Academic Left and Its Quarrel with Science.* Baltimore and London: Johns Hopkins University Press.

Gross, Paul R., Norman Levitt, and Martin W. Lewis (Eds.). 1996. *The Flight from Science and Reason.* New York: New York Academy of Sciences.

Grosskurth, Phyllis. 1991. *The Secret Ring: Freud's Inner Circle and the Politics of Psychoanalysis.* Reading, MA: Addison-Wesley.

Grünbaum, Adolf. 1984. *The Foundations of Psychoanalysis: A Philosophical Critique.* Berkeley: University of California Press.

———. 1993. *Validation in the Clinical Theory of Psychoanalysis: A Study in the Philosophy of Psychoanalysis.* Madison, CT: International Universities Press.

Gunn, Giles (Ed.). 2005. *A Historical Guide to Herman Melville.* New York: Oxford University Press.

Guze, Samuel B. 1992. *Why Psychiatry Is a Branch of Medicine.* New York: Oxford University Press.

Hacking, Ian. 1995. *Rewriting the Soul: Multiple Personality and the Sciences of Memory.* Princeton: Princeton University Press.

Hammond, D. Corydon. 1992. "Hypnosis in MPD: Ritual Abuse." Paper delivered at the Fourth Annual Eastern Regional Conference on Abuse and Multiple Personality, Alexandria, VA, June 25.

———. 1997. "Investigating False Memory for the Unmemorable: A Critique of Experimental Hypnosis and Memory Research." Tape-recorded talk delivered at the 14th International Congress of Hypnosis and Psychosomatic Medicine, San Diego, June.

Harrington, Evan. 1996. "Conspiracy Theories and Paranoia: Notes from a Mind-Control Conference." *Skeptical Inquirer,* 20:35–42.

Harris, Adrienne. 1996. "False Memory? False Memory Syndrome? The So-Called False Memory Syndrome?" *Psychoanalytic Dialogues,* 6:155–187.

Hartman, Geoffrey. 1980. *Criticism in the Wilderness: The Study of Literature Today.* New Haven: Yale University Press.

Haught, John H. 2000. *God After Darwin: A Theology of Evolution.* Boulder, CO: Westview.

Hawthorne, Nathaniel. 1882–89. *The Complete Works of Nathaniel Hawthorne*. 13 vols. Ed. George Parsons Lathrop. Boston and New York: Houghton Mifflin.

Hedges, Lawrence E. 1994. "Taking Recovered Memories Seriously." *Issues in Child Abuse Accusations*, 6:1–31.

Herman, Judith. 1992. *Trauma and Recovery*. New York: Basic Books.

Himmelfarb, Gertrude. 1994. *On Looking into the Abyss: Untimely Thoughts on Culture and Society*. New York: Knopf.

———. 1995. *The De-moralization of Society: From Victorian Virtues to Modern Values*. New York: Knopf.

———. 1996. *Darwin and the Darwinian Revolution*. (1959). Chicago: Ivan R. Dee.

———. 1999. *One Nation, Two Cultures*. New York: Knopf.

———. 2001. "Two Nations or Two Cultures?" *Commentary*, January, pp. 29–30.

Holmes, David S. 1990. "The Evidence for Repression: An Examination of Sixty Years of Research." In Singer 1990, pp. 85–102.

Hopkins, Budd. 1981. *Missing Time: A Documented Study of UFO Abductions*. New York: Marek.

Horgan, John. 1999. *The Undiscovered Mind: How the Brain Defies Replication, Medication, and Explanation*. New York: Free Press.

Horner, Thomas M. 1993. "The Biases of Child Sexual Abuse Experts: Believing Is Seeing." *Bulletin of the American Academy of Psychiatry Law*, 21:281–292.

Hutchinson, Peter. 1977. "Red Herrings or Clues?" In Flores 1977, pp. 206–215.

Hynek, J. Allen. 1972. *The UFO Experience: A Scientific Inquiry*. New York: Regnery.

Israëls, Han, and Morton Schatzman. 1993. "The Seduction Theory." *History of Psychiatry*, 4:23–59.

Jacobs, David M. 1998. *The Threat: Revealing the Secret Alien Agenda*. New York: Simon & Schuster.

Jameson, Fredric. 1994. *The Political Unconscious: Narrative as a Socially Symbolic Act*. (1981). Ithaca: Cornell University Press.

Janet, Pierre. 1914–15. "Psychoanalysis." *Journal of Abnormal Psychology*, 9:1–35, 153–187.

Jehlen, Myra. 2005. "Melville and Class." In Gunn 2005, pp. 83–103.

John Paul II. 1997. "Message to the Pontifical Academy of Sciences." Reprinted in "The Pope's Message on Evolution and Four Commentaries." *Quarterly Review of Biology*, 72:382–383.

Johnson, Barbara. 1980. *The Critical Difference: Essays in the Contemporary Rhetoric of Reading*. Baltimore: Johns Hopkins University Press.

————. 1985. "Teaching Deconstructively." In *Writing and Reading Differently*, ed. Douglas Atkins and Michael L. Johnson. Pp. 140–148. Lawrence: University Press of Kansas.

————. 1987. *A World of Difference*. Baltimore: Johns Hopkins University Press.

Johnson, K. Paul. 1994. *The Masters Revealed: Madame Blavatsky and the Myth of the Great White Lodge*. Albany: State University of New York Press.

————. 1995. *Initiates of Theosophical Masters*. Albany: State University of New York Press.

Johnson, Phillip E. 1991. *Darwin on Trial*. Downers Grove, IL: InterVarsity Press.

————. 1995a. *Reason in the Balance: The Case Against Naturalism in Science, Law, and Education*. Downers Grove, IL: InterVarsity Press.

————. 1995b. "Daniel Dennett's Dangerous Idea." *The New Criterion*, October, pp. 9–14.

————. 1997. *Defeating Darwinism by Opening Minds*. Downers Grove, IL: InterVarsity Press.

————. 1998. *Objections Sustained: Subversive Essays on Evolution, Law, and Culture*. Downers Grove, IL: InterVarsity Press.

————. 2000. *The Wedge of Truth: Splitting the Foundations of Naturalism*. Downers Grove, IL: InterVarsity Press.

Johnston, Moira. 1997. *Spectral Evidence: The Ramona Case: Incest, Memory, and Truth on Trial in the Napa Valley*. Boston: Houghton Mifflin.

Jones, Ernest. 1953–1957. *The Life and Work of Sigmund Freud*. 3 vols. New York: Basic Books.

Jung, Carl G. 1934. "Zur gegenwärtigen Lage der Psychotherapie." *Zentralblatt für Psychotherapie*, 7:1–16.

Kafka, Franz. 1977. *Letters to Friends, Family, and Editors*. Trans. Richard and Clara Winston. New York: Schocken.

————. 1982– . *Schriften Tagebücher Briefe*, ed. Gerhard Neumann, Malcolm Pasley, and Jost Schillemeit. Frankfurt-am-Main: Fischer Verlag.

————. 1995– . *Historisch-kritische Ausgabe sämtlicher Handschriften, Drucke und Typoskripte*. Ed. Roland Reuss and Peter Staengle. Basel: Stroemfeld/Roter Stern.

————. 1998a. *The Trial*. Trans. Breon Mitchell. (1925). New York: Schocken.

————. 1998b. *The Castle*. Trans. Mark Harman. (1926). New York: Schocken.

————. 2002. *Amerika: The Man Who Disappeared*. Trans. Michael Hofmann. (1927). New York: New Directions.

Kelley, Charles R., and Eric C. Kelley. 1994. *Now I Remember: Recovered Memories of Sexual Abuse*. Vancouver, WA: K/R Publications.

Kerr, John. 1993. *A Most Dangerous Method: The Story of Jung, Freud, and Sabina Spielrein*. New York: Random House.

Kihlstrom, John F. 1987. "The Cognitive Unconscious." *Science*, 237:1445–1452.

Kimball, Roger. 1990. *Tenured Radicals: How Politics Has Corrupted Higher Education*. New York: Harper & Row.

———. 1992. "The Periphery vs. the Center: The MLA in Chicago." In *Debating P.C.: The Controversy over Political Correctness on College Campuses*, ed. Paul Berman. Pp. 61–84. New York: Laurel.

Klass, Philip J. 1974. *UFOs Explained*. New York: Random House.

———. 1988. *UFO-Abductions: A Dangerous Game*. Buffalo, NY: Prometheus.

———. 1997. *The Real Roswell Crashed-Saucer Coverup*. Amherst, NY: Prometheus.

Koertge, Noretta. 1998. *A House Built on Sand: Exposing Postmodernist Myths about Science*. New York: Oxford University Press.

Kristol, Irving. 1984. "The Political Dilemma of American Jews." *Commentary*, July, pp. 23–29.

Kutchins, Herb, and Stuart A. Kirk. 1997. *Making Us Crazy: DSM: The Psychiatric Bible and the Creation of Mental Disorders*. New York: Free Press.

Lakoff, Robin Tolmach, and James C. Coyne. 1993. *Father Knows Best: The Use and Abuse of Power in Freud's Case of "Dora."* New York: Teachers College Press.

Lanning, Kenneth V. 1989. "Satanic, Occult, Ritualistic Crime: A Law Enforcement Perspective." *The Police Chief*, Oct., pp. 62–83.

Lear, Jonathan. 1990. *Love and Its Place in Nature: A Philosophical Interpretation of Freudian Psychoanalysis*. New York: Farrar, Straus & Giroux.

———. 1996. [Review of Crews et al., *The Memory Wars*]. *Journal of the American Psychoanalytic Association*, 44:580–587.

———. 1998. *Open Minded: Working Out the Logic of the Soul*. Cambridge, MA, and London: Harvard University Press.

Lehrer, Ronald. 1995. *Nietzsche's Presence in Freud's Life and Thought: On the Origins of a Psychology of Dynamic Unconscious Mental Functioning*. Albany: State University of New York Press.

Lemonick, Michael D. 1998. *Other Worlds: The Search for Life in the Universe*. New York: Simon & Schuster.

Lentricchia, Frank. 1983. *Criticism and Social Change*. Chicago: University of Chicago Press.

Leys, Ruth. 2000. *Trauma: A Genealogy*. Chicago: University of Chicago Press.

Lilienfeld, Scott O., Steven Jay Lynn, and Jeffrey M. Lohr (Eds.). 2003. *Science and Pseudoscience in Clinical Psychology*. New York: Guilford Press.

Lind, Michael. 1995. "Rev. Robertson's Grand International Conspiracy Theory." *New York Review of Books*, Feb. 2, pp. 21–25.

Livingston, Paisley. 1995. "The Poetic Fallacy." In Eddins 1995, pp. 150–165.

Loftus, Elizabeth, and Katherine Ketcham. 1994. *The Myth of Repressed Memory: False Memories and Allegations of Sexual Abuse*. New York: St. Martin's.

Loundon, Sumi D. (Ed.). 2001. *Blue Jean Buddha: Voices of Young Buddhists*. Boston: Wisdom Publications.

Love, Patricia. 1990. *The Emotional Incest Syndrome: What to Do When a Parent's Love Rules Your Life*. New York: Bantam.

Mack, John E. 1984. "An Approach to Helping Abductees." In *Alien Discussions: Proceedings of the Abduction Study Conference*, ed. Andrea Pritchard, David E. Pritchard, John E. Mack, Pam Kasey, and Claudia Yapp. Pp. 478–484. Cambridge, MA: North Cambridge Press.

———. 1994. *Abduction: Human Encounters with Aliens*. New York: Scribner's.

MacLean, Harry N. 1994. *Once Upon a Time: A True Story of Memory, Murder, and the Law*. New York: HarperCollins.

Macmillan, Malcolm. 1997. *Freud Evaluated: The Completed Arc*. (1991). Cambridge, MA: MIT Press.

Mahony, Patrick. 1984. *Cries of the Wolf Man*. Madison, CT: International Universities Press.

Masson, Jeffrey Moussaieff. 1984. *The Assault on Truth: Freud's Suppression of the Seduction Theory*. New York: Farrar, Straus & Giroux.

———. 1992. *The Assault on Truth: Freud's Suppression of the Seduction Theory*. 2nd ed. New York: HarperPerennial.

———. 2003. *The Assault on Truth: Freud's Suppression of the Seduction Theory*. 3rd ed. New York: Random House.

McCarthy, Thomas. 1978. *The Critical Theory of Jürgen Habermas*. Cambridge, MA: MIT Press.

McGuire, William (Ed.). 1974. *The Freud-Jung Letters: The Correspondence between Sigmund Freud and C. G. Jung*. Trans. Ralph Manheim and R. F. C. Hull. Princeton: Princeton University Press.

McHugh, Paul R. 1992. "Psychiatric Misadventures." *American Scholar*, 61:497–510.

———. 1994. "Psychotherapy Awry." *American Scholar*, 63:17–30.

McNally, Richard J. 2003. *Remembering Trauma*. Cambridge, MA, and London: Belknap Press of Harvard University Press.

Melville, Herman. 1962. *Billy Budd, Sailor (An Inside Narrative)*. Ed. Harrison Hayford and Merton M. Sealts, Jr. Chicago: University of Chicago Press.

———. 1983. *Redburn: His First Voyage; White-Jacket; or, The World in a Man-of-War; Moby-Dick; or, The Whale*. New York: Library of America.

———. 1991. *Clarel: A Poem and Pilgrimage in the Holy Land*. Ed. Harrison Hayford et al. Evanston and Chicago: Northwestern University Press and The Newberry Library.

———. 1993. *Correspondence*. Evanston and Chicago: Northwestern University Press and The Newberry Library.

Menzel, Donald H., and Ernest H. Taves. 1977. *The UFO Enigma: The Definitive Explanation of the UFO Phenomenon*. New York: Doubleday.

Micale, Marc. 1995. *Approaching Hysteria: Disease and Its Interpretations.* Princeton: Princeton University Press.

Michels, Robert. 1996. [Review of F. Crews et al., *The Memory Wars*]. *Journal of the American Psychoanalytic Association*, 44:573–579.

Middleton, Anne. 1992. "Medieval Studies." In *Redrawing the Boundaries: English and American Literary Studies*, ed. Stephen Greenblatt and Giles Gunn. Pp. 12–39. New York: MLA.

Milder, Robert. 2000. "'The Ugly Socrates': Melville, Hawthorne, and Homoeroticism." *ESQ*, 46:1–49.

———. 2005. "Herman Melville, 1819–1891: A Brief Biography." In Gunn 2005, pp. 17–58.

Miller, J. Hillis. 1987. "The Triumph of Theory, the Resistance to Reading, and the Question of the Material Base." *PMLA*, 102:281–291.

Miller, Jonathan. 1995. "Going Unconscious." In *Hidden Histories of Science*, ed. Robert B. Silvers. Pp. 1–35. New York: New York Review Books.

Miller, Kenneth R. 1999. *Finding Darwin's God: A Scientist's Search for Common Ground between God and Evolution.* New York: Cliff Street Books.

Moreland, J. P. (Ed.). 1994. *The Creation Hypothesis: Scientific Evidence for an Intelligent Designer.* Downers Grove, IL: InterVarsity Press.

Murphy, William M. 1995. *Family Secrets: William Butler Yeats and His Relatives.* Syracuse: Syracuse University Press.

Murray, Nicholas. 2004. *Kafka.* New Haven: Yale University Press.

Nagel, Thomas. 1994. "Freud's Permanent Revolution." *New York Review of Books*, May 12, pp. 34–38.

Nathan, Debbie, and Michael Snedeker. 1995. *Satan's Silence: Ritual Abuse and the Making of a Modern American Witch Hunt.* New York: Basic Books.

National Science Board. 1996. *Science and Engineering Indicators—1996.* U.S. Government Printing Office, NSB 96–21.

Nealon, Jeffrey T. 1992. "The Discipline of Deconstruction." *PMLA*, 107:1266–1279.

Noll, Richard. 1994. *The Jung Cult: Origins of a Charismatic Movement.* Princeton: Princeton University Press.

Norris, Christopher. 1992. *Uncritical Theory: Postmodernism, Intellectuals, and the Gulf War.* London: Lawrence & Wishart.

Nunberg, Herman, and Ernest Federn (Eds.). 1967. *Minutes of the Vienna Psychoanalytic Society: Volume II, 1908–1910.* New York: International Universities Press.

Obholzer, Karin. 1982. *The Wolf-Man Sixty Years Later: Conversations with Freud's Controversial Patient.* Trans. Michael Shaw. London: Routledge and Kegan Paul.

Ofshe, Richard, and Ethan Watters. 1994. *Making Monsters: False Memories, Psychotherapy, and Sexual Hysteria.* New York: Scribner's.

Ofshe, Richard J., and Richard A. Leo. 1997. "The Social Psychology of Police

Interrogation: The Theory and Classification of True and False Confessions." *Law, Politics, and Society*, 16:185–247.

Orne, Martin T. 1959. "The Nature of Hypnosis: Artifact and Essence." *Journal of Abnormal Social Psychology*, 58:277–299.

———. 1962. "On the Social Psychology of the Psychological Experiment: With Particular Reference to Demand Characteristics and Their Implications." *American Psychologist*, 27:776–783.

Ornstein, Peter, Stephen J. Ceci, and Elizabeth Loftus. 1996. "Reply to the Alpert, Brown, and Courtois Document: The Science of Memory and the Practice of Psychotherapy." In *Final Report of APA Working Group on Investigation of Memories of Childhood Abuse*. Pp. 106–131. Washington, DC: American Psychological Association.

Otter, Samuel. 1999. *Melville's Anatomies*. Berkeley, Los Angeles, and London: University of California Press.

Parker, Barry. 1998. *Alien Life: The Search for Extraterrestrials and Beyond*. New York: Plenum Trade.

Parnell, June. 1998. "Measured Personality Characteristics of Persons Who Claim UFO Experiences." *Psychotherapy in Private Practice*, 6:159–165.

Pasley, Malcolm. 1977. "Semi-private Games." In Flores 1977, pp. 188–205.

Patton, Phil. 1998. *Dreamland: Travels Inside the Secret World of Roswell and Area 51*. New York: Villard.

Pavel, Thomas G. 1989. *The Feud of Language: A History of Structuralist Thought*. Oxford and Cambridge, MA: Blackwell.

Pease, Donald E. 1985. "*Moby Dick* and the Cold War." In *The American Renaissance Reconsidered: Selected Papers from the English Institute, 1982–83*, ed. Walter Benn Michaels and Donald E. Pease. Pp. 113–155. Baltimore: Johns Hopkins University Press.

Pendergrast, Mark. 1996. *Victims of Memory: Sex Abuse Accusations and Shattered Lives*. (1995). Hinesburg, VT: Upper Access.

Pennock, Robert T. 1999. *Tower of Babel: The Evidence against the New Creationism*. Cambridge, MA: MIT Press.

Podhoretz, Norman. 1995. "In the Matter of Pat Robertson." *Commentary*, August, pp. 27–32.

Polanyi, Michael. 1958. *Personal Knowledge: Towards a Post-Critical Philosophy*. Chicago: University of Chicago Press.

Pollack, Robert. 2000. *The Faith of Biology and the Biology of Faith: Order, Meaning, and Free Will in Modern Medical Science*. New York: Columbia University Press.

Pope, Harrison G., Jr., Paul S. Oliva, and James I. Hudson. 1999. "Repressed Memories: The Scientific Status." In *Modern Scientific Evidence: The Law and Science of Expert Testimony*, ed. David L. Faigman et al. Vol. 1, Pocket Part, pp. 115–155. St. Paul, MN: West Publishing.

Pope, Kenneth S., and Laura S. Brown. 1996. *Recovered Memories of Abuse:*

Assessment, Therapy, Forensics. Washington, DC: American Psychological Association.

Prozan, Charlotte Krause. 1992. *Feminist Psychoanalytic Psychotherapy.* Northvale, NJ: Jason Aronson.

———. 1993. *The Technique of Feminist Psychoanalytic Psychotherapy.* Northvale, NJ: Jason Aronson.

Rabinowitz, Dorothy. 2003. *No Crueler Tyrannies: Accusation, False Witness, and Other Terrors of Our Times.* New York: Wall Street Press Books/Free Press.

Rice, James L. 1993. *Freud's Russia: National Identity in the Evolution of Psychoanalysis.* New Brunswick, NJ: Transaction.

Ricoeur, Paul. 1970. *Freud and Philosophy.* New Haven: Yale University Press.

Robertson, Ritchie. 1985. *Kafka: Judaism, Politics, and Literature.* Oxford and New York: Clarendon Press.

———. 1994. "In Search of the Historical Kafka: A Selective Review of Research, 1980–92." *Modern Language Review,* 89:107–137.

Robins, Richard W., Samuel D. Gosling, and Kenneth H. Craik. 1999. "An Empirical Analysis of Trends in Psychology." *American Psychologist,* 54:117–128.

Roche, David. 2001. "A Bit Confused: Creationism and Information Theory." *Skeptical Inquirer,* March/April, pp. 40–42.

Rorschach, Hermann. 1975. *Psychodiagnostics: A Diagnostic Test Based on Perception.* Trans. Paul Lemkau and Bernard Kronenberg. (1921). New York: Grune & Stratton.

Rosenthal, Robert. 1994. "Interpersonal Expectancy Effects: A 30-Year Perspective." *Current Directions in Psychological Science,* 3:176–179.

Ruse, Michael. 2001. *Can a Darwinian Be a Christian? The Relationship between Science and Religion.* Cambridge and New York: Cambridge University Press.

Sagan, Carl. 1996. *The Demon-Haunted World: Science as a Candle in the Dark.* New York: Random House.

Said, Edward. 1983. *The World, the Text, and the Critic.* Cambridge, MA: Harvard University Press.

Scharnberg, Max. 1993. *The Non-Authentic Nature of Freud's Observations.* 2 vols. Stockholm: Almqvist & Wiskell International.

Schatzman, Morton. 1992. "Freud: Who Seduced Whom?" *New Scientist,* March 21, pp. 34–37.

Scheflin, Alan W., and Daniel Brown. 1999. "The False Litigant Syndrome: 'Nobody Would Say That Unless It Was the Truth.'" *Journal of Psychiatry and Law,* 27:649–705.

Scheflin, Alan W., and Jerrold Lee Shapiro. 1989. *Trance on Trial.* New York: Guilford Press.

Schimek, Jean G. 1987. "Fact and Fantasy in the Seduction Theory: A Historical Review." *Journal of the American Psychoanalytic Association*, 35:937–965.

Share, Lynda. 1994. *If Someone Speaks, It Gets Lighter: Dreams and the Reconstruction of Infant Trauma*. Hillsdale, NJ: Analytic Press.

Shorter, Edward. 1996. *A History of Psychiatry: From the Era of the Asylum to the Age of Prozac*. New York: Wiley.

Showalter, Elaine. 1985. *The Female Malady: Women, Madness, and English Culture, 1830–1980*. New York: Pantheon.

———. 1997. *Hystories: Hysterical Epidemics and Modern Culture*. New York and Chichester, England: Columbia University Press.

Sicha, Mary Hunter. 1939. "A Study of the Rorschach 'Erlebniss-Typus' [sic] of Comparable White and Negro Subjects." Doctoral dissertation, Faculty of Philosophy, Columbia University.

Simon, Bennett. 1992. "'Incest—See under Oedipus Complex': The History of an Error in Psychoanalysis." *Journal of the American Psychoanalytic Association*, 40:955–988.

Singer, Jerome L. (Ed.). 1990. *Repression and Dissociation: Implications for Personality Theory, Psychopathology, and Health*. Chicago: University of Chicago Press.

Skues, Richard A. 2001. "On the Dating of Freud's *Aliquis* Slip." *International Journal of Psychoanalysis*, 82:1185–1204.

Sokal, Alan, and Jean Bricmont. 1998. *Fashionable Nonsense: Postmodern Intellectuals' Abuse of Science*. (1997). New York: St. Martin's.

Sokel, Walter H. 1985. "Zwischen Gnosis und Jehovah: Zur Religionsproblematik Franz Kafkas." In *Franz Kafka Symposium 1983*, ed. Wilhelm Emrich and Bernd Goldmann. Pp. 37–79. Mainz: Hase & Koehler.

Spanos, Nicholas P. 1996. *Multiple Identities and False Memories: A Sociocognitive Perspective*. Washington, DC: American Psychological Association.

Spanos, Nicholas P., Patricia A. Cross, Kirby Dickson, and Susan C. Dubereuil. 1993. "Close Encounters: An Examination of UFO Experiences." *Journal of Abnormal Psychology*, 102:624–632.

Spanos, William V. 1995. *The Errant Art of Moby-Dick: The Canon, the Cold War, and the Struggle for American Studies*. Durham and London: Duke University Press.

Spurling, Laurence (Ed.). 1989. *Sigmund Freud: Critical Assessments*. 4 vols. London: Routledge.

Stove, David. 1999. *Against the Idols of the Age*. New Brunswick, NJ: Transaction.

Strieber, Whitley. 1988. *Communion: A True Story*. (1987). New York: Avon.

———. 1995. *Breakthrough: The Next Step*. New York: HarperCollins.

———. 1998a. *Transformation: The Breakthrough*. New York: Avon.

———. 1998b. *Confirmation: The Hard Evidence of Aliens Among Us*. New York: St. Martin's.

Strieber, Whitley, and Ann Strieber. 1997. *The Communion Letters*. New York: HarperPrism.

Sulloway, Frank J. 1991. "Reassessing Freud's Case Histories: The Social Construction of Psychoanalysis." *Isis*, 82:245–275.

———. 1992. *Freud, Biologist of the Mind: Beyond the Psychoanalytic Legend.* (1979). Cambridge, MA: Harvard University Press.

Sundquist, Eric J. 1993. *To Wake the Nations: Race in the Making of American Literature.* Cambridge, MA: Belknap Press of Harvard University Press.

Suzuki, Shunryu. 1970. *Zen Mind, Beginner's Mind.* Ed. Trudy Dixon. New York: Weatherhill.

Swales, Peter J. 1982a. "Freud, Minna Bernays, and the Conquest of Rome: New Light on the Origins of Psychoanalysis." *New American Review*, 1:1–23.

———. 1982b. "A Fascination with Witches." *The Sciences*, 27(8):21–25.

———. 1983. "Freud, Cocaine, and Sexual Chemistry: The Role of Cocaine in Freud's Conception of the Libido." Privately published by the author.

———. 1986. "Freud, His Teacher, and the Birth of Psychoanalysis." In *Freud: Appraisals and Reappraisals: Contributions to Freud Studies.* Vol. 1, ed. Paul E. Stepansky. Pp. 3–82. Hillsdale, NJ: Analytic Press.

———. 1988. "Freud, Katharina, and the First 'Wild Analysis.'" In *Freud: Appraisals and Reappraisals: Contributions to Freud Studies,* Vol. 3, ed. Paul E. Stepansky. Pp. 81–164. Hillsdale, NJ: Analytic Press.

———. 1989a. "Freud, Johann Weier, and the Status of Seduction: The Role of the Witch in the Conception of Fantasy." In Spurling 1989, 1:331–358.

———. 1989b. "Freud, Krafft-Ebing, and the Witches: The Role of Krafft-Ebing in Freud's Flight into Fantasy." In Spurling 1989, 1:359–365.

Terr, Lenore. 1991. "Childhood Traumas: An Outline and Overview." *American Journal of Psychiatry*, 148:10–20.

———. 1992. *Too Scared to Cry: Psychic Trauma in Childhood.* (1990). New York: Basic Books.

———. 1994. *Unchained Memories: True Stories of Traumatic Memories, Lost and Found.* New York: Basic Books.

van der Kolk, Bessel, and Onno van der Hart. 1991. "The Intrusive Past: The Flexibility of Memory and the Engraving of Trauma." *American Imago*, 48:425–454.

Victor, Jeffrey S. 1993. *Satanic Panic: The Creation of a Contemporary Legend.* Chicago and La Salle, IL: Open Court.

Vitz, Paul C. 1988. *Sigmund Freud's Christian Unconscious.* New York: Guilford Press.

Walker, Lenore E. A. 1994. *Abused Women and Survivor Therapy: A Practical Guide for the Psychotherapist.* Washington, DC: American Psychological Association.

Washington, Peter. 1995. *Madame Blavatsky's Baboon: A History of the Mystics, Mediums, and Misfits Who Brought Spiritualism to America*. New York: Schocken.

Watts, Steven. 1991. "The Idiocy of American Studies: Poststructuralism, Language, and Politics in the Age of Self-Fulfillment." *American Quarterly*, 43:625–660.

Wells, Jonathan. 2000. *Icons of Evolution: Science or Myth? Why Much of What We Teach about Evolution Is Wrong*. Washington, DC: Regnery.

White, Graham, and John Maze. 1995. *Henry A. Wallace: His Search for a New World Order*. Chapel Hill: University of North Carolina Press.

Wieseltier, Leon. 2005. "The Wake." *New Republic*, Jan. 17, p. 34.

Wilcocks, Robert. 1994. *Maelzel's Chess Player: Sigmund Freud and the Rhetoric of Deceit*. Lanham, MD: Rowman & Littlefield.

Williams, Rowan. 2005. "Of Course This Makes Us Doubt God's Existence." *Sunday Telegraph* (London), Jan. 2, p. 22.

Wilson, Edmund. 1962. "A Dissenting Opinion on Kafka." (1947). Reprinted in *Kafka: A Collection of Critical Essays*, ed. Ronald Gray. Pp. 91–97. Englewood Cliffs, NJ: Prentice-Hall.

Wollheim, Richard. 1993. *The Mind and Its Depths*. Cambridge, MA: Harvard University Press.

Wood, James M., M. Teresa Nezworski, Scott O. Lilienfeld, and Howard N. Garb. 2003. *What's Wrong with the Rorschach? Science Confronts the Controversial Inkblot Test*. San Francisco: Jossey-Bass.

Working Group on Investigation of Memories of Childhood Abuse. 1996. *Final Report*. Washington, DC: American Psychological Association.

Wortis, Joseph. 1940. "Fragments of a Freudian Analysis." *American Journal of Orthopsychiatry*, 10:843–849.

Wright, Lawrence. 1994. *Remembering Satan*. New York: Knopf.

Young, Allan. 1995. *The Harmony of Illusions: Inventing Post-Traumatic Stress Disorder*. Princeton: Princeton University Press.

INDEX

Achebe, Chinua, 311
Acocella, Joan, 250, 369–370
Ad hominem argument, 11–12, 15, 75
Adler, Alfred, 24, 365
"AE." *See* Russell, George
Alpert, Judith, 142, 157
Alter, Robert, 320
Althusser, Louis, 297, 307, 359
American Psychiatric Association,
 159–160, 163, 166–169
American Psychoanalytic Association,
 163–164, 366
American Psychological Association,
 141–142, 163, 164–166, 187, 197
Anderson, Reb, 290
Anima, Jungian, 38, 249
"Anna O." *See* Pappenheim, Bertha
Antiscientific sentiment, 7, 46–61,
 74–75, 183–184, 265–269, 358–359
Anzieu, Didier, 54
Appleman, Philip, 375
Arac, Jonathan, 313
Ariosophy, 236, 247–248
Aron, Lewis, 369

Baker, Richard, 283–293
Balducci, Corrado, 372
Barrett, Kirk, 102–103
Barthes, Roland, 297, 307, 313, 360
Bass, Ellen, and Laura Davis, 92–93,
 113–117, 119, 122, 124, 127, 131,
 132, 155, 371
Bauer, Felice, 322
Bauer, Ida, 27–30, 185
Beck, Samuel, 195
Behe, Michael, 258, 260–261, 262,
 263, 274
Bennett, William, 361
Berlinski, David, 258, 266, 374
Bernays, Martha, 39
Bernheim, Hippolyte, 144, 156, 369

Bersani, Leo, 82–84
Berthoff, Warner, 329–330, 331, 333,
 378
Besant, Annie, 227–228
Binder, Hartmut, 376
Bjerre, Poul, 37
Blackmore, Susan, 372
Blacky test, 66
Blavatsky, H. P., 220–231, 233,
 234–237, 238, 239, 244–250, 373
Bleuler, Eugen, 36
Bloch, Grete, 316
Blume, E. Sue, 114–116
Boa, Elizabeth, 321–323
Bonaparte, Marie, 18
Borch–Jacobsen, Mikkel, 69, 142,
 144, 241, 243, 369, 370
Bornstein, Robert, 64–65
Bradshaw, John, 113, 116
Branch, Glenn, 343–350
Braun, Bennett, 161, 370
Brenneis, C. Brooks, 44
Breuer, Josef, 59, 123, 144, 149, 173,
 175, 177, 239, 241, 242
Bricmont, Jean, 358, 359
Brod, Max, 315, 316, 327
Brooks, Peter, 71, 87
Brown, Daniel, 156, 159, 160,
 162–163, 370
Brown, Jerry, 283, 287
Brown, Laura, 138, 166
Brown, N. O., 246
Brownmiller, Susan, 114
Bruck, Maggie, 139
Bryan, C. D. B., 372
Bush, George W., 257
Butler, Judith, 79–82

Calasso, Roberto, 323–327
Carotenuto, Aldo, 365
Ceci, Stephen, 139

Chadwick, David, 375
Charcot, J.-M., 144, 148–149, 173, 175–177, 185, 239, 241
Chase, Thomas, 351–360
Cheit, Ross, 95
Cheney, Lynne, 181, 361
Cioffi, Frank, 17, 32, 44, 63–64
Circular reasoning, 22, 56, 69–70, 72, 74, 76, 85, 87, 96, 142, 157, 243, 257, 297, 303, 305–306
Cixous, Hélène, 182, 183
Clancy, Susan, 200
Clément, Catherine, 182
Clever Hans, 142
Clinical evidence, 16–18, 32, 34–35, 37, 46–47, 69–70, 78–79, 86, 93–94, 132, 141–142, 145, 164, 165, 193, 195, 199, 243, 354, 356, 363, 367
Cold War, 212–213, 230, 316, 334, 377
Commentary, 266–268, 344, 374
"Committee," Freud's, 37–38, 42
Commonweal, 345, 346–347
Comprehensive System, Rorschach. *See* Exner, John
Confirmation bias, 66–67, 68, 76, 78, 82, 84–85, 116, 139–140, 142, 176, 193
Cooper, Arnold, 366–367
Corngold, Stanley, 318–323, 325, 327
Countertransference. *See* Transference
Coyne, James. *See* Lakoff, Robin
Coyne, Jerry, 349
Crabtree, Adam, 374
Creationism, 6–8, 254–269, 270–281, 343–350. *See also* Intelligent design
Cronbach, Lee, 195
Culley, Margo, 371
Cultural studies, 315, 321–323

Darwin, Charles, and Darwinism, 6–8, 58, 225, 235, 254–269, 270–281, 343–350, 375
Davies, Jody, 146, 251
Davis, Laura. *See* Bass, Ellen

Davis, Percival, 374
Dawes, Robyn, 117, 371
Dawkins, Richard, 256, 267, 274, 348
Daycare abuse allegations, 112, 137–139, 154, 369
Dean, Jodi, 201, 211–216
Deconstruction, 269, 304, 308–314, 315, 318–321, 358, 361, 378
Delbanco, Andrew, 330–342, 377–378
de Man, Paul, 308, 310, 314, 318–320
Dembski, William, 258, 261–262, 263, 267, 274, 374
Demonology, 130, 134–152
Dennett, Daniel, 256, 267, 274
Denton, Michael, 258
Derrida, Jacques, 297, 300, 307, 310, 314, 359, 378
Determinism, Freudian, 53, 59
DeWolf, David, 374
Diagnostic and Statistical Manual of Mental Disorders, 167–169
Disciplinary discourse, 305–306, 312–314
Discovery Institute, 258, 266
Dissociation, of consciousness, 143, 146–147, 155, 157–159, 166, 167, 169, 251. *See also* Multiple personality
Dolnick, Edward, 63
"Dora." *See* Bauer, Ida
Dostoevsky, Fyodor, 21–22, 23, 30, 53
Dowden, Stephen, 316
Downing, Michael, 282–294
Dreams, interpretation of, 24, 31, 55–56, 67, 68, 70, 102, 107, 116, 126, 127, 129, 130, 131, 145, 154, 163–164, 194, 199, 210, 243, 244–245, 366
Drury, Shadia, 351–356
Dworkin, Andrea, 114

Eckstein, Emma, 18, 20, 150
Eldredge, Niles, 280, 374
Ellenberger, Henri, 17, 67, 69, 242, 374

Ellis, John, 299, 304
Ellison, Ralph, 336
Ellmann, Richard, 372
Empiricism, 5–12, 46–61, 62–70, 76–82, 132, 191, 238, 259, 362–363, 371
Erdelyi, Matthew, 66, 352, 367
Erikson, Erik, 27, 83
Erwin, Edward, 48, 64, 66
Esotericism, 373. *See also* Gnosticism, Theosophy
Esterson, Allen, 20, 31–35, 64, 370
Evidence. *See* Circular reasoning, Clinical evidence, Experimental tests
Evolution. *See* Darwin, Charles
Exner, John, 196–199
Experimental tests, of psychological theory, 47, 62, 63, 65–68, 78, 94–96, 99, 141–142, 160–161, 176, 195
Eysenck, Hans, 66

Faivre, Antoine, 223
False Memory Syndrome Foundation, 109, 117, 156, 160
Farmer, Kevin, 368
Fascism, 229, 234, 236–238
Female psychology, psychoanalytic, 21, 41, 76, 131, 182–184, 194, 312–313, 355, 356, 365
Feminism, 7, 27, 32, 83, 92, 113, 116, 119, 122, 151–152, 155, 163, 174–175, 180–186, 211, 293, 298, 308, 310, 312–313, 322–323, 356, 361, 371
Ferenczi, Sándor, 130, 144, 152, 186, 246
Feyerabend, Paul, 268, 359
Fields, Rick, 375
First Things, 267
Fisher, Philip, 313
Fisher, Seymour, 66
Fliess, Wilhelm, 18, 20, 30, 34, 150, 151, 185, 244, 365–366, 368
Fortune, Christopher, 369
Foucault, Michel, 49, 50, 297, 300, 301, 307, 310, 313, 314, 359, 376

Franklin, George, 96–105, 367
"Frau Cäcilie M." *See* von Lieben, Anna
Frazier, Kendrick, 372
Fredrickson, Renee, 114–116, 125, 368
Free association, psychoanalytic, 18, 26, 51, 57, 70, 76, 102, 191, 243, 367
Freud, Anna, 18
Freud, Sigmund, 11–12, 15–42, 43–61, 62–70, 71–87, 93, 95–96, 122–131, 132, 133, 135–136, 141–152, 155, 158, 163, 173, 175–177, 183–186, 188, 193, 197, 239, 241, 242–246, 247–248, 249, 250–251, 253, 265, 300, 337, 341, 345, 351–359, 365, 366, 367, 368, 369, 370, 374, 376, 377. *See also* "Committee," Dreams, Experimental tests, Free association, Hysteria, Lamarckism, "Little Hans," Oedipus complex, Pankeev, Paranormal claims, Pseudoscience, Psychoanalysis, "Seduction theory," Suggestion, Symptoms, Transference, Unconscious
Freyd, Jennifer, 156–157
Freyd, Pamela, 156
Frink, Horace, 19–20

Garb, Howard, 188, 371
Gartner, Richard, 44, 251, 370
Gasché, Rodolphe, 313
Gay, Peter, 16, 32
Gellner, Ernest, 54, 57, 146
Gilman, Sander, 184, 321–323, 376
Gnosticism, 57, 60, 151, 221, 325
Godwin, Joscelyn, 223
Goethe, Johann, 53, 59
Goldstein, Eleanor, 368
Goodheart, Eugene, 46, 48–52, 60, 366
Goodrick-Clarke, Nicholas, 236–237
Gordon, Bruce, 374
Gould, S. J., 276–280
Graff, Gerald, 310–311, 376

Greenberg, Roger, 66
Gross, Paul, 375
Grosskurth, Phyllis, 17, 365
Grünbaum, Adolf, 16, 51, 64, 69–70
Gulf War syndrome, 177, 178
Gunn, Giles, 329–330
Gurdjieff, G. I., 207, 228–230, 232, 234, 373
Guttmacher Award, 159–160, 163
Guze, Samuel, 145, 152

Hacking, Ian, 369
Hall, Barry, 263
Hammond, Corydon, 159, 161–163, 370
Harrington, Evan, 370
Harris, Adrienne, 251, 369
Hartman, Geoffrey, 308, 309, 311, 314
Haught, John, 271–272, 274, 278, 280, 346–347, 348
Hawthorne, Nathaniel, 52, 134–136, 151, 304, 350, 366
Hedges, Lawrence, 131
Herman, Judith, 92, 93, 109, 157, 159, 369
Hertz, Marguerite, 195
Hesemann, Michael, 372
Hill, Barney and Betty, 372
Himmelfarb, Gertrude, 265–266, 374
Himmler, Heinrich, 237
Hitler, Adolf, 237
Holland, Norman, 62–70
Holmes, David, 94, 158
Holt, Robert, 40
Hopkins, Budd, 203, 205–207, 209, 212, 214
Horgan, John, 71
Horner, Thomas, 368
Humanities, and criteria of knowledge, 10, 16, 46–61, 74–87, 173, 183–184, 351–363
Hume, David, 202, 373
Hutchinson, Peter, 317
Huxley, Aldous, 224
Hynek, J. A., 202

Hypnosis, 18, 102–103, 116, 120, 123, 130, 140, 142, 144–145, 149, 154, 156, 158, 160–162, 164, 165, 168, 175, 176, 180, 204, 209–211, 240–243, 245, 252, 369, 370, 372
Hysteria, 21, 26–30, 32, 34, 74, 80, 120, 122–123, 126, 128, 130, 144, 148–150, 158, 168, 173–186

Ingram, Paul, 106–111, 130, 139, 367–368
Intelligent design, 7, 11, 258–267, 274, 275, 280, 343–348, 374
Interdisciplinary inquiry, 10, 173, 306
Interrogation, of children, 112, 137, 139
Intuition, as source of knowledge, 6–9, 46–52, 60, 68–69, 132–133, 147, 151, 191, 192, 237, 303, 325, 347, 355, 373
Irigaray, Luce, 182
Israëls, Han, 17, 365

Jacobs, David, 201, 203–205, 208, 209, 210, 212
James, William, 37
Jameson, Fredric, 303, 304
Janet, Pierre, 67, 142, 143, 146, 149, 158, 173, 177, 239, 369
Jehlen, Myra, 336
Jesenská, Milena, 315, 316, 322
John Paul II, Pope, 6, 277
Johnson, Barbara, 308–309, 310
Johnson, K. P., 223–224
Johnson, Phillip, 258, 259, 266, 267, 268–269, 270, 274, 278, 343–346, 350, 374
Johnston, Moira, 368
Jones, Ernest, 16, 37, 52, 74, 242–246, 365
Jung, C. G., and Jungianism, 19–20, 24, 35–40, 188, 191, 192, 246–250, 252, 253

Kabbalah, 221, 325
Kafka, Franz, 315–327

Kelley, Charles and Eric, 368
Kenyon, Dean, 374
Kerr, John, 31, 35–40, 365
Ketcham, Katherine, 94, 97, 101, 118
Kihlstrom, John, 66
Kimball, Roger, 267, 298, 299, 312, 362, 375
King, Stephen, 98, 367
Kirk, Stuart, 371
Klass, Philip, 202, 372
Klopfer, Bruno, 192–194, 195, 197, 198
Koertge, Noretta, 375
Kris, Ernst, 18
Krishnamurti, Jiddu, 228–230
Kristeva, Julia, 182, 297, 359
Kristol, Irving, 265–266, 268
Kuhn, Thomas, 49–50, 268, 359
Kutchins, Herb, 371

Lacan, Jacques, and Lacanianism, 83, 182, 297, 301, 310, 312–313, 355–359
Laing, R. D., 357–358
Lakoff, Robin, and James Coyne, 27–30, 31
Lamarckism, Freud's, 56–57, 127, 150
Lanning, Kenneth, 368
Lawrence, D. H., 52, 219, 229, 234, 330
Leadbeater, Charles, 227–228
Lear, Jonathan, 46–48, 60, 246, 366, 369
Lehrer, Ronald, 54–55
Lemonick, Michael, 372
Lentricchia, Frank, 309
Leo, Richard, 139
Lévi–Strauss, Claude, 301–302
Levitt, Norman, 375
Lewontin, Richard, 274, 344
Leys, Ruth, 370
Library of Congress, and Freud archives, 18, 19
Lilienfeld, Scott, 188, 371
Lind, Michael, 375
Lindner, Robert, 194, 199

Lipsker, Eileen, 96–105, 367
"Little Hans," 352
Livingston, Paisley, 305
Loftus, Elizabeth, 94–99, 101, 105, 118
Loundon, Sumi, 293
Love, Patricia, 115
Luborsky, Lester, 66
Lyell, Charles, 255

Mack, John, 203, 252, 372
MacLean, Harry, 97, 100
Macmillan, Malcolm, 16, 44, 48, 63–64, 352, 354, 374
Mahony, Patrick, 24–25, 69
Malthus, Thomas, 255
Mann, Thomas, 52
Mansfield, Katherine, 229–230
Marcuse, Herbert, 265, 341
Marx, Karl, and Marxism, 45, 55, 265, 299, 300, 303, 307, 310, 316, 357, 359, 361
Masson, Jeffrey, 32, 122–123, 155, 369, 370
Materialism, scientific, and its detractors, 7–8, 207, 220, 223, 256, 268, 320, 345, 346, 374
Matthiessen, F. O., 333–334, 335
Maze, John, 230–231
McCall, Dan, 333
McCarthy, Thomas, 376
McHugh, Paul, 117, 132–133, 371
McMartin Preschool case, 112, 369
McNally, Richard, 44, 153–170
Mead, G. R. S., 247
Melville, Herman, 328–342, 377
Memory, recovered. See Recovered memory
Menzel, Donald, 372
Mesmer, Franz, and Mesmerism, 130, 210, 239–240, 241, 242, 251
Meyer, Stephen, 258
Meyers, F. W. H., 242
Micale, Marc, 174
Michael Polanyi Center, 374
Michelle Remembers, 178

Michels, Robert, 71, 77–79, 366, 369
Middleton, Anne, 312
Milder, Robert, 339, 341, 378
Miller, Alice, 155
Miller, Arthur, 136, 138, 143
Miller, J. H., 308, 309–310
Miller, Jonathan, 240
Miller, Kenneth, 262, 274–276, 346
Modern Language Association, 173, 184, 307, 362
Moll, Albert, 37
Morris, Michael, 117
Muir, Willa and Edwin, 315, 316
Multiple personality, 119–120, 140, 155, 161, 167, 250–251, 370. See also Dissociation
Murphy, William, 372
Murray, Nicholas, 315, 376
Mysticism, 207, 220–232, 233–253, 363, 373. See also Gnosticism

Nabokov, Vladimir, 135
Nagel, Thomas, 129–130, 132, 133, 369
NASA, 212–213
Nathan, Debbie, 370
National Association of Biology Teachers, 348
National Center for Science Education, 340, 348–349
Naturalism, methodological vs. metaphysical, 7–8, 259, 345–347
Nazi Party. See Fascism
Nealon, Jeffrey, 314
Neoconservatism, 265–268
Neuhaus, Richard, 267
New Age, 238
"New Americanists," 377
New Criterion, The, 267
New Criticism, 309, 360–361
New Left, 212–213, 307–308, 333–335, 341
Nezworski, M. T., 188, 371
Nietzsche, Friedrich, 20, 53, 54–55, 67
Noll, Richard, 247

Norris, Christopher, 313, 376
Numerology. See Paranormal claims

Obholzer, Karin, 24–25
Occultism, 373. See also Paranormal claims
Ockham's razor, 66, 140, 202
Oedipus complex, 12, 22, 34, 44, 51–52, 53, 57, 67, 76, 123, 146, 152, 183, 184, 185, 186, 354, 357, 366
Ofshe, Richard, 44, 97, 101, 102–104, 110, 118–120, 124, 139
Olcott, Henry, 220–223, 229, 235
Orne, Martin, 142
Ornstein, Peter, 142
Otter, Samuel, 377
Ouspensky, P. D., 232

Padian, Kevin, 344
Paley, William, 256, 266
Pankeev, Sergei, 22–26, 30, 31, 33, 37, 41, 69
Pappenheim, Bertha, 144–145, 175, 177, 241–242
Paranormal claims, 60, 132, 204, 219–232, 233–253
Parker, Barry, 372
Parnell, June, 372
Pasley, Malcolm, 317
Patton, Phil, 372
Pearcey, Nancy, 258
Pease, Donald, 334, 377
Pendergrast, Mark, 91, 101, 113–114, 118, 120–121, 130, 368, 369
Penis envy. See Female psychology
Pennock, Robert, 262, 264
Pius XII, Pope, 276–277
Plantinga, Alvin, 345, 347–348
Podhoretz, Norman, 268, 375
Polanyi, Michael, 299–300
Pollack, Robert, 271, 280
Pope, Harrison, 158
Pope, Kenneth, 138, 166
Positivism, 59, 76, 79, 353
Postmodernism. See Poststructuralism

Poststructuralism and postmodernism, 159, 211–216, 269, 297–314, 351–363
Post–traumatic stress disorder, 167–170
Pound, Ezra, 219, 220
Provine, William, 274, 276
Prozan, Charlotte, 131–132
Pseudoscience, 12, 34–35, 61, 63–70, 113, 170, 191, 210, 306, 351
Psychoanalysis, 11–12, 15–42, 43–61, 62–70, 71–87, 94, 122–133, 163–164, 174–175, 176, 182–186, 188, 191, 192, 193, 194, 240, 243, 245–246, 249, 251, 299, 301–302, 310, 343–344, 351–363, 365, 366. *See also* Freud
Putnam, James, 37

Question begging. *See* Circular reasoning

Rabinowitz, Dorothy, 370
Radicalism, political, 307–310, 333–335, 359
Ramona, Gary, 368
"Rat Man" case, 40
Recovered memory, 12, 41, 44, 91–111, 112–133, 153–170, 177, 179–182, 185–186, 199, 210, 239, 250–251
Religious belief, 3–10, 253, 254–269, 270–281, 316, 320–321, 343–350. *See also* Gnosticism, Theosophy
Repression, psychic, 32, 36, 54, 69, 92–98, 100–101, 104, 105, 108–110, 113, 116–117, 121, 123, 126, 127, 128–129, 143, 157–160, 164, 242, 304, 341, 351–353, 354, 367
Rice, James, 20–26, 31
Ricoeur, Paul, 55
Rinpoche, C. T., 284
Ritvo, Harriet, 313
Rivera, Geraldo, 108, 155, 368
Roazen, Paul, 17
Robertson, Pat, 268

Robertson, Ritchie, 376
Robins, Richard, 62
Robinson, Paul, 84
Roche, David, 374
Róheim, Geza, 246
Rorschach, Hermann, and his test, 66, 187–199, 371
Rosenthal, Robert, 142
Ross, Colin, 161
Ruse, Michael, 272–274, 279, 280, 346, 348–350
Russell, George ("AE"), 230

Sagan, Carl, 214, 215, 238–239, 250–251
Said, Edward, 309
Salter, Stephanie, 117
Satanic ritual abuse, 106–110, 112, 118–119, 130, 137, 150, 154, 160–162, 239, 368. *See also* Demonology
Saussure, Ferdinand de, 301, 302, 304, 357
Scharnberg, Max, 44, 145
Schatzman, Morton, 17, 365
Scheflin, Alan, 159–163, 370
Schimek, Jean, 32
Science. *See* Antiscientific sentiment, Circular reasoning, Clinical evidence, Empiricism, Materialism, Pseudoscience
Scott, Eugenie, 348
"Seduction theory," Freud's, 31–35, 74, 122–126, 143, 144, 148, 152, 155, 186, 251, 352, 365, 369, 370
Self–ratifying discourse, 305–306. *See also* Circular reasoning
Sexual abuse allegations. *See* Daycare abuse allegations, Recovered memory
Shapiro, Jerrold, 163
Share, Linda, 131
Shaw, Lemuel, 334, 335
Shorter, Edward, 77
Showalter, Elaine, 173–186, 209
Sicha, Mary, 371
Sifford, Darrell, 117

Simon, Bennett, 152, 371
Sinnett, A. P., 235, 249
Skepticism, 9–12, 58, 207, 214–215,
    221, 299–300, 320, 324, 347
Skura, Meredith, 85
Sleep paralysis, 120, 202, 209
Smith, Huston, 348
Snedeker, Michael, 370
Snyder, Gary, 285, 294
Sokal, Alan, 358, 359
Sokel, Walter, 376
Spanos, Nicholas, 144, 370, 372
Spanos, William, 334–335, 377
Spielrein, Sabina, 35, 38–39, 365
Spiritualism, 373. See also Paranormal
    claims
Steiner, Rudolf, 222
Stove, David, 267
Strieber, Whitley, 200, 201, 203–208,
    209, 212, 372
Suggestion, therapeutic, 41, 105–111,
    112, 118–120, 124–125, 138–140,
    144–145, 369, 370
Sulloway, Frank, 17, 26, 40, 69
Sundquist, Eric, 377
Suzuki, Shunryu, 288–294, 375
Swales, Peter, 17, 39, 60, 242–243,
    366, 369
Sybil, 155, 178, 370
Symptom checklist, diagnostic,
    115–116, 125, 155, 165–167
Symptoms, symbolic meaning
    assigned to, 24, 40, 56, 57, 58, 65,
    84, 98, 101, 115–116, 125–126, 129,
    149, 155, 166–167, 185, 198, 239,
    241, 243, 251, 365, 368, 369

Taves, Ernest, 372
Tavris, Carol, 117
Taylor, Bill, 117
Teilhard de Chardin, Paul, 272, 346
Telepathy. See Paranormal claims
Terr, Lenore, 96–105, 117, 126, 157,
    367, 368
Theodicy, 3–5
Theosophy, 219–232, 233–253, 373

Thornton, E. M., 17
Three Faces of Eve, The, 178
Todorov, Tzvetan, 359
Transference, therapeutic, and
    countertransference, 40, 58, 70, 76,
    86–87, 145–147, 243
Trilling, Lionel, 60, 335, 337, 341,
    366, 377
Tsunami of December 2004, 3, 5, 6

UFO lore, 11, 132, 177, 200–216,
    252, 372
Unconscious, the, 36, 51, 55–56, 59,
    66–67, 74, 82, 100, 127, 128–129,
    132, 144, 149–150, 157, 183, 185,
    240, 245, 247–249, 253, 301, 351
Updike, John, 338

Validation. See Circular reasoning,
    Clinical evidence, Empiricism,
    Intuition, Pseudoscience
van der Hart, Onno, 155
van der Kolk, Bessel, 155
Victor, Jeffrey, 368, 370
Vitz, Paul, 366
von Lieben, Anna, 175, 242–243

Walker, Lenore, 165–166
Wallace, Henry, 230–231, 232, 373
Washington, Peter, 224–230, 233, 234
Watts, Steven, 302–303, 307
Webster, Richard, 184
Wedgwood, James, 227
Weier, Johann, 147–148, 369
Weinberg, Steven, 344–345
Weininger, Otto, 366
Wells, Jonathan, 258, 260, 343
White, Graham, 230–231
Whitehorn, John, 145
Wieseltier, Leon, 4
Wilcocks, Robert, 368–369
Williams, Jeffrey, 359–360
Williams, Rowan, 4–6, 9
Wilson, Edmund, 316–317, 327
Wilson, E. O., 274
Wilson, Glenn, 66

Witchcraft. *See* Demonology
Wittgenstein, Ludwig, 56
"Wolf Man." *See* Pankeev
Wollheim, Richard, 85–87, 129
Wood, James, 66, 188–199, 371
Wortis, Joseph, 26
Wright, Lawrence, 106–109, 139

Yeats, W. B., 219–222, 231–232
Young, Allan, 371

Zaretsky, Eli, 357
Zen Buddhism, 282–294, 375